Railway Records

A guide to sources

Cliff Edwards

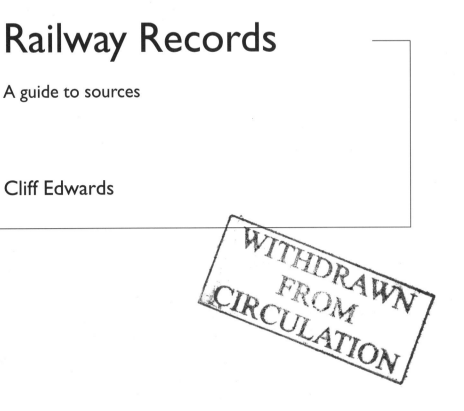

PUBLIC RECORD O.

Public Record Office
Richmond
Surrey
TW9 4DU

ISBN 1 903365 10 4

British Library Cataloguing-in-Publication Data
A catalogue record for this book is available from the British Library

For Marion

Front cover:

Clock-face bookplate recording the presentation to the Southern Railway of a collection of documents and photographs mainly relating to the London, Brighton & South Coast Railway. Curiously, it is dated November 1957 – ten years after nationalization and the demise of the SR. RAIL 414/554

Coniston Lake station, Furness Railway. At the platform is railmotor No 1, a passenger carriage with driving compartments at both ends and a steam loco-motive built into it – its chimney can be seen protruding from the carriage roof under the overbridge. The photograph is tentatively dated 1910. RAIL 214/91

Printed by Cromwell Press, Trowbridge, Wiltshire

Contents

Acknowledgements   iv
List of abbreviations   v
How to use this book   vii
How to use the PRO   viii

1   THE HISTORY OF BRITAIN'S RAILWAYS   1

2   WHERE TO FIND RAILWAY RECORDS   11

3   RECORDS CREATED AND USED BY THE RAILWAYS   17

4   GOVERNMENT POLICY AND CENTRAL CONTROL OF RAILWAYS   24

5   RAILWAY STAFF RECORDS   69

6   MAPS, PLANS AND TECHNICAL DRAWINGS   89

7   PHOTOGRAPHS   99

Appendix 1: BTHR Codes   105
Appendix 2: Contents of RAIL and AN series   121
Appendix 3: List of Designated Repositories   213

Bibliography   218

Index   219

Acknowledgements

I should like to thank Anne Kilminster and Sheila Knight, successive Publications Officers at the PRO, for their unfailing encouragement and patience, and Peter Leek who prepared the book for press.

David T. Hawkings provided suggestions for several of the examples in Chapter 5 and for illustrations.

Dr Terry Gourvish, of the London School of Economics and historian of British Railways, read the manuscript in draft and gave useful advice.

My greatest debt is to Robin Linsley, former Records Officer of the BRB, who gave up a considerable amount of time over a period of years to assist me with research on the records in the PRO. He also read and commented on drafts of the book. Any errors and omissions are, however, mine.

Finally, my heartfelt thanks to my wife, Marion, who probably worried more about this book than did I, and who now has her weekends back.

List of abbreviations

BR	British Railways/British Rail
BRB	British Railways Board
BR (E)	British Railways Eastern Region
BR (LM)	British Railways London Midland Region
BR (NE)	British Railways North Eastern Region
BR (S)	British Railways Southern Region
BR (Sc)	British Railways Scottish Region
BR (W)	British Railways Western Region
BTC	British Transport Commission
BTHR	British Transport Historical Records
Cal R	Caledonian Railway
CLC	Cheshire Lines Committee
Co(s)	Company/Companies
Cttee(s)	Committee(s)
E	East
FR	Furness Railway
GCR	Great Central Railway
GER	Great Eastern Railway
GNoER	Great North of England Railway
GNR	Great Northern Railway
GNR(I)	Great Northern Railway (Ireland)
GNSR	Great North of Scotland Railway
GSWR	Glasgow and South Western Railway
GWR	Great Western Railway
H&BR	Hull and Barnsley Railway
Jct	Junction
Jt	Joint
L&YR	Lancashire and Yorkshire Railway
LBSCR	London, Brighton and South Coast Railway
LCDR	London, Chatham and Dover Railway
LMSR	London Midland and Scottish Railway
LNER	London and North Eastern Railway
LNWR	London and North Western Railway
LPTB	London Passenger Transport Board
LSWR	London and South Western Railway
LTE	London Transport Executive
Lt R	Light Railway
LTSR	London, Tilbury and Southend Railway
M&GNJR	Midland and Great Northern Joint Railway
Met	Metropolitan

MR	Midland Railway
MSLR	Manchester, Sheffield and Lincolnshire Railway
MSWJR	Midland and South Western Junction Railway
N	North
NAS	National Archives of Scotland
NBR	North British Railway
NER	North Eastern Railway
NRM	National Railway Museum
OWWR	Oxford, Worcester and Wolverhampton Railway
PRO	Public Record Office
R	Railway
RCH	Railway Clearing House
RHC	Railway Heritage Committee
Rys	Railways
S	South
S&DR	Stockton and Darlington Railway
SECR	South Eastern and Chatham Railway
SER	South Eastern Railway
SR	Southern Railway
TVR	Taff Vale Railway
W	West

How to use this book

This Reader's Guide is designed to introduce railway records to the newcomer and to provide further help to those who may already have used the Public Record Office (PRO) to research railway history. There are so many records in the PRO that possible sources of information may be overlooked. This guide is intended to help the user of the PRO learn about the basic record series (formerly known as classes) containing information about railways, and to open other avenues of research. It looks at the records created by the railways themselves and the records of government that complement them; it also refers to other repositories that hold records about railways.

Those who are new to the PRO should begin with the section 'How to use the PRO'. It explains how the PRO works, what you have to do to become a reader there, and how to prepare for visits. Chapter 1 of this guide is a brief history of the railways of Britain, and provides helpful background material. Chapter 2 explains how the railway records came to the PRO and where else you might look for records about railways. Chapter 3 briefly describes the kinds of records to be found in the archives of the railway companies and British Railways themselves, which are held by the PRO. Appendix 2 expands on Chapter 3 and is in the form of an index to railway company and institution names showing which record series contain information on each one. Appendix 2 can also be used with Chapter 5, which describes railway staff records, Chapter 6, railway maps and plans, and Chapter 7, photographs.

Chapter 4 describes records, of potential interest to railway researchers, created by government departments. It demonstrates the great diversity of these records and refers to difficulties that can be encountered when using them. In most government departments railways were not uppermost in the minds of civil servants when they designed lists and indexes to help them find papers. Original subject indexes can be particularly unreliable in this respect and should be approached with lateral thinking (because it is not under 'R' for 'railways' that does not mean there is nothing about railways there)[1]. Some government record series are frustrating because the finding aids do not give enough information. Perhaps the list gives only dates and one must make educated guesses about where records of a particular event may be. Using such series can be time-consuming; unfortunately so is the creation of better finding aids, and series of records may wait decades before attention can be given to them. On the other hand, a difficult finding aid tends to make the series underused. There are nuggets to be found for those patient enough to dig.

---

1 A favourite ploy used in the research for this book was to look under 'G', because a significant number of railway titles began with 'Great', or 'L' because so many were called the 'London and . . . Railway'.

How to use the PRO

The Public Record Office is primarily the national repository for government records in the UK. The surviving records of government from the Domesday Book (1086) to the present are held at its main site at Kew. So are the railway records.

The PRO, Kew, about 10 minutes' walk from Kew Gardens underground station, which is on both the London Underground District Line and the Silverlink Metro Service. If you intend to drive, the PRO is signposted from the South Circular Road (A205). There is a public car park, as well as a public restaurant, a shop, self-service lockers and an extensive library. The newly-opened Education and Visitor Centre offers an Internet Cafe and an exhibition of historic documents selected from the PRO's extensive archives.

You do not need to make an appointment to visit the PRO, but you will need a reader's ticket to gain access to the research areas. To obtain a ticket, bring with you an identity document such as a full UK driving licence, a UK banker's card or a passport if you are a British subject; a passport or a national identity card if you are not a British subject. New readers are invited to take a short induction tour, which will help you to familiarize yourself with the various reading and research facilities.

The protection and preservation of the unique records held by the PRO are very important. You will not be permitted to use ink in the research areas; pencils and notebooks only are allowed in the reading rooms. Bags and other containers, which could be used to conceal stolen records, must be left in the ground floor lockers. Eating, drinking and smoking are strictly forbidden anywhere in the research areas.

Opening times are:

Monday	9 a.m. to 5 p.m.
Tuesday	10 a.m. to 7 p.m.
Wednesday	9 a.m. to 5 p.m.
Thursday	9 a.m. to 7 p.m.
Friday	9 a.m. to 5 p.m.
Saturday	9.30 a.m. to 5 p.m.

The PRO is closed on Sundays, public holidays, and for annual stocktaking.

The PRO's address is Public Record Office, Kew, Richmond, Surrey TW9 4DU. Telephone numbers are 020 8876 3444, enquiries 020 8392 5200, advance ordering of documents (exact references only) 020 8382 5260.

The PRO website http://www.pro.gov.uk provides all the above details, as well as

information about events, popular documents, and information leaflets. It will also allow you to access the PRO's extensive on-line catalogue (the 'series lists'). The home page provides entrance to several areas of enquiry, the series lists are accessed by clicking 'finding aids'. By the time this book is published the PRO catalogue (PROCAT) will be on-line. PROCAT is the catalogue of the contents of the PRO, complete with high level descriptive material (information on departmental histories and series details) as well as the record descriptions at piece level. It has a search system capable of making sophisticated interrogations of the database, shaped by the user.

Ordering documents

To read documents in the reading rooms you need to call for them by their correct references. PRO call numbers usually have three parts. First the 'Department', followed by the 'Series' and then the 'Piece'.

The 'department' is a letter, or number of letters (never more than four) indicating the government department that transferred the records to the PRO. Most are mnemonic (e.g. ADM for the Admiralty, HO for the Home Office) but, in the 1970s, a move to non-mnemonic codes was made for new departments. Although not from a government department, the records of the railways were classified, in the traditional way, RAIL. It so happened that when it came to the creation of a new code for the nationalized railway records the change had just been made to non-mnemonic codes; AN, the next available code in alphabetical sequence, was allocated. AN stands for nothing except nationalized railways but many refer to it as meaning 'After Nationalization'. Departments were until recently called 'Lettercodes', and before that, 'Groups', and you may see them so referred to.

The series is a number (again, never more than four digits long) specifying a distinct series of records.

The piece is the production unit within the series, be it a volume, file, bundle of papers, map, etc.

Together the department, series and piece number (e.g. RAIL 543/10) form the reference used to order the particular record. This book gives examples of call numbers and, where necessary, indicates where they have more than three elements. Ordering of records is computerized. Records are usually delivered to the search rooms within 30 minutes of ordering.

Swindon, Great Western Railway, showing mixed broad and narrow gauge track. The loco-motives and most of the vehicles are narrow gauge but some broad gauge vehicles can be seen at the extreme left. The photograph was registered for copyright on 24 August 1885 by R.H. Bleasdale, Aston, Birmingham. COPY 1/373

The History of Britain's Railways

The concept of the 'railway'

The idea of guiding vehicles by the use of 'rails' is said to go back to the Romans. In Britain it came into use (or, perhaps, came back into use) in the seventeenth century when wooden tracks were laid down to improve the ground surface for carts to travel on. In the eighteenth century this idea was refined into a trackway with an 'L'-shaped rail, which increasingly would have been of iron or faced with iron. Ordinary wagon wheels would have run on the horizontal part of the rail while being guided, and confined to the track, by the vertical portion of the 'L' inside the wheels. This kind of track was sometimes called an 'Outram way' (after Benjamin Outram who first cast iron plates in this form in the 1770s), a 'tramway' or a 'plateway' (because it was composed of 'L'-section 'plates' fastened together). These were horse-powered lines, generally laid out to convey minerals from mines to canals and rivers or the sea, water still providing the most efficient form of long distance transport. The transport of passengers by such means was not important. The earliest railways considered in this book were projected in this form, though some intended to use, and all quickly came to use, the newer edge rails. These are the kinds of rails we are familiar with now. The top of the rail is the running surface and guidance is provided by slightly inclining the rails inward and coning the wheel treads to suit. The flange on the inside of the wheel is not the primary guiding device but prevents the wheel climbing over the rail where centrifugal forces in a sharp curve might overcome the natural centring effect of the coned wheels.

It was to the plateways that steam locomotion was first applied. In 1804 Richard Trevithick first demonstrated a steam railway locomotive on the Pen-y-darren plateway in South Wales. It was successful, but in repeated use it broke up the track which was not strong enough consistently to bear the weight. Trevithick designed a locomotive in the following year for the Wylam colliery railway near Newcastle. It was at Wylam that the next developments in the design of reliable railway locomotives were made by William Hedley, whose famous 'Puffing Billy' ran on the railway from 1813 until the 1860s. George Stephenson, who had been born at Wylam and who worked on stationary steam engines in the area, was well aware of Hedley's engines. Stephenson was appointed enginewright at Killingworth colliery in 1812 and began to design his own locomotives for the Killingworth railway. By 1821, when the Act authorizing the construction of the Stockton & Darlington Railway was passed,

Stephenson was the most experienced locomotive engineer in the country and was able to present himself to the proprietors, and be accepted, as the engineer for the construction of the line.

Public railways

The Stockton & Darlington Railway, opened in 1825, was the first to use steam locomotives. But the technology was still not entirely trustworthy and Stephenson used them only on parts of the railway. Some of the inclines were powered by stationary winding engines. The company's Parliamentary Act permitted the carriage of passengers but until 1833 passengers were conveyed by horse-drawn vehicles. The first railway regularly to convey passengers by steam was the Canterbury & Whitstable Railway which opened in 1830, the same year as the first railway to adopt steam traction throughout, and for all traffic, the Liverpool & Manchester Railway. The L&M too was laid out by George Stephenson and the success of the locomotive 'Rocket', largely designed by George's son Robert and a much more refined machine than anything before it, was crucial to the acceptance of steam as the motive power for railways.

The tramways that were built to convey minerals were usually of short length. Their builders found it relatively easy to obtain the right to use land required for the route by agreement with the few landowners involved. A favoured method, especially in the north east of England, was the 'wayleave' by which the landowner granted leave to use the land without giving it up. When longer railways were contemplated, proposing to use the land of many owners, it was found necessary to obtain compulsory purchase powers. These, and the right to raise capital, were granted by an Act of Parliament that also formally incorporated the railway company. (See Chapter 2 for the parliamentary system of approving railway Bills.)

In the late 1820s a spate of railway promotions occurred, not all intending to use steam. Some, like the Canterbury & Whitstable, the Bolton & Leigh and the Liskeard & Looe railways, were quite short, linking adjacent towns. In the 1830s more ambitious railways opened, many adopting distant town names in their titles; the Newcastle & Carlisle, London & Birmingham and London & Southampton railways, for example.

In the case of the Liverpool & Manchester Railway, its independent existence lasted fifteen years. In 1845 it was absorbed, along with the Bolton & Leigh and the Kenyon & Leigh Junction railways into the Grand Junction Railway, which had already absorbed the Warrington & Newton Railway in 1834 and the Chester & Crewe Railway in 1840. In 1846, the Grand Junction, the Manchester & Birmingham and London & Birmingham railways amalgamated to form the London & North Western

Railway which became, by some measures and certainly by its own estimation, the kingdom's 'Premier Line'. This process of gradual amalgamation of railway companies to form the great trunk routes was repeated across Britain in the nineteenth century. The LNWR eventually stretched from Euston in London, via several routes to the Scottish border north of Carlisle, across the north of Wales, north-east as far as Leeds, and east to Peterborough. It also had an interest in the Dundalk, Newry & Greenore Railway in Ireland as well as the sea transport link with Ireland. The 'West Coast' route of the LNW and the Caledonian railways rivalled the 'East Coast' route to Edinburgh of the Great Northern, North Eastern and North British railways.

Government intervention

The British government was far less concerned to direct the development of the emerging railway network than were its continental neighbours. Where many European countries directed the strategy of building and running railways, to forward military ends and to promote economic development, Britain left it to the railway companies and parliamentary scrutiny. The railway companies' strategic considerations, however, extended only so far as their own business interests. The needs of the country were usually secondary to the advantage of a company over its rivals. The result was that sections of main routes might be duplicated and, conversely, that some much fought-over areas of the country had to wait decades for connection to the railway system while companies opposed each other's schemes. In such cases the railways that were finally built as a consequence might not have been the most advantageous to the districts but the best compromise solutions. It became clear that the guidance of government was required and some legislation appeared in the first years. In 1830 railways were made subject to the Carriers Act. As the 1830s progressed, there were other Acts requiring such things as the maintenance of gates and attendants at level crossings (Highways Acts 1835 and 1839), the payment for special constables to maintain order at railway premises (Constables Act 1838), and the obligation to carry mail (Railways (Conveyance of Mails) Act 1838). The first major piece of legislation came in 1840 with the Regulation of Railways Act. It is interesting to see what the government took notice of after ten or fifteen years' experience of public railways. By the Regulation Act, the Board of Trade was:

- to be notified a month in advance of the opening of a railway;
- to appoint inspectors of railways;
- to be sent all railway company bye-laws and allow or disallow them;
- to settle disputes between companies and landowners over connections between main and branch railways.

The inspectors were not given power to prevent the opening of railways if they did not consider them fit, though that loophole was filled two years later in the Regulation

of Railways and Conveyance of Troops Act 1842. Thereafter there was a succession of Acts making law on the procedures for building railways and obtaining additional powers, on standard clauses to be included in railway Acts, on the kinds of bridges and crossings the railways could build, etc. However, *where* railways were to be built remained a matter for commerce and parliamentary hearings to decide. Some politicians did understand the economic and strategic significance of railways as a national asset. By Gladstone's Railway Regulation Act 1844 the Treasury were authorized to purchase new railways (i.e. those authorized after the Act) after 21 years. However, this nationalization procedure was never taken up, because the railway companies did not achieve the level of profitability required by the Act.

The gauge war

One of the most important results of the involvement of George Stephenson and his son Robert with the first major railways was the adoption of the 4ft 8½in track gauge (the gauge used by the Northumberland colliery railways) on the public railways they constructed. It became, and in its metric equivalent is still, the standard gauge in mainland Britain. (It is also used in many parts of the world including most of Europe and America.) Remarkably, there were few exceptions to the use of this gauge in Britain. The Irish standard gauge was fixed at 5ft 3in but that was confined to that island. The only major rival to the Northumberland gauge on the mainland was the 7ft ¼in. gauge used on I. K. Brunel's Great Western Railway and its associated companies. The difficulties of transferring traffic (particularly goods) between broad and narrow gauge at the places where they met made company rivalry even worse; the narrow gauge camp being determined to keep the broad gauge out of their areas and the broad gauge companies fighting to extend. Government intervention to deal with this problem was largely ineffective. In 1845 a Gauge Commission was appointed to investigate and report to parliament. It conducted comparative trials on the GWR and the 4ft 8½in gauge Great North of England Railway. Their report, in 1846, concluded that despite certain technical superiorities of the broad gauge, breaks of gauge were 'a very serious evil' and the narrow gauge should be the standard. They recommended that the narrower gauge be declared the gauge to be used by all public railways from then on and that either the broad gauge ones should be narrowed or that all broad gauge lines should be made useable by trains of both gauges. The resulting Gauge of Railways Act 1846, however, watered this down so much that it left the situation almost as it had been before. The narrower gauge was to be assumed if no mention of gauge was made in new railway Acts but it was still possible for parliamentary committees to approve new broad gauge ones. Indeed, new ones continued to be built (though several Acts contained stipulations for mixed gauge track) a notable one being the South Wales Railway which took the broad gauge across the breadth of south Wales from Gloucester to Haverfordwest and was not completed until 1854.

Government departmental organization[1]

The Board of Trade had been given responsibility for the oversight of railways. Its Railway Department was set up in 1840. In 1844 a Railway Board was established in an attempt to remove railways from the direct responsibility of the President of the Board of Trade. In fact, the Railway Board was never truly separated from the parent, but it was the nearest Britain came to having a body with the effective power to recommend to parliament which railway Bills were the best for the needs of the country. It set out to report to parliament on all railway Bills. But a sudden craze for floating railway schemes nearly swamped the system. 'Railway mania' began in earnest in 1844 when 248 railway Bills were presented. In 1845 there were 788 Bills. The mania collapsed for economic reasons, but the Railway Board's strategic monitoring had not materialized. It had scotched some worthless schemes but was barely able to keep up with the work it had to do on individual Bills. Both the Railway Board and its successors, the new Whig government's independent Commissioners of Railways, had little impact on the overall development of the railway system. In 1851 the work returned to the Board of Trade and the Railway Department was reinstated.

Government effort in the rest of the nineteenth century was mainly directed towards the regulation of railway powers and railway safety and some social provision. It could be argued that by 1900, the regulations were such that the industry was approaching government control. The great social measure, the provision of 'parliamentary trains' by which every railway company had to provide at least one train for third class passengers in each direction, stopping at every station, and charging no more than 1 penny a mile, had been passed in 1844 (Railway Regulation Act 1844). In Ireland some effort was made to alleviate economic problems by giving governmental financial help to the building of railways to open up remote areas for trade and to create employment (Railway Companies (Ireland) Temporary Advances Act 1866, and subsequent amendments).

Railway Clearing House

Given that there was no central operational control of Britain's railways, the apportionment of fares for through journeys (travel over the tracks of more than one railway in the course of a single journey) was complicated. It frequently required the passenger to re-book for each stage. In 1842 some of the railway company managers set up an organization to deal with such matters. It was called the Railway Clearing House and was similar to bank clearing houses. In the course of its long life (it was not disbanded until 1963) it set up a large organization, mainly of clerks to apportion fares

---

1 For a good account of the history of governments' relations with railways *see* Parris, Henry, A. *Government and the Railways in the Nineteenth Century*, Routledge & Kegan Paul, London, 1965.

for journeys and the movement of goods. In order to do that effectively it investigated the exact mileage of each company's lines, exactly where the boundaries between companies were at junctions, and produced definitive line maps and junction diagrams. It also produced common classifications of the types of goods carried, introduced standardized telegraphic codes, and provided a venue at which managers of companies could meet for conferences on rates, etc.[2]

Joint railways

Railway companies frequently fought each other. It often happened, however, that companies found it better to share lines and facilities rather than squabble unproductively over them. One way of cooperating was to allow the trains of one railway to use the tracks of another. This was known as granting 'running powers' over the line and was very frequently adopted. Another way was to run a line or a station jointly. A Joint Committee would be formed of senior officers of the companies concerned (there were several joint committees of four or more railways). Very often these committees ran the joint railway as a separate railway company, indeed many had separate legal status and promoted their own parliamentary Bills. Some joint railways were large; the Midland and Great Northern Joint Railway (formed by the Midland Railway and the Great Northern Railway) was the longest with 186 miles of track in Lincolnshire and North Norfolk. Other large ones were the Cheshire Lines Committee (GCR, GNR and MR) which operated a network of lines between Manchester, Liverpool, and Chester, and the Somerset and Dorset Joint Railway (LSWR and MR) between Bath and Bournemouth. Where railways converged on a town they might set up a Joint Station Committee to operate a single station to serve them all. Examples were Leeds Central station (GNR, L&YR, LNWR and NER) and Birkenhead Park (Mersey Railway and Wirral Railway) but there were many more. These joint committees continued after the grouping of the railways in 1923 (*see* 'The grouping' below) in cases where their constituent companies fell into different grouped companies.

Light railways

The Light Railways Act 1896, was intended to bring railways into agricultural areas, even into the fields, to enable farmers to transport, and thereby market, their produce more efficiently and profitably. The idea was to reduce the cost of establishing railways by waiving some of the rules about signalling and the solidity of the track, and making construction affordable by permitting subsidy from local authorities and the Treasury. The cumbersome and expensive requirement to procure an authorizing

2 *See* Bagwell, Philip, *The Railway Clearing House in the British Economy 1842–1922*, Allen & Unwin, London, 1968.

Act was also done away with in favour of a certificate issued by the Board of Trade on the recommendation of a new Light Railway Commission. Thus both initial cost and some of the constant costs of manning and running a conventional railway were to be avoided. Many railways were built under light railway orders but the vision of the rural railway was rarely approached. Some light railways were entirely urban (street tramways began to be built under this legislation). Some of the large railway companies took advantage of the Act to build otherwise uneconomic branch lines. Within a few decades the idea had lost most of its force with the development of motorized road transport, a more flexible means of transporting produce from the field.

The Railway Executive Committee

At the beginning of the First World War, the railways were taken over by the government under clause 16 of the Regulation of the Forces Act 1871, which empowered the government, in emergency, to take control of all or any of the railways in the United Kingdom. Any warrant effecting the take-over was to run for a week only but could be renewed from week to week (and so it was until the end of 1919). The railways were placed under the control of a Railway Executive Committee chaired by the President of the Board of Trade but effectively run by the acting chairman, H. A. Walker of the London & South Western Railway. The committee members were drawn from senior officers of the largest railways: the Caledonian, Great Central, Great Eastern, Great Northern, Great Western, Lancashire & Yorkshire, London & North Western, London, Brighton & South Coast, Midland, North Eastern, and South Eastern & Chatham railways. As a public announcement put it, 'The control of the railways has been taken over by the government for the purpose of ensuring that the railways, locomotives, rolling stock and staff shall be used as one complete unit in the best interests of the state for the movement of troops, stores and food supplies'. The profits of the railways were controlled, as were the dividends they could pay their shareholders. Rolling stock was pooled (i.e. the stock of any railway could be used by any other as was most convenient for the traffic). Workshops were largely given over to work for the Ministry of Munitions. Many locomotives and thousands of wagons were sent overseas for the war effort. At the end of it all the railways had much recovery work to do to bring back the standard of operations to pre-war levels. There had been, since the 1890s, a lobby for the nationalization of railways. Many people confidently expected that now was the time for it.

The grouping

In 1919 a new Ministry of Transport took over responsibility from the Board of Trade and considered the fate of the railways. Despite many predictions, the Railways Act

1921 produced a solution very different from nationalization. The prejudice against commercial monopoly was still not quite powerful enough to outweigh that against government ownership in peacetime. The Act required all the large railways and almost all the small ones to amalgamate into four large regional companies. These emerged as the London Midland & Scottish Railway, the London & North Eastern Railway, the Great Western Railway (the only one to retain a pre-group name) and the Southern Railway. By far the biggest of these was the LMSR, which included two of the largest pre-group companies, the LNWR and the Midland Railway as well as the L&YR, Caledonian and numerous others. The main constituents of the LNER were the GCR, GER, GNR, GNSR, NBR, and NER. The GWR included the old GWR, the Cambrian, Rhymney, Taff Vale and several other Welsh and West Country railways. The Southern consisted essentially of the LSWR, LBSCR and SECR with minor additions. In all 123 companies were amalgamated. The Act was to come into force at the beginning of 1923 but a year before that the amalgamations began, the LNWR absorbing the L&YR, for example.

The 'big four', as the new grouped companies were often called, made great efforts to maintain standards of service and produced some eye-catching events like the speed competition between the LMS and the LNE lines to Scotland. The LNER captured the speed record for a steam-powered train (126 mph) in 1938, a record that still stands.

There were outstandingly good modern services, but the generality of rail transport was still essentially Victorian. Much Victorian equipment remained in service. Competition from roads, the old-fashioned practice of using small, badly maintained, wagons owned privately by collieries, coal factors and merchants for coal traffic, the Depression and gains in pay and conditions of service of staff after it, all contributed to increased costs and reduced profit. The 'big four' maintained some profitability. The GWR was the best, paying reasonable dividends to its shareholders. The LNER, on the other hand, paid poorly.

The Second World War and nationalization[3]

There was a second Railway Executive Committee to run the railways in the Second World War. This time there was new legislation, the Minister of Transport issuing the Emergency Control Order 1939 under section 1 of the Emergency Powers (Defence) Act 1939. The committee was drawn from the 'big four' and the London Passenger Transport Board (LPTB) which had been set up in 1933 to run London's road and rail (Underground) passenger transport. The railways had as much to contribute as they did in the First World War but were also hit harder by bombing. At the end the

---

3 For the full story of the first 25 years of the nationalized railway *see* Gourvish, T. R. *British Railways 1948–73, A Business History*, Cambridge University Press, 1986.

railways were in a deplorable state, badly maintained, underfunded and in no condition to repair to pre-war standard. There was a new mood in the country with a disposition to nationalize industry (many of the documents of the period refer to 'socialization' rather than 'nationalization'). The Transport Act 1947 created the British Transport Commission (BTC) with the idea of integrating transport of all types. On 1 January 1948 the Commission took over the railways along with much of the road transport industry (passenger and freight), and the waterways and docks. The BTC formed Executives for each of these and the LPTB became the London Transport Executive. The Railway Executive was the biggest of the Executives and was in operational control of six railway Regions. The Regions bore a striking resemblance to the 'big four' and even, in one case, to pre-group divisions. There were the London Midland Region (essentially the LMS up to the Scottish border), the Eastern Region (corresponding to the former GC, GE and GN railways), the North Eastern Region (very much the old NER territory), the Southern Region (virtually the former Southern Railway), Western Region (corresponding to the grouped GWR) and the Scottish Region, the only one to take territory from two of the Grouped railways.

The structure of the BTC and the Executives created problems for British Railways (as it styled itself). Relations between the Railway Executive and the Commission were strained. The Commission was keen to keep policy making to itself while the Executive tried to coordinate the regions in its own way. This was not an effective decision making structure for British Railways (it worked better for the smaller units like the LTE). The railways were starved of investment in the 'austerity' period.

In 1953 the Railway Executive was abolished and Area Boards controlled the Regions. There was a Railway Sub-commission between the BTC and the Regional General Managers. This organization produced a greater vision, resulting in the modernization plan of 1955. More money was to be invested in the technical development of the railways. The result was the rapid switch from steam to diesel locomotion, and plans to improve freight handling, track and signalling. Such plans depended for their effect on a correct understanding of the trend of business. In the freight area especially, the modernization plan underestimated the migration of traffic to the roads. By the time they came into use, many of the new large freight marshalling yards were virtually redundant.

Since 1955 British Railways had been in trading deficit. The government wanted to make radical changes and by the Transport Act 1962 the BTC was abolished. The railways were to be controlled by a new British Railways Board (BRB). Regional Boards replaced the Area Boards, though most decision making was made in the BRB itself. Some new managers were recruited from outside the industry and the Chairman was Dr Richard Beeching from ICI. In 1963 the 'Beeching Report'[4] was

---

4 *The Reshaping of British Railways*, HMSO, London, 1963.

published. It 'intended to shape the railways to meet present day requirements by enabling them to provide as much of the total transport of the country as they can provide well'. This meant removing some of the services it was inefficient for railways to provide. The report reflected the realization that the pattern of the railway business had to be changed and that many services, stations and whole lines of railway would have to be closed if the business was to work efficiently. The 'Beeching cuts' were controversial but, although in the following years some services were reprieved for social reasons, most of them were effected.

Between the 1960s and the 1980s the railways continued to rationalize and improve the marketing of their business. The concept of the trading unit within British Rail is exemplified by British Railways Engineering Ltd (BREL) set up in 1970 as a company owned by the BRB to trade not only as a provider of workshop facilities for the home railway but to seek business elsewhere. Several of these companies were formed by the BRB. In the 1980s the move towards privatization was begun. Instead of Regions running everything in their territories, operating sectors came into being and names like InterCity, Network South East and Regional Railways became well known. These sectors transcended regional boundaries and were operators of particular kinds of railway services. From them were developed the shadow franchise companies of the 1990s that became the privatized Train Operating Companies of today. Only Railtrack, which maintains the track and buildings of the railway, is the provider for the whole country.

2 Where to Find Railway Records

Records of the railway companies and the nationalized railway

Britain has a rich archive of records created by those who ran the railways. Many of these records are now in the PRO, but there are several important railway archives elsewhere. This chapter shows where records are and how they came to be there. At the chapter's end is a list of repositories, other than the PRO, which hold railway records.

History

From the start of steam railways there appears to have been a concern within the companies to preserve the evidence of the activities of the industry and pass it on to future generations. As companies were taken over by larger ones their records passed with them and were preserved as part of the heritage of the larger railway. This was partly practical, to preserve records of ownership and legal entitlement, and partly a matter of pride. When the railways were nationalized in 1948, the record keepers of the 'big four' railway companies handed over to the British Transport Commission a huge archive of their own and their predecessors' records. (The BTC also inherited archives of canal and road companies that also survive in the PRO and elsewhere.) The BTC kept these records in various places, the largest part of them in the former Great Western Railway Deeds Registry at Porchester Road, Paddington, the contents of which became known as the British Transport Historical Records (BTHR). There were also repositories in York and Edinburgh. Public access to the BTHR was allowed in reading rooms in these offices. When the BTC was abolished, by the Transport Act 1962, the records were put into the charge of the new British Railways Board.

The Transport Act 1968 removed from the BRB the obligation to preserve its records and historical artifacts. The locomotives and other objects formerly stored in railway museums in Clapham (South London) and in York were to be exhibited in a new National Railway Museum (NRM) which was established in York. It was proposed that the records should accompany them, but pressure from the research community, which wanted the records to be in London where they could be used in conjunction with the records of government in the PRO, caused the Minister of Transport to think again. As a result, the PRO, in 1972, took over the BTHR and continued the operation

of the record office in Paddington while preparing the records for transfer to the new PRO building at Kew. The railway records transferred from Paddington were the first to be housed in the new Kew record office in 1977. The records from York had been sent to Porchester Road and also came to the PRO.

Distribution of the records

The PRO took the administrative records; minutes of meetings, staff and financial records, and the other evidence of the bureaucracy of the railways. It also took technical records about the railway lines themselves; the bridges, buildings, embankments and cuttings. Technical records about locomotives and rolling stock went to the NRM, which also became the repository for the photographic collections. At the same time, administrative and technical records about railways in Scotland were taken by the then Scottish Record Office, now the National Archives of Scotland (NAS), and records about London Transport were transferred to the London Transport Executive. The London Transport archives are now in the London Metropolitan Archive, formerly the Greater London Record Office. These broad divisions of interest continue so that the records still being processed through the Porchester Road store (now the BRB Records Centre) are directed to an appropriate record repository according to its collecting policy.

Despite what has been said above, the PRO does hold some records about locomotives and rolling stock that might be expected to be in the NRM. Similarly, the NRM has some administrative records that might have been placed in the PRO. The PRO also has records about Scottish railways[1] and those of London Transport and its predecessor companies (*see* **Appendix 2**). Quite often records about Scottish railways were collected by companies based in England, and appear among their records in the PRO.

Another explanation of apparent misplacement is that over the 170 or so years of the existence of railways, there has been constant, though minor, disposal into private hands. Those finding or inheriting such records are likely to offer them to an institution they have heard of, which may not necessarily be the most appropriate one, so it is hardly surprising that records are to be found in unlikely places. It must be remembered that even the nationalized railway records have never been subject to the Public Records Acts[2] so that there has been no legal impediment to their disposal into private hands.

---

1 In the 'grouping' period two companies, the LMSR and the LNER operated the railways of Scotland as well as railways south of the border. The records dealing with the general operations of these companies are in the PRO even though, inevitably, they include administration of Scottish lines with others.

2 It was proposed at the time of the drafting of the Transport Bill in 1947 that the records of the BTC should be subject to the Public Records Act but the proposal was rejected on the grounds that the BTC was likely to create an extremely large quantity of documents, down to tickets and waybills, all of which would have to be considered for preservation. At the time it was thought inappropriate to make a public record body of a creator of such quantities of records.

Local record offices

In 1984 an advisory panel on railway records designated certain county record offices to receive records of particular railway companies that were deemed to be of local interest. A list of these local repositories and the railway companies allocated to them is in **Appendix 3**.

Irish railways

Irish railways ought to be outside the scope of this book since the repositories for Irish railway records are in Ireland (*see* the list of repositories at the end of the chapter) but, as **Appendix 2** shows, the PRO does hold a few records of Irish railways. For the most part they reflect the interests of English companies in Ireland, tariff agreements between Irish and mainland companies, and annual reports and accounts. They also include copies of documents created for and by parliamentary committee hearings into proposed Irish companies. Many of these documents appear to have been collected by mainland companies as part of their gathering of business intelligence.

Parliamentary records

Parliamentary papers relating to the promotion of railways in all four nations of the British Isles are held by the House of Lords Record Office, but it is helpful to know that some are also available in the PRO. These even include some deposited plans, though nothing approaching a complete set (*see* Chapter 5). Other papers include subscription contracts, estimates of costs, and records of the committee hearings of the Commons and Lords (*see* **Appendix 2**). Of more immediate reference use may be the printed Acts of Parliament held in the PRO's Resource Centre (the Library). The great majority of railway companies obtained authorization to form their companies, raise money, and compulsorily purchase land by Local Acts of Parliament. In the Resource Centre will be found complete runs of bound printed copies of the Local Acts (as well as General and Private Acts) with their published index volumes. The indexes are divided into several categories of which railways is one and light railways and railway certificates under the Railways Construction Facilities Act 1864[3] are others. The railways are indexed according to their exact titles, often referring the reader to a subsection of the entry for a larger, absorbing, company. The references to the Acts are printed under each company's name with some description of the purpose of each Act (e.g. incorporation; powers to build a particular branch; further borrowing powers). All Acts are referred to by the year of the reign of the monarch and the 'chapter'

---

3 This Act permitted the Board of Trade to issue certificates authorizing the construction of railways without an Act in cases where all the relevant landowners agreed to the use of their land.

number within that year (each Act is a 'chapter'). Local and Private Acts' chapter numbers are referred to by Roman numerals like this, '27&28 V[ictoria] c[hapter] cxxiii' and General Acts carry arabic numerals, like this, '27&28 V c.123'. The regnal years and chapter numbers included in each volume of the printed Acts are stamped on its spine.

Records of the commercial railway industry

Most railway companies established workshops for the manufacture, as well as maintenance, of their own locomotives, rolling stock and other equipment, but there was also a sizable commercial railway equipment manufacturing industry. Indeed, some railway companies relied on the products of commercial manufacturers and even the largest ordered from them occasionally. The PRO has none of the records created by these companies but it does have some records about them in returns and other material received by government departments (*see* **Chapter 4**). In many cases the original records of commercial companies have been preserved in archives local to their activities. For example, the records of Beyer Peacock & Co, locomotive engineers, are preserved at the Museum of Science and Industry in Manchester. The Royal Commission on Historical Manuscripts (RCHM) maintains the National Register of Archives which can be used, either at the RCHM office in London or remotely by Internet access, to find out the whereabouts of the records of such companies (*see* list of addresses at the end of the chapter). The RCHM itself holds no records but it is a useful source of information on what records survive and where they are kept.

Government records about railways

The PRO is essentially the archive of government. It includes the surviving records of the government departments that controlled and influenced railways throughout the British Isles, though records of purely local events in Scotland and Ireland will be found in those countries. The principal departments regulating railways were the Board of Trade and the Ministry of Transport though others also had influence. Chapter 4 describes the government records.

Records of the new private companies

The PRO regards the newly privatized railways as outside its scope. Records about the regulation of railways will continue to be deposited in the PRO by the Strategic Rail Authority and the Office of the Rail Regulator but the records of Railtrack and the railway operating companies will not. A unique body, the Railway Heritage Committee (RHC) has been set up by the Railways Act 1993. The RHC's remit is to

designate for preservation records and artefacts it deems to be of historical importance and to direct them to an appropriate repository. Its powers cover the private companies set up from the shadow companies of the BRB. As this book is being written, the RHC is trying to find the means to institute a Railway Industry National Archive to receive records of the new railway that it has designated for preservation. The RHC's address and website are given in the list of addresses below.

Among the privatized railway companies, the largest holder of records is Railtrack. Railtrack maintains the structure of the railway, its track and buildings, and has inherited from the BRB a great many records and plans of structures still in use, many of which are from the nineteenth century. There is no right of access to these records (they are the records of a working business) but access may be arranged in certain circumstances. A fee is likely to be charged for access to information. Enquiries should be made to the Head of Records Management whose address is given below.

Major repositories of records other than the PRO

House of Lords Record Office
House of Lords, London SW1A 0PW
Telephone 020 7219 3074
http://www.parliament.uk
Records of railway Acts of Parliament and proposals for Acts.

London Metropolitan Archives
40 Northampton Road, London EC1R 0HB
Telephone 020 7332 3820
Records of London Transport and its predecessors.
http://www.corpoflondon.gov.uk/archives/lma

National Archives of Scotland
HM General Register House, Edinburgh EH1 3YY
Telephone 1031 535 1314
http://www.nas.gov.uk
Records of Scottish railway companies and the nationalized railway in Scotland.

National Railway Museum
Leeman Road, York YO2 4XJ
Telephone 01904 621261
http://www.nmsi.ac.uk/nrm
Technical records including plans and drawings mainly relating to railway locomotives and rolling stock. Photographic records of the railway companies and private railway photographers.

Public Record of Office of Northern Ireland
66 Balmoral Avenue, Belfast BT9 6NY
Telephone 02890 251318
http://proni.nics.gov.uk
Public and private records of the railways in Northern Ireland. Records of the Railway Preservation Society of Ireland.

Irish Railway Record Society
Heuston Station, Dublin 8
http://www.irrs.ie
Private society holding a large archive of Irish railway records.

For information about the whereabouts of records of the railway industry

Royal Commission on Historical Manuscripts
Quality House, Quality Court, Chancery Lane, London WC2A 1HP
Telephone 020 7242 1198
http://www.hmc.gov.uk
Operates the National Register of Archives. Holds copy listings of records.
(*Note* Does not itself hold records.)

Private railway records

The Secretary
Railway Heritage Committee
British Railways Board Records Centre, 66 Porchester Road, London W2 6ET
http://www.rhc.gov.uk
Responsible for the designation, and direction to repositories, of records of the current railway deemed to be of historical value.

The Head of Records Management, Railtrack plc
Room 210, East Side Offices, Kings Cross Station, London N1 9AP
Telephone 020 7465 9265
Records of, and inherited by, the company.

3 Records Created and Used by the Railways

This chapter considers the kinds of records, created by the railways themselves, that have survived in the PRO. All these records are in the **RAIL** and **AN** departments. **Appendix 2**, which is in the form of an index, shows where the records of each company or other railway organization can be found among the record series in RAIL and AN. We should also note here the library material inherited by the PRO from BTHR. This consists of several series of books on railway history and other railway subjects. These are now available to readers, to order as though they were records, in the series in the department **ZLIB**. Similarly a large collection of railway and other periodicals is available in **ZPER**. There is also a single 'special collection' in **ZSPC** (other such series have been given RAIL references). This is a comprehensive collection of articles and ephemera about railways in the British Isles donated to BTHR by Mr W. E. Hayward.

The largest single collection of railway company records in the PRO is that of the Great Western Railway. Since the GWR was unique in perpetuating its name at the grouping of the railways in 1923, the GWR series include both pre-grouping and grouped company records. As can be seen from the long list of GWR record series shown in **Appendix 2** the potential variety of railway records in the PRO is great. Because of the size of its archive the GWR has separate series for many types of records; other companies frequently have but a single series to their name. Almost anything may appear in these single series, but the variety of records found in the GWR and other large company records cannot be expected there.

Where, in **Appendix 2**, a record series appears immediately after the name of the company, that series contains the main surviving records of the company. Even so substantial numbers of records may be in other series (miscellaneous series can contain more than a main series) so subsidiary series containing records of or about the company are indented below its title. Many company entries do not show a main series; they have only secondary series indented under the company name.

Organization of administrative records

Pre-group period records are frequently bound in registers (this can apply to correspondence as well as to minutes of meetings). They can also survive as single items removed from their original series, perhaps because of their curiosity value. In the latter case it may be difficult to relate items to their originating departments. (The custodians of company records have indulged in a good deal of reorganization of records, putting them into artificial series by type, e.g. share certificates, and creating 'miscellanies' of records taken out of context as 'historical' examples.) Contextual organization of records improves with the grouped railways, which began to keep records in file series. The nationalization period saw a great increase in the paper record and a corresponding need to organize it. There are large file series in the records of British Railways and British Rail; their origins are usually evident.

The following are the principal series of records to be found in the records of the railways.

High office holders

Most company series contain records of **directors' meetings**. These are the main decision-making meetings and deal with company strategy (though they often deal with relatively mundane matters relating to the running of the line as well). There may also be records of **shareholders' meetings**, sometimes called **'proprietors' meetings'**. In a way these are the most important, because the proprietors, the major shareholders, appointed the directors who, in turn, appointed the general manager who appointed the departmental heads of the railway. Below the directors, in a large company, would be the general manager and below him the departmental structure would typically be divided between goods and passenger traffic and engineering. The chief goods manager would be in charge of managers for the districts and, on the passenger side, a superintendent of the line would control district superintendents. In engineering, a chief engineer would be in charge with civil engineers and mechanical and electrical engineers below him. The latter would control superintendents of the locomotive and carriage and wagon departments. There may also have been a marine and dock superintendent in the chief engineer's sphere.

Committees

Policy committees and sub-committees appear frequently. Depending on their importance they might be chaired by a director or the head of a department. Examples are **Traffic Committees, Way and Works Committees** and **Finance Committees** (the

Great Northern Railway, for example, has records of all of these in its general series RAIL 236). In the records of the London & Brighton Railway in the 1840s are records of the **Audit, Coaching, Construction, Finance, General Purposes, Land, Locomotive, Stores** and **Traffic Committees** (RAIL 386). Other companies had similar committees, though they may have called some of them by different titles.

Joint Committees and negotiating bodies

Frequently two or more companies joined forces to run a particular line or system of lines. They would form a **Joint Committee** in which high-level representatives of each company would meet at regular intervals to decide their policy for running the joint line. Records of their meetings are often of equal status with the main company directors' records. Several joint committees had the status of companies in their own right. The major companies sometimes formed consolidated joint committees to administer several of their joint lines together. For example, the Great Western and Midland Railways Joint Committee series (RAIL 241) deals with the administration of the Severn & Wye, Halesowen, and Clifton Extension joint railways as well as the Bristol, Worcester and Churchdown joint stations. At towns where several railways came together they might build a joint station to serve all their traffic. The GWR/MR ones mentioned above are three, another was the station at Normanton, Yorkshire, owned originally by the L&YR, the MR and the York & North Midland railways. A joint committee ran it and its records now have their own series, RAIL 546. The Carlisle Citadel joint station committee (Cal R/LNWR) series, RAIL 98, also contains records of the Carlisle Goods Traffic Committee (Cal R/G&SWR/LNWR/MR), a committee set up to prevent destructive competition between the companies in this area.

Several of the joint committees have record series of their own; for example the Norfolk and Suffolk Joint Railways Committee (GER/GNR/MR), RAIL 518. Since at the grouping the MR fell into the LMSR group while the other two became part of the LNER, the N&S Joint Committee carried on after 1923 as an LMSR/LNER joint committee.

It is worth mentioning here that names died hard on the railways. The Manchester, Sheffield & Lincolnshire and the Midland railways had a joint committee that continued when the MS&L became the Great Central in 1897, and when the GCR became part of the LNER and the MR part of the LMS at grouping in 1923. Even in the grouping period this joint committee was still known as the 'Sheffield and Midland Joint Committee'. The same can apply to sections of the line too; it is not uncommon for railwaymen, even in the nationalized period, to write of a line by its pre-group title.

The Irish and English Traffic Conference (RAIL 327) was not a joint committee but a negotiating body setting rates for traffic between Ireland and the mainland. A large number of companies was involved, some, especially the Irish ones, quite small.

In the LNER records are the minutes of the LMSR/LNER Main Pooling Committee of the 1930s (RAIL 390). This was set up to negotiate 'closer working' in agreeing the handling of traffic at certain locations by one or other company rather than both, the object being to economize by preventing duplication of effort and reducing manpower.

In **Appendix 2** joint committees and negotiating bodies are indexed under the entries for each of their contributing companies. Often records of them are found in several series. All are shown in **Appendix 2**.

Legal and contractual records

Considering, promoting and opposing legislation was a vital part of the railway business. Almost all the railway companies owed their existence to local Acts of Parliament and depended on supplementary Acts to vary and extend their powers. They were also very watchful of their rival companies' proposals to legislate, and tried, by all the influence they could bring to bear, to prevent them achieving advantages. By the middle of the nineteenth century the major railways were promoting annual Bills which might include proposals to alter capital, build new lines and to vary powers together in one Act. Records arising from the parliamentary process may be found in the record series of individual companies as well as several series devoted to them. There are series of:

● Parliamentary Bills and Minutes of Evidence (RAIL 1066 and 1067);
● Special Acts (RAIL 1063);
● Supplementary Acts (RAIL 1064);
● Miscellaneous Acts, North Eastern Area (RAIL 1065).

These are printed copies of parliamentary records and will also be found, more completely, in the House of Lords Record Office. Indeed, it may be easier, in the PRO, to consult the printed Acts in the Resource Centre (Library) (*see* **Chapter 2**, under the heading 'Parliamentary records'). There is also a series containing bye-laws of many railways (RAIL 1001).

Records of contracts, for anything from building sections of the line to the supply of quite mundane services, are often present, as are agreements for services like the Southern Railway's with Stephenson Clarke Ltd for the supply of coal (RAIL 647/29). There are bonds binding signatories to deliver services as promised, and indemnities

allowing, for example, a contractor to enter railway premises to examine and repair wagons, or a person to walk on the line, without risk to the railway company in the case of injury.

Estates and rating

Land was another vital part of the railways' existence. Records relating to land, its ownership, use and disposal are often found, though they are not necessarily systematically organized. Maps and plans may be found useful in this area (*see* **Chapter 6**). The GWR has a series of records devoted to estates and rating (RAIL 274) which includes much about railways taken over as well as joint lines.

Finance

Ledgers, cash books and journals are likely to be present even where few records of a particular company survive. Sometimes the annual and bi-annual reports to shareholders have also survived and there are several series devoted to them (RAIL 1110, 1111, 1114, 1116 and 1117). (**Appendix 2** notes all the companies included in these series.)

Management of staff

Railway companies, at least from the second half of the nineteenth century, were generally keen to show that they cared about the welfare of their staff. The rise of labour unions also spurred these efforts to an extent. Records survive relating to pension funds, welfare funds and the various philanthropic activities of the companies. The latter are particularly evident in the records of the largest companies. The GWR has series of records about its provisions at the works town, Swindon (the mechanics institution, the New Swindon Improvement Company and schools, *see* **Appendix 2**), and the LMSR has records of the endowment of churches at Crewe and Wolverton inherited from the LNWR (RAIL 424/30). Staff registers and records are described in more detail in **Chapter 5**.

Engineering

The engineering history of some railway companies is hardly mentioned in their surviving records except perhaps in board minutes. The larger companies, however, have left us some records of locomotives and rolling stock and something of their civil engineering history. Where records of locomotives and rolling stock survive in the

PRO, they usually take the form of registers of locomotives and sometimes carriages and wagons. Occasionally diagram books are found (*see* **Chapter 6**) and photographs (*see* **Chapter 7**) although the main sets of works drawings and official photographs are preserved in the National Railway Museum. Most of the surviving records, pre- and post-grouping, are in the grouped railways' series. It is always worth looking in the records of the grouped railways if the information sought is not in the pre-group records. They may include such things as locomotive and boiler repair registers, locomotive tender records and wagon repair registers.

Civil engineering is mainly recorded in contracts and specifications (which may be found in almost any general series) and maps and plans (*see* **Chapter 6**), though the LMSR has a series of Civil Engineer's records (RAIL 430). While it can be said that the engineering records surviving in the PRO give a good general impression of the technical side of the industry, particular examples of engineering may be difficult to find. Relative to the vast amount of construction of buildings, bridges, locomotives and the permanent way itself that the railways undertook, only a small proportion of records of the total now survive.

Other forms of transport and railway business

The railways had interests in many activities apart from the running of railways. Canals were frequently the progenitors of railways. The early railway companies had interest in canals and this continued until the canals were placed in a different Executive under the BTC on nationalization. **Appendix 2** does not list canal records. They are generally in separate RAIL series (mostly between RAIL 800 and 899) and represent a large body of records which, beyond this note, are not addressed in this book.

Ferry services became important quite early and the railways owned ships. There are records of the marine activities of the 'big four' (*see* **Appendix 2**) but pre-group shipping activity is less well represented.

In the twentieth century diversification into bus and even airline operation occurred. The records of bus operations are not separately covered in this book, though air operations are noted in **Appendix 2** partly because they are few.

The 'big four' railways acquired an interest in haulage companies, such as Pickfords, Hays Wharf and Carter Paterson. The main records relating to these concerns have been indexed in **Appendix 2**.

Tramway companies

The concept of a railway easily embraces street tramways and they are included in **Appendix 2**. Mostly their records in the PRO are about their promotion. Most of them were local authority responsibilities and their main records are likely to be found in local record offices.

4 Government Policy and Central Control of Railways

It is convenient for research that the major archive of railway administrative records of England and Wales should be held in the PRO together with the records of government departments. Governmental influence on railways has always been important and it increased in the mid-twentieth century. The PRO's holdings of government departmental records are, of course, vast. It would be impossible, in a book of this size, to be definitive about the extent of government records about railways. Indeed, there are few government departments that had no dealings with the railways. This chapter presents a way in to the main sources with the hope that further possibilities for research will occur to the reader as a result.

There are, of course, several different levels of government control, from the creation of national policy at prime ministerial and cabinet level, through the departmental policy decisions taken by responsible government departments, down to the actions of inspectors and individual civil servants in carrying out the policy. At the highest level, in the records of the Prime Minister's Office and the Cabinet Office, will be found quite brief statements of policy decisions with some distilled background material. At departmental level more background detail can be found and some detailing of the results of policy in practice.

This chapter is divided into sections:

High policy – dealing with the records of the Prime Minister and the Cabinet.
Regulatory departments – describing the records of the Board of Trade and the various Ministries of Transport.
Finance and tax – about the Treasury, Inland Revenue, and Customs & Excise.
Railways and the Armed Services – dealing with records of the Admiralty and the War Office and their interest in the construction and use of railways. This section also describes the records of the Air Ministry concerning railways.
Other sources – briefly picking out other government departmental records of potential interest to railway research.

High policy

Prime Minister's Office   **PREM**

The Prime Minister (PM) is the chief minister of the government, chairing the cabinet and guiding ministers, informing the sovereign of events in government and receiving deputations from those concerned in government policy.

The department, the Prime Minister's Office, was not set up until 1916 and is very small, consisting of the PM's private and appointments secretaries and a small staff of civil servants. Its records consist mainly of the PM's correspondence and papers.

PREM I Correspondence, 1916–1940
These are folders of letters, sometimes containing only one. They include:

- a letter from the Minister of Transport on the excessive claims of railway companies (1920);
- pressure on railways to provide work for the unemployed (1923);
- prospects of a Channel Tunnel (1924–1930);
- London Passenger Transport Bill (1929–1931);
- electrification of suburban railways (1929–1933);
- proposed legislation to remove inequalities between road and rail (1932–1933).

PREM 3 Operations papers of the Second World War
(The PM was also Minister of Defence)
Subjects include:

- air raid shelters (including underground stations);
- evacuation of coastal areas (some mention of railways and railway infrastructure);
- railways as part of inland transport for 'Operation Overlord';
- supplies to Russia (including some mention of railway equipment).

PREM 4 Confidential papers of the Second World War
These include:

- Railway companies' plan for air transport (1944);
- Beveridge committee report on skilled men in the services, with a little on railwaymen (1941–1942);
- Bethnal Green underground shelter disaster (1943).

PREM 8 Correspondence and papers, 1945–1951
Dealing with:

- movement of coal;
- shortage of railway wagons;
- delay (1947) in returning 'austerity' locomotives from France;
- nationalization;
- appointment of a Channel Tunnel committee (1949);
- railway wages and disputes.

PREM 11 Correspondence and papers, 1951–1964
Including, among many railway-related subjects:

- discussions on a fixed Channel link;
- industrial relations, wages and strikes;
- nationalized industries in general;
- railway revenues;
- safety and manning;
- reorganization, including the establishment of the British Railways Board and the Beeching proposals.

PREM 13 Correspondence and papers, 1964–1970
Records open so far include:

- Channel Tunnel, 1964–1965;
- policy on rail closures;
- coordination of road and rail services;
- industrial disputes on the railway.

Cabinet Office   CAB

The cabinet is the central policy making body of government and is composed of the most senior ministers. It makes decisions about every aspect of policy, transport being one. The Cabinet Office originated in December 1916 when the cabinet began to record its deliberations systematically, taking as a model the system used from 1904 by one of its committees, the Committee of Imperial Defence. Before that no central record was kept, copies of papers being held by the ministers concerned who might destroy them or include them in their private records. Some earlier memoranda were

returned to the Cabinet Office and are now in CAB 1. In the early 1960s the PRO made an effort to photocopy those it could find in private and other collections. Some 3,300 were copied, some duplicating those in CAB 1, and were placed in CAB 37. The PRO also holds, in CAB 41, copies of letters in the Royal Archives sent by prime ministers to the King or Queen reporting proceedings of the cabinet.

Since CAB series record government business at high level they usually lack detail. The minutes ('conclusions' from August 1919) usually describe each matter agreed in a short paragraph; they are definitely not minutes of the kind that record what was said at meetings. The memoranda, which are the papers used by the cabinet as reference material, are usually distillations devoid of all but essential detail, though they sometimes include supporting documents.

Since the Cabinet Office originated in the First World War, and there are now in the PRO relatively few surviving records of earlier periods, there is in its records a preponderance of warlike themes. Even in the interwar period records about railways seem to deal largely with preparations for future conflict. A major topic after the Second World War is nationalization. Transport planning also figures; railways playing less and less part as the 1960s progress.

Earliest surviving records (up to 1916)

CAB 41 Records copied from the Royal Archives
Prime ministers' letters to the King or Queen about cabinet proceedings, 1868–1916. These are briefings at the highest level and can be very brief, in some cases merely stating that a topic was discussed. Among railway topics mentioned are:

- railway legislation, 1871, 1873, 1913;
- proposed railway amalgamations, 1872, 1909;
- Irish railways, 1872, 1883;
- the Channel Tunnel, 1883, 1892, 1907;
- industrial relations (including strikes), 1907, 1911, 1912, 1916.

Some of these topics are covered in more detail in CAB 37, *see below*.

CAB 37 Copies of cabinet papers in collections outside the PRO
These cover much the same topics as CAB 41 (*above*) though not always the same incidents. There is more detail than in CAB 41 but these papers are also confined to the essential.

CAB 1 Miscellanea

Only a few references to railways have been found in this series which includes the surviving original cabinet memoranda returned to the cabinet, 1866–1916. All those noted date from the First World War. They deal with:

- railway ferries;
- carriage of beer;
- delays;
- the Channel Tunnel;
- provision of railway wagons to Italy.

CAB 2 Committee of Imperial Defence minutes

Some records about railways, notably the Channel Tunnel (1907 and 1914) and distribution of supplies in war.

CAB 3 Committee of Imperial Defence memoranda on home defence

Channel Tunnel again (1906–1914).

CAB 4 Committee of Imperial Defence miscellaneous memoranda

Some records are about distribution of supplies in war including the use of railways.

CAB 38 Committee of Imperial Defence copies of minutes and memoranda

Copies of records in CAB 2, 3, 4 and 18.

CAB 16 Committee of Imperial Defence ad hoc sub-committees

Here are a couple of pieces about:

- supply in time of war (1914) including rail access to ports, particularly Southampton;
- the economic position of London (including statistics of rail-borne freight). (*See* post-1916 records below for more in this series.)

CAB 17 Committee of Imperial Defence correspondence and miscellaneous papers

Among these are:

- Channel Tunnel (1906–1916);
- supplies of British locomotives and rolling stock for the British army in France (1916).

CAB 18 Committee of Imperial Defence miscellaneous volumes

This has another piece on the Channel Tunnel (1906–1914) which brings together much of the material in CAB 2 and 3.

Records after 1916

CAB 21 Registered files

These are the surviving files of the officials of the Cabinet Office. They contain more background information about the subjects considered by the cabinet than the conclusions and memoranda. The files cover the period from 1916 to the latest openings. Among other topics related to railways, they deal with:

- rail freight delays (1917 and 1919);
- Channel Tunnel at various dates;
- civil aviation policy, including a little on the railway companies' air services in the 1930s;
- nationalization of railways, proposed in 1920 and carried out in the 1940s (when it was called 'socialization');
- general transport policy.

CAB 23 Cabinet minutes (conclusions from 1919–1939)

There are several series of minutes of different types. Original subject indexes are pieces within the series so they have to be ordered before you can find out which minute pieces you need to order. Entries do appear in them under 'railways' but it is just as likely that railway subjects are indexed under other terms. The minutes and conclusions are all preserved so every cabinet decision should be here. (*See also* **CAB 128**.)

CAB 24 Cabinet memoranda, 1915–1939

Subject indexes are either in the pieces themselves or are, themselves, separate pieces. Indexes for 1937 and 1938 are included in the series list. (*See also* **CAB 129**.)

CAB 26 Printed minutes of the Home Affairs Committee

There is a subject index to this series. Among others about railways are minutes on:

- supply of alcoholic spirits to railway refreshment rooms (1919–1920);
- the 1921 Railways Bill and the grouping of the railways;
- the settlement of Irish railway claims;
- the Post Office (London) Railway Bill 1924 (extension of time to build the PO railway);
- London Passenger Transport Bill 1931 (London Underground).

CAB 27 Records of committees to 1939

This includes some substantial records of committees including the Supply and Transport Committee, set up in 1919 specifically to deal with strikes and to maintain supplies, which includes records of the railway strikes of 1919, 1924, and the General Strike of 1926. Other subjects are:

- grouping of railways;
- transport policy;
- railway air operations (Cadman Report on civil aviation, 1938).

CAB 16 Committee of Imperial Defence, ad hoc sub-committees

Here is a record of a sub-committee on supplies of coal (1937–1939) which deals with the adequacy of railway wagon stocks. (*See above* for pre-1916 records in this series.)

CAB 33 Post-war Priority and Demobilization Committee, 1918–1919

It appears that only the Permanent (Labour) Sub-committee of the War Priorities Committee has records about railways. The minutes and circulated papers include records about the dilution of labour in railway workshops (to release men for the forces or munitions work).

CAB 40 War Priorities Committee

There are certainly three pieces on supply of locomotives, wagons and railway materials (1917–1919) and there may be other railway-related records lurking under general descriptions.

CAB 46 Committee of Imperial Defence, Air Raid Precautions Committee, 1924–1939

Railways figure in these records (e.g. the vulnerability to gas of underground railways used as air raid shelters). The difficulty is that the list for the most part gives only the date and minute or memoranda numbers. There are contents lists at the beginning of pieces but, of course, you have to order the pieces before you can examine them.

CAB 57 Committee of Imperial Defence, Manpower Committee

This has a few records of the 1920s and 1930s about skilled men required for the forces, including railwaymen, and lists of reserved occupations also including railwaymen.

CAB 58 Economic Advisory Council, 1925–1939

This series contains records of a sub-committee on the Channel Tunnel, 1929–1930, (including a proposal for a 7ft gauge London to Paris railway). The list gives only dates and committee titles but not what the committees considered so there may be more railway-related material hidden here.

CAB 60 Committee of Imperial Defence, Principal Supply Officers Committee

This has one piece containing a list of locomotives and rolling stock sent to France in the First World War.

CAB 61 Irish Boundary Commission, 1924–1925

Under 'Submissions, Evidences and Exhibits' are listed submissions from the **Belfast & County Down Railway** and the **Bessbrook & Newry Tramway Company**. There may well be other records about railways here.

CAB 71 War Cabinet, Lord President's Committees, 1940–1945

In this series there are separate pieces for minutes and memoranda. It appears to contain a good deal about transport policy and railways in the Second World War including such diverse matters as the acquisition of Thomas Cook & Son by the grouped railways, railwaymen's wages and the carriage of flowers by rail.

CAB 72 War Cabinet, Committees on Economic Policy

Records of the Second World War, among which are:

- aggregated railway statistics in statistical digests;
- brief mention of railway needs for materials (in the records of the Sub-committee on Substitute Materials);
- very slight mention of railway production for export (Sub-committee on Encouragement of Exports).

CAB 73 War Cabinet Committees on Civil Defence

Records of the Second World War. Those about railways mainly deal with blackout restrictions.

CAB 78 War Cabinet Committees, miscellaneous and general

Railways are here considered under *Socialization of Industries* (1945).

CAB 87 War Cabinet, Committees of Reconstruction

There is some mention of railways under *reconstruction problems*. These are Second World War records.

CAB 92 War Cabinet, Committees on Supply, Production, Priority and Manpower

Contains a few records about railway equipment and supply of British equipment to allies in the Second World War.

CAB 102 Historical Section, Official War Histories (Second World War)

Records about the research and drafting of the published histories of the Second World War. Railways were specifically covered in *Inland Transport* and also figure in *Civil Defence, Air Raid Shelters* and several others. (*See also* **CAB 103**.)

CAB 103 Historical Section, registered files

Has general files on the war histories (*see* **CAB 102**). Only the *Inland Transport* file appears to deal with railways.

CAB 108 Central Statistical Office, minutes and memoranda

Some basic statistics on traffic receipts, production of locomotives and freight traffic (1940s and 1950s) are included.

CAB 115 Central Office for North American Supplies

A couple of pieces are about British requirements for locomotives and railway equipment (1940–1943).

CAB 117 Reconstruction Secretariat files

Records of the Official Committee on the Planning and Timing of Investment consider the LPTB and whether there should be similar boards in Birmingham, Liverpool and Manchester. There is also a piece on post-war transport and highways policy including railways. These are Second World War records.

CAB 123 Lord President of the Council, Secretariat files

These are Second World War records on:

- coal distribution;
- main-line railway traffic;
- transport of flowers.

CAB 124 Minister for Reconstruction, Lord President of the Council and Minister for Science, Secretariat files

Here are records about:

- post-war planning for railways (mid- to late 1940s);
- rail nationalization, much of it in *socialization of industry* records (1940s);
- rail connections for new towns (1940s);
- transport of radioactive materials (1960s).

CAB 127 Private collections: ministers and officials

Among the records of Sir William Jowitt are some (1942–1944) on town and country planning, planning in general and post-war organization of transport, all of which deal in some measure with railways.

CAB 128 Minutes from 1945

Here are all the cabinet conclusions. The memoranda in **CAB 129** will have a little more detail. (*See also* **CAB 23**.)

CAB 129 Memoranda from 1945

(*See also* CAB 24.)

CAB 130 Ad hoc Committees, general and miscellaneous

Included here are records about:

- railway wages and industrial disputes (late 1940s and 1950s);
- railway policy linked to the modernization plan (1956);
- papers on reorganization leading to the establishment of the British Railways Board (1960).

CAB 132 Lord President's Committee and sub-committees

Only the main committee seems to consider railway and urban tramway subjects (one is the replacement of London's trams by trolley buses, 1946). Minutes of meetings are in separate pieces from their background papers.

CAB 134 Committees: general series

Includes records of committees on:

- investment programmes (1947–1951);
- socialization of industries (1940s) and nationalized industries (1950s and 1960s);
- road and rail transport and transport policy (1950s and 1960s);
- fixed Channel link (1963–1965);
- reorganization of railways (dealing with the Beeching proposals, 1963–1964).

CAB 139 Central Statistical Office: correspondence and papers

Includes records about:

- locomotive stocks and production (1942–1947);
- capital expenditure (1945 to the mid-1950s) some of it about railways;
- national income, including statistics of rail passenger travel;
- examination of reports of railway accidents (1948–1949).

CAB 140 Central Statistical Office: selected working papers

Among these are two files on production of locomotives and rolling stock for home and foreign orders (1939–1949).

Regulatory departments

Board of Trade and Ministry of Transport   BT and MT

The Board of Trade became the principal department involved in regulating railways. Its records therefore contain a great deal about the early railway companies and their progress through the nineteenth century. It also had responsibility for the regulation of companies and the development of policy on industry in general. The commercial railway equipment manufacturers feature in the records of these functions. The Ministry of Transport was established in 1919 and took over many of the transport responsibilities of the Board of Trade and others.

When the railway age began the Board of Trade was a small department of government acting more as an adviser on trade matters than an executive body. Its business was small enough to be given the personal attention of 'the Board' – the President and Vice-president assisted by their secretaries. As the nineteenth century proceeded the Board set up specialist departments, including the Railway Department, though much of its business was recorded centrally. The Board's practice in the early years of railways was to refer correspondence to the relevant specialist department (such as the Railway Department or another government department), receive its response and then, itself, respond to the original correspondent.

The Regulation of Railways Act 1840 gave the Board powers to appoint inspectors of railways, to approve and disallow railway company bye-laws, to receive returns of traffic, accidents and charges from railway companies and to enforce compliance with parts of their Acts that railway companies had not carried out. The Regulation of Railways and Conveyance of Troops Act 1842 gave the Board power to prevent the opening of a railway until the inspector was sure of its safety, and a succession of Acts thereafter refined and extended the Board's powers. In order to deal with the considerable business created by these powers the Railway Department was set up in 1840. In 1844 the responsibility for railways passed to the Railway Board (theoretically outside the responsibility of the President of the Board of Trade but never entirely detached from it). In 1846 the Railway Commissioners took over and in 1851 the Railway Department was reinstated. The Department lasted until 1919 when responsibility for railways was taken over by the new Ministry of Transport. Board of Trade Railway Department records (including those of the Railway Board and Commissioners) were transferred to that department and have come to the PRO in several Ministry of Transport (MT) series.

Railway Department records

MT 6 Correspondence and papers

This is the main series of Railway Department records. Its contents have been heavily weeded. Even so, it contains a wealth of information from 1840 to 1919. **Indexes and registers** to MT 6 are in **MT 7** covering the whole period. An index of railway company and station names, with the numbers of the MT 6 pieces in which they appear, is also available in the PRO (it has also been published by the List and Index Society, 1984).

Railway Department **out-letters** are in **MT 11** though, as a set, they survive for the early period only (1840–1855). Some draft out-letters are in **MT 6**. Curiously, the **indexes to out-letters, MT 12** survive from 1855 to 1917 so some idea of the business done can be gained but no specific detail.

MT 13 Minute books

These were kept only between 1844 and 1857 but they include the minutes of the Railway Commissioners.

MT 8 Railway Commissioners returns of iron bridges

Returns made by railway companies (1847) describing their iron bridges, in response to a circular from the Commissioners after the collapse of the Dee bridge.

The **Railway Department** still has a series of **correspondence and papers** in the BT lettercode, **BT 22**, but this contains records of the functions that remained in the Board of Trade after 1919. A few pieces relate tangentially to railways, e.g. **BT 22/36/12** Tramways Institute of Great Britain: articles of association, 1885.

MT 91 Drawings and plans

A small series including a register to drawings, *c*.1840–1886, almost all of which are now destroyed. The examples surviving here consist of drawings of:

- details of the Wishaw Viaduct, Caledonian Railway;
- bridges on the Limerick & Ennis Railway, *c*.1857;
- a proposed Channel Tunnel 1866–1868;
- summit tunnel on the Manchester & Leeds Railway 1841;
- I.K. Brunel's plans for mixed gauge railways with Robert Stephenson's report thereon.

In the context of the Railway Department we should also look at the general Board of Trade series.

BT 5 Minutes to 1952

These are notes of the correspondence and submissions dealt with by the Board and its actions on each item of business, some of which touch on railways. Up to July 1839 (**BT 5/46**) the minutes are the best means of over-viewing the work of the Board and finding original in-coming letters. Up to that time they are in indexed volumes describing the papers received and briefly indicating the action to be taken on each. They might, for example, indicate the line to be taken by the secretary when replying to a correspondent, that the matter was to be referred elsewhere (perhaps to the Railway Department), or that no action was to be taken, in which case the single word 'read' appeared. Many of the entries have annotations in red ink giving the numbers of the bundles in which the papers were originally stored. These red numbers can easily be related to pieces in the **BT 1** list. The presence of a red number indicates that the paper will be found in **BT 1** rather than **BT 2** (in-letters, Foreign Office) or **BT 6** (Miscellanea).

From July 1839 until 1857 the minutes consist of unbound drafts. After 1857 the minutes record only establishment matters and appointments (e.g. formal appointments of railway inspectors).

BT 4 General registers and indexes up to 1864

Until 1864 each incoming item of correspondence was given a registered number which, with a note of its contents, was entered in the general register (this series) as well as being noted in the Minutes (**BT 5**). As noted above it is usually easier to trace documents using BT 5 up to 1839.

In BT 4 there are index volumes and registers. **Indexes** have sections A to Z for the initial letter of each subject (e.g. railway passenger duty under 'R'). They also have separate sections for government departments' correspondence. It requires ingenuity and persistence to find entries here (e.g. Grand Junction Railway entered under 'Treasury'). The indexes give the page numbers in the corresponding registers where will be found entries for each paper giving the paper number.

Registers record the registered paper numbers as well as referring backward to previous papers and forward to subsequent ones, again, giving the paper numbers. They also provide a basic record of business dealt with on papers now destroyed. They are used for finding the registered numbers of in-coming papers in **BT 2** and **BT 6** and must be used to find papers in **BT 1** after July 1839. If a matter was referred to (say) the Railway Department, that department's reply to the Board was given its own registered number like any other piece of in-coming correspondence and had its own entries in BT 4 (and **BT 5**).

It has to be said that there is not a great deal on railways in the correspondence series **BT 1**, **BT 2** and **BT 6** to which the registers relate. Before the setting up of the Railway Department, of course, any railway-related matters will be there, but afterwards, unsurprisingly, the main record is in **MT 6**, etc.

In-coming papers

Original incoming items of correspondence were bound in volumes and now form series **BT 1**, **BT 2** and part of **BT 6**.

BT 1 is the main series of **in-letters** up to 1863. Most original papers on railways will be found here. They are bound generally (but not infallibly) in numerical order of their registered numbers. Up to 1845 the papers survive complete but have been weeded thereafter. Use **BT 4** and **BT 5** as finding aids. The series is listed by date only up to 1846 (**BT 1/462**) and descriptively listed thereafter. **BT 19 Indexes to papers retained** can be used as a finding aid to the papers in BT 1.

Examples of items from the descriptive part of the list of BT 1:

- **BT 1/463/2177** Plan of Holyhead Harbour including railway, 1846.
- **BT 1/464/594** Memorial against Chester & Holyhead R becoming owners of steam vessels, 1847.
- **BT 1/464/598** Papers on Lord Dalhousie's Railway Dissolution Act, including memorial of proprietors of shares in proposed Staffordshire & Shropshire Jct R, 1847.
- **BT 1/464/850** Companies' Registration Office on renewal of certificate of provisional registration of a railway company, 1847.
- **BT 1/1827a/52** Resignation of Capt. Laffan from the Railway Department, 1852.

BT 2 In-letters: Foreign Office, 1824–1845

Some of the correspondence from the Foreign Office is here but, curiously, a good deal of it is in the ordinary series, **BT 1**. Most railway items here concern foreign railways but some touch on British ones. Papers may be here if they cannot be found in **BT 1** or **BT 6**.

BT 6 Miscellaneous papers up to 1921

The series contains records about railways, though much of what was there has been removed to **MT 6** (*see* Railway Department below). In-letters may be in BT 6 if they cannot be found in **BT 1** or **BT 2**.

A few maps were extracted from **BT 1** and are now in **BT 9 Maps, 1851–1853**. Only one piece is of railway interest: **BT 9/9** (now a map reference **MPI 1/140**), seven plans

of proposed railway from the coalfield in Llandil Tal-y-bont, Glamorgan, to the Spitty extension of the Bynea Branch of the Llanelly Railway, 1851.

Out-going papers

BT 3 Copies of out-letters up to 1863

Bound in chronological order. More railway subjects are covered here than in the latter part of **BT 1** since these records have been preserved entire except for some routine correspondence. The series is listed by date only. From April 1837 (**BT 3/27**) each volume has its own index, but the normal means of reference is by the date of each letter which will be found in the **BT 4** registers or, up to July 1839, in **BT 5**.

BT 198 Board of Trade Council, minutes and papers, 1917–1927

Records of the 'morning meetings' to discuss administrative action involving policy. Railway subjects are treated as any other industry.

BT 55 Records of departmental committees, 1910–1959

Several committees deal with railways as an industry.

Other Board of Trade departmental records

As time went on the Board divided its work among various specialist departments and divisions. They are given below in alphabetical order of their titles.

Civil Aviation Departments

(*See also* Air Ministry records, *below*.)

BT 217 R series files

This series includes information on railway run airlines in the 1930s and 1940s.

BT 247 Aerodromes group

One file includes correspondence with Great Western and Southern Airlines about Cardiff Airport.

Commercial Department

BT 11 Correspondence and papers, 1866 onwards
Few pieces of any sort dated before 1914 survive and relatively few relating to railways in any period. Those that are here deal with:

- commercial production and export of railway locomotives and equipment in the late 1940s;
- two pieces on the export of electric railway equipment to Russia and Poland in the early 1960s.

BT 12 Out-letters, 1864–1921
There is railway material here but finding it requires effort. Earlier records are flimsy wet-process copies of manuscript letters, later come carbon copies of typed letters. Because they were bound into volumes there has been no selection, though between 1864 and 1913 (**BT 12/1–74**) a significant number of the volumes are wanting. Non-selection, however means that much routine work has survived. Up to 1914 (**BT 12/87**) the letters are in chronological order, after that the arrangement is alphabetical by name of addressee. As an example:

- **BT 12/91** (1915) has letters to the Great North of England, Clarence & Hartlepool R, the Great Southern & Western R of Ireland and the GWR all under 'G'.

Commercial Relations and Exports Department

BT 246 Export Licensing Branch files
Has a little on land transport, (including railway) equipment in the 1950s.

Commodity and General Division

BT 213 Files
A few records, of the 1960s, are about railways especially rail closures and the Channel Tunnel.

Companies Department

BT 58 Correspondence and papers, 1850 onwards
Includes records about railways and commercial railway equipment manufacturing companies.

Companies Registration Office

BT 41 Files of joint stock companies registered under the 1844 and 1856 Acts

Among them files of dissolved railway companies and railway equipment manufacturers. The kinds of papers that may be found are:

- prospectuses;
- provisional registrations;
- lists of directors;
- returns of shares;
- changes to lists of shareholders.

BT 31 Files of dissolved companies registered after 1856

Similar to **BT 41** (above) with selected annual returns and, after 1932, liquidators' accounts.

BT 34 Dissolved companies, liquidators' accounts, 1890–1932

After 1932 the accounts are in **BT 31**.

BT 288 Miscellaneous records of dissolution and winding up of companies

Records of the process of dissolution, 1891 onwards, including records of several railway and tramway companies.

BT 285 Railway Companies Act 1866, returns

Returns of half-yearly capital accounts of railway companies under the Railway Companies Securities Act 1866.

BT 283 Returns under section 39 of the Railway and Canal Traffic Act 1888

Canal owners were required to report to the companies registrar the name and description of their canal, the principal officer and main office. This series includes the returns of railway companies in respect of the canals they owned.

Establishment Department

BT 13 Correspondence and papers, 1865 onwards

Staff matters, including appointments of officials such as railway inspectors and Railway Rates Tribunal members and the loan of railway officers to government departments in the First World War, and legislation, including railway bills and orders. Registers and indexes to this series are in **BT 14**. (**BT 19 Indexes to papers retained** can also be used as a finding aid.) The series is worth checking for oddities too, e.g. **BT 13/10/16** 'Fish: returns of amount conveyed by railway in 1878'.

BT 14 Registers and indexes of correspondence, 1865–1917

Original indexes to **BT 13**, including reference to all the records surviving in BT 13 plus all the correspondence now destroyed, important and trivial, with some indication of what it was about and what happened. The series is arranged alphabetically by subject or personal name.

BT 20 Out-letters, 1865–1921

These deal with similar subjects to those in **BT 13**. Indexes to this class are in **BT 21, Indexes to out-letters, 1865–1921**.

Finance Department

BT 15 Correspondence and papers, 1865 onwards

Files on expenses and a few relatively minor financial matters involving railways. Examples are:

- **BT 15/2/A658/66** Dover Harbour: amount due (from SER and LCDR) for pier dues, 1866;
- **BT 15/20/F893/82** Tay Bridge Inquiry: expenses, 1882;
- **BT 15/52/F4675/06** Vauclain's Patent: Act for rendering valid letters patent for improvements in compound steam locomotives, 1906.

Indexes are in **BT 16**.

BT 16 Indexes and registers, 1864–1919

Indexes to **BT 15** starting a year earlier than BT 15 and including reference to all the correspondence of the department surviving and destroyed. Indexes refer to entries in registers by the registered number of the letter and folio number of the BT 15 letter book. The index references are mostly to people, though company names are also used.

BT 17 Out-letters, 1864–1919

These volumes are arranged chronologically. Sampling shows much (mainly routine) on railways. They are indexed in **BT 18**.

BT 18 Indexes to out-letters, 1869–1918

Arranged alphabetically, these give the registered number of each letter and the folio in the relevant **BT 17** letter book. Examples from **BT 18/23**, 1891:

- LCDR and SER, Dover Pier dues and expenses;
- LNWR, payment for parcels from Poplar;
- GWR, warrants for travel of seamen.

BT 62 Controller of Trading Accounts, correspondence and papers, 1919–1930

Includes:

- a file on traffic on government controlled railways;
- a couple of files on timber for railways.

Finance Division

BT 279 Files, 1921 onwards

Contains a few files, 1958–1969, on a loan to the North British Locomotive Co. under the Distribution of Industry Act 1945.

Harbour Department

MT 10 Correspondence and papers, 1864–1919

Contains material on railway bridges, railway works in harbours and railway land on foreshores. Access to it is by **BT 19 Indexes to papers retained**. Like all subject indexes, BT 19 has its limitations. It is not especially concerned to identify railways. The best approach is to look for locations.

Industries and Manufactures (I&M) Department

BT 64 Correspondence and papers, 1919 onwards

Deals with the effects of transport and industrial policy on railways and on the

commercial railway manufacturing industry. There is a subject index covering BT 64/97–4135.

BT 85 Out-letters, 1918–1921
Few letters appear to be about railways or railway manufacturers.

BT 56 Chief Industrial Adviser
Sir Horace Wilson was advisor to the Department of Overseas Trade and the Ministry of Labour as well as to the Board of Trade, 1929–1932. The staff was absorbed into the I&M Department in 1932. The records concern several railway schemes, large and small, for example:

- **BT 56/5/E/228** Southwold harbour: light railway scheme, 1929;
- **BT 56/10/B/355** Plan for Outer-London goods railway, 1929;
- **BT 56/30/CIA/1640/2** Survey of proposed railway schemes under the Development Act 1930.

Power Transport and Economic Department

The Industrial Power and Transport Department was set up in 1918 but became the Power Transport and Economic Department after the Ministry of Transport took much of its transport work in 1919.

BT 65 Correspondence and papers, 1906–1929
There are several files dealing with railway matters including the Channel Tunnel.

Solicitor's Department

BT 23 Indexes and registers of correspondence, 1879–1902
None of the correspondence to which these finding aids relate survives, though some solicitor's papers may be found in departmental files and solicitor's subject files are in **BT 103** (below). There was, however, a considerable amount of correspondence on railway matters, and with railway companies, as these registers show. A certain amount of information about each item of correspondence is given.

BT 103 Files, 1860 onwards

Includes files on:

- the Tay Bridge Inquiry, 1880;
- the Channel Tunnel, 1882–1919;
- some twentieth century legal matters involving railway companies and the export of railway equipment by commercial manufacturers.

Statistics Department/Division

The Statistics Department was renamed Statistics Division in 1945.

BT 70 Correspondence and papers, 1918 onwards

Includes files on:

- production of railway equipment by railway companies and commercial makers;
- censuses of production.

Other Ministry of Transport records

MT 24 Transport Arbitration Tribunal, 1947–1957

A court set up to determine the values of transport shares and securities to enable compensation to be made to the owners on the nationalization of transport undertakings. It also dealt with disputes involving the BTC. The records include assessments of value of minor and light railways, including annual accounts, details of dividends and shareholders.

MT 41 Ferries Committee, 1946

Some selected files on ferry services of the 'big four'.

MT 43 Transport Advisory Council, 1934–1944

The Council advised the Minister of Transport on the coordination of transport and its improvement and development. The records consist of the formal Minutes of the Council and Committee files, mostly about roads but with railway subjects among them.

MT 49 Geddes papers

Records of the private office of Sir Eric Geddes, the first Minister of Transport. There is a great deal on railways and transport by railway and the Railways Bill 1921 which grouped the railways.

MT 50 Defence Planning and Emergency Transport Committees

Records of the preparation of transport for war and the committees on transport that met during the Second World War (1924–1948). Railways are relatively poorly represented here. Nevertheless it is a large series and holds a significant amount of records relating to railways.

MT 51 Ministry of Transport Council, 1919–1922

The Council discussed transport problems with the minister. One of its concerns was the state of the railways after the First World War. It also considered the Channel Tunnel, and matters affecting individual railways.

MT 56 Rates and charges

Records of formal meetings and files about rates charged by transport undertakings including a great deal about railway and street tramway fares and charges (1940s and 1950s)

MT 62 Private Office papers, 1928–1953

Records of ministers. They include records of:

- the Official Committee on Inland Transport, 1944;
- government control of railways, 1941;
- transport legislation of the 1950s.

MT 63 Port and Transit, correspondence and papers

There are several files on railway owned ports and co-ordination of railways in port working (1930s–1950s).

MT 65 Statistics files

Contains files on post-war planning including:

- some dealing specifically with railway needs (1942–1948);
- investigations into railway traffic (1950s and 1960s);

- the Beeching report and channel crossings.

It should be said that many files are *about* the results rather than containing the statistical results themselves.

MT 74 Transport Act 1947, files and papers

Records (1941–1948) about proposals for the nationalization of transport undertakings. As well as general files on transport there are specific files about:

- minor railway companies;
- the Railway Clearing House;
- future organization of the BTC.

MT 80 Transport Tribunal proceedings

A court to deal with rates and charges. The records cover road, rail (including London Transport) and waterborne transport. The tribunal issued fares orders setting permitted charges. The records run from 1947 to 1964.

MT 87 Nationalized Transport Division files

These files cover the whole decade of the 1960s. There is much about:

- railway workshops;
- manning of the railways;
- conditions of service;
- pensions;
- extensions of the London Underground.

MT 92 Road Safety files

This series is mentioned only for one piece, **MT 92/239** which is about accident prevention and half-barrier level crossings, 1963–1966.

MT 94 Tramways inspection registers, 1871–1949

Records of the Board of Trade under the Tramways Act 1870 and the Light Railways Act 1896. The powers of the Board of Trade were transferred to the Ministry of Transport in 1919 and those of the Light Railway Commission in 1921. These records are register entries of inspections of street tramways arranged in alphabetical order of company in each register. The registers refer to papers and plans and orders which may be found in **MT 6, MT 54 Light Railway Plans** and **MT 58 Light Railway Orders**.

MT 95 Highway engineering files
Files, 1950s and 1960s, on:

- accidents on level crossings;
- railway bridges crossing roads.

MT 96 General Division files
Files, 1940s–1960s, on:

- pensions of employees of the BTC and the regulations thereon;
- the Railway Bill (1962–3);
- the policy and political balance of the Transport Users Consultative Committees;
- studies of road and rail transport costs;
- suburban railway electrification;
- extension of the London Underground to Heathrow.

MT 97 Road Transport files
Files, 1940s–1960s, on subjects including:

- the replacement of trams by buses;
- the Victoria Line tube;
- the effects of the Beeching plan;
- Liner trains.

MT 100 Highways N Division files
Files, 1960s, on the effects of the Beeching rail closures and use of abandoned railways as roads.

MT 106 London Highways Division files
Includes:

- a file (1930–1966) on level crossings in London;
- several files (1960s) on railway bridges crossing roads;
- files on the effect on traffic of Beeching rail cuts.

MT 118 Bridges Engineering Division files

Files, 1950s–1970s, on:

- the effect on road bridges of overhead electrification of railways;
- railway bridges crossing roads;
- the effect on traffic of rail closures in the Isle of Wight.

MT 132 Finance Transport and Shipping Division

Files, 1950s and 1960s, on general transport financial matters, including:

- the policy for investment in railways;
- the financial winding up of the BTC;
- a file (with papers going back to the 1920s) about the sale of the Welsh Highland Railway to the Festiniog Railway.

MT 135 London Policy Division

Records from the 1960s and early 1970s on:

- the London Transport Board including Board membership;
- extensions of the tube;
- power supply and capital investment in the Underground.

There are also files on:

- schemes for rail links to Heathrow Airport;
- electrification of the Great Northern suburban lines;
- the Transport Co-ordinating Council for London.

MT 147 Public Transport A Division files

These records deal with:

- legislation, including the Transport Bill 1968;
- Passenger Transport Authorities' concerns about railways.

MT 149 Directorate General of Economic Planning

Files, 1960s, about:

- railway policy review and white papers on transport policy and the national freight plan (1967);
- railway capital projects;
- corporate planning in British Railways;
- the future of railway workshops;
- the policy for preventing closure of socially desirable rail services designated to be closed by the Beeching plan.

Finance and tax

The Treasury   T

The Treasury is the department of the Chancellor of the Exchequer and is responsible for financial policy at home and abroad. It retains a link with the Prime Minister who has the title First Lord of the Treasury. The Treasury's financial policy concerns include tax, foreign exchange and the entire economic state of the country. It controls all government expenditure and approves the amounts of money voted to each government department each year, having a powerful effect on the use made of it. This means that the Treasury records contain a great deal of information about the work of government departments. It receives information from other departments as well as undertaking its own research. In a sense, Treasury records stand between those of the Cabinet Office and those of the subject departments. They are often concerned with policy at the highest level but also dip into more mundane levels of detail. They can be useful in drawing together information on topics to which several government departments have contributed. Since railways were regulated by government and contributed to the economy of the country, they figure quite strongly in Treasury records.

T 1 Treasury Board papers

This is an extremely large series containing the in-coming papers to the Treasury from the sixteenth century to 1920. It has been extensively weeded but still retains an enormous amount of information. To give some idea of the material on railways in T 1, here are some examples taken from the descriptive list entries:

- **T 1/13125,** *1882, Post Office and Board of Trade: Irish mail contract.*
- **T 1/13387,** *1883, Metropolitan Railway: workmen's trains; employment of sergeant of Royal Engineers to make observations* (but *note*, this is about his employment rather than his investigations).

- **T 1/15310,** *1883, Midland Railway and others: percentages claimed on telegraph works.*
- **T 1/11331/13890/11,** *1911, Board of Trade: financial position of Leek & Manifold Valley Light Railway; status of loans by Treasury and Staffordshire County Council.* (*Note* that the reference for the last piece has four elements; **T 1/11331** together make the piece reference, but it is necessary to add the 1911 paper number, **13890/11** to get the specific item).

T 1 has a descriptive list from the latter part of the nineteenth century but up to about the 1870s we have to rely on contemporary registers and indexes to find papers. There are three contemporary finding aids, **T 2, T 3** and **T 108**.

T 2 Registers of papers

These are large index volumes. The object of consulting them is to find the paper number of a relevant record to translate into a T 1 reference. These indexes are cumbersome to use. They are alphabetical but they group certain topics under a particular letter. For example, entries for the Commissioners of Stamps may be found grouped under 'S'. At the beginning of each letter of the alphabet is a contents list. The paper numbers take the form of a year (there are several T 2 registers for each year) and a paper number within that year. In many ways it is easier, though less thorough, to use **T 108**.

T 108 Subject registers

This is a much smaller series, on open access in the reference room, which lists paper numbers under subject headings. For example under 'Railroads' in **T 108/30** is a lengthy list of papers including *'The Greenwich & Gravesend Railway 8200/35'*. In this case **8200** is the paper number, **35** means 1835. Another example is *'The Commissioners of Stamps report on memorials of proprietors of railways to compound for passenger duty'*. One of several paper numbers quoted here is **503/34**. Whether you find your paper number in T 2 or T 108 the next step is the same; consult the relevant register in **T 3**.

T 3 Skeleton registers

These are simple registers listing papers for each year in numerical order. By the side of each paper number may be a tick, in which case it ought to be in **T 1**, or a blank, which means it does not survive, or another paper number. Another number means that the original paper has been associated with a later paper and taken the later paper's reference. In the 1834 T 3 register, paper **503/34**, which we found in **T 108**, has written beside it, **24838/35**. Consulting the register for 1835 we find a blank so our paper and the later one have been destroyed. This is a very frequent result. One has to be patient using the finding aids to T 1. A paper can be followed for years as it transfers from one number to another only to be destroyed in the end.

Another reference under 'Railroads' in **T 108/30** is *'Railroad contracts, 6941/38'*. In the 1838 T 3 register there is a tick by that number indicating survival. Looking up the series list for **T 1** we find that paper 6941 of 1838 is within the range of papers in **T 1/3258**. The call reference we use is **T 1/3258/6941**. The item turns out to be about contracts between the railways and the Post Office for carrying mail.

Should a paper number listed in a T 3 register have an 'L' by it, it means it has been placed in a 'long bundle'. These are bundles of papers on the same subject put together by the Treasury clerks to keep like with like. The practice was stopped in 1840. Long bundles are in **T 1/3411–4404**. The best way to find a paper in them is to find a likely subject bundle. The titles are listed in the T 1 series list. Examples are:

- **T 1/3652** Dean Forest Railway;
- **T 1/4145** Railways: England;
- **T 1/4166** Railways: Ireland and Shannon navigation.

Out-letters

These are registers of Treasury letters, hand copied or in the form of flimsy copies of originals both manuscript and, later, typed. The series lists give dates only, so one can only pick a likely piece and check its internal index having ordered it.

T 5 Admiralty, 1849–1920
Railway matters would appear to occur regularly though not in quantity. (For the Admiralty's interest in railways, *see* Records of the Armed Services *below*.)

T 8 Corporations, 1849–1913
Mostly correspondence to local mayors. Railway matters usually concern land for railways.

T 9 Council
Letters to the Privy Council Office from before the beginning of railways to 1922. Letters to the Boards of Trade, Education and Agriculture are sometimes included. Sampling found letters about the railway inspectorate, light railways and individual companies including Irish ones.

T 14 Ireland, 17th century to 1924
Contains some correspondence on the finance of Irish railways.

T 27 General, from before steam railways to 1920

The series is quite difficult to use because the list is by date only and the indexes are in each volume of correspondence. Railway subjects are to be found but are rare. Railway companies are not always indexed by name. Examples of content:

- letters to railways about lines proposed to pass through the Crown Estate of the Royal Military College;
- to the Rother Valley Light R refusing grant in aid of construction.

From 1921 the Treasury put its papers into subject files in a succession of series. The immediate successors of T 1 were **Finance Files, T 160; Supply Files, T 161; Establishment Files, T 162** and **General Files, T 163**.

T 163 General files 1921–c.1945

Railway records here are mainly about railway Bills including several on London underground railways, including the London Passenger Transport Bill 1933–4, various electric tramways and several mainline railways.

Thereafter Treasury records were placed in divisional series of which the following have some significance for railway history.

T 224 Agriculture, Trade and Transport Division

The series includes several files, 1950s and 1960s, on:

- Channel Tunnel;
- Victoria Line of the London underground;
- public transport in Northern Ireland;
- payments to BTC for maintenance of bridges and crossings.

T 228 Trade and Industry Division

Files, 1940s and 1950s, including:

- nationalization of railways;
- BTC finance, receipts and expenditure, and capital investment programme;
- London Transport;
- Railway (London Plan) Committee.

T 233 Home (Finance) Division

Files, 1930s to 1960s, including:

- nationalization of railways;
- BTC finance;
- British Transport Stock;
- Railway Savings Bank;
- railways in Northern Ireland including the split of the GNR(I) between North and South;
- Channel Tunnel Study Group.

T 298 National Resources Divisions

Records of the 1960s including:

- BTC finance;
- pay and conditions of BTC staff;
- BTC requirements for locomotives and equipment;
- electrification of London Midland main line;
- Channel Tunnel Working Party.

T 311 National Economy Group

High level files (Chancellor, Ministers, Chairman of BRB) on the application of incomes policy on the railways, 1960–1964.

T 312 Finance Overseas and Co-ordination Division

Files of the first half of the 1960s, mainly about foreign railways owned in Britain but also about export guarantees to British railway equipment manufacturers for exports.

Senior officers' and committee records

Three other Treasury series are worthy of note, two series of senior officers' papers and records of a committee.

T 172 Private Office Papers and Private Collections, Chancellor of the Exchequer's Office

These range in date from 1915 to 1945 and include:

- deputations from the Railway Companies Association about taxes and losses from road competition, 1920s and 1930s;

- financial position of railways, including Irish railways, 1918–1919;
- London Underground;
- notes and reports on various aspects of railways.

T 186 Hardman Lever papers

Between 1919 and 1921 Sir Hardman Lever was Treasury representative in the Ministry of Transport. He supervised all financial transactions relating to roads, railways and canals. Records include:

- Irish railways, 1920–1922 including the split between North and South;
- Railway Advisory Committee, 1920;
- terms of acquisition of privately owned wagons, 1919;
- terms of hire of government pool of rolling stock;
- Channel Tunnel.

T 191 Development (Public Utility) Advisory Committee, 1929–1939

This committee scrutinised projects requiring government aid from the points of view of relief of unemployment, improved public amenity and use of British products. It approved applications for assistance. The class contains a series of files on schemes of the GWR, LMSR, LNER, Metropolitan Railway and the rest of the London Underground.

Taxation   CUST, IR

Several taxes are covered here, the main ones being Stamp Duty and Railway Passenger Duty. The Duties on the Stage Carriages Act 1832 imposed a duty of a halfpenny per mile for every four passengers. Railway companies were required to keep a record of the number of paying passengers carried and the number of miles they were conveyed and to inform the Commissioners of Stamps monthly. The Lords of the Treasury were empowered to compound with the railway companies for payment of an agreed sum instead of a calculated amount of tax due. The Duties on the Passengers Act 1842 took into account the apportionment of tax between companies in respect of through journeys between them. The 'Parliamentary' trains were exempted in 1844. The tax was modified several times in the nineteenth century and was not repealed until 1929. Records about it are in Treasury series (*above*) and in those of the Inland Revenue and Customs and Excise. Passenger duty was at first collected by the Commissioners of Stamps, then, from 1847, by the Board of Excise. In 1849 the Board of Excise combined with the Board of Stamps to form the Board of Inland Revenue. In 1909 the Commissioners of Excise left the Inland Revenue to join

the Board of Customs as H. M. Customs and Excise. Excise functions remained separate throughout these changes. The two distinct parts of Customs and Excise dealt with customs (duties imposed on goods brought into the country 'from foreign') and excise (duties on goods and services produced and sold within the country including Railway Passenger Duty). The records of all tax matters are dealt with below in departmental groups beginning with the Inland Revenue.

IR 32 Railway Assessment Authority

The Authority was set up under the Railways (Valuation for Rating) Act 1930 to assess the net receipts of railway companies, make a valuation, and apportion a part of the valuation to each railway land holding. Between 1936 and 1948 it made a series of valuation rolls for each of the 'big four' grouped railway companies. This series contains the valuation rolls as well as the records of meetings, and the papers, of the Authority.

IR 40 Stamps and Taxes Division

A very large series of files, from the 1800s to the 1990s, covering the whole range of inland tax collection and policy. Railways figure in it quite strongly. Files here deal with individual railway companies' liability to stamp duty, income tax, inhabited house duty and tax matters affecting employees of the railways.

IR 59 Selected Death Duty Accounts

Files on the estates of deceased celebrities, including George Stephenson and I. K. Brunel. There may be others with railway connections too.

IR 82 Chief Inspector of Taxes

This series contains a few files about railways dealing with:

- depreciation and renewals allowances requested by the Locomotive Manufacturers' Association, 1922–1930;
- wear and tear allowances (depreciation) for railway wagons, 1925–1929;
- BTC and London Transport pension schemes, 1955–1956;
- British Rail and London Transport, PAYE.

IR Miscellanea

Mentioned solely because **IR 83/13** contains the 1849 instructions to Excise officers concerning stage carriage and railway duties.

It might be thought that the records of customs would be irrelevant to the history of railways in a country largely bordered by sea, but since 1922 the United Kingdom has had a land boundary between Ulster and the Irish Republic. Not the least of the problems for customs control has been the railways crossing the border. Customs and Excise series therefore contain excise material on internal railway taxes and some records concerning customs and railways in Britain.

CUST 45 Excise registered papers

There appear to be only two files of railway interest here:

- a proposal to abolish railway passenger duty, 1897;
- sale of wines and spirits in railway dining cars, 1880–1900.

CUST 49 Customs and Excise registered papers, 1909 onwards

This is the main series of records of the combined Board of Customs and Excise. There are many files in this series. Railway subjects include:

- Channel Tunnel;
- railway quays for the landing of passengers and goods;
- Irish railways and the effect of the Irish land boundary;
- railway bonded warehouses;
- conveyance of dutiable goods by railways;
- continental train ferries and connecting trains.

CUST 121 Excise Treasury papers, 1816–1887

Correspondence with the Treasury of the Board of Excise and the Excise Branch of the Inland Revenue. The list gives only the paper numbers within each piece; **CUST 122 registers** are used to find the paper numbers. The records relating to railways concern railway passenger duty, including the cheap trains, and other duties to which they were liable.

CUST 122 Excise registers of Treasury papers

These must be used to find paper numbers in **CUST 121**. They are indexed alphabetically; 'railways' seems to find most entries but it is as well to look elsewhere too.

Railways and the Armed Services

From the beginning of railways the Admiralty and War Office had an interest in them. From 1842 the railways were statutorily required to provide transport for the army and the same provision was extended to the navy in 1853. From 1845 the Admiralty was required to make sure that the construction of new railways should not interfere with the use of navigable waterways.

From the 1870s the railways were an essential part of plans for mobilization for war. In both world wars they were crucial to the mobility of the forces at home and in supplying the country. They were also a strategic target and there are some records of the bombing of home railways which are described here.

In the 1930s the railway companies developed their own air services. At that time the Air Ministry controlled civil as well as military aviation, so some records of railway air services occur in **AIR** and are dealt with here.

Admiralty   ADM

ADM 1 Admiralty and Secretariat papers

A huge series of in-letters which begins in the seventeenth century and extends to the 1970s. It seems to contain a great deal of railway historical material but searching in it is not always easy. After 1914, ADM 1 is descriptively listed in chronological order. Before 1914, the records consist of bundles of loose papers, some of which are in imperfect order. For this period the series list gives only the dates and categories of records in each bundle (e.g. 'Architect', 'Surveyor', 'Captains and Yards'), so to get at the particular contents **ADM 12**, which contains indexes and digests, has to be consulted.

ADM 12 Admiralty and Secretariat indexes and compilations Series III, 17th century to 1938

A leaflet describes the use of this series which is the Admiralty's own contemporary finding aid. The leaflet gives a fuller explanation of the series than can be given here but, simply, it contains subject indexes and digests, the latter arranging references under subject code systems. Do not expect everything (or anything) to appear under 'R' for Railways in these indexes; the Admiralty was more interested in the names of correspondents, places, ships, etc., rather than railways as a subject. As will be seen from the examples below, this can make identifying railway-related records a matter of lateral thinking or prior knowledge.

As an example of records in the nineteenth century part of **ADM 1**, a bundle was taken at random and records from it concerned with railways are given below. Index terms in ADM 12 are in bold:

ADM 1/5809 *In-letters, Promiscuous* (i.e. miscellaneous) *1862, A–H*
Under 'F' were found:
Freshfields and Newman's report on the LCDR No. 1 Bill which includes a provision for communication with the Admiralty Pier at Dover;
Falmouth as a postal port, including an 1843 statement of facts referring to the forthcoming railway connection.
Under 'H':
Correspondence with John **Hawkshaw** acting for the LNWR on improvements to the pier at **Holyhead** for Irish postal traffic;
Defence of Portsmouth by advanced seaworks. A proposal for a long mole carrying a branch railway from **Havant**, LBSCR and LSWR;
Arrangements with the London, Tilbury & Southend Extension Railway for a special train to take the Special Committee on Iron to Shoeburyness to test an iron shield. (I do not know why this is under 'H'.)

Names, of places or correspondents, are the index terms usually used. Discoveries are clearly there to be made in **ADM 1** if one is prepared to be patient. Before 1914, the most likely sources would seem to be the 'Dockyards' and 'Promiscuous' categories. Further random sampling of those has found records about:

- proposed coastal railways;
- development of docks and harbours by railway companies;
- railway owned ferries;
- proposals for railway bridges across navigable water;
- various Channel Tunnel projects.

ADM 12 will also give a clue to the whereabouts of related **Out-letters** in **ADM 2** (although ADM 2 seems to contain less railway material than ADM 1) and **Minutes** in **ADM 3** (though almost no mention of railways was found in ADM 3). ADM 12 also gives brief digests of the contents of records that no longer survive.

ADM 7 Miscellanea

This series contains 'cases' which are really early examples of subject files. Two of them certainly deal with railways:

- **ADM 7/616**, in which **Case 93** is about Dunleary (*sic*) Harbour and an extension of the **Dublin & Kingstown R** there, 1834–1843;
- **ADM 7/617**, in which **Case 148** contains papers dating from 1835–1846 on the effect

of a railway extension on the instruments of the Greenwich Observatory, including vibration tests by Robert Stephenson on the **London & Birmingham R** and the **Dublin & Kingstown R**.

It is possible that some of the **ADM 7** records about dockyards may also deal with railways.

ADM 13 Admiralty and Secretariat: supplementary

Records are listed here under 'Registers of Correspondence: Legal Branch' which include notes (mainly financial accounting) of dealings with railways in the mid-nineteenth century. As an example:

ADM 13/65 is a large volume containing accounting entries. Under 'Surveys and Exploring Expeditions' there is, among other entries of railway interest, an 1861 entry about a survey of the Barnstaple River, the expense of which was paid by the **North Devon R**.

Unfortunately, the letter books to which ADM 13 related, which would have fleshed out the notes, are not known to have survived.

ADM 46 Accountant General's Admiralty Orders and ADM 47 Record Books

Both these series contain routine accounting records some of which are about transactions with railway companies.

ADM 65, 66, 67, 74, 75, 76, 79, 80 and 169

These are all **Greenwich Hospital Estates** series containing, to greater and lesser extent, records relating to railways. The Admiralty administered the Greenwich Hospital and, with it, the Greenwich Hospital Estates which included not only land in Greenwich itself but also in Cumberland, Northumberland and Durham. References to relations with the local railways (including the **London & Blackwall, Hexham & Allandale, Newcastle & Carlisle, Spittal & Tweedmouth**, and the **Scremerston Colliery R** among others) occur in the records.

ADM 106 Navy Board in-letters and out-letters

Until 1832, the civil administration of the navy was the responsibility of the Navy Board (the Admiralty until then dealing only with the fighting aspects). This is a general series which ends in 1837 when railways were beginning, but it contains at least one railway subject:

ADM 106/1781, charge for carriage of Navy timber on a proposed railway between Foxes Bridge and Purton Pill, Forest of Dean, dated 1831.

The series may repay searching for more.

ADM 116 Admiralty and Secretariat: cases, late 19th century to the 1960s

Another large series containing information about:

- harbour railways;
- tramways;
- the effect of railway strikes;
- use of railways in wartime.

The latter part of the list is by subject codes, so some imagination is needed in picking the likely ones to search.

Station records

Several series, some of which have separate index series, are records of naval stations. These have some routine records about arrangements for rail travel (e.g. travel warrants) but may also contain a few items on other railway matters. **ADM 131 Station Records: Plymouth, 1842–1926,** for example, has some undetailed papers on First World War ambulance trains (**ADM 131/6**) and some papers on the **Bere Alston & Calstock Light R (ADM 131/42)**. The class is indexed in **ADM 143**, for the period 1876–1912.

Other Station Records series are:

- **ADM 149, Ireland, 1816–1912,** indexed in **ADM 150**;
- **ADM 151, Nore, 1805–1939,** indexed in **ADM 152**;
- **ADM 179 Portsmouth, 1880–1948.**

ADM 174, Dockyard records: Plymouth, 17th century to 1950

The series includes, among other things, a plan of the Royal Victoria Yard, Deptford, 1888, showing **LBSCR** connection and sidings. (There are a number of records of dockyards other than Plymouth in this series).

Civil Engineer-in-Chief's records

ADM 195 Photographs, 1857–1961

The series consists of albums of photographs of the progress of construction work at dockyards, often including contractors' railways, locomotives and wagons as well as main-line railway equipment. The photographs of several dockyards include railways, principal among them being, Chatham, Devonport, Dover, Haulbowline (Cork), Keyham, Portsmouth and Rosyth. Others show railways to a lesser extent. (*See also* **ADM 214** below.)

ADM 214 Papers

Agreements, contract papers, specifications, photographs and plans of naval installations. Reports on visits to docks in 1904 include the **Caledonian R** basin at Grangemouth. Here are contract documents for the works at Dover, Keyham and Rosyth photographed in **ADM 195**.

War Office   WO

WO 32 General registered papers, 1845–1985

A large series listed under subject codes. The following are examples of the kinds of records to be found here:

Code 0 (AD) Overseas: Ireland
Files on the use and control of Irish railways in the First World War and immediately after it.
Code 3(A) Parliamentary Bills
Files on the **Romney, Hythe & Dymchurch Light R** Order and Extension Order, 1926–1928.
Code 5(A) Defence of the Realm Acts: General
Records of the preparation, and execution, of the control of railways under the National Defence Act 1888 and Regulation of the Forces Act 1871, 1909–1919. Also included are amendments to Orders under these Acts following the creation of the Irish Free State, 1923–1924.
Code 9(A) Travelling and Transport: General
This covers many aspects of the transport of troops and equipment by rail, 1907–1942, as well as records about the Army Railway Council, 1897–1920.
Code 14(A) Army Organization: General
Here is a file on the Bartyan Committee proposals for the formation of a separate Transport Corps, 1950.
Code 14(E) Army Organization: Engineers
Contains files on the transport services of the Royal Engineers including the railway

units, 1900s and 1946–1953.
Code 14(F) Army Organization: Medical
Includes files of the 1950s on ambulance trains.

WO 33 Reports, memoranda and papers

Formal reports. Railway related subjects include:

- Channel Tunnel, 1882;
- mobilization arrangements for both First and Second World Wars;
- report of a committee on the working of railways in the event of a general mobilization, 1896;
- protection of railways in war, 1930s.

WO 35 Army of Ireland, Administrative and Easter Rising records

Includes records of defence of Ireland schemes including surveys of Irish railways, 1870s and 1900s.

WO 185 Ministry of Supply files

This includes some files on the use of railway company and commercial works for the war effort, Second World War.

WO 199 War of 1939–1945: Military Headquarters papers, Home Forces

There is much of railway interest in this series. Subjects include:

- railway requirements for home defence;
- protection of railways;
- movements by rail;
- immobilization of railways in invasion;
- railway company Home Guard units;
- armoured trains.

Air Ministry   AIR

Only one of the AIR series has any quantity of railway-related records:

AIR 2 Correspondence

Railway material seems to be in the First World War to 1930 period and consists of:

- items on travel warrants;
- several pieces on railways and light railways in or to RAF (and Royal Flying Corps) sites;
- land for railways;
- sidings and level crossing agreements.

The list is subject coded but not all the railway records are listed under 'Transport: Railways'.

Of the other AIR series, the following have *some* railway content:

AIR 1 Air Historical Branch Records: Series I

Railway material is sparse, mainly from the First World War. It includes:

- several pieces on the effects of air raids on Britain with a little on railway targets;
- **AIR 1/621/16/15/371** is about visibility of objects on the ground at night including lights of trains and railway installations;
- **AIR 1/633/17/122/89** reports a Zeppelin raid on London comparing flares with flashes from electric railways.

(*N.B.* The whole six-element reference has to be used when calling for these records.)

AIR 5 Air Historical Branch: Series II

Records deal with, among other things:

- the railway strike, 1919;
- railway wireless telegraphy services, 1919–1920;
- the light railway at Farnborough, 1919–1925;
- the railway and steamer Irish mail service, 1919–1921;
- GWR plans of docks at Swansea, Newport, Falmouth and Barry, 1930s.

AIR 8 Chief of the Air Staff

Of these:

- Piece **14** has a chart showing the effect of the 1919 rail strike;
- Piece **25** is about the Channel Tunnel, 1924–1930.

AIR 14 Bomber Command

Records of:

- bomb damage to British towns, including some mention of railways, Second World War;
- reports, 1939–1940 on the vulnerability of railways to air attack;
- tactical aspects of attacking railways including bombing trials on a railway at the Railway Training Centre, Longmoor, Hants. and at Porton, 1938–1939.

AIR 19 Private Office Papers

Piece **38** consists of correspondence with Sir Josiah Stamp, LMSR, on air services between England and the Irish Free State, including railway interests, 1938.

Other sources

This section notes briefly records of other government departments that may shed sidelights on, and add different perspectives to, railway research. It works alphabetically through the departmental codes, pointing out where records are known to be and noting some curiosities.

AB

The **Atomic Energy Authority (AB),** has some files on the transport of radioactive materials in **AB 6, AB 8, AB 9** and **AB 62**.

AVIA

In **Ministry of Aviation (AVIA)** records. **AVIA 12** and **22** have a few files on supply of locomotives in the Second World War. (These are **Ministry of Supply** records. Some other Supply records are noted in **WO** above.)

AY

In **AY** are **Transport and Road Research Laboratory** reports on rail traffic, 1970s and 1980s.

BD

The **Welsh Office (BD)** has some files on Welsh railways and rail closures in **BD 23** and **BD 24**, 1950s and 1960s.

BS

BS 1 contains records of the **Channel Tunnel Advisory Group** of 1972–1975.

CAOG

The **Crown Agents for Oversea Governments (CAOG)** has some records about commercial supply of rail equipment abroad by British manufacturers. In **CAOG 13** are some records about British railway personnel recruited for Commonwealth railways.

COAL

COAL contains records of the **National Coal Board** including supply of coal to railways, 1930s and 1940s. **COAL 4**, and several other COAL classes, have records about rail operations. **COAL 27** has the NCB's own specifications for railway equipment.

COU

The **Countryside Commission (COU)** has some records about rail access to national parks, 1950s and 1960s.

CRES

The **Crown Estate Commission (CRES)** is worth exploring for records about railways that crossed, or attempted to cross, crown land. (There is a great deal of crown land all over the country.)

D

In **D 4** are the **Development Commission** records on advances of money to light railways, 1912–1918.

EF

In **EF 2** are **Explosives Inspectorate** reports on explosions on railways, 1876–1916.

EW

The **Department of Economic Affairs (EW)** has 1960s files on rail closures, the Channel Tunnel, railway fares and rates of charging in **EW 7**. Elsewhere in EW are files on transport policy and finance and the powers of British Railways to manufacture commercially.

F

Forestry Commission records sometimes relate to railways. In **F 26** are three files on promotion of railways in the Forest of Dean, 1851–1894.

FS

Several **Registry of Friendly Societies (FS)** series contain records about railway and tramway trade unions.

HLG

The **Ministry of Housing and Local Government** records in **HLG** contain railway topics including street tramways, traffic surveys, new towns (transport access to them was important) and the effects of rail closures.

HO

The **Home Office (HO)** has several series dealing with railways. **HO 185, Ministry of Munitions and Home Office** has records about the government control of liquor and on the state management of the Carlisle Citadel Station refreshment rooms, 1916–1949 (*see also* **HO 190**). **HO 186, Ministry of Home Security: Air Raid Precautions** has some files on the bombing of railways in the Second World War, as do **HO 191, HO 192, HO 196** and **HO 198. Tube Shelter Committee** records are in **HO 200**; and the 'Great Train Robbery' records are to be found in **HO 242, HM Inspectorate of Constabulary**.

LAB

The **Ministry of Labour** had interaction with railways. Its code is **LAB**, several classes dealing with employment on railways, records of the **Industrial Court (LAB 3)**, health safety and welfare, statistics, and trade disputes.

MAF

The **Ministry of Agriculture and Fisheries** and its successor the **Ministry of Agriculture Fisheries and Food** had some concerns about railways. Land drainage where railways ran was important (*see* **MAF 218**). Transport of food in wartime is covered in several series. There are three files on lineside fires in **MAF 142**. Records concerning tube shelter feeding and the feeding of railway employees, 1939–1945, are in **MAF 99**.

The Ministry ran its own railway, the **Wissington Light R**, and records about that are in **MAF 48, MAF 105, MAF 143** and **MAF 147**, 1913–1961.

MUN

The **Ministry of Munitions (MUN)** series **3**, **4**, **5** and **7** contain records about the production of armaments during the First World War. Since both railway companies' and commercial railway manufacturers' works were used for munitions work, records about them are present in these series.

TS

Finally, the **Treasury Solicitor** has records about legal matters affecting railways in **TS 18** and **TS 25**. Admiralty Solicitor records in **TS 4** include the scrutiny of new railway Bills for Admiralty interest, 1830s-1850s. **TS 5** too has records about railway Bills, as well as advances to light railways and much besides.

5 Railway Staff Records

Since the railways employed a large number of staff, their records are likely to be an important source for the family historian. It is not known precisely how many men and women were employed at any one time but, as an indicator of the numbers there must have been, a medium-sized railway, the LSWR, is said to have employed about 7,000 weekly paid and 700 salaried staff in 1872.[1] In 1897, the general manager of the LNWR claimed his was the largest of all railway companies in Britain; it then employed about 70,000 people.[2] From this it may be assumed that, at any but the earliest period, the railways employed some hundreds of thousands of staff at any one time and, with the turnover of staff as time went on, the total must have been in millions. At the beginning of the nationalized railway in 1948, British Railways employed 641,000 people.[3]

There are several types of records containing information about railway staff. The most important are the staff registers, but other records are of potential value and, in many cases, are all we have. No staff registers survive for the great majority of smaller railways. It may be that staff can be traced in the records of successor companies but, otherwise, there is little chance of finding named staff unless they happen to be mentioned in the minutes of directors' meetings, committee meetings or financial records.

Staff registers

Staff registers are usually found among the records of the larger companies. As usual the GWR has the most (there is a separate series for them). It is clear that, even where registers survive, there are gaps in their sequences. It would be impossible now to establish what registers were compiled; we only know that many have not survived. Staff registers, with some exceptions, provide a very basic record. The companies did not compile them out of curiosity about their staff; they wanted to know:

---

1 Williams, R. A. *The London & South Western Railway*, David & Charles, Newton Abbot, 1973, vol. 2, p. 330.
2 Interview with Sir Frederick Harrison in the *Railway Magazine,* September 1897, PRO ref. ZPER 39/1.
3 Gourvish, *British Railways 1948–73, a Business History*, p. 99 (*see* Bibliography).

- who were employed;
- what they were employed to do;
- how good their performance was;
- how much they were paid.

It is as well to be wary of the dates of staff registers as given in the series lists. They tend to exaggerate the age of the earliest records. The listers appear to have taken the earliest date on the first page of a register, called that its start date and taken the latest date on the last page as the terminator. Since the earliest date on the first page is likely to be a date of birth, rather than the date of first employment of the individual, the actual date of commencement of the register (which is what should have been recorded) is rendered misleading. That the earliest date of birth on the first page is unlikely to be the earliest in the register makes the dating even more meaningless. Similarly, the last date might be the last event in the last individual's history rather than the date the register was closed. The difficulty for the listers was that the first entries in a register were likely to have been retrospectively entered. The register may not settle down to record new staff as they enter service until a substantial part of the book has been filled. Registers compiled in the earliest years of the railways are rare, though long-serving staff may be recorded in later ones.

The illustration from RAIL 226/204 (Figure 1) is a typical example of an entry in a staff register. It is from the Great Central Railway at the beginning of the twentieth century and shows, in a very basic way, when A. E. Shaw joined the railway and how old he was then, what he was employed as, what he was paid, and when his pay was increased and by how much. It also shows (rectangular stamp in top right corner) that he attested himself under Lord Derby's scheme. This was the last attempt to meet the army's needs for recruits in the First World War without resorting to conscription. Every man aged between 19 and 41 was asked either to join up at once or to attest

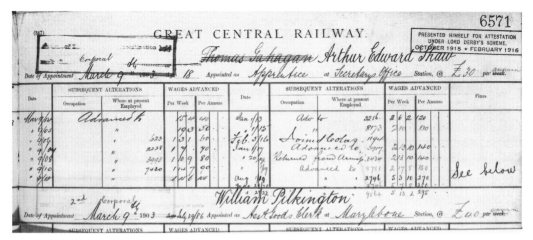

Figure 1 Extract from a Great Central Railway staff register. RAIL 226/204

willingness to join when called upon. The youngest unmarried attesters would be called up first followed by the older unmarried and then the married men. It failed to gain enough support and compulsory conscription followed in May 1916. This entry shows that Shaw 'joined colours' in February 1916 and returned on 20 January 1919. His entry, to 1924, continues lower down the page. By 1924 the GCR had been grouped into the LNER so it might be possible to follow his career further in the records of the LNER (RAIL 394). Indeed, in tracing older employees of the GCR who might have joined it when it was still called the Manchester, Sheffield & Lincolnshire R, one might follow careers through the records of all three companies (MSLR records are in RAIL 463). This is something to bear in mind when searching for information on staff; if they cannot be found in the records of the company they joined, they may be

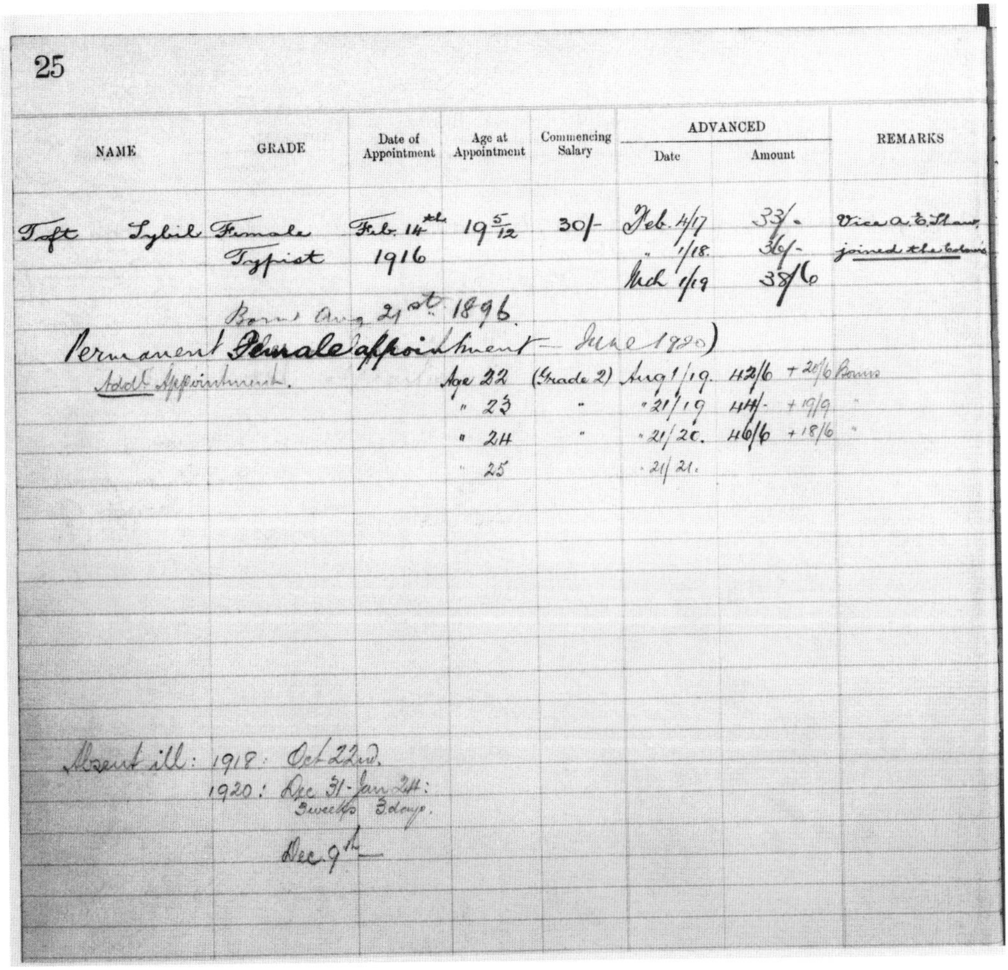
25

NAME	GRADE	Date of Appointment	Age at Appointment	Commencing Salary	ADVANCED Date	ADVANCED Amount	REMARKS
Toft Sybil	Female Typist	Feb. 14th 1916	19 5/12	30/-	Feb. 4/17 " 1/18. Mch 1/19	33/- 36/- 38/6	Vice A. E. Shaw, joined the colours

Born Aug 21st 1896.

Permanent Female appointment — June 1920)

Addl Appointment.

Age 22	(Grade 2)	Aug 1/19.	42/6	+ 20/6 Bonus
" 23	"	" 21/19	44/-	+ 19/9 "
" 24	"	" 21/20.	46/6	+ 18/6 "
25		" 21/21.		

Absent ill: 1918: Oct 22nd.
1920: Dec 31-Jan 24:
3 weeks 3 days.
Dec 9th

Figure 2 Extract from a Great Central Railway staff register. RAIL 226/194

recorded by a successor company. There are also overlaps in the use of old company registers and those of the new. In this example, the GCR register was still being added to two years after absorption into the LNER.

Another example from the GCR, this time involving a woman, is the illustration from RAIL 226/194 (Figure 2). Sybil Toft was one of the women recruited to replace men serving in the forces in the First World War, indeed, officially she replaced Shaw (though her career goes on long after he had returned). Lord Derby's scheme had required that, in order to be exempted from military service, it was essential to show a tribunal that the man's occupation was vital, of national importance and that efforts had been made to replace him with a man over enlistment age, or a woman. GCR records show that Miss Toft continued as a Woman Clerk with the railway at least until 1926. It may be that LNER records carry the story forward.

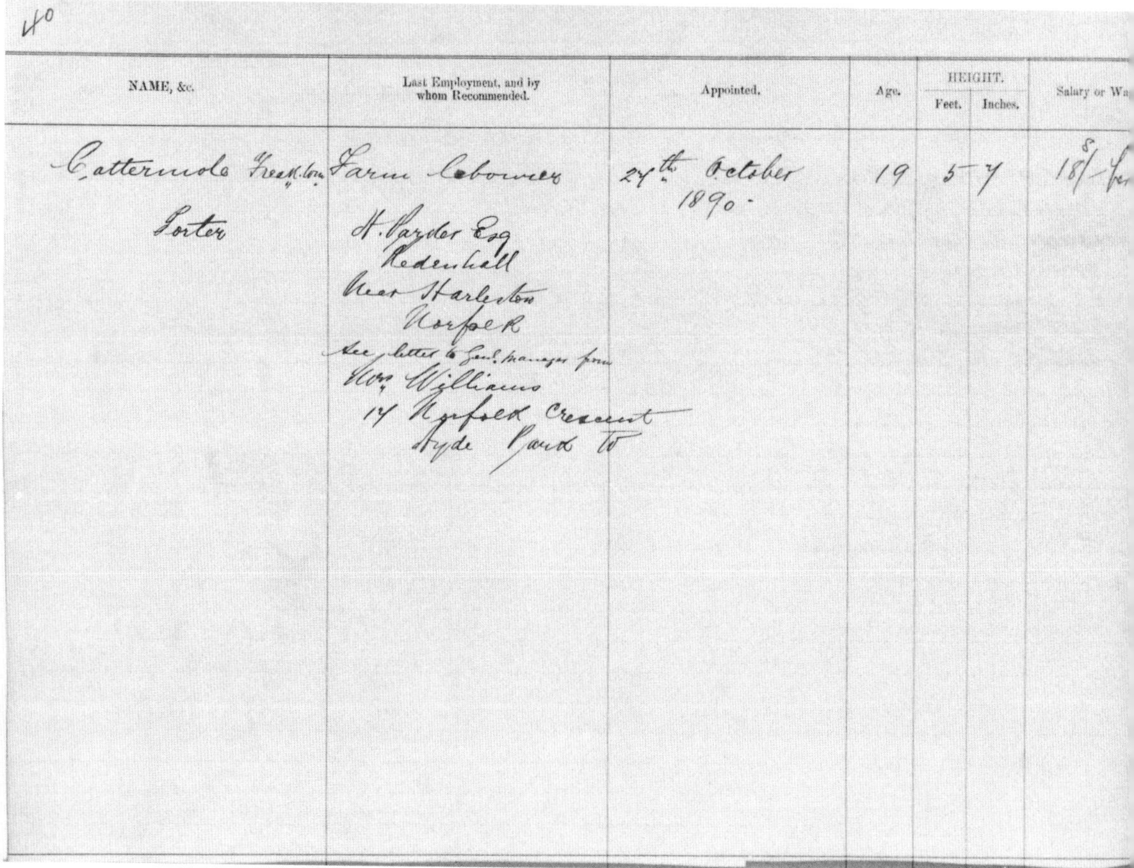
40

NAME, &c.	Last Employment, and by whom Recommended.	Appointed.	Age.	HEIGHT. Feet.	HEIGHT. Inches.	Salary or Wa
Cattermole Frederk. Porter	Farm Labourer H. Cayder Esq Redenhall Near Harleston Norfolk See letter to Genl. Manager from Rev. Williams 14 Norfolk Crescent Hyde Park W	24th October 1890.	19	5	7	18/- per

Figure 3 Extract from a North London Railway staff register. RAIL 529/135

The illustration from RAIL 529/135 (Figure 3) is an example from a register of the North London Railway. This is very similar in content to the GCR example, but it is rare in that it gives information about previous employment including the address of, in this case, the farm where F.W. Cattermole had been a labourer. Mrs Williams of Hyde Park presumably sent a letter recommending the young man. This register also records the subject's height, which is not quite so rare but still unusual. (There are a few staff records that also give eye and hair colour.) This career might again be pursued elsewhere - the entries end in 1909, when he was clearly still employed, and when the NLR came into common management with the LNWR (the NLR was formally taken over by the LNWR in 1922). It would, therefore, be worth looking in the staff records of the LNWR to see whether it recorded Cattermole's later service.

Sometimes entries in this NLR register say what happened to the employee on leaving. For example Alfred Clark joined the railway as a train register boy in 1889 aged 14 (having previously been a draper's errand boy in Islington), stayed, working

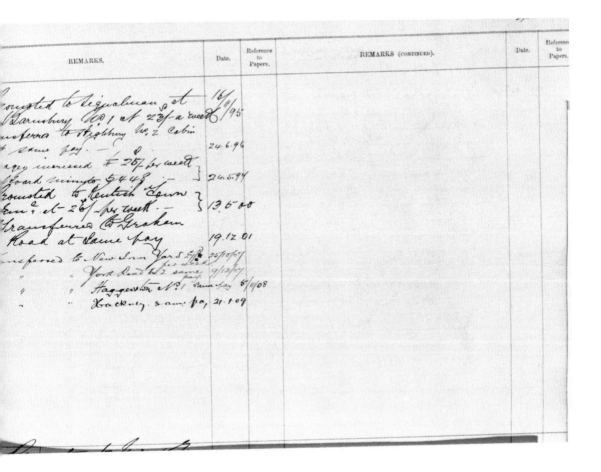

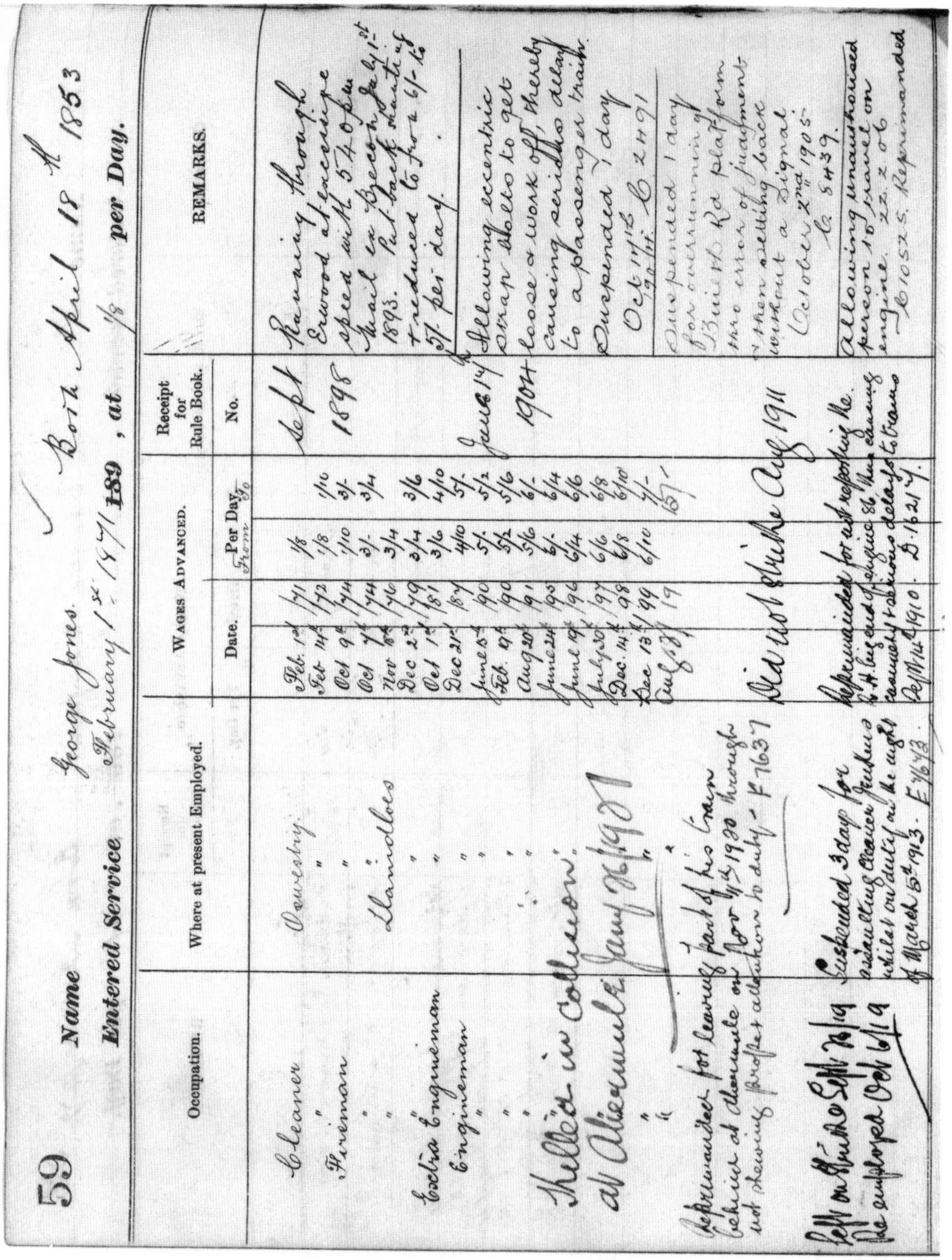

59 Name George Jones Born April 18th 1853

Entered Service February 1st 1871 ~~189~~, at 1/8 per Day.

Occupation.	Where at present Employed.	Wages Advanced. Date.	Per Day From	Per Day To	Receipt for Rule Book. No.	Remarks.
Cleaner	Oswestry	Feb. 1st /71	1/8	1/10	Sept 1898	Running through Erwood at excessive speed with 5.40 a.m. Mail ex Brecon July 1st 1893. Put back instead of reduced to 6/- to 5/- per day.
Fireman	"	Feb 14 /72	1/8	1/10		
"	"	Oct 9 /74	1/10	3/-		
"	Llanidloes	Oct 1 /74	3/-	3/4		
Extra Engineman	"	Nov /76	3/4	3/6	June 14 1904	Allowing eccentric strap bolts to get loose & work off thereby causing serious delay to a passenger train.
Engineman	"	Dec 2 /79	3/4	3/6		Suspended 1 day Oct 1912 C 2491
"	"	Oct 1 /81	3/6	4/10		Suspended 1 day for overrunning Builth Rd platform thro error of judgment & then setting back without a signal. October 2nd 1905. C 8439.
"	"	Dec 21 /87	4/10	5/-		Allowing unauthorised person to travel on engine. 22.2.06. C 10525. Reprimanded.
		June /90	5/-	5/2		
		Feb /90	5/2	5/6		
		Aug 20 /91	5/6	6/-		
		June /95	6/-	6/4		
		June /96	6/4	6/6		
		July 30 /97	6/6	6/8		
		Dec 14 /98	6/8	6/10		
		Dec 13 /99	6/10	7/-		
		Aug /19		15/-		

Killed in collision at Abermule Jany 26/1921

Reprimanded for leaving part of his train behind at Abermule on Nov 4th 1920 through not showing proper attention to duty. F 7637

Did not strike Aug 1911

Left on strike Sept 26/19. Re-employed Oct 6/19.

Suspended 3 days for assaulting Station Foreman at Talerddig whilst on duty on the night of March 15th 1913. E 7642.

Reprimanded for not reporting the S.H. tugs and fire of engine 86, thus causing casualty & serious delays to trains. Sept 14th 1910. D 1621.

Figure 4 Extract from a Cambrian Railways register of enginemen. RAIL 92/142

at various places, until 1894 when he 'resigned to go into the baking trade' (it does not, unfortunately, say for whom he then worked).

Finally, the illustration from RAIL 92/142 (Figure 4) is an example of a register that records, as many do, offences and disciplinary action. It is from the Cambrian Railways. The entry for George Jones covers a long career in the locomotive department during which he suffered suspensions from work and reductions in pay for various mishaps. Over such a long period the offences are relatively few, but they add greatly to our knowledge of this individual. Jones was part-author of his own death. The entry records that he was killed in the collision at Abermule in 1921, one of the worst head-on collisions on a single-line in the history of Britain's railways. Jones's train simply should not have been where he took it. Its presence was the result of slack working at Abermule station, in which basic checks were not made by several people, the last of whom was Jones himself. He failed to check that the single-line token he was handed was the right one. Despite the apparent infallibility of the operating procedure, he had been handed the token for the line of track he had just left rather than that for the section ahead. Assuming he had the correct token he drove his train into the next section and into the path of an express approaching Abermule at speed.[4]

Pay records

Some railways have left accounting records of wages and salaries paid to staff. They may take the form of wages lists giving names and job titles. The illustration from RAIL 315/30 (Figure 5) is an example from the Hull & Selby R. This is one account from a series of monthly tabulations giving salaries of clerks in the goods department. Obviously, the next month's account (they become fortnightly in 1853) will record much the same list of people but, over time (the volume covers 1845–1854 and 1874–1875) changes and advancements will be recorded. The virtue of this record is that it is relatively early; records of this period are harder to find than those of the end of the century.

The illustration from RAIL 205/1 (Figure 6) is an example of staff records surviving almost accidentally. It is taken from a 'voucher book' of the Festiniog & Blaenau R. The voucher book is a large volume of blank pages onto which receipts, vouchers, cashed cheques and invoices have been pasted as a record of transactions. Included are pay lists like the one shown. One supposes that this list represents the entire staff of the railway. A number of smaller railways have such voucher books. One, at least, was kept by a solicitor administering a railway in receivership.

---

4 A vivid account of this accident, and the history of the development of railway safety as a result of accidents, is in Rolt, L. T. C. *Red for Danger*, published by Bodley Head, London, in 1955, with later editions.

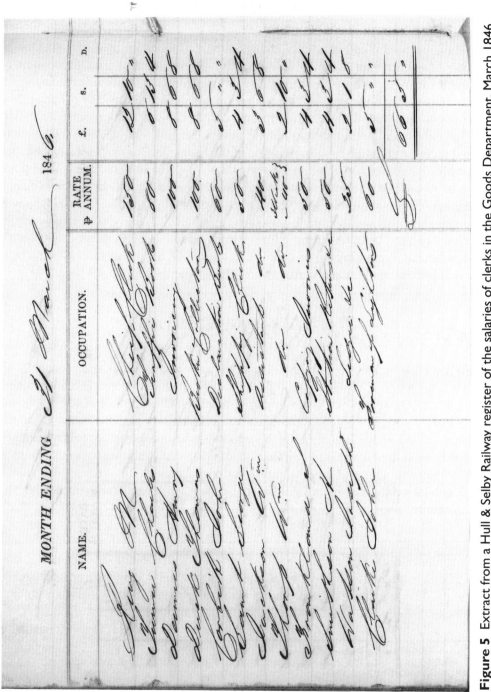

Figure 5 Extract from a Hull & Selby Railway register of the salaries of clerks in the Goods Department, March 1846. RAIL 315/30

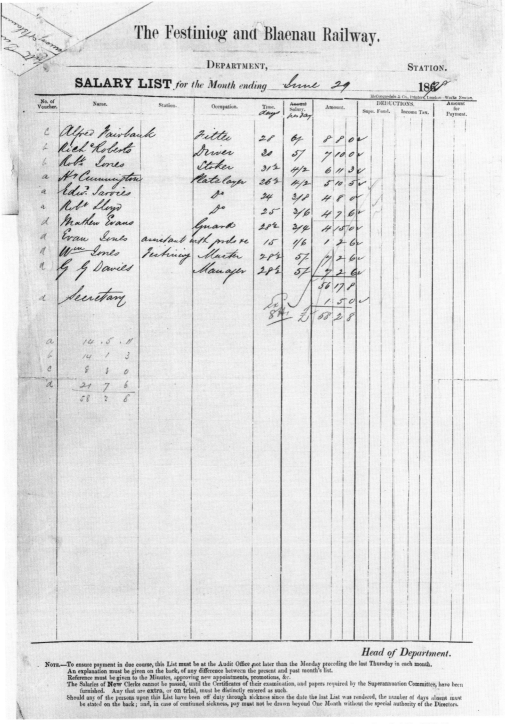

Figure 6 Extract from a Festiniog & Blaenau Railway voucher book. RAIL 205/1

Committee minutes

A particularly useful source of names and some detail about staff are the minutes of joint committees. Joint committees were committees of high-ranking officials from more than one company who met to administer lines of railway and stations owned by the companies jointly. These were often treated as companies in their own right and, while they drew staff from the parent companies, they controlled them as though they were their own. This means that movements of staff, promotions, retirements and disciplinary matters all received attention in committee and were recorded in the minutes.

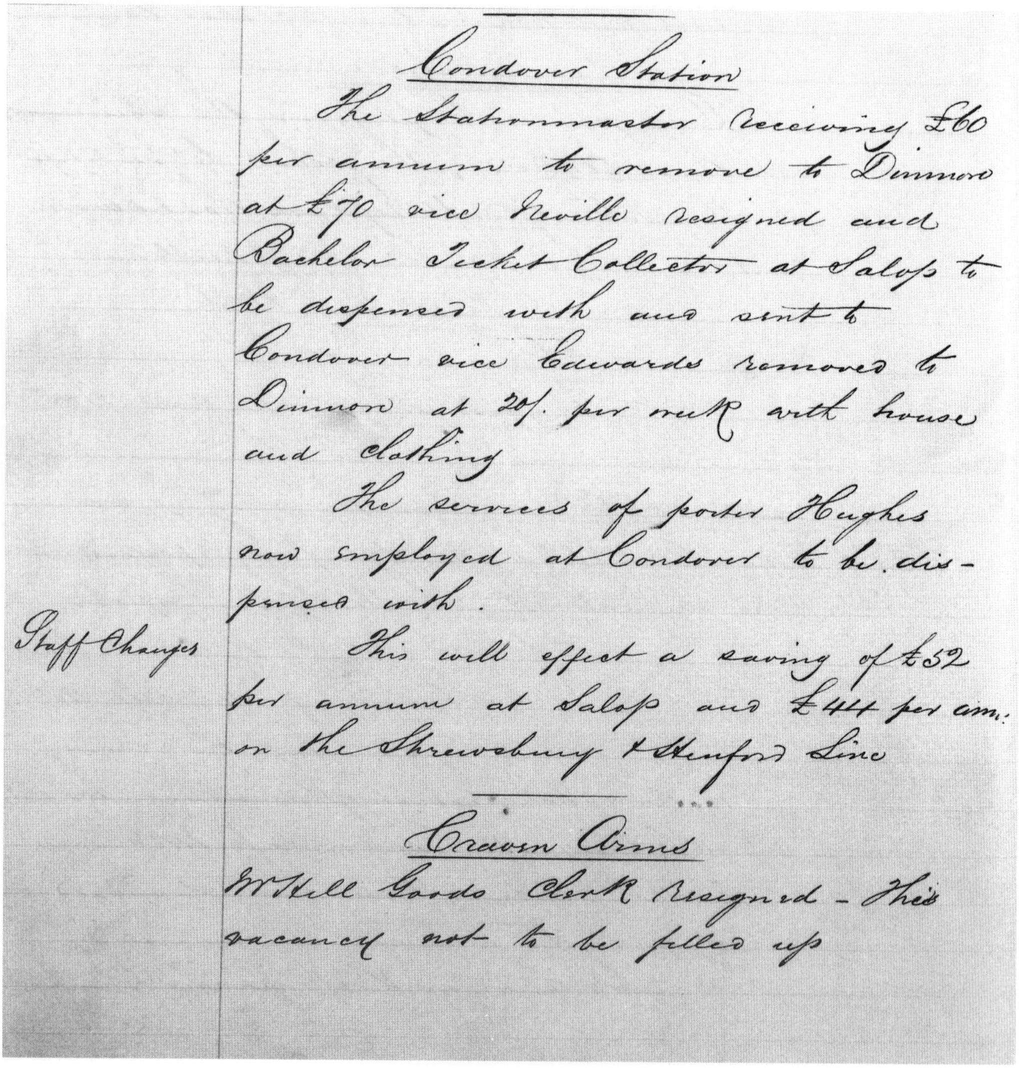

Condover Station

The Stationmaster receiving £60 per annum to remove to Dinmore at £70 vice Neville resigned and Bachelor Ticket Collector at Salop to be dispensed with and sent to Condover vice Edwards removed to Dinmore at 20/. per week with house and clothing

The services of porter Hughes now employed at Condover to be dispensed with.

Staff Changes

This will effect a saving of £52 per annum at Salop and £44 per ann: on the Shrewsbury & Hereford Line

Craven Arms

Mr Hill Goods Clerk resigned - This vacancy not to be filled up

Figure 7 Extract from minutes of the Shrewsbury & Hereford Joint Committee, 20 October 1863. RAIL 617/12

[15 MAY.89]

41

5.   It was agreed to make the following recommendations to the Board as to the appointment and salaries of Clerks &

That the following increases of salary be sanctioned :—

				Present salary	Salary allowed
Mr L. C. Owen	Assistant	Engineers Office	Reading	150	10
" E. W. Baynon	Draughtsman	"	"	107½	14½
" D. J. Price	Chief Clerk	"	Neath	185	10
" James Thomd	Clerk	"	"	65	10
" F. W. Pitts	"	Dist Eng.r Office	Paddington	80	10
Henry Moodly	Lad Clerk	"	"	20	15
Wm H. Short	"	Engineers Office	Plymouth	15	10
L. B. W. Carter	"	"	Reading	20	5

That Mr William A. Cashman be appointed to the Permanent Staff as Assistant in the Engineers Office, Paddington at a salary of £110 per annum in place of Mr Hargreaves resigned :—

That the following Lad Clerks who have served their term of probation be appointed at the salaries set against their respective names :—

A. E. Hicks	Telegraph Dept.	Taunton at £20 per annum.
Ernest Ryder	"	"	" 20 "

Figure 8 Extract from minutes of the Great Western Railway Engineering Committee, 15 May 1889. RAIL 250/168

The illustration from RAIL 617/12 (Figure 7) shows minutes of the Shrewsbury & Hereford Joint Committee (GWR/LNWR). This is typical of joint committee minutes on staff. Often the pay rates of staff are recorded in minutes like these, and sometimes lists of staff are given.

Other committees might deal with staff. The illustration from RAIL 250/168 (Figure 8) is a GWR example from its Engineering Committee. The Lad Clerk, A.E. Hicks referred to here is traceable in the registers of Lad Clerks in the GWR staff records series, RAIL 264. His entry in Vol 3 of the Lad Clerks' registers (RAIL 264/387) is reproduced below as Figure 9. This tells us a little more than the committee minute, notably his date of birth and when he joined the GWR. These particular registers are indexed separately; the index to this one is the next piece, RAIL 264/388, which gives the page number of Hicks's entry in this register. His entry in the register also has a note, which (after some deciphering) reads 'LC 4/56'. This refers to Lad Clerks Register 4, page 56, which is where his record was continued, as is confirmed by the index to that register, RAIL 264/389. Unfortunately, Register 4 no longer survives. I have not been able to trace Hicks in any other GWR staff record, so perhaps he did not continue with the company.

Figure 9 Extract from a Great Western Railway register of lad clerks. RAIL 264/387

Pensions and benefits

Many railway companies ran superannuation and benefit funds to which employees and employer contributed.

In RAIL 258/532, a GWR record series, are correspondence and notes of meetings, etc., about the Taff Vale Railway's Employees Accident Fund and its take-over by the GWR at the grouping. In the file are papers of 1947 listing signalmen of the TVR who retired at the end of the nineteenth century, with their ages and length of service. This was in an effort to establish what had been TVR policy on retirement. It illustrates the point that information on individuals can appear long after they ceased to be employed on the railways in a successor company's records.

The illustration from RAIL 667/228 (Figure 10) is an example from an early superannuation society minute book of the Stockton & Darlington Railway. This is dated 4 March 1862. Subsequent entries in later minutes confirm that the transaction was carried out.

The Railway Benevolent Institution was a general body granting gratuities and annuities to subscribing railway staff, former railway staff, and their families in need.

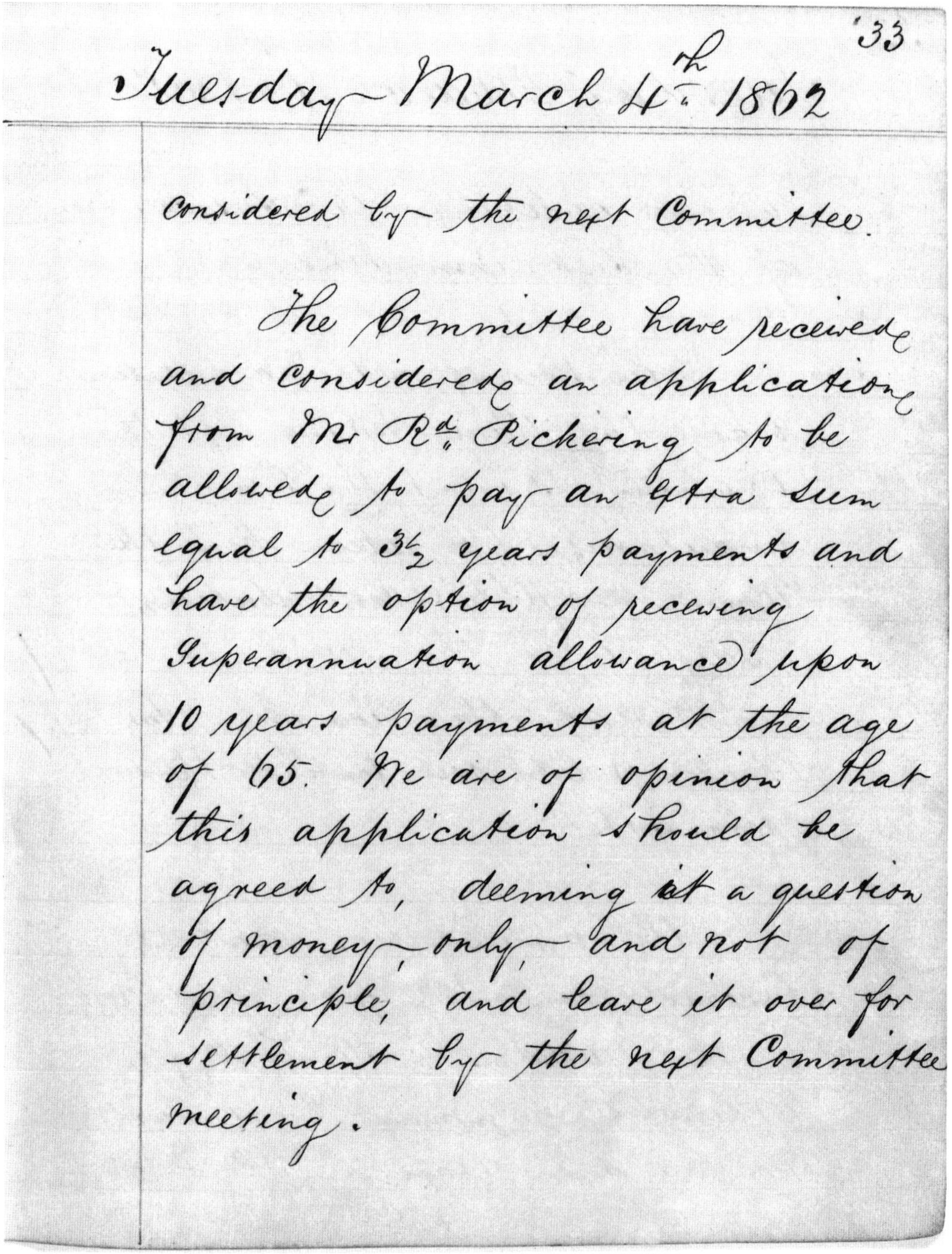

'33

Tuesday ~ March 4ᵗʰ 1862

Considered by the next Committee.

The Committee have received
and considered an application
from Mr Rd. Pickering to be
allowed to pay an extra sum
equal to 3½ years payments and
have the option of receiving
Superannuation allowance upon
10 years payments at the age
of 65. We are of opinion that
this application should be
agreed to, deeming it a question
of money only, and not of
principle, and leave it over for
settlement by the next Committee
meeting.

Figure 10 Extract from a minute book of the Stockton & Darlington Railway Superannuation Society, March 1862. RAIL 667/228

226

Gratuities

Widows   Children

Servants

1900

Mr. William Schofield

Case 827

April 10073. Read—Application for assistance from Mr. William Schofield, aged 58 years, widower and having one daughter aged 19 years, 28 years' service. Engine-driver Lancashire and Yorkshire Railway, Low Moor; he left the Company's service in 1886, and has since been employed in collecting for an insurance company, and earns about 4s. per week, but will probably be unable to continue to do so owing to heart disease. He collected for the Derby Orphanage prior to the amalgamation in 1881, and has no means of support.

Resolved—That a gratuity of £15 be allowed for the assistance of Mr. W. Schofield.

15 . .

A.F. 9/245   Apr. 1901 Sur. 10634 . Further gratuity. (Last wages)   £18.67 22539   15 . 1 .
                                        22.745.24704
                                        23822.01
" 1902 " 10932 "   23401-2   15 . .
" 1903 " 11200 "   Admit   15 . .
June 1904 " 11391 " Admit 24059.03   Died May 1st 1904 16/10/04

The illustration from RAIL 1166/83 (Figure 11) is an extract from a volume of records of its cases. The end of W. Schofield's life is quite well described here, and the record includes something of his railway service, his family circumstances and his death.

Other sources

Other sources can help to flesh out the lives of railway staff. Some railways kept records of **accidents** that record who was hurt and who was responsible.

A few have separate records about **sickness**. The LBSCR, for example, has a register of staff sickness in RAIL 414/636. It is extremely basic, giving name, rank (i.e. job title), station at which employed, dates of absence (early twentieth century) and cause.

In the records of the MSLR there is a **rent roll**, a volume containing the addresses of

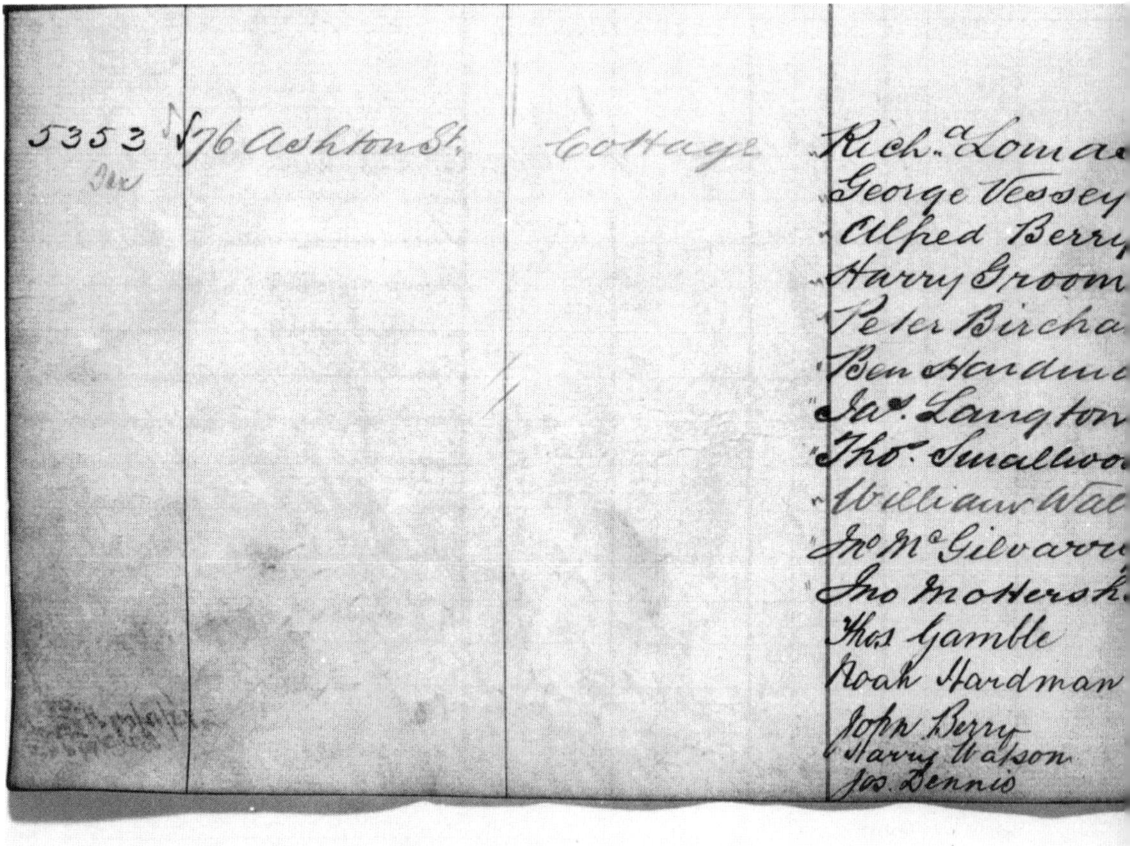

5353 | 76 Ashton St. | Cottage
Rich.d Loma
George Vessey
Alfred Berry
Harry Groom
Peter Bircha
Ben Hardma
Jas. Langton
Thos. Smallwoo
William Wal
Jno McGilvarr
Jno Mottersh
Thos Gamble
Noah Hardman
John Berry
Harry Watson
Jos. Dennis

Figure 12 Extract from a rent roll of the Manchester, Sheffield & Lincolnshire Railway. RAIL 463/164

company-owned property and tenants. The illustration from RAIL 463/164 (Figure 12) is the entry for a cottage in Dukinfield with names of its successive tenants and the amount of their rent. There is an index to tenants' names in the volume.

Finally, it has to be said that the more trouble a staff member caused the company the more likely it was that detail about the individual would be recorded. Persistent disciplinary offenders, the accident prone and poor attenders are much more likely to have left a full record of their lives than the exemplary. The gentleman referred to in the illustration from RAIL 186/100 (Figure 13) must have caused the Eastern Counties Railway (and, presumably, its successor the GER) a good deal of trouble for them to have created a separate record of his activities.

There are no records of the Eastern Counties Railway devoted to staff, but How would have finished his career in the successor company, the GER. He has eluded me in the GER registers – but, since they are not indexed, it may be that my search has not been

<u>GEORGE HOW.</u>

Entered service of Eastern Counties Railway at Brentwood in 1851 and remained there about 3 years.   In 1853 met with accident in the Cattle Dock, slipping between 2 Cattle Trucks.   Removed to Witham, was there about 4 years, being promoted to Goods Guard.   Run as Guard about 8 years during which time he was knocked down and fell through coal pits at Tottenham.   Was in a collision that occurred at Bishops Stortford about 1865, and about 1873 in another collision at Beccles Swing Bridge on the single line between the Up Fish train and the Down Norwich Goods train.

On promotion to Inspector he was attached to Devonshire Street for about 2 years, and then moved to Brick Lane and Spitalfields.   Remained at Spitalfields for 8½ years and whilst there (in 1871) was knocked down by Carriage train and run over by engine and carriages.   Was Travelling Inspector for about 25 years.   Met with accident at Bethnal Green Jct. December 29th, 1900, breaking one of his legs and injuring ankle.

Retired 6th July, 1901.   Died July 1917.   Aged 85.

Figure 13 Minute from a volume of miscellaneous records and pamphlets, Eastern Counties Railway (presumably typed for the Great Eastern Railway). RAIL 186/100

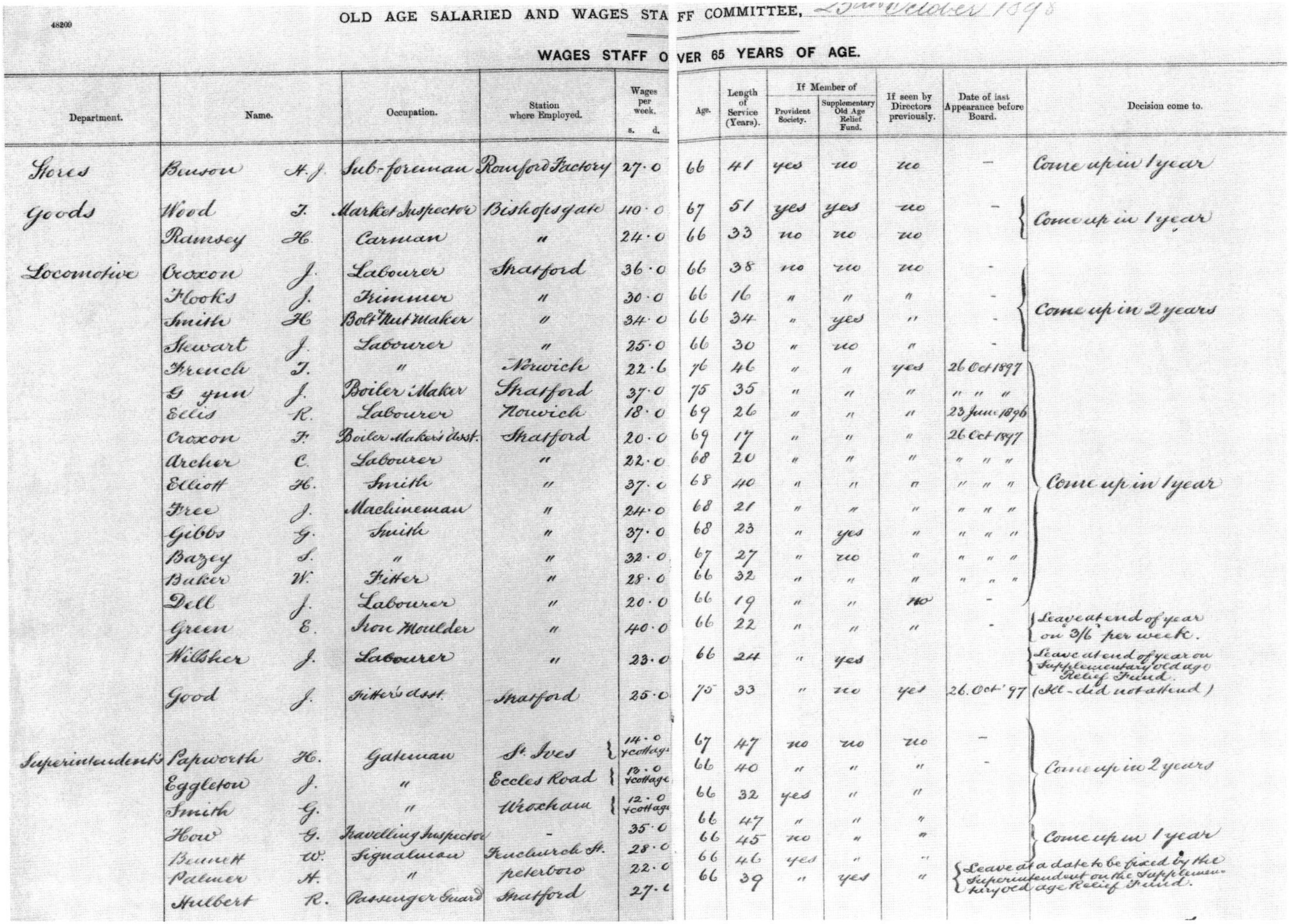

48200

OLD AGE SALARIED AND WAGES STAFF COMMITTEE, 25th October 1898

WAGES STAFF OVER 65 YEARS OF AGE.

Department.	Name.		Occupation.	Station where Employed.	Wages per week. s. d.	Age.	Length of Service (Years).	If Member of Provident Society.	If Member of Supplementary Old Age Relief Fund.	If seen by Directors previously.	Date of last Appearance before Board.	Decision come to.
Stores	Benson	H. J.	Sub-foreman	Romford Factory	27·0	66	41	yes	no	no	–	Come up in 1 year
Goods	Wood	J.	Market Inspector	Bishopsgate	40·0	67	51	yes	yes	no	–	Come up in 1 year
	Ramsey	H.	Carman	"	24·0	66	33	no	no	no		
Locomotive	Croxon	J.	Labourer	Stratford	36·0	66	38	no	no	no	-	Come up in 2 years
	Flooks	J.	Trimmer	"	30·0	66	16	"	"	"	-	
	Smith	H.	Bolt & Nut Maker	"	34·0	66	34	"	yes	"	-	
	Stewart	J.	Labourer	"	25·0	66	30	"	no	"	-	
	French	J.	"	Norwich	22·6	76	46	"	"	yes	26 Oct 1897	Come up in 1 year
	Gynn	J.	Boiler Maker	Stratford	37·0	75	35	"	"	"	" " "	
	Ellis	R.	Labourer	Norwich	18·0	69	26	"	"	"	23 June 1896	
	Croxon	F.	Boiler Maker's Asst.	Stratford	20·0	69	17	"	"	"	26 Oct 1897	
	Archer	C.	Labourer	"	22·0	68	20	"	"	"	" " "	
	Elliott	H.	Smith	"	37·0	68	40	"	"	"	" " "	
	Free	J.	Machineman	"	24·0	68	21	"	"	"	" " "	
	Gibbs	G.	Smith	"	37·0	68	23	"	yes	"	" " "	
	Bazey	S.	"	"	32·0	67	27	"	no	"	" " "	
	Baker	W.	Fitter	"	28·0	66	32	"	"	"	" " "	
	Dell	J.	Labourer	"	20·0	66	19	"	"	no	-	
	Green	E.	Iron Moulder	"	40·0	66	22	"	"	"	-	Leave at end of year on 3/6 per week.
	Wilsher	J.	Labourer	"	23·0	66	24	"	yes			Leave at end of year on Supplementary Old Age Relief Fund.
	Good	J.	Fitter's Asst.	Stratford	25·0	75	33	"	no	yes	26 Oct '97	(He did not attend)
Superintendent's	Papworth	H.	Gateman	St. Ives	14·0 + cottage	67	47	no	no	no	–	Come up in 2 years
	Eggleton	J.	"	Eccles Road	12·0 + cottage	66	40	"	"	"	-	
	Smith	G.	"	Wroxham	12·0 + cottage	66	32	yes	"	"		
	How	G.	Travelling Inspector	-	35·0	66	47	"	"	"		Come up in 1 year
	Bennett	W.	Signalman	Fenchurch St.	28·0	66	45	no	"	"		Leave at a date to be fixed by the Superintendent on the Supplementary Old Age Relief Fund.
	Palmer	H.	"	Peterboro	22·0	66	46	yes	"	"		
	Hulbert	R.	Passenger Guard	Stratford	27·0	66	39	"	yes	"		

Figure 14 Extract from records of the Great Eastern Railway Superintendent's Department, 25 October 1898. RAIL 227/195

thorough enough. There are, however, records of him in the GER Old Age Salaried and Wages Staff Committee. The committee met every few months to consider staff over sixty years of age and whether they should be continued in employment. How was seen twice, in 1898 and 1900. The illustration from RAIL 227/195 (Figure 14) is the record of the first appearance. It does, at least, prove that he finished as a travelling inspector as the earlier note of his service said.

6 Maps, Plans and Technical Drawings

The railway companies and the nationalized railways created and used maps and plans in large numbers. Many of them are now held by the PRO. Government also, for business related to the railways directly, and for other purposes, used maps and plans that can now be of use to railway researchers.

The terms 'map' and 'plan' are often used indiscriminately in descriptions of records in the PRO. 'Map' can be taken to mean a representation of land and the features on it; 'plan' is often used for the same thing but it can also mean a drawing of an object. In this chapter maps may be referred to as plans because they were so called by those who used them, but a distinction is drawn between them and technical drawings.

Maps in the PRO range from freehand sketches to highly detailed, large-scale printed maps (some very large indeed). Technical drawings, given the PRO's selection policy (*see* **Chapter 1**), usually have to do with track, signalling and railway buildings. They range from sketch diagrams to finished, frequently coloured, drawings, often showing the minute details of structures. In both cases it will be noticed that in different time periods there were different styles of drawing and finish: line drawings, sometimes printed as lithographs, and finely detailed and coloured drawings in the nineteenth century, blueprints and a more functional style in the twentieth century. Frequently the plans, however well drawn, are on flimsy paper that requires careful conservation. It is clear that these were, for the most part, working documents and signs of a hard life are frequently apparent.

Drawings of locomotives and rolling stock should usually be sought in the NRM which holds the surviving sets of the drawings from the railways' workshops, but the PRO does have some.

In order to preserve maps in the best way, it is the policy of the PRO to remove those found folded within files to separate map references. You will be asked to order such maps as items in their own right using map references. Because of their size (depending on which they will be stored either flat or rolled) most maps have to be examined in the map and large document reading room on the second floor of the PRO. There are a number of different reference series for rolled and flat maps reflecting ideas in vogue at different times. Where rolled maps have been given map references they are usually in one of the four series **MR**. Flat maps may be referenced as **MPA**, **MPB**, etc., according to

the department of origin (e.g. maps from the War Office are in **MPH**). This system dates from the 1920s. Where a flat map is extra large the suffix letter is doubled (e.g. **MPHH**). From 1997 newly extracted flat maps are all given references in the series **MF**. The process of removing maps from files is still continuing and readers are asked to fill in a form reporting maps they find in files and to hand it to the production staff.

This chapter is divided into two main sections, the records of the railways themselves, and the records of government – but two series which do not readily fall into either part must be described first.

The **MPS** series contain maps that were held in BTHR as a kind of map library. They came from the railway companies and commercial publishers. Their BTHR references were MPS and they have been quoted as such in publications. Recently the PRO has reclassified them. Their new and former references are:

- **RAIL 1029 Maps, Plans and Surveys: Canals and Inland Waterways**
  formerly **MPS 1**
- **RAIL 1030 Maps, Plans and Surveys: Individual Railway Companies**
  formerly **MPS 2**
- **RAIL 1031 Maps, Plans and Surveys: Railways, Canals and Inland Waterways**
  formerly **MPS 3**
- **RAIL 1032 Maps, Plans and Surveys: Railway Clearing House**
  formerly **MPS 4**
- **RAIL 1033 Maps, Plans and Surveys: Ports and Local Areas**
  formerly **MPS 5**
- **RAIL 1034 Maps, Plans and Surveys: London and London Transport**
  formerly **MPS 6**
- **RAIL 1035 Maps, Plans and Surveys: General and Atlases**
  formerly **MPS 7**
- **RAIL 1036 Maps, Plans and Surveys: British Empire and Foreign**
  formerly **MPS 8**
- **RAIL 1037 Maps, Plans and Surveys: York Collection**
  formerly **MPS(Y)**.[1]

The **ZMAP** series contain maps and atlases formerly held by the library of the PRO but now given record call references to make them more easily available to readers. Maps of potential interest to railway research have been noted in:

- **ZMAP 1 Miscellaneous Maps and Atlases**
- **ZMAP 4 Maps of London Reproduced by the London Topographical Society**
- **ZMAP 5 Facsimile Reproductions of Miscellaneous Maps and Plans.**

---

1 Although the York collection deals mainly with the north-east of England it does include maps of other areas.

Maps and plans produced and used by the railways

Maps and plans are frequently found in the record series of particular companies, yet, as can be seen from **Appendix 2**, there are relatively few series devoted to them. This is understandable in that records are usually kept in their working context and not artificially separated by type, but it means that, if information about a particular physical detail of the railway at a particular time is wanted, the hunt may be difficult. Futhermore there is no guarantee that the information is available since many maps and plans have not been selected for preservation. The PRO policy now is to preserve only those maps that record major changes. Although rather more was kept in the past, still a great deal did not survive. Many maps have been passed to local record offices as being of purely local interest (*see* the list of designated local record offices in **Appendix 3**) and a few are in private hands. Some old maps are still relevant to work on the existing railway and are held by Railtrack plc.

Prospectuses

The railways made maps for many different purposes. The first map made for a company proposing a railway might be the map incorporated into its prospectus. The prospectus is usually a printed document describing the proposed route of the line, what people it will serve, what it will carry, and how to subscribe for shares. There are two series, **RAIL 1075** and **1076**, devoted to prospectuses. In many, but by no means all, cases a small map indicating the general route is present. These two series are not the only places where prospectuses can be found. The main record series of the company may have them, and it is also worth checking the records of other companies, especially the large ones, because they often collected prospectuses of rival lines and those they absorbed as well as their own. The series of miscellanea contain prospectuses too.

Parliamentary plans

These are the maps required to be deposited in Parliament at the time of the application for a Bill. They are generally called 'deposited plans'. The House of Lords Record Office holds the original series of these maps with their books of reference (giving the owners of plots of land required to be purchased by the railway) but the PRO has some of the companies' copies. Other possible sources of plans and books of reference are local record offices. Standing orders of the House of Commons required the railway company to deposit copies of these documents with the Clerk of the Council or Town Clerk of every county and borough through which the railway was to go. These copies may have found their way into local archives. The deposited plans

give detailed information on the route, its limits of deviation and the land required to be purchased for it. Part of the deposited plan was the 'section' which was a diagram, a slice, as it were, through the ground along the route, representing the gradients, earthworks, bridges and tunnels. There is a series devoted to parliamentary deposited plans, **RAIL 1071**, but they also occur in company series. Note that, even where deposited plans exist in the PRO, the books of reference are rarely to be found there.

Two-chain surveys

Similar to the parliamentary plans are the linear maps tracing the routes of railways often to the scale of 2 chains = 1 inch ('two-chain surveys'), but sometimes to larger or smaller scales. They can be large sheet maps, one following another in bound volumes, or long narrow maps cleverly folded so that, when opened, they follow the curves of the railway but closing into a small rectangular shape the size of a small book. They are often colour-washed and show boundaries, ownership of adjoining land, culverts, crossings and the names of roads crossing the railway. Using them it is possible to follow the line of the railway noting the earthworks and buildings en route. The ground plans of many buildings outside the boundary as well as those within are shown and the scale is big enough to show platelayers' huts and the like as well as the exact track layout. The **Great Northern Railway** has a whole series of this type of map in **RAIL 796**. Maps of the same, or similar, type are sometimes found in other company series.

Contract drawings

These are plans for the construction, by contractor, of a particular section of railway. For example, in **RAIL 491** are contract plans for the **Midland Railway's Settle to Carlisle line** with 'land plans' and 'route plans'.

Gradient diagrams

These are similar to the parliamentary sections showing the railway as a longitudinal slice through the earth with an exaggerated vertical scale to show the line of the top of the running rails, their gradients, and the cuttings, embankments and tunnels through which they run. Although they are to scale, gradient diagrams are more schematic than realistic.

Distance or mileage diagrams

Entirely schematic, they show the lines of rail in stylized form and, particularly the distances between features like junctions, level crossings, bridges, culverts, etc., so that the engineers have all the details they need in compressed form. **RAIL 798** is a series of mileage diagrams devoted to the **LNER**.

Station plans

Station plans are perhaps on the borderland of technical drawings. They are maps, often large-scale and detailed, of the layouts of individual stations. Sometimes more detailed drawings of individual buildings are associated with them.

Siding diagrams

They show the physical arrangements of sidings to private traders' premises. Typically they show the junction with the railway company's line, how far the siding is maintained by the railway and at what physical point the trader becomes responsible. They vary between hand-drawn sketches with manuscript additions to small printed maps.

Wayleave plans

Some railways, especially in the north-east of England, were constructed and operated by wayleaves which were agreements by the landowner to the use of a railway over the land. In some cases wayleave plans are associated with wayleave agreements, several appearing in **NER** records in **RAIL 527** and some in the **Pontop & South Shields Railway** series, **RAIL 569**.

Railway Clearing House plans

The Railway Clearing House (RCH) produced plans showing the routes of railways coloured to indicate the ownership of each separately owned stretch of line. Many of these can be found in **RAIL 1032** and **RAIL 1037**. Those series also include similar maps published by John Airey, whose rights in the maps were sold to the RCH in 1895. In **ZMAP 1/59** will be found a schedule compiled in 1958 for the *Journal of the Railway and Canal Historical Society*, showing the whereabouts of all known maps of Airey and the RCH in twelve public collections, including those in the PRO. The schedule quotes MPS references for those in the PRO.

The RCH also produced junction diagrams that showed, again by coloured line diagrams, the exact ownership of track at junctions where the lines of different companies met. Those that the PRO holds are in **RAIL 1082**.

Technical drawings

Drawings of buildings

These are architectural drawings either recording existing buildings (perhaps to be modified) or drawn for the construction of new buildings. Some are contract drawings. Often they are colour-washed to indicate the different materials used in their construction. Occasionally they can be very detailed, for example the drawings of porches, roofs, ironwork, etc., of **Midland Railway** stations, Wellingborough to Leicester, in 1858 to 1 inch = 1 foot scale, in **RAIL 491/753**. Sometimes the plans relate solely to sections of buildings, such as iron roofs.

Drawings of bridges and viaducts

A more specialized form of architecture or engineering, bridges were built of timber, brick, stone, iron and steel. The drawings of them can be minutely detailed down to the shape of bolt heads, and there may be several sheets of details accompanying a main drawing.

Standard lineside buildings

Some railways produced standard drawings of frequently repeated buildings such as culverts, road bridges, fences and gates, etc. Some of these are in the PRO, e.g. an **Ashton, Stalybridge & Liverpool Junction Railway** plan of culverts and drains by John Hawkshaw in the **LNWR** series **RAIL 410/2071**.

Signalling plans and diagrams

These tend to take the form of stylized diagrams of track layouts showing the positions of signals and signalling equipment on the ground and relating signals and points to the numbered levers in the signal boxes. Occasionally the signal box diagrams which hung above the levers in the box have survived.

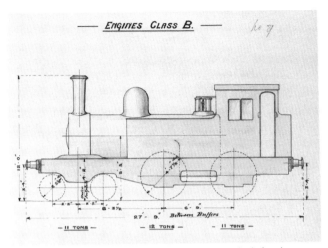

Locomotive class B. Seven of these were built for the
E & MR by Hudswell, Clarke between 1879 and 1881.

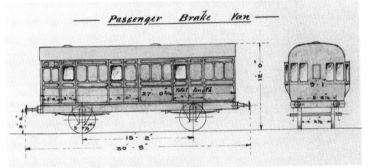

Passenger brake van built in the E & MR workshops.

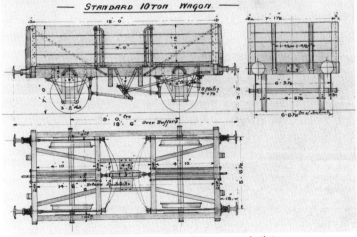

Standard 10 ton wagon. Six of these were built in
the E & MR workshops in 1892.

Figure 15 Diagrams from a book of drawings and miscellaneous papers of the
Eastern & Midlands Railway. The originals are colour-washed. RAIL 184/3

Track

There appear to be very few drawings of track and track components in the PRO but some can be found, like the specification and plans of permanent way of the **Warrington & Stockport Railway**, 1852, in **RAIL 710/6**. Some are from manufacturers rather than the railways themselves, for example drawings of Parsons' patent switches and crossings, 1850, in **Taff Vale Railway** miscellanea, **RAIL 1008/128**.

Locomotives and rolling stock

With a few exceptions, the drawings of rolling equipment in the PRO consist of diagram books. These give a basic outline of the vehicles with main dimensions and, especially in the case of locomotives, the weights on each axle. Detailed drawings are very rare in the PRO (the proper place to look for them is the NRM), but there are a few. In **RAIL 56/60**, for example, are drawings, dated 1860, of carriage bodies (without underframes) of the **Blyth & Tyne Railway** built by Joseph Wright of Birmingham. In **RAIL 102/9, Carnarvonshire Railway**, are some large-scale drawings of railway wagons (some to 1 inch = 1 foot scale) by Wright's successors, the Metropolitan Carriage & Wagon Company. An unusual survival, which can perhaps be included here since the rolling stock was produced by British industry although for a foreign railway, is the set of drawings among the **Daniel Gooch papers** in **RAIL 1008/28**. Gooch was the Locomotive Superintendent of the GWR but took on other work among which, in the mid-1850s, was a consulting engineer role to the Geelong & Melbourne Railway in Australia. He drew up specifications for locomotives and rolling stock (as well as civil engineering items) and supervised construction by various British manufacturers. His papers contain technical drawings of many of the locomotives and rolling stock by various manufacturers including Joseph Wright, Robert Stephenson & Co and the Stothert & Slaughter company.

Maps in the records of government

Ordnance Survey maps

The PRO does not collect Ordnance Survey (OS) maps for their own sake (the British Library has the deposited sets of published maps). Nevertheless it does hold tens of thousands of them, annotated and overprinted for diverse uses by government departments. Although the government uses of them may not be of especial interest to the railway researcher, the large-scale maps, which show accurate railway track layouts, etc., may be of value. The three basic scales that include accurate railway

track layouts are the 1:10 650 (6 inches = 1 mile) scale[2], 1:2500 (approximately 25 inches = 1 mile) scale, and the 1:1250 (approximately 50 inches = 1 mile) scale. OS mapping at smaller scales[3] is not dealt with here.

Continuous revision of OS maps was not introduced until after the Second World War. Before that revisions could wait two, three or four decades. Maps were frequently issued with basic survey information two or more decades old or with minor revisions to, for example, boundaries. This means that although the latest edition may have been used for a particular purpose, its survey information may have related to an earlier time. I have tried to indicate the range of issue dates of the maps described below, but this point should be borne in mind if information of a particular date is required.[4]

The largest collection of OS maps in the PRO comes from the **Inland Revenue Valuation Office Agency**. They record plot numbers for each separately owned plot of land in England and Wales and were required for administering the tax imposed on the accrued value of land changing hands, which was imposed between 1910 and 1919. They are to be found in **IR 121 (London)** and **IR 124** to **135** inclusive, a series for each region of England and one (**IR 131**) for **Wales**. The 'valuation maps' are generally to 1:2500 scale but some were specially enlarged by the OS to 1:1250 scale. The valuers appear to have used the latest available OS maps at the time so the issue dates vary from the 1880s to the First World War. In a few cases, particularly town maps that had heavy use, replacement maps of the 1920s may be found. Some of the valuation maps were destroyed by Second World War bombing, so the collection is not complete.

There is an incomplete collection of 1:10 650 scale OS maps for England and Wales that came to the PRO from the House of Commons Library. These are referenced **ZOS 12** but are in volumes on the open shelves in the map and large document reading room in the PRO. They range in date from the 1880s to 1968. Some are provisional maps, some are definitive.

Among the records of the **National Coal Board** and its predecessors is **COAL 40 Registration of Assets: Maps**, a series of 1:2500 scale maps of the colliery areas of England and Wales. A random check shows them to be mainly from 1913–1921 editions, with some from the 1930s, but none of them are complete sheets and they do not always carry information as to survey dates, etc.

---

2 From 1969 mapping at 1:10 000 scale began.
3 In 1961 the Ordnance Survey took the decision to generalize railway track layouts in the 1:10 650 and 1:10 000 scales. Individual tracks ceased to be shown at these scales.
4 For further information about the history of OS mapping, *see* J. B. Harley, *Ordnance Survey Maps, a Descriptive Manual* Ordnance Survey, Southampton, 1975.

OS maps are also to be found mixed up with other records in some series and have been noted in the following:

BD 5 is a series transferred from the **Welsh Office** relating to the review of Welsh county districts under the Local Government Act 1929. The records are of the 1930s and, occasionally, the 1940s. Generally the records here deal with county and large area boundaries, with appropriate small-scale maps, but where particular towns or districts are concerned 6-inch maps are present. For example, **BD 5/39** is about the boundary between Conway Borough and Llandudno Urban District Council and contains a 1931 reprint 6-inch map sheet for that area.

BD 28, records of the **Welsh Office Town and Country Planning Division**, contains some extracts from 6- and 25-inch maps. These records relate to the 1940s to 1960s.

Crown Estate records

Although several **CRES** series have a few plans concerning railways, there are three that have a significant number. They are the registered file series, **CRES 35**, **CRES 37** and **CRES 58**. In many of these the maps are still in the files. Where railways occur in the title deeds series, **CRES 38**, maps often accompany the records.

The Land Revenue Record Office map series, **LRRO 1**, contains many maps about railways. These have generally been removed to **MPE**, **MPEE** and **MR** references.

Other mapping

BK 25 National Dock Labour Board: Maps and Plans of Docks and Harbours

An example of a series of maps from various sources and to various scales which happen to show railway layouts in docks. It includes two 6-inch OS maps, for Lowestoft and Poole, used in 1927 and 1937 respectively.

BT 356 Marine Maps and Plans of the Board of Trade

This series contains maps of foreshores and other marine maps. Some show coastal railways, for example **BT 356/12757**, a 1 inch = 200 feet scale map of Dover Harbour showing existing and proposed railways, dated 1905. Some of the maps here are parliamentary sessional plans.

Finally, mention must be made of the main **Board of Trade Railway Department** series, **MT 6**. Many of the files here still contain maps and plans, although a great many have been extracted to map references. Where maps have been extracted, there is always a link from the file to the map reference.

7 Photographs

Photographs from the railways' own records

The PRO has nothing to match the photographic collections of the NRM. Indeed, it is probable that the PRO holds few, if any, images created for or by the railways not also held by the NRM. The photographs in the PRO are prints, whereas the NRM holds negatives of many of its images. The PRO's photographs occur in the odd album or file, and sometimes as single images associated with other documents. There are some striking pictures among them, although very often the prints have suffered blemishes in the course of their use.

Bristol & Exeter Railway No 58 built by Rothwell, 1859. RAIL 1014/37/6 (1)

One cannot point to a series devoted to photographs although a department, **CN**, has been allocated to photographs extracted from other documents. **CN 18** has been created for extracts from RAIL series but very few items have been placed there as yet; apart from some photographs of documents, it holds two or three prints of the Southwold Railway and a picture of the site of an accident at Rhiwbwa Halt, Cardiff Railway, *c*.1920.

Sometimes photographs of locomotives carriages and wagons are found in rolling stock diagram books (*see* **Chapter 6**) as illustrations of the types of vehicles on a particular railway. For example **RAIL 437/42** is an album of photographs and diagrams of the stock of the **London, Tilbury & Southend R**. The same album also contains photographs of steamships and locomotive depots. Elsewhere are albums of photographs of miscellaneous subjects, like the set of albums of the **GCR** showing munitions work at the company's workshops at Gorton and Dukinfield in the First World War, **RAIL 226/103–108**. Pieces 103 and 104 of these also include pictures of locomotives, ambulance trains constructed by the company, wagons constructed for the War Department and outsize loads. These particular albums strongly feature women workers in heavy industry, a novelty of the war. In the same series, **RAIL 226/384** contains some documentary shots of volunteer workers during the rail strike of 1919 which also show the crowding of stations caused by the delays.

In **RAIL 254/31** is an album of **GWR** photographs of locomotives, rolling stock and rolling stock parts from railways taken over at the grouping. Many of them appear to have been recorded just before they were scrapped.

Other favourite themes are accidents, stations, hotels and other buildings, pictures of vehicles (including road vehicles) and equipment, group photographs, and images of civil engineering projects. In the **Furness Railway** series **RAIL 214**, pieces **91** and **92** include, as well as pictures of bridges, docks, ships, and war damage on the railway (First World War), views of places reachable by using the railway. These include a photograph of a large group on a confectioners' outing to Furness Abbey.

War damage in both world wars, as well as peacetime accidents are relatively prominent. There are a few photographs of Second World War damage on the **LNER** in **RAIL 393/328**. The **GWR** has two albums of war damage pictures of the same period in **RAIL 253/ 641** and **642,** and there are more air raid damage photographs in **RAIL 253/ 74** and **75.**

Aftermath of the explosion of the boiler of GWR broad gauge locomotive 'Perseus' in the engine shed at Westbourne Park, West London, 8 November 1862. The locomotive was thrown 30 feet and part of the boiler went through the roof and landed 100 yards away. Three locomotive department employees were killed. RAIL 1014/37/6 (5)

Construction gang at West Norwood Station, LBSCR, c. 1909. RAIL 414/554

Railway photographs in government departmental records

COPY I Copyright Office: entry forms etc.

Under the Copyright Acts, photographs (as well as books, paintings and drawings, advertisements, etc.) could be registered by publishers or originators to assert their proprietorial rights. From 1842 until 1912 a copy of the work was attached to each application form for registration. COPY 1 contains the application forms to the Copyright Office with examples of work, among them a great variety of photographs of railways. Interest lies not only in the images, but also in the details of the photographers and, where different, proprietors of these photographs. It must be said that the quality of the prints is not always of the best (some are fading) and, because the print had to be made to fit the size of the form, some have been folded. Nevertheless, they are an interesting collection.[1] Pictures of street tramways are also to be found here. In the early years of this series photographs are relatively few and are

A Great Eastern Railway tram engine on the quay at Great Yarmouth. The photograph was taken by Joseph Nock and registered for copyright on 14 October 1899 by G.W. Wilson, Aberdeen. COPY 1/ 443

---

1 About 70 per cent of the railway images have been published in Linsley, Robin, *Railways in Camera, 1860–1913*, Alan Sutton, Stroud, 1996.

included in the general run of registrations along with literary works, etc. From the 1860s, when photography became popular, many more photographs came forward for registration and their applications are kept in separate sequences.

COPY 1 is the only series of government records to contain many photographs of railways. Otherwise, railway subjects are relatively few among government records. In the remaining part of this chapter government records are taken in the alphabetical order of their department codes, indicating the variety of subjects to be found in them. This should not be taken as a definitive or exhaustive list. In some cases the notes relate to a single image.

ADM 195 Civil Engineer-in-Chief: photographs
(already mentioned in **Chapter 4**)
These are albums of photographs of building work in naval dockyards. Some of the images contain contractors' railways, locomotives and wagons. Occasionally, main-line wagons also come into shot. The railway images date to the 1890s and 1900s.

AY 18 Princes Risborough Laboratory reports
AY 18/1278–1282 are records of experiments in the antiseptic treatment of railway sleepers to prevent rot. Pieces **1279** and **1280** include photographs of sleepers at experimental sites on each of the 'big four' railways.

BK 12 National Dock Labour Board
BK 12/4 has a photograph of the view from the new headquarters building of the NDLB showing the tracks towards Vauxhall Station, London, and the Albert Embankment, 1956. (The series also has some snapshots taken in docks including a little railway content.)

COAL 13 National Coal Board, 'Cobb photographs'
The Rev. F. W. Cobb took these photographs of Barber Walker & Co's collieries around Eastwood, Nottinghamshire between 1907 and 1914. Some of his images record pit railways.

CRES 35 Crown Estate Commissioners files on estates remaining in Crown Possession after 1940
CRES 35/3216, 4085 and **4089** have photographs of the outside of Piccadilly Circus and Trafalgar Square underground stations showing proposed signs, *c.*1910.

HLG 131 Ministry of Housing and Local Government: Local Government Planning Divisions

HLG 131/78 is about development of the Enfield London Underground station, 1961–1963, with photographs.

HLG 131/100 records a Working Group on Commuting in London and also has some photographs, 1962–1964.

HO 242, Home Office Inspectorate of Constabulary: reports and papers

This series contains records of the 'Great Train Robbery', 1963. Piece **3** includes photographs, some of which show the train and the signal that was tampered with.

MAF 49 Ministry of Agriculture, Fisheries and Food: land drainage and water supply

MAF 49/ 1872 has photographs of Bodorgan railway viaduct, Anglesey, in a file about the Malltraeth Marsh drainage scheme.

MUN 5 Ministry of Munitions: Historical Records Branch

In the list of MUN 5, under *External Productive Organization: Co-ordinating Committee Papers*, will be found some pieces about ammunition factories of the First World War that include photographs of railways and guided ways within, and associated with, the factories.

It is impossible, at present to produce a complete list of photographs among government records, although work on cataloguing photographs is progressing. Usually, the presence of photographs (though not their exact content) is noted in lists. Recent listings will include such notes as a matter of policy, but the lists of earlier transfers to the PRO may not. The practice of removing photographs to the series in **CN** (*see* p. 100) will continue.

Appendix 1: BTHR Codes

In the British Transport Historical Records office at Paddington records were classified using a system of mnemonic codes. When the PRO took over the records they were reclassified as RAIL and AN 'classes', now known as 'series'. The BTHR codes are reproduced here, in alphabetical order, keyed to their RAIL and AN equivalents to help in the finding of records cited in books and articles published before the change to RAIL and AN. References to AN series are listed separately at the end of this Appendix.

BTHR code	Records	RAIL series	BTHR code	Records	RAIL series
ABB	Abbotsbury Railway Company	1	BAW	Bishop Auckland and Weardale Railway Company	46
ABD	Aberdare Railway Company	2	BBA	Blackburn, Burnley, Accrington and Colne Railway Company	51
ABG	Abingdon Railway Company	5			
ABV	Aberdare Valley Railway Company	3	BBJ	Buckingham and Brackley Junction Railway Company	85
AD	Alexandra (Newport and South Wales) Docks and Railway Company	7	BBR	Bristol and Birmingham Railway Company	74
AGR	Avon and Gloucestershire Railway Company	12	BCC	Brighton and Croydon Railways Committee of Amalgamation	71
ALC	Alcester Railway Company	6	BCD	Banbury and Cheltenham Direct Railway Company	18
ANBE	Ambergate, Nottingham and Boston and Eastern Junction Railway Company	8	BCH	Brighton and Chichester Railway Company	70
ANJ	Ashby and Nuneaton Joint Committee	11			
AP	Parliamentary: Acts	1062–1064	BCR	Bedford and Cambridge Railway Company	27
AP(Y)	Parliamentary: Acts: North Eastern	1065			
ARR	Andover and Redbridge Railway Company	9	BDB	Bishop's Stortford, Dunmow and Braintree Railway Company	48
ASD	Ashburton, Newton and South Devon Junction Railway Company	10	BDG	Bridgewater Railway Company	68
AWC	Aberystwyth and Welsh Coast Railway Company	4	BDJ	Birmingham and Derby Junction Railway Company	36
AXJ	Axholme Joint Railway Committee (North Eastern and Lancashire and Yorkshire Railways)	13	BDK	Barnoldswick Railway Company	21
			BDL	Bedale and Leyburn Railway Company	26
AXL	Axminster and Lyme Regis Light Railway Company	14	BDT	Bridport Railway Company	69
AYL	Aylesbury Railway Company	15	BDW	Bodmin and Wadebridge Railway Company	57
B&E	Bristol and Exeter Railway Company	75	BED	Banstead and Epsom Downs Railway Company	20
BAD	Bala and Dolgelly Railway Company	16			
BAF	Bala and Festiniog Railway Company	17	BEI	Bradford, Eccleshill and Idle Railway Company	63

BEK	Berwick and Kelso Railway Company	31
BEX	Bideford Extension Railway Company	33
BFD	Briton Ferry Dock and Railway Company (Briton Ferry Floating Dock Company)	82
BGC	Bangor and Caernarvon Railway Company	19
BGH	Blaydon, Gateshead and Hebburn Railway Company	55
BGN	Bognor Railway Company	58
BGR	Birmingham and Gloucester Railway Company	37
BHA	Birmingham and Henley in Arden Railway Company	38
BHE	Berks and Hants Extension Railway Company	29
BHR	Berks and Hants Railway Company	30
BHW	Birmingham West Suburban Railway Company	43
BIR	Bacton and Immingham Light Railway Company	24
BIW	Bishop's Waltham Railway Company	49
BKL	Brackenhill Light Railway Company	61
BKT	Brighton, Uckfield and Tunbridge Wells Railway Company	73
BLA	Blackburn Railway Company	52
BLB	Beckenham, Lewes and Brighton Railway Company	25
BLH	Brighton, Lewes and Hastings Railway Company	72
BLL	Blackpool and Lytham Railway Company	53
BLM	Birmingham, Lichfield and Manchester Railway Company	41
BLP	Blackburn and Preston Railway Company	50
BLR	Byelaws and Regulations	1001–1003
BMC	Birkenhead, Manchester and Cheshire Junction Railway Company	34
BMR	Brecon and Merthyr Tydfil Junction Railway Company	65
BNN	Bedford and Northampton Railway Company	28
BNS	Bristol and North Somerset Railway Company	77
BOP	Bolton and Preston Railway Company	59
BOW	Bourton-on-the-Water Railway Company	60
BOX	Birmingham and Oxford Junction Railway Company	39
BPA	Bishop Auckland Station Joint Committee (North Eastern and Stockton and Darlington Railways)	47
BPG	Burry Port and Gwendreath Valley Railway Company	89
BPL	Blackpool Railway Company	54
BPP	Bristol Port Railway and Pier Company (including Clifton Extension Railway)	81
BRD	Bridgend Railway Company	67
BRH	Bristol Harbour Railway Company	79
BRI	Bricklayer's Arms Extension Railway Company	66
BRJ	Brandling Junction Railway Company	64
BRK	Birkenhead Railway Company	35
BRM	Bromley Direct Railway Company	83
BRY	Barry Railway Company	23
BSC	Birmingham and Sutton Coldfield Extension Railway Company	40
BSN	Bristol Joint Station Committee	80
BSVR	Birmingham, Wolverhampton and Stour Valley Railway Company	45
BSW	Bristol and South Wales Union Railway Company	78
BTD	Buckfastleigh, Totnes and South Devon Railway Company	84
BTG	Bristol and Gloucester Railway Company	76
BTR	Bradford and Thornton Railway Company	62
BTY	Blyth and Tyne Railway Company	56
BUC	Buckley Railway Company	87
BUD	Budleigh Salterton Railway Company	88
BUK	Buckinghamshire Railway Company	86
BUT	Bury and Tottington District Railway Company	90
BWD	Birmingham, Wolverhampton and Dudley Railway Company	44

BWS	Birmingham, North Warwickshire and Stratford-upon-Avon Railway Company	42
BXH	Bexley Heath Railway Company	32
BYR	Barnsley Coal Railway Company	22
C&C	Chester and Crewe Railway Company	776
CAA	Cowbridge and Aberthaw Railway Company	140
CAB	Corwen and Bala Railway Company	136
CAM	Cambrian Railways Company	92
CAR	Cardiff Railway Company	97
CBE	Colne and Bradford Extension Railway	127
CCR	Cork City Railway Company	131
CDJ	County Donegal Railways Joint Committee	137
CER	Stock and Share Certificates	1158
CER(Y)	Stock and Share Certificates (York Collection)	1159
CFJ	Cleator and Furness Railway Committee	118
CGW	Cheltenham and Great Western Union Railway Company	109
CHA	Chard Railway Company	106
CHB	Chester and Birkenhead Railway Company	112
CHF	Charnwood Forest Railway Company	108
CHH	Chester and Holyhead Railway Company	113
CHM	Cheshire Midland Railway Company	111
CHP	Cromford and High Peak Railway Company	144
CKM	Cannock Mineral Railway Company	94
CKP	Cockermouth, Keswick and Penrith Railway Company	123
CLA	Clarence Railway Company	117
CLC	Cheshire Lines Committee	110
CLJ	Coventry and Leicester Junction Railway Company	138
CLL	Carnarvon and Llanberis Railway Company	101

CLT	Conway and Llanrwst Railway Company	130
CLW	Cleator and Workington Junction Railway Company	119
CLY	Cambridge and Lincoln Extension and Lincoln, York and Leeds Junction Railway Company	93
CMC	Carmarthen and Cardigan Railway Company	99
CMD	Cleobury Mortimer and Ditton Priors Light Railway Company	120
CMGW	Cornwall Minerals and Great Western Railway Companies Joint Committee	132
CMR	Cornwall Minerals Railway Company	133
CMT	Carmarthenshire Railway or Tramroad Company	100
CMU	Coleford, Monmouth, Usk and Pontypool Railway Company	125
CNBL	Coventry, Nuneaton, Birmingham and Leicester Railway Company	139
CNE	Calne Railway Company	91
CNR	Cowes and Newport Railway Company	142
CNV	Carnarvon Railway Company	102
COL	Coleford Railway Company	126
CON	Coniston Railway Company	129
COR	Cornwall Railway Company	134
COV	Cardiff and Ogmore Valley Railway Company	95
COW	Cowbridge Railway Company	141
CP	Road Service Companies: Carter Paterson & Co Ltd	1130
CPB	Cardiff, Penarth and Barry Junction Railways Company	96
CPS	Crystal Palace and South London Junction Railway Company	146
CRM	Chichester and Midhurst Railway Company	115
CRP	Cranbrook and Paddock Wood Railway	143
CRS	Corris Railway Company	135
CSB	Crowhurst, Sidley and Bexhill Railway Company	145

CSC	Carlisle Citadel Station Committee	98
CSN	Chester Joint Station Committee	114
CSV	Colchester, Stour Valley, Sudbury and Halstead Railway Company	124
CTH	BTHR: Railway Hotels: Miscellanea	1022
CTR	Chard and Taunton Railway Company	105
CVD	Cleveland Railway Company	121
CVH	Colne Valley and Halstead Railway Company	128
CVL	Culm Valley Light Railway Company	147
CVR	Chipstead Valley Railway Company	116
CWC	Central Wales and Carmarthen Junction Railway Company	104
CWR	Cockermouth and Workington Railway Company	122
CWS	Cawood, Wistow and Selby Light Railway Company	103
CXB	Charing Cross Railway Company	107
DAC	Devon and Cornwall Railway Company	154
DAS	Devon and Somerset Railway Company	155
DBC	Darlington and Barnard Castle Railway Company	149
DCR	Dorset Central Railway Company	159
DEV	Dearness Valley Railway Company	151
DHD	Disley and Hayfield Railway Company	158
DJR	Durham Junction Railway Company	165
DLO	Direct London and Portsmouth Railway Company (Atmospheric)	157
DLP	Duffryn, Llynvi and Porthcawl Railway Company	161
DMJ	Dursley and Midland Junction Railway Company	166
DNG	Dundalk, Newry and Greenore Railway Company	162
DNS	Didcot, Newbury and Southampton Railway Company	156
DNV	Dearne Valley Railway Company	150
DR	Dunstable Railway Company	163
DRU	Denbigh, Ruthin and Corwen Railway Company	152
DSF	Downham and Stoke Ferry Railway Company	160
DSR	Durham and Sunderland Railway Company	164
DSW	Derbyshire, Staffordshire and Worcestershire Junction Railway Company	153
DVR	Dare Valley Railway Company	148
EAR	East Anglian Railway Company	171
EAS	Easingwold Railway Company	167
EC	Eastern Counties Railway Company	186
ECH	Easton and Church Hope Railway Company	188
ECL	Ely and Clydach Valleys Railway Company	192
ECSJ	Eastern Counties and East Suffolk Joint Committee	185
ECT	East Coast (Railway Companies) Conference	172
EDE	Epsom Downs Extension Railway Company	198
EDN	Eden Valley Railway Company	189
EGG	East Grinstead, Groombridge and Tunbridge Wells Railway Company	174
EGL	East Gloucestershire Railway Company	173
EGW	Exeter Great Western Railway Company	202
EHL	Edgware, Highgate and London Railway Company	190
EKL	East Kent Light Railway Company	175
ELA	East Lancashire Railway Company	176
ELI	East Lincolnshire Railway Company	177
ELJC	East London Railway Joint Committee	179
ELR	East London Railway Company	178
ELV	Elham Valley Railway Company	191
EMR	Eastern and Midlands Railway Company	184
ENM	Ely and Newmarket Railway Company	193
ENR	East Norfolk Railway Company	180
EPL	Epsom and Leatherhead Railway Company	197

EPP	Epping Railways Company	196
ERR	Evesham and Redditch Railway Company	199
ERSJ	Evesham, Redditch and Stratford-upon-Avon Junction Railway Company	777
ESO	East Somerset Railway Company	181
ESR	East Suffolk Railway Company	182
EST	Ely and St Ives Railway Company	194
EUK	East Usk Railway Company	183
EUR	Eastern Union Railway Company	187
EVL	Ely Valley Railway Company	195
EWJ	East and West Junction and Stratford-upon-Avon, Towcester and Midland Junction Railway Companies Joint Committee	168
EWY	East and West Yorks Union Railways Company	170
EWYJ	East and West Yorkshire Junction Railway Company	169
EXC	Exeter and Crediton Railway Company	201
EXE	Exeter Railway Company	203
EXV	Exe Valley Railway Company	200
FAR	Faringdon Railway Company	204
FBN	Festiniog and Blaenau Railway Company	205
FCT	Forcett Railway Company	208
FDC	Forest of Dean Central Railway Company	209
FDR	Forest of Dean Railway Company	210
FIR	Fishguard and Rosslare Railways and Harbours Company	206
FMJ	Furness and Midland Railways Joint Committee	213
FPW	Fleetwood, Preston and West Riding Junction Railway Company	207
FRS	Frosterley and Stanhope Railway Company	212
FUR	Furness Railway Company	214
FYN	Freshwater, Yarmouth and Newport Railway Company	211
GCHB	Great Central, Hull and Barnsley, and Midland Railways Joint Committee	225

GCMJ	Great Central and Midland Railways Joint Committee	224
GCNW	Great Central and London and North Western Railways Joint Committee	222
GCR	Great Central Railway Company	226
GDF	Gloucester and Forest of Dean Railway Company	217
GE	Great Eastern Railway Company	227
GEN	LMSR: Record Office Files	1007
GEN	Archivist's Historical Miscellanea	1005
GEN(Y)	Archivist's Historical Miscellanea (York Collection)	1006
GJR	Grand Junction Railway Company	220
GKE	Garstang and Knott End Railway Company	215
GLC	Garston and Liverpool Railway Committee	216
GMEJ	Great Central and Metropolitan Railways Joint Committee	223
GML	Goole and Marshland Light Railway Company	219
GMW	Great Marlow Railway Company	230
GN	Great Northern Railway Company	236
GNC	Great North of England, Clarence and Hartlepool Junction Railway Company	231
GNE	Great North of England Railway Company	232
GNGE	Great Northern and Great Eastern Railways Joint Committee	233
GNML	Great Northern and Manchester, Sheffield and Lincolnshire Joint Committee	235
GNNW	Great Northern and London and North Western Railways Joint Committee	234
GRV	Gravesend Railway Company	221
GSS	Great Grimsby and Sheffield Junction Railway Company	228
GSSL	Great Grimsby and Sheffield Junction Railway and Sheffield and Lincolnshire Junction Railway Joint Committee	229
GVR	Golden Valley Railway Company	218
GW	Great Western Railway Company	250–282

GWB   Great Western and Brentford Railway
       Company   237

GWBD   Great Western, Bristol and Exeter,
       and South Devon Railways' Joint
       Committee   249

GWBE   Great Western and Bristol and Exeter
       Railways Joint Committee   238

GWD   Gwendreath Valleys Railway
       Company   285

GWGC   Great Western and Great Central
       Railways Joint Committee   239

GWM   Great Western and West Midland
       Railway Companies   248

GWMR   Great Western and Midland Railway
       Companies Joint Committee   241

GWPT   Great Western and Port Talbot
       Railways and Docks Companies   242

GWRS   Great Western and Rhondda and
       Swansea Bay Railway Companies   243

GWRY   Great Western and Rhymney Railway
       Companies   244

GWSA   Great Western and Stratford-upon-
       Avon Railway Companies   246

GWSC   Great Western, Shrewsbury and
       Chester, and Shrewsbury and
       Birmingham Railway Companies   283

GWSR   Great Western and Southern Railways'
       Joint Committee   245

GWSW   Great Western and London and South
       Western Railways Joint Committee   240

GWU   Great Western and Uxbridge Railway
       Company   247

GWWM   Great Western, West Midland, and
       South Wales Railway Companies   284

HAD   Hexham and Allendale Railway
       Company   303

HAH   Hull and Hornsea Railway Company 314

HAL   Halesowen Railway Company   286

HAR   Harborne Railway Company   292

HAS   Harrow and Stanmore Railway
       Company   293

HAY   Hayling Railways Company   298

HBG   Hayling Bridge and Causeway
       Management Committee   297

HBGC   Hull and Barnsley and Great Central
       Railways Joint Committee   310

HBJ   Hull and Barnsley Junction Railway
       Company   311

HBR   Hull and Barnsley Railway
       Company   312

HCR   Horncastle Railway Company   305

HDL   Horsham, Dorking and Leatherhead
       Railway Company   307

HDR   Hartlepool Dock and Railway
       Company   294

HEL   Helston Railway Company   299

HGD   Horsham and Guildford Direct
       Railway Company   306

HHB   Hereford, Hay and Brecon Railway
       Company   300

HHL   Halifax High Level and North and
       South Junction Railway Company   289

HHLJ   Halifax High Level Railway Joint
       Committee   290

HHR   Hundred of Hoo Railway Company   320

HJR   Hampstead Junction Railway
       Company   291

HL   Various Transport Undertakings   1008

HLN   Halesowen Railway Joint Committee 287

HMC   Humber Conference   318

HOJ   Halifax and Ovenden Joint
       Committee   288

HOL   Holywell Railway Company   304

HOT   BTHR: Railway Hotels: Miscellanea 1022

HRD   Humber Commercial Railway and
       Dock Company   317

HRG   Hereford, Ross and Gloucester
       Railway Company   302

HRP   Railway Collections: various
       companies   1014–1018

HRP   Miscellanea   1020

HRP(Y) Miscellanea: North Eastern   1021

HSA   Hatfield and St Albans Railway
       Company   295

HSB   Hull South Bridge Company   316

HSE   Hull and Selby Railway Company   315

HSJ   Huddersfield Joint Station
       Committee   309

HSM   Hylton, Southwick and Monkwearmouth
       Railway Company   322

HSN	Hereford Joint Station Construction and Traffic Committees	301
HSR	Hythe and Sandgate Railway Company	323
HUH	Hull and Holderness Railway Company	313
HUM	Huddersfield and Manchester Railway and Canal Company	308
HWC	Road Services Companies: Hay's Wharf Cartage Co Ltd	1131
HWM	Hawes and Melmerby Railway Company	296
HWN	Hunstanton and West Norfolk Railway Company	321
HWT	Humber Warehousing and Transport Company Limited	319
IBE	Ipswich and Bury St Edmunds Railway Company	326
IETC	Irish and English Traffic Conference	327
ILF	Ilfracombe Railway Company	325
IOW	Isle of Wight Railway Company	330
IRC	International Railway Congress Association	1023–1024
ISR	Idle and Shipley Railway Company	324
IWC	Isle of Wight Central Railway Company	328
IWN	Isle of Wight (Newport Junction) Railway Company	329
KBS	Kingsbridge and Salcombe Railway Company	335
KCR	Kent Coast Railway Company	333
KER	Knott End Railway Company	337
KES	Kent and East Sussex Light Railway Company	332
KLD	King's Lynn Docks and Railway Company	334
KNE	Kington and Eardisley Railway Company	336
KWV	Keighley and Worth Valley Railway Company	331
LAC	Lancaster and Carlisle Railway Company	346
LAN	Lampeter, Aberayron and New Quay Light Railway Company	339
LAS	Labour and Staff Matters	1025
LAS(Y)	Labour and Staff Matters (York Collection)	1026
LAU	Lancashire Union Railways Company	345
LBH	Leeds, Bradford and Halifax Junction Railway Company	352
LBM	London and Birmingham Railway Company	384
LBR	London and Brighton Railway Company	386
LBS	London, Brighton and South Coast Railway Company	414
LBW	London and Blackwall Railway Company (formerly Commercial)	385
LCA	Law Cases and Arbitration	1027
LCA(Y)	Law Cases and Arbitration (York Collection)	1027
LCCJ	London and Chatham and Chatham and Portsmouth Junction Railway Company	387
LCD	London, Chatham and Dover Railway Company (formerly East Kent Railway Company)	415
LCH	Ludlow and Clee Hill Railway Company	442
LCP	Leeds, Castleford and Pontefract Junction Railway Company	353
LCR	London and Croydon Railway Company	388
LCS	Liverpool, Crosby and Southport Railway Company	372
LDE	Lancashire, Derbyshire and East Coast Railway Company	344
LDM	Leeds, Dewsbury and Manchester Railway Company	355
LEB	Leeds and Bradford Railway Company	350
LEC	Leeds Central Station	354
LEG	Lewes and East Grinstead Railway Company	364
LET	Leicester and Tamworth Junction Railway Company	361
LEU	Lewes and Uckfield Railway Company	365
LGJ	London, Midland and Scottish and Great Western Railways Joint Committee	416

LGR   London and Greenwich Railway
      Company   389

LHR   Lynn and Hunstanton Railway
      Company   444

LIB   Library series – now orderable
      as ZLIB

LIC   Liskeard and Caradon Railway
      Company   366

LIS   Liskeard and Looe Union Canal
      Company (afterwards Liskeard and
      Looe Railway Company)   367

LLA   Llanelly Railway and Dock
      Company   377

LLG   Llangollen and Corwen Railway
      Company   378

LLN   Llanidloes and Newtown Railway
      Company   379

LLV   Llynvi Valley Railway Company   383

LMB   Leominster and Bromyard Railway
      Company   362

LMGJ London and North Western;
      Manchester, Sheffield and Lincolnshire;
      and Great Northern Railway
      Companies Joint Committee   408

LMK   Leominster and Kington Railway
      Company   363

LMLN London, Midland and Scottish, and
      London and North Eastern Railway
      Companies Joint Committee   417

LMM   Llanelly and Mynydd Mawr
      Railway Company   376

LMMJ London and North Western;
      Midland; and Manchester, Sheffield
      and Lincolnshire Railway
      Companies Joint Committee   409

LMS   London, Midland and Scottish
      Railway Company   418–433

LMV   Leek and Manifold Valley Light
      Railway Company   358

LNBM London and North Western and Brecon
      and Merthyr Joint Committee   402

LNE   London and North Eastern
      Railway Company   390–401

LNF   London and North Western and
      Furness Railways Joint Committee   403

LNGW London and North Western and
      Great Western Joint Committee   404

LNLY London and North Western, and
      Lancashire and Yorkshire Railways
      Joint Committee   405

LNM   London and North Western and
      Midland Railways Joint Committee   406

LNO   Leeds Northern Railway Company   357

LNRY London and North Western and
      Rhymney Railway Companies Joint
      Line Committee   407

LNW   London and North Western Railway
      Company   410

LOC   London, Oxford and Cheltenham
      Railway Company   434

LOE   Louth and East Coast Railway
      Company   439

LOER Liverpool (Overhead) Electric
      Railway Company   778

LOJ   Llynvi and Ogmore and Great
      Western Railways Joint Committee   381

LOL   Louth and Lincoln Railway
      Company   440

LOR   Llynvi and Ogmore Railway
      Company   382

LOS   Lee-on-the-Solent Railway Company 349

LPJ   Lancaster and Preston Junction
      Railway Company   347

LRH   Lowestoft Railway Company   441

LRM   London Road Station Committee,
      Manchester   435

LRS   Leicester and Swannington Railway
      Company   359

LSB   Lynn and Sutton Bridge Railway
      Company   445

LSD   Launceston and South Devon
      Railway Company   348

LSL   Liverpool, St Helens and South
      Lancashire Railway Company   374

LSN   Leeds New Joint Station Committee 356

LSO   London and Southampton Railway
      Company   412

LSP   Liverpool, Southport and Preston
      Railway Company   375

LSR   Leeds and Selby Railway Company   351

LSW   London and South Western Railway
      Company   411

LSY	London, Salisbury and Yeovil Junction Railway Company	436
LTC	Leicester, Tamworth, Coventry, Birmingham and Trent Valley Junction Railway Company	360
LTS	London, Tilbury and Southend Railway Company	437
LTV	Llantrissant and Taff Vale Junction Railway Company	380
LVB	Liverpool and Bury Railway Company	368
LVC	Liverpool and Chester Railway Company	369
LVL	Liverpool and Leeds Railway Company	370
LVM	Liverpool and Manchester Railway Company	371
LVO	Liverpool, Ormskirk and Preston Railway Company	373
LVR	Lambourn Valley Railway Company	338
LWRA	London and West Riding Association	413
LWS	London, Worcester and South Staffordshire Railway Company	438
LY	Lancashire and Yorkshire Railway Company	343
LYB	Lynton and Barnstaple Railway Company	446
LYD	Lydd Railway Company	443
LYGE	Lancashire and Yorkshire and Great Eastern Railways Joint Committee	340
LYGN	Lancashire and Yorkshire and Great Northern Joint Stations Committee	341
LYLU	Lancashire and Yorkshire and Lancashire Union Joint Committee	342
MAC	Maryport and Carlisle Railway Company	472
MAL	Malmesbury Railway Company	452
MAM	Manchester and Milford Railway Company	456
MAR	Marlborough Railway Company	470
MAS	Maidstone and Ashford Railway Company	450
MAWJ	Manchester South Junction and Altrincham, and Warrington and Stockport Joint Committee	464

MBB	Manchester, Bolton and Bury Canal Navigation and Railway Company	458
MBD	Merrybent and Darlington Railway Company	474
MBM	Macclesfield, Bollington and Marple Railway Company	448
MBU	Manchester, Buxton, Matlock and Midland Junction Railway Company	459
MC	Midland Counties Railway Company	490
MDG	Middlesbrough and Guisborough Railway Company	483
MDJ	Malton and Driffield Junction Railway Company	453
MDY	Mawddwy (Mowddwy) Railway Company	473
MEA	Midland and Eastern Railway Company	485
MER	Mersey Railway Company	475
MFD	Mitcheldean Road and Forest of Dean Junction Railway Company	494
MGNJ	Midland and Great Northern Railways Joint Committee	487
MGR	Marlborough and Grafton Railway Company	469
MGSW	Midland and Glasgow and South Western Joint Committee	486
MGW	Monmouthshire Railway and Canal and Great Western Railway Companies Consultation Committee	499
MHJ	Marple, New Mills and Hayfield Junction Railway Company	471
MHP	Muswell Hill and Alexandra Palace Railway Company	503
MID	Midland Railway Company	491
MIL	Milford Railway Company	492
MIN	Minehead Railway Company	493
MKR	Mid-Kent (Bromley to St Mary Cray) Railway Company	478
MKW	Macclesfield and Knutsford Railway Company	447
MLD	Mold and Denbigh Junction Railway Company	495
MLH	Manchester, Leeds and Hull Associated Railway Company	460

MNB	Manchester and Birmingham Railway Company	454
MNE	Midland and North Eastern Railway Companies Committee (Swinton and Knottingley Railway)	488
MNH	Monmouth and Hereford Railway Company	497
MNRC	Monmouthshire Railway and Canal Company	500
MOL	Mold Railway Company	496
MON	Monmouth Railway Company	498
MPJ	Manchester and Milford, and Pembroke and Tenby Railway Companies Joint Committee	455
MPR	Miscellaneous Papers and Records	1057
MPR(Y)	Miscellaneous Papers and Records (York Collection)	1058
MPS	BTHR: Maps, Plans and Surveys	1030–1032
MPS(Y)	BTHR: Maps, Plans and Surveys (York Collection)	1037
MPX	Mansfield and Pinxton Railway Company	467
MRC	Middlesbrough and Redcar Railway Company	484
MRJ	Methley Railway Joint Committee	477
MRS	Miscellaneous Letters and Statistics	1059
MRS(Y)	Miscellaneous Letters and Statistics (York Collection)	1060
MRY	Mansfield Railway Company	468
MSD	Mortonhampstead and South Devon Railway Company	501
MSF	Mid-Suffolk Light Railway Company	479
MSGN	Manchester, Sheffield and Lincolnshire and Great Northern Railway Companies Joint Line Committee	461
MSJ	Manchester South Junction and Altrincham Railway Company	465
MSL	Manchester, Sheffield and Lincolnshire Railway Company	463
MSM	Mid-Sussex and Midhurst Junction Railway Company	480
MSMD	Manchester, Sheffield and Lincolnshire and Midland Joint Lines Committee	462
MSN	Macclesfield Joint Station Committee	449
MSP	Manchester and Southport Railway Company	457
MSU	Manchester South Union Railway Company	466
MSW	Midland and South Western Junction Railway Company	489
MSX	Mid-Sussex Railway Company	481
MT	Law Cases and Arbitration	1027
MT	Board of Trade Railway Department and Ministry of Transport	1038; 1044; 1052–1054; 1056
MT(Y)	Law Cases and Arbitration (York Collection)	1027
MT(Y)	Board of Trade Railway Department and Ministry of Transport (York Collection)	1038; 1053; 1055
MTA	Merthyr, Tredegar and Abergavenny Railway Company	476
MW	Mid-Wales Railway Company	482
MWB	Maldon, Witham and Braintree Railway Company	451
MWS	Much Wenlock and Severn Junction Railway Company	502
NAB	Neath and Brecon Railway Company	505
NAH	Newport, Abergavenny and Hereford Railway Company	513
NAS	Norfolk and Suffolk Joint Railways Committee	518
NBG	Nottingham, Vale of Bevoir and Grantham Railway Company	548
NBJ	Northampton and Banbury Junction Railway Company	538
NCC	Northern Counties Railway Committee	542
NCR	North Cornwall Railway Company	522
NCU	Northern Counties Union Railway Company	543
NDC	North Devon and Cornwall Junction Light Railway Company	523
NDD	North Devon Railway and Dock Company	524
NDW	Newcastle, Derwent and Weardale Railway Company	508
NEB	Newcastle and Berwick Railway Company	506

NEHB	North Eastern Railway and Hull and Barnsley and West Riding Junction Railway and Dock Company Joint Committee	525
NELY	North Eastern Railway and Lancashire and Yorkshire Railway Joint Committee	526
NEN	Northern and Eastern Railway Company	541
NER	North Eastern Railway Company	527
NEW	Newent Railway Company	510
NGS	Newport, Godshill and St Lawrence Railway Company	514
NJS	Nottingham Joint Station Committee	546
NKR	Newmarket Railway Company	512
NL	North London Railway Company	529
NLL	North Lindsey Light Railway Company	528
NM	Newtown and Machynlleth Railway Company	517
NMD	Nantwich and Market Drayton Railway Company	504
NNS	Newcastle and North Shields Railway Company	507
NOB	Northampton and Banbury Railway Company	539
NOBC	Northampton, Banbury and Cheltenham Railway Company	540
NOG	Nottingham and Grantham Railway and Canal Company	545
NOM	North Midland Railway Company	530
NOW	North Western Railway Company	536
NPF	North Pembrokeshire and Fishguard Railway Company	531
NQC	Newquay and Cornwall Junction Railway Company	516
NRL	Norfolk Railway Company	519
NS	North Staffordshire Railway Company	532
NSD	Newhaven and Seaford Sea Defence Commissioners	511
NSJ	Newport Street Joint Committee	515
NSN	Normanton Joint Station Committee	520

NSP	Norwich and Spalding Railway Company	544
NSU	North Sunderland Railway Company	533
NSW	North and South Western Junction Railway Company	521
NTS	Nottingham Suburban Railway Company	547
NUR	North Union Railway Company	534
NWC	Newcastle-upon-Tyne and Carlisle Railway Company	509
NWL	North Wales and Liverpool Railway Committee	535
NYC	North Yorkshire and Cleveland Railway Company	537
OAG	Oldham, Ashton-under-Lyne and Guide Bridge Railway Company	551
OEW	Oswestry, Ellesmere and Whitchurch Railway Company	553
OGM	Ogmore Valley Railway Company	549
OIJ	Otley and Ilkley Joint Line Committee	554
OLD	Oldbury Railway Company	550
OSN	Oswestry and Newtown Railway Company	552
OWW	Oxford, Worcester and Wolverhampton Railway Company	558
OXB	Oxford and Bletchley Junction Railway Company	555
OXD	Oxford Railway Company	557
OXR	Oxford and Rugby Railway Company	556
PAT	Patents	1072–1073
PAT(Y)	Patents (York Collection)	1074
PCN	Pontypool, Caerleon and Newport Railway Company	570
PDP	Parliamentary: Deposited Plans	1071
PDS	Plymouth, Devonport and South Western Junction Railway Company	567
PEM	Pembroke and Tenby Railway Company	559
PEN	Penarth Harbour Dock and Railway Company	561

PER   Periodicals – now orderable as ZPER

PET   Petersfield Railway Company   565

PEX   Penarth Extension Railway
        Company   560

PHS   Road Services Companies: Pickfords
        and Hay's Wharf Shipping and
        Forwarding Company   1132

PIC   Road Services Companies:
        Pickfords Ltd   1133

PLD   Plymouth and Dartmoor Railway
        Company   566

PLJ   Preston and Longridge Railway
        Joint Committee   576

PNR   Penrith Joint Station Committee
        (London and North Western,
        Stockton and Darlington and
        Cockermouth, Keswick and Penrith
        Railway Companies)   563

POB   Poole and Bournemouth Railway
        Company   572

PRE   Princetown Railway Company   578

PRM   Portsmouth Railway Company   575

PROS   Prospectuses   1075

PROS(Y) Prospectuses (York Collection) 1076; 1079

PSN   Plymouth Joint Station Committee   568

PSS   Pontop and South Shields Railway
        Company   569

PTC   Port Talbot Company   573

PTJ   Penarth Harbour Dock and Railway
        Company and Taff Vale Railway
        Company Joint Committee   562

PTR   Port Talbot Railway and Docks
        Company   574

PTY   Pontypridd, Caerphilly and Newport
        Railway Company   571

PWS   Peterborough, Wisbech and Sutton
        Railway Company   564

PWY   Preston and Wyre Railway Harbour
        and Dock Company   577

PYB   Parliamentary: Bills etc   1066; 1068; 1070

PYB(Y) Parliamentary: Bills etc: North
        Eastern   1067; 1069

RAC   Reports and Accounts   1110; 1114–1116

RAC(Y) Reports and Accounts (York
        Collection)   1111; 1117

RB   Rules and Regulations   1134–1136

RB(Y)   Rules and Regulations (York
        Collection)   1134–1136

RC   Reports of Commissions   1119

RCA   Railway Companies Association
        1098; 1100

RCA(Y) Railway Companies Association
        (York Collection)   1099

RCB   Ringwood, Christchurch and
        Bournemouth Railway Company   585

RCH   Railway Clearing House   1080; 1082;
        1084–1085; 1087; 1089;
        1090; 1093; 1095–1097

RCH(Y) Railway Clearing House
        (York Collection)   1081; 1086; 1092

RDH   Redditch Railway Company   580

RGR   Reading, Guildford and Reigate
        Railway Company   579

RHR   Royston and Hitchin Railway
        Company   588

RHY   Rhymney Railway Company   583

RIC   Richmond Railway Company   584

RNR   Ryde and Newport Railway
        Company   591

ROS   Ross and Ledbury Railway
        Company   586

RPC   Ryde Pier Company   592

RRT   Railway Rates Tribunal   1101

RSA   Railway Students' (Study)
        Association   1107

RSB   Rhondda and Swansea Bay Railway
        Company   581

RSM   Ross and Monmouth Railway
        Company   587

RUL   Rugby and Leamington Railway
        Company   589

RUM   Rumney Railway Company   590

RVH   Rhondda Valley and Hirwain
        Junction Railway Company   582

SAD   Stockton and Darlington Railway
        Company   667

SAH   St Helens Canal and Railway
        Company   593

SAL   Strabane and Letterkenny Railway
        Company   672

SAM	Sheffield, Ashton-under-Lyne and Manchester Railway Company	610
SAR	Stratford-upon-Avon Railway Company	675
SAT	Stanhope and Tyne Railway Company	663
SBR	Spalding and Bourn Railway Company	657
SBS	Stalybridge Joint Station Committee	661
SBW	Scarborough, Bridlington and West Riding Junction Railways Company	597
SC	Reports of Committees	1124
SCL	Southport and Cheshire Lines Extension Railway Company	656
SCR	Somerset Central Railway Company	628
SDC	South Devon, Cornwall and West Cornwall Railway Companies	630
SDJ	Salisbury and Dorset Junction Railway Company	594
SDJC	Somerset and Dorset Joint Line Committee	626
SDL	South Durham and Lancashire Union Railway Company	632
SDR	South Devon Railway Company	631
SDT	South Devon and Tavistock Railway Company	629
SDW	Stockport, Disley and Whaley Bridge Railway Company	665
SEA	Seaton and Beer Railway Company	601
SEB	South Eastern, Brighton, Lewes and Newhaven Railway Company	634
SEC	South Eastern and Chatham Railway Companies Managing Committee	633
SER	South Eastern Railway Company	635
SES	Stamford and Essendine Railway Company	662
SEVT	Great Western Railway Company: Severn Tunnel Railway	775
SFD	Sheffield District Railway Company	611
SFR	Spilsby and Firsby Railway Company	658
SGM	Shareholders' Guides and Manuals	1140; 1142; 1144
SHB	Shrewsbury and Birmingham Railway Company	615

SHC	Shrewsbury and Chester Railway Company	616
SHD	Seacombe, Hoylake and Deeside Railway Company	599
SHH	Shrewsbury and Hereford Railway Company (including Shrewsbury and Hereford Joint Committee)	617
SHN	Shortlands and Nunhead Railway Company	614
SHP	Shropshire Railways Company	622
SHW	Shrewsbury and Wellington Joint Line Committee	618
SIR	Sirhowy Railway Company	624
SIW	Stokes Bay Railway and Pier Company	669
SJN	South Yorkshire Junction Railway Company	642
SLE	South Leicestershire Railway Company	636
SLML	Sheffield and Lincolnshire Junction Railway and Manchester and Lincoln Union Railway and Canal Companies Joint Committee	608
SLR	Sheffield and Lincolnshire Junction Railway Company	607
SMA	Swindon, Marlborough and Andover Railway Company	683
SMD	Somerset and Dorset Railway Company	627
SMJ	Stratford-upon-Avon and Midland Junction Railway Company	674
SML	Shropshire and Montgomeryshire Light Railway Company	621
SMN	Stratford and Moreton Railway Company	673
SMR	South Midland Railway Company	637
SNB	Severn Bridge Railway Company	605
SNC	Swindon and Cheltenham Extension Railway Company	681
SNH	Swindon and Highworth Light Railway Company	682
SNV	Severn Valley Railway Company	606
SNW	Scotswood, Newburn and Wylam Railway Company	598
SOD	Southampton and Dorchester Railway Company	644

SOK	Sevenoaks, Maidstone and Tunbridge Railway Company	602
SOL	Shireoaks, Laughton and Maltby Railway Company	613
SOS	South Staffordshire Railway Company	638
SOU	Southern Railway Company	645–655
SOW	South Wales Railway Company	640
SPC	Special Collections 1147–1151; 1155–1157 ZSPC 11	
SRB	Sheffield, Rotherham, Barnsley, Wakefield, Huddersfield and Goole Railway Company	612
SRM	Sheffield and Rotherham Railway Company	609
SSJ	Seaforth and Sefton Junction Railway Company	600
SSN	Shrewsbury Joint Station Committee	619
SSR	Sittingbourne and Sheerness, and London, Chatham and Dover Railways Joint Traffic Committee	625
SSX	Surrey and Sussex Junction Railway Company	676
STA	Stockport, Timperley and Altrincham Junction Railway Company	666
STH	Stockton and Hartlepool Railway Company	668
STP	Stonehouse Pool Improvement Company	670
STR	Stourbridge Railway Company	671
SUB	Subscription Contracts	1160; 1163
SUB(Y)	Subscription Contracts (York Collection)	1161
SURC	Shropshire Union Railways and Canal Company	623
SVR	Swansea Vale Railway Company	679
SWD	Staines and West Drayton Railway Company	659
SWH	Scarborough and Whitby Railway Company	596
SWJ	Stockport and Woodley Junction Railway Company	664
SWM	South Wales Mineral Railway Company	639
SWN	Swansea and Neath Railway Company	678
SWR	Severn and Wye Railway and Canal Company	604
SWS	Shrewsbury, Wolverhampton and South Straffordshire Junction Railway Company	620
SWV	Swansea Valley Railway Company	680
SWW	Staines, Wokingham and Woking Railway Company	660
SWY	Sutton and Willoughby Railway Company	677
SYB	Severn and Wye and Severn Bridge Railway Company	603
SYD	South Yorkshire Railway and River Dun Company	643
SYJ	South Yorkshire Joint Line Committee	641
SYR	Salisbury and Yeovil Railway Company	595
TAG	Trent, Ancholme and Grimsby Railway Company	698
TBY	Tebay Joint Station Committee	686
TEB	Tenbury and Bewdley Railway Company	689
TEN	Tenbury Railway Company	690
TEV	Tees Valley Railway Company	687
TFG	Tottenham and Forest Gate Railway Company	696
TGN	Teign Valley Railway Company	688
THD	Tendring Hundred Railway Company	691
THJ	Tottenham and Hampstead Junction Railway Company	697
THW	Thetford and Watton Railway Company	694
TLR	Tanat Valley Light Railway Company	685
TNN	Tenterden Railway Company	692
TRV	Trent Valley Railway Company	699
TT	Timetables: various companies 900; 902–909; 911–927; 929–939; 941–963; 965–967; 969–970; 972–987	
TT(Y)	Timetables: various companies (York Collection)	940; 968

TV	Taff Vale Railway Company	684
TVD	Tiverton and North Devon Railway Company	695
TVR	Thames Valley Railway Company	693
ULR	Ulverstone and Lancaster Railway Company	700
URR	Uxbridge and Rickmansworth Railway Company	701
VOG	Vale of Glamorgan Railway Company	702
VOL	Vale of Llangollen Railway Company	703
VON	Vale of Neath Railway Company	704
VOT	Vale of Towy Railway Company	706
VRL	Vale of Rheidol Light Railway Company	705
VSP	Victoria Station and Pimlico Railway Company	707
WAC	Whitland and Cardigan Railway Company	747
WAL	Warwickshire and London Railway Company	712
WAP	Weymouth and Portland Railway Company	741
WAR	Windsor and Ascot Railway Company	754
WAS	Warrington and Stockport Railway Company	710
WBA	Wivenhoe and Brightlingsea Railway Company	758
WBL	Worcester, Bromyard and Leominster Railway Company	763
WCC	West Coast Conference	727
WCE	Whitehaven, Cleator and Egremont Railway Company	745
WCH	West Cheshire Railway Company	724
WCJ	West Cornwall Railway Joint Committee	726
WCO	West Cornwall Railway Company	725
WCP	Weston, Clevedon and Portishead Light Railway Company	779
WCR	Wimbledon and Croydon Railway Company	751
WDJ	Wear and Derwent Junction Railway Company	716

WDR	Wellington and Drayton Railway Company	719
WDS	Widnes Railway Company	748
WDU	West Durham Railway Company	728
WEN	Wenlock Railway Company	723
WFJ	Whitehaven and Furness Junction Railway Company	744
WFM	Wells and Fakenham Railway Company	721
WHB	Ware, Hadham and Buntingford Railway Company	709
WHG	Worcester, Hereford, Ross and Gloucester Railway Company	764
WHH	West Hartlepool Harbour and Railway Company	730
WHJ	Whitehaven Junction Railway Company	746
WHR	Worcester and Hereford Railway Company	762
WID	Wimbledon and Dorking Railway Company	752
WIM	Wimbledon and Sutton Railway Company	753
WIR	Wirral Railway Company	756
WIT	Witney Railway Company	757
WJC	Wolverhampton Joint Committees	759
WJR	Wigan Junction Railway Company	749
WLA	West Lancashire Railway Company	731
WLC	West End of London and Crystal Palace Railway Company	729
WLER	West London Extension Railway Company	732
WLL	Welshpool and Llanfair Light Railway Company	722
WLR	West London Railway Company	733
WLU	Warwick and Leamington Union Railway Company	711
WMQ	Wrexham, Mold and Connah's Quay Railway Company	767
WMR	West Midland Railway Company	734
WMV	Westerham Valley Railway Company	740
WNJ	West Norfolk Junction Railway Company	735

WNS	Watton and Swaffham Railway Company	714
WOC	Waterloo and City Railway Company	713
WOD	Woodstock Railway Company	761
WPR	Whitby and Pickering Railway Company	742
WRG	West Riding and Grimsby Railway Company	736
WRM	Whitby, Redcar and Middlesbrough Union Railway Company	743
WRV	Wear Valley Railway Company	718
WSC	Woodside and South Croydon Railway Company and Joint Committee	760
WSM	West Somerset Railway Company	737
WSR	Wellington and Severn Junction Railway Company	720
WSS	Windsor, Staines and South Western Railway Company	755
WSW	Wiltshire, Somerset and Weymouth Railway Company	750
WVE	Wear Valley Extension Railway Company	717
WVR	Wye Valley Railway Company	769
WVY	Waveney Valley Railway Company	715
WWH	West Wickham and Hayes Railway Company	738
WWR	Wallingford and Wellington Railway Company	708
WXE	Wrexham and Ellesmere Railway Company	765
WXM	Wrexham and Minera Railway Joint Committee (London and North Western and Great Western Railways)	766
WYB	Wycombe Railway Company	768
WYR	West Yorkshire Railway Company	739
YDR	Yorkshire Dales Railway Company	774
YLNJ	York, Newcastle and Berwick; York and North Midland; and Leeds Northern Railways Joint Committee	773
YNB	York, Newcastle and Berwick Railway Company	772
YNM	York and North Midland Railway Company	770
YSN	York Joint Station Committee	771

BTHR code	AN series
BB	94
BR	7, 14, 17, 82, 84, 87, 91, 94
BRB	17–20, 22, 82, 84
BTC	5, 7, 8, 11, 12, 83, 84, 91
LMS	90
MPR	109
PN	79
RB	94
RB(Y)	94
RCH	94
RCH(Y)	94
RCR	82
REC	1–3
RER	14, 23–25, 27–29, 56, 82, 84, 87, 90–92
REX	4–7, 27, 84, 87–88

BTHR code	AN series
RGR	92
RHE	54
RLM	6–7, 14, 30–31, 35, 37–39, 82, 90–95
RNE	7, 27–28
RPE	50, 56–57, 91
RSC	68
RSO	7, 44, 82, 87, 90
RWR	7, 17, 38, 45–46, 49, 51–53, 87–88, 90–91
TDK	73
THC	69
THCF	70
TRT	80
TRT(Y)	80

Appendix 2: Contents of RAIL and AN series

This appendix lists, in strict alphabetical order the names of railway companies, the various organizations of the nationalized transport industry (so far as their records relate to railways), and some other bodies concerned with railways. It is confined to records in the **RAIL** and **AN** departments (*see* Chapter 3 for a general description of the kinds of records to be found in RAIL and AN).

Under each company or organization are given the series in which its records appear. Entries are based on the contents of the original records as well as the published series lists. In some cases, the information given is not included in search room or Internet finding aids. This is particularly true of series of a general nature (e.g. reports and accounts) where only dates are given in the search room lists. The appendix can be used to find out which companies' records appear in particular general series. It can also indicate the presence of records of one company among those of another.

Records of jointly run railways are cross-referenced to each of the companies concerned. To avoid repetition of the same information under several companies, such cross-references are sometimes made to entries for the joint committees themselves. It is worth looking for these cross-references at the end of 'joint committees' sections.

Where use was made of more than one form of a company's name, the name given it by its Act of Incorporation has usually been chosen. As an example, the railway commonly called the 'Newcastle & Carlisle Railway' (sometimes 'Railroad') was given the title 'Newcastle-upon-Tyne and Carlisle Railway' by its Act and that is how it appears in this index.

The full name of each organization is given at the beginning of its entry but elsewhere more common names are abbreviated (*see* List of Abbreviations at the beginning of the book). Entries for companies that were proposed but failed to achieve parliamentary approval have '(proposed)' after their titles. (Note that not all the railways authorized by Act managed to build their railways.)

References in the singular (e.g. *'map'*, *'prospectus'*) show that only one example is present. Plural references (e.g. *'reports and accounts'*, *'share certificates'*), however, should be taken as including single items as well as multiples. For clarity, keywords of larger entries are set in **Bold**.

Abbotsbury Railway, **RAIL 1**
  Prospectuses etc, **RAIL 1075; RAIL 1110**
  Railway and Canal Traffic Acts proceedings,
    RAIL 1038
  Reports and accounts, **RAIL 1110**
Aberdare and Central Wales Junction Railway
  (proposed)
    Parliamentary papers, **RAIL 1066**
Aberdare Northern Railway (proposed)
  Parliamentary papers, **RAIL 1066**
Aberdare Railway, **RAIL 2**
  Miscellanea, **RAIL 1020**
Aberdare Urban District Council Tramways
  Parliamentary papers, **RAIL 1068**
Aberdare Valley and Caerphilly Junction Railway
  (proposed)
    Parliamentary papers, **RAIL 1066**
Aberdare Valley Railway, **RAIL 3**

Parliamentary papers, **RAIL 1163**
Aberdeen and Turriff Railway
  Reports and accounts, **RAIL 1116**
Aberdeen Joint Station Committee (LMSR/LNER)
  Reports and accounts, **RAIL 1116**
Aberdeen Railway
  Parliamentary papers, **RAIL 1163**
  Reports and accounts, **RAIL 1116; RAIL 1117**
Abergavenny and Monmouth Railway
  Parliamentary papers, **RAIL 1066**
Abergavenny and Raglan Railway (proposed)
  Miscellanea, **RAIL 1057**
Aberlady, Gullane and North Berwick Railway
  Share certificates, **RAIL 1158**
Aberystwyth and Welsh Coast Railway, **RAIL 4**
  Reports and accounts, **RAIL 1110**
  Subscription contracts, **RAIL 1160**
Abingdon Railway, **RAIL 5**

Miscellanea, **RAIL 1057**
Railway and Canal Traffic Acts proceedings,
    RAIL 1038
Reports and accounts, **RAIL 1110; RAIL 1116**
Subscription contract, **RAIL 1163**
Aboyne and Braemar Railway
    Reports and accounts, **RAIL 1116**
Acton and Brentford Railway
    Miscellanea, **RAIL 1057**
    Parliamentary papers, **RAIL 1066**
Acton and Hammersmith Railway (proposed)
    Parliamentary papers, **RAIL 1066**
Acton and Twickenham Railway (proposed)
    Parliamentary papers, **RAIL 1066**
Alba Railway
    Share certificates, **RAIL 1158**
Alcester Railway, **RAIL 6**
    Prospectuses etc, **RAIL 1075**
    Reports and accounts, **RAIL 1110**
Alcester, Stratford-upon-Avon and Warwick
    Junction Railway (proposed)
    Parliamentary papers, **RAIL 1066**
Alexandra (Newport and South Wales) Docks and
    Railway, **RAIL 7** (*includes records of* Newport
    Dock Co *and* Alexandra (Newport) Dock Co)
    Byelaws and regulations, **RAIL 1001**
    Law cases and arbitration, **RAIL 1027**
    Maps, **RAIL 1030**
    Miscellanea, **RAIL 1057**
    Parliamentary papers, **RAIL 1066;**
        RAIL 1067
    Railway and Canal Traffic Acts proceedings,
        RAIL 1038
    Reports and accounts, **RAIL 1110; RAIL 1116;**
        RAIL 1117
    Timetables, **RAIL 981**
See also GWR locomotives and rolling stock
Alexandra (Newport) Dock Company
    Miscellanea, **RAIL 1057**
    Prospectus, **RAIL 1110**
    Reports and accounts, **RAIL 1110**
See also Alexandra (Newport & South Wales)
    Docks & R
Alford Valley Railway
    Reports and accounts, **RAIL 1116**
Alloa Railway
    Parliamentary papers, **RAIL 1066**
Althorpe-on-Trent and Lincoln Railway (proposed)
    Parliamentary papers, **RAIL 1066**
Alton, Alresford and Winchester Railway
    Reports and accounts, **RAIL 1116**
Alyth Railway
    Share certificates, **RAIL 1158**
Ambergate, Nottingham and Boston and Eastern
    Junction Railway (and Canal Company), **RAIL 8**
    Miscellanea, **RAIL 1008**
    Parliamentary papers, **RAIL 1163**

Prospectuses etc, **RAIL 1075**
Reports and accounts, **RAIL 1110; RAIL 1116;**
    RAIL 1117
Timetables, **RAIL 981**
See also Nottingham & Grantham R & Canal Co
Ambleside Railway (proposed)
    Parliamentary papers, **RAIL 1147**
Amesbury and Military Camp Light Railway
    Parliamentary papers, **RAIL 1066**
Andover and Great Western Railway (proposed)
    Parliamentary papers, **RAIL 1066**
Andover and Redbridge Railway, **RAIL 9**
    Parliamentary papers, **RAIL 1066**
Andover, Redbridge and Southampton Railway
    (proposed)
    Parliamentary papers, **RAIL 1066**
Andoversford and Stratford-upon-Avon Railway
    (proposed)
    Miscellanea, **RAIL 1057**
    Parliamentary papers, **RAIL 1066**
Anglesey Central Railway
    Miscellanea, **RAIL 1007**
    Prospectuses etc, **RAIL 1075**
    Reports and accounts, **RAIL 1116**
Anglesey Railway (proposed)
    Prospectuses etc, **RAIL 1075**
Anstruther and St Andrews Railway
    Share certificates, **RAIL 1158**
Arbroath and Forfar Railway
    Miscellanea, **RAIL 1015**
    Reports and accounts, **RAIL 1116;**
        RAIL 1117
    Share certificates, **RAIL 1158**
See also LMSR amalgamation
Ardrossan Railway
    Reports and accounts, **RAIL 1116**
Ascot, Windsor and Aldershot Railway (proposed)
    Parliamentary papers, **RAIL 1066**
Ashburton, Newton and South Devon Junction
    Railway, **RAIL 10**
    GWR miscellanea, **RAIL 1014**
Ashby and Nuneaton Joint Committee
    (LNWR/MR), **RAIL 11; RAIL 410**
    Rule books, **RAIL 1134**
Ashton, Stalybridge and Liverpool Junction
    Railway *see* L&YR, LNWR
Associated Society of Locomotive Engineers and
    Firemen
    Labour and staff matters, **RAIL 1025;**
        RAIL 1026
    National conditions of service, **RAIL 1174**
Association of Railway Shareholders
    Reports and accounts, **RAIL 1116**
Athenry and Ennis Junction Railway
    Prospectus, **RAIL 1117**
    Reports and accounts, **RAIL 1116;**
        RAIL 1117

Athenry and Tuam Extension to Claremorris
    Railway
        Reports and accounts, **RAIL 1116**
Athenry and Tuam Railway
        Reports and accounts, **RAIL 1116; RAIL 1117**
Avon and Gloucestershire Railway, **RAIL 12**
        Miscellanea, **RAIL 1014; RAIL 1021**
See also GWR miscellanea
Avon and South Wales Railway (proposed)
        Miscellanea, **RAIL 1057**
Avonmouth Light Railway *see* LMSR Solicitor's
    records; GWR/LMS jt cttees
Axholme Joint Railway Committee (L&Y/NER; *in
    1922* LNWR/NER; *from 1923* LMSR/LNER,
    managing Isle of Axholme Lt R *and* Goole &
    Marshland Lt R, *q.v.*), **RAIL 13; RAIL 410**
    (LNWR/NER)
        Miscellanea, **RAIL 1057**
        Parliamentary papers, **RAIL 1163**
        Reports and accounts, **RAIL 1116**
            (LMSR/LNER)
        Timetables, **RAIL 981**
        Traders' ledger credit agreements, **RAIL 1165**
See also L&YR/NER jt cttees
Axminster and Lyme Regis Light Railway, **RAIL 14**
        Prospectuses etc, **RAIL 1075**
        Share certificates, **RAIL 1158**
Aylesbury and Buckingham Railway
        Miscellanea. **RAIL 1057**
        Railway and Canal Traffic Acts proceedings,
            RAIL 1038
        Reports and accounts, **RAIL 1110; RAIL 1116**
Aylesbury and Rickmansworth Railway (proposed)
        Parliamentary papers, **RAIL 1066**
Aylesbury Railway, **RAIL 15**
        Miscellanea, **RAIL 1014**
        Prospectuses etc, **RAIL 1075**
        Reports and accounts, **RAIL 1110**
Ayr and Maybole Junction Railway
        Reports and accounts, **RAIL 1116**
Ayr and Maybole Railway (proposed)
        Parliamentary papers, **RAIL 1066**
Ayrshire and Galloway (Smithstown and
    Dalmellington) Railway
        Parliamentary papers, **RAIL 1163**
Ayrshire and Wigtownshire Railway
        Parliamentary papers, **RAIL 1066**
        Railway and Canal Traffic Acts proceedings,
            RAIL 1038
        Reports and accounts, **RAIL 1116**
Bagenalstown and Wexford Railway
        Reports and accounts, **RAIL 1116**
Baker Street and Waterloo Railway
        Miscellanea, **RAIL 1014; RAIL 1057**
        Parliamentary papers, **RAIL 1066**
        Reports and accounts, **RAIL 1110; RAIL 1116**
        Rule books, **RAIL 1134**

See also London Electric R
        Underground Electric Rys Co
Bala and Dolgelly Railway, **RAIL 16**
        Reports and accounts, **RAIL 1110**
Bala and Festiniog Railway, **RAIL 17**
        Parliamentary papers, **RAIL 1066**
        Railway and Canal Traffic Acts proceedings,
            RAIL 1038
        Reports and accounts, **RAIL 1110**
See also GWR estates and rating
Ballinascarthy and Timoleague Junction Light
    Railway
        Railway and Canal Traffic Acts proceedings,
            RAIL 1038
Ballochney Railway
        Miscellanea, **RAIL 1157**
Ballycastle Railway
        Railway and Canal Traffic Acts proceedings,
            RAIL 1038
        Reports and accounts, **RAIL 1116**
Ballymena and Larne Railway
        Reports and accounts, **RAIL 1116**
See also Irish & English Traffic Conference
Ballymena, Ballymoney, Coleraine and Portrush
    Junction Railway
        Parliamentary papers, **RAIL 1163**
Banbridge, Newry, Dublin and Belfast Junction
    Railway
        Reports and accounts, **RAIL 1116**
Banbury and Cheltenham Direct Railway, **RAIL 18**
        Parliamentary papers, **RAIL 1066**
        Prospectuses, **RAIL 1014; RAIL 1110**
        Railway and Canal Traffic Acts proceedings,
            RAIL 1038
        Reports and accounts, **RAIL 1110**
Banff, Macduff and Turriff Extension Railway
        Reports and accounts, **RAIL 1116**
Banff, Macduff and Turriff Junction Railway
        Parliamentary papers, **RAIL 1163**
        Reports and accounts, **RAIL 1116**
Banffshire Railway
        Reports and accounts, **RAIL 1116**
Bangor and Caernarvon Railway, **RAIL 19**
Banstead and Epsom Downs Railway, **RAIL 20**
        Share certificates, **RAIL 1158**
Bantry Extension Railway (*constructed by
    Cork Bandon & S Coast R)
        Reports and accounts, **RAIL 1116**
Bardfield and Sible Hedingham Light Railway
    (proposed)
        Miscellanea, **RAIL 1057**
Barking Town Urban District Council
    Tramways
        Reports and accounts, **RAIL 1114**
Barnard Castle and Bishop Auckland Junction
    Railway (proposed)
        Prospectuses etc, **RAIL 1076**

Barnet and Willesden Railway (proposed)
    Parliamentary papers, **RAIL 1163**
    Prospectuses etc, **RAIL 1075**
Barnet, Hendon and Midland Junction Railway
  (proposed)
    Parliamentary papers, **RAIL 1066**
Barnoldswick Railway, **RAIL 21**
Barnsley Coal Railway, **RAIL 22**
    Parliamentary papers, **RAIL 1066; RAIL 1067**
Barnsley Junction Railway (proposed)
    Prospectus, **RAIL 1151**
Barrow, Darlington and Sunderland Railway
  (proposed), **RAIL 1152**
Barry Dock and Railway Company
    Byelaws and regulations, **RAIL 1001**
    Law cases and arbitration, **RAIL 1027**
    Maps, **RAIL 1030**
    Miscellanea, **RAIL 1057**
    Parliamentary papers, **RAIL 1066**
    Railway and Canal Traffic Acts proceedings,
      RAIL 1038
    Reports and accounts, **RAIL 1110;**
      RAIL 1116
See also Barry R
Barry Railway, **RAIL 23** (*includes records of*
  predecessor Barry Dock & R)
    Byelaws and regulations, **RAIL 1001**
    Instructions to staff, **RAIL 1135**
    Labour and staff matters, **RAIL 1025**
    Law cases and arbitration, **RAIL 1027**
    Maps, **RAIL 1030**
    Miscellanea, **RAIL 1014; RAIL 1020;**
      RAIL 1057
    Parliamentary papers, **RAIL 1066; RAIL 1067**
    Reports and accounts, **RAIL 1116; RAIL 1117**
    Rule books, **RAIL 1134**
    Timetables, **RAIL 981**
      Working timetables appendixes,
      RAIL 1136
See also GWR locomotives and rolling stock
Barton and Immingham Light Railway, **RAIL 24**
Barton and Stretford Light Railway (proposed)
    Parliamentary papers, **RAIL 1066**
Barton and Stretford Railway (proposed)
    Parliamentary papers, **RAIL 1066**
Barton, Blyton and Gainsborough Railway
  (proposed)
    Prospectus, **RAIL 1151**
Basing and Bath Railway (proposed) (*also known as*
  Bath & Basing R)
    GWR miscellanea, **RAIL 1014**
    Prospectuses, **RAIL 1075; RAIL 1076**
Basing, Bath and Bristol Railway (proposed)
    Prospectuses, **RAIL 1057; RAIL 1075**
Basingstoke, Alton and Petersfield Railway
  (proposed)
    Parliamentary papers, **RAIL 1066**

Basingstoke and Alton Light Railway
    Parliamentary papers, **RAIL 1066**
Bath and Basing Railway (proposed) *see* Basing &
  Bath R
Bath and Weymouth Great Western Union Railway
  (proposed)
    Miscellanea, **RAIL 1014; RAIL 1057**
Bath Electric Tramways
    Reports and accounts, **RAIL 1114**
Bawtry and Trent Railway and Dock Company
    Parliamentary papers, **RAIL 1066**
Bayswater, Paddington and Holborn Bridge
  Railway *see* N Metropolitan R
Beaconsfield, Uxbridge and Harrow Railway
    Parliamentary papers, **RAIL 1066**
Beckenham and Sydenham Junction Railway
  (proposed)
    Parliamentary papers, **RAIL 1066**
Beckenham, Lewes and Brighton Railway
  (proposed), **RAIL 25**
    Parliamentary papers, **RAIL 1066**
    Prospectuses etc, **RAIL 1075**
Beckenham, South Norwood Park and Crystal
  Palace Railway (proposed)
    Parliamentary papers, **RAIL 1066**
Bedale and Leyburn Railway, **RAIL 26**
    Parliamentary papers, **RAIL 1067**
    Reports and accounts, **RAIL 1116**
    Timetables, **RAIL 981**
Bedford and Cambridge Railway, **RAIL 27**
  (*includes records of predecessor* Bedford,
  Potton & Cambridge R *q.v.*), **RAIL 410**
    Prospectuses etc, **RAIL 1075**
    Reports and accounts, **RAIL 1116**
See also LNWR
Bedford and Northampton Railway, **RAIL 28**
    Prospectus etc, **RAIL 1147**
    Reports and accounts, **RAIL 1116**
    Share certificates, **RAIL 1158**
Bedford, Northampton and Weedon Railway
  (proposed)
    Parliamentary papers, **RAIL 1066**
Bedford, Potton and Cambridge Railway
    Prospectuses etc, **RAIL 1075; RAIL 1076**
    Reports and accounts, **RAIL 1116**
See also Bedford & Cambridge R
Belfast and Ballymena Railway
    Reports and accounts, **RAIL 1116; RAIL 1117**
Belfast and County Down Railway
    Parliamentary papers, **RAIL 1163**
    Railway and Canal Traffic Acts proceedings,
      RAIL 1038
    Reports and accounts, **RAIL 1110; RAIL 1116;**
      RAIL 1117
    Rule books, **RAIL 1134**
    Timetables, **RAIL 941**
See also Irish & English Traffic Conference

Belfast and Northern Counties Railway
    Joint committee with:
        Portpatrick & Wigtownshire R (Larne &
        Stranraer Steamboat Co), **RAIL 1116**
        (reports and accounts)
    Miscellanea, **RAIL 1007**
    Parliamentary papers, **RAIL 1066**
    Railway and Canal Traffic Acts proceedings,
      RAIL 1038
    Reports and accounts, **RAIL 1110; RAIL 1116;**
      RAIL 1117
    Share certificates, **RAIL 1158**
    Timetables, **RAIL 941; RAIL 981**
See also Irish & English Traffic Conference
    Northern Counties R Cttee
Belfast Central Railway
    Parliamentary papers, **RAIL 1066**
    Reports and accounts, **RAIL 1116**
See also Irish & English Traffic Conference
Belfast City Central Railway
    Parliamentary papers, **RAIL 1066**
Belfast, Holywood and Bangor Railway
    Reports and accounts, **RAIL 1116**
Belfast Traffic Conference, **RAIL 1080**
See also Irish & English Traffic Conference
Belfast Traffic Meeting, *see* Irish & English Traffic
  Conference
Bentley and Bordon Light Railway (LSWR)
    Parliamentary papers, **RAIL 1066**
Berks and Hants Extension Railway, **RAIL 29**
    Prospectuses etc, **RAIL 1075**
    Reports and accounts, **RAIL 1110; RAIL 1116**
Berks and Hants Railway, **RAIL 30**
    Parliamentary papers, **RAIL 1066**
    Prospectuses etc, **RAIL 1075**
See also GWR miscellanea
Berwick and Kelso Railway, **RAIL 31**
Berwickshire Railway
    Reports and accounts, **RAIL 1116**
    Share certificates, **RAIL 1158**
Bessbrook and Newry Tramway
    Railway and Canal Traffic Acts proceedings,
      RAIL 1038
Beverley and East Riding Railway
    Parliamentary papers, **RAIL 1067**
Bexhill and St Leonards Tramroads (proposed)
    Parliamentary papers, **RAIL 1068**
Bexhill Direct Railway (proposed)
    Parliamentary papers, **RAIL 1066**
Bexley Heath Railway, **RAIL 32**
    Parliamentary papers, **RAIL 1066**
Bexley Urban District Council Tramways
    Reports and accounts, **RAIL 1114**
Bicslade Tramway *see* BTC Chief Secretary's Office
Bideford Extension Railway, **RAIL 33**
    Reports and accounts, **RAIL 1116**
    Subscription contracts, **RAIL 1160**

Billingham and Willington Railway (proposed)
    Map, **RAIL 1030**
Birkenhead and Liverpool Railway (proposed)
    Parliamentary papers, **RAIL 1066**
Birkenhead, Chester and North Wales Railway
    Parliamentary papers, **RAIL 1066**
Birkenhead, Chester, Mold, Ruabon and Vale of
  Llangollen Railway (proposed)
    Share certificate, **RAIL 1159**
Birkenhead County Borough Tramways
    Reports and accounts, **RAIL 1114**
Birkenhead Dock Railways *see* Mersey Docks &
  Harbour Board
Birkenhead Docks and West Cheshire Junction
  Railway (proposed)
    Bill, **RAIL 1147**
Birkenhead, Lancashire and Cheshire Junction
  Railway *later* Birkenhead R
    Byelaws and regulations, **RAIL 1001**
    Joint committees:
      LNWR, **RAIL 35** (Birkenhead R)
    See also Chester Jt Station Cttee
    Miscellanea, **RAIL 1057**
    Parliamentary papers, **RAIL 1163**
    Reports and accounts, **RAIL 1110; RAIL 1116;**
      RAIL 1117
    Share certificates, **RAIL 1158**
See also Birkenhead R
Birkenhead, Manchester and Cheshire Junction
  Railway (proposed), **RAIL 34**
    Subscription contracts, **RAIL 1163**
Birkenhead, North Wales and Stafford Railway
  (proposed)
    Parliamentary papers, **RAIL 1066**
Birkenhead Railway, **RAIL 35** (*includes records of
  predecessor* Birkenhead, Lancashire & Cheshire
  Jct R/LNWR *and* GWR/LNWR jt cttees)
    Joint committee GWR/LNWR, **RAIL 114**
      (Chester jt station)
    Miscellanea, **RAIL 1057**
    Parliamentary papers, **RAIL 1066**
    Reports and accounts, **RAIL 1116**
    Share certificates and dividend warrants,
      RAIL 1158
    Subscription contracts, **RAIL 1160**
    Timetables, **RAIL 981**
Birmingham and Derby Junction Railway,
  RAIL 36
    Miscellanea, **RAIL 1008; RAIL 1014;**
      RAIL 1157
Birmingham and Gloucester Railway, **RAIL 37**
    Miscellanea, **RAIL 1008; RAIL 1014;**
      RAIL 1020
    Parliamentary papers, **RAIL 1066**
    Parliamentary plans, **RAIL 1071**
    Prospectuses etc, **RAIL 1075**
    Subscription contracts, **RAIL 1160**

Birmingham and Halesowen Junction Railway
(proposed)
   Parliamentary papers, **RAIL 1066**
Birmingham and Henley-in-Arden Railway,
   RAIL 38
   Miscellanea, **RAIL 1057**
   Prospectuses etc, **RAIL 1075**
   Reports and accounts, **RAIL 1110**
Birmingham and Lichfield Junction Railway
   Map, **RAIL 1015**
   Miscellanea, **RAIL 1057**
   Parliamentary papers, **RAIL 1066**
Birmingham and Oxford Junction Railway,
   RAIL 39 (*includes records of* GWR)
   Miscellanea, **RAIL 1014**
   Parliamentary plans, **RAIL 1071**
   Reports and accounts, **RAIL 1110**
See also GWR miscellanea
Birmingham and Sutton Coldfield Extension
   Railway, **RAIL 40**
Birmingham, Bristol and Thames Junction Railway
   Miscellanea, **RAIL 1005; RAIL 1014**
   Prospectuses etc, **RAIL 1075**
See also W London R
Birmingham Corporation Tramways
   Reports and accounts, **RAIL 1114**
Birmingham, Dudley and Wolverhampton
   Railway (proposed)
   Prospectus, **RAIL 1016**
   Share certificates, **RAIL 1158**
Birmingham, Erdington and Sutton Coldfield
   Railway (proposed)
   Prospectuses etc, **RAIL 1075**
Birmingham Junction Railway (proposed)
   Prospectus, **RAIL 1057**
Birmingham, Lichfield and Manchester Railway,
   RAIL 41
   Parliamentary plans, **RAIL 1071**
Birmingham, North Warwickshire and
   Stratford-upon-Avon Railway, **RAIL 42**
   Parliamentary papers, **RAIL 1066**
   Parliamentary plans, **RAIL 1071**
Birmingham Railway Carriage and Wagon
   Company
   Reports and accounts, **RAIL 1116**
Birmingham, Walsall and Cannock Chase Railway
   (proposed)
   Parliamentary papers, **RAIL 1066**
Birmingham West Suburban Railway, **RAIL 43**
Birmingham, Wolverhampton and Dudley
   Railway, **RAIL 44** (*includes records of* GWR)
   Parliamentary papers, **RAIL 1066**
   Reports and accounts, **RAIL 1110**
Birmingham, Wolverhampton and Stour Valley
   Railway, **RAIL 45; RAIL 410**
   Byelaws and regulations, **RAIL 1001**
      (LNWR)

Joint committee with Shrewsbury &
      Birmingham R, **RAIL 759** (Wolverhampton
      High Level station)
   Parliamentary papers, **RAIL 1066**
   Parliamentary plans, **RAIL 1071** (*as* Stour
      Valley R)
   Timetables, **RAIL 981**
See also LNWR
Bishop Auckland and Weardale Railway, **RAIL 46**
   Miscellanea, **RAIL 1021**
   Prospectuses etc, **RAIL 1076**
   Share certificate, **RAIL 1159**
   Timetables, **RAIL 981**
Bishop Auckland Station Joint Committee
   (NER/S&DR), **RAIL 47**
Bishops Castle Railway
   Parliamentary papers, **RAIL 1066**
   Prospectuses etc, **RAIL 1075**
   Railway and Canal Traffic Acts proceedings,
      RAIL 1038
   Reports and accounts, **RAIL 1116**
See also GWR Secretary's papers
      LMSR amalgamation
Bishop's Stortford, Dunmow and Braintree
   Railway, **RAIL 48**
Bishops Waltham Railway, **RAIL 49**
   Share certificates, **RAIL 1158**
Blackburn and Preston Railway, **RAIL 50**
   Joint committee with E Lancashire R,
      RAIL 176
Blackburn, Burnley, Accrington and Colne
   Extension Railway, **RAIL 51**
Blackburn, Chorley and Wigan Railway
   (proposed)
   Prospectuses etc, **RAIL 1075**
Blackburn, Clitheroe and North Western Junction
   Railway
   Parliamentary plans, **RAIL 1071**
See also Blackburn R
Blackburn, Darwen and Bolton Railway *see*
   Blackburn R
Blackburn Railway, **RAIL 52** (*includes records of*:
   Blackburn, Clitheroe & N Western Jct R
   Blackburn, Darwen & Bolton R
   Bolton, Blackburn, Clitheroe & W Yorkshire R
   E Lancashire R/L&YR jt cttee)
   Parliamentary papers, **RAIL 1066**
   Reports and accounts, **RAIL 1116;**
      RAIL 1117
Blackpool and Fleetwood Railway (proposed)
   Parliamentary papers, **RAIL 1066**
Blackpool and Lytham Railway, **RAIL 53**
   Reports and accounts, **RAIL 1110; RAIL 1116**
Blackpool County Borough Tramways
   Reports and accounts, **RAIL 1114**
Blackpool Railway, **RAIL 54**
   Parliamentary papers, **RAIL 1066**

Blaenavon Railway
    Miscellanea, **RAIL 1057**
Blane Valley Railway
    Reports and accounts, **RAIL 1116**
    Share certificates, **RAIL 1158**
Blaydon, Gateshead and Hebburn Railway,
    RAIL 55
    Miscellanea, **RAIL 1157**
    Prospectuses etc, **RAIL 1075; RAIL 1076**
Blyth and Tyne Railway, **RAIL 56**
    Miscellanea, **RAIL 1152; RAIL 1157**
    Parliamentary papers, **RAIL 1163**
    Reports and accounts, **RAIL 1110; RAIL 1116;**
        RAIL 1117
    Share certificates, **RAIL 1159**
Bodmin and Wadebridge Railway, **RAIL 57**
    Miscellanea, **RAIL 1017**
    Parliamentary papers, **RAIL 1066**
    Share certificates, **RAIL 1158**
    Timetables, **RAIL 981**
Bognor Railway, **RAIL 58**
    Parliamentary papers, **RAIL 1163**
Bolton and Leigh Railway
    Miscellanea, **RAIL 1015; RAIL 1057**
Bolton and Preston Railway, **RAIL 59**
    Miscellanea, **RAIL 1008; RAIL 1014**
    Timetables, **RAIL 981**
Bolton, Blackburn, Clitheroe and West Yorkshire
    Railway *see* Blackburn R
Bolton Junction Railway (proposed)
    Parliamentary papers, **RAIL 1066; RAIL 1147**
    Parliamentary plans, **RAIL 1071**
Bolton, Wigan and Liverpool Railway *see*
    Liverpool & Bury R
Border Counties Railway
    Share certificates, **RAIL 1158**
    Reports and accounts, **RAIL 1116; RAIL 1117**
Boston and Midland Counties Railway and Dock
    Company (proposed)
    Parliamentary papers, **RAIL 1066**
    Prospectuses etc, **RAIL 1075**
Boston Ocean Dock and Railway (proposed)
    Parliamentary papers, **RAIL 1066**
Boston, Sleaford and Midland Counties Railway
    Miscellanea, **RAIL 1057**
    Reports and accounts, **RAIL 1116; RAIL 1117**
Bourne Valley Light Railway (proposed)
    Miscellanea, **RAIL 1057**
Bourton-on-the-Water Railway, **RAIL 60**
    Parliamentary papers, **RAIL 1066**
    Reports and accounts, **RAIL 1110**
Brackenhill Light Railway, **RAIL 61**
    Reports and accounts, **RAIL 1110;**
        RAIL 1117
See also Swinton & Knottingley Jt R
Bradford and Thornton Railway, **RAIL 62**
    Parliamentary papers, **RAIL 1066**

Bradford Corporation Tramways
    Parliamentary papers, **RAIL 1068**
    Reports and accounts, **RAIL 1114**
Bradford, Eccleshill and Idle Railway, **RAIL 63**
Bradford Junction and Thornton Valley Railway
    (proposed)
    Prospectuses etc, **RAIL 1075**
Bradford, Wakefield and Leeds Railway
    Parliamentary papers, **RAIL 1066; RAIL 1067**
    Reports and accounts, **RAIL 1116; RAIL 1117**
    Share certificates, **RAIL 1158**
See also W Yorkshire R
Brading Harbour Improvement and Railway
    Map, **RAIL 1057**
Bradshaw *see* Shareholders' Guides and Manuals;
    Timetables
Bramley Moor and Eckington Railway
    Miscellanea, **RAIL 1153**
Brandling Junction Railway, **RAIL 64**
    Miscellanea, **RAIL 1021; RAIL 1152;**
        RAIL 1157
    Prospectuses etc, **RAIL 1076**
    Rule books, **RAIL 1134**
    Timetables, **RAIL 981**
Bream Down Harbour and Railway
    Miscellanea, **RAIL 1057**
Brechin and Edzell District Railway
    Reports and accounts, **RAIL 1116**
    Share certificates, **RAIL 1158**
See also LMSR amalgamation
Brecon and Llandovery Junction Railway
    Reports and accounts, **RAIL 1116**
Brecon and Merthyr Tydfil Junction Railway
    (*commonly called* Brecon & Merthyr R), **RAIL 65**
    Byelaws and regulations, **RAIL 1001**
    Instructions to staff, **RAIL 1135**
    Joint committees with:
        LNWR, **RAIL 402; RAIL 410; RAIL 421**
            Rule books, **RAIL 1134**
    Labour and staff matters, **RAIL 1025**
    Maps, **RAIL 1030**
    Miscellanea, **RAIL 1008; RAIL 1020;**
        RAIL 1057
    Parliamentary papers, **RAIL 1066**
    Prospectus, **RAIL 1110**
    Railway and Canal Traffic Acts proceedings,
        RAIL 1038
    Reports and accounts, **RAIL 1110; RAIL 1116;**
        RAIL 1117
    Rule books, **RAIL 1134**
    Share certificates, **RAIL 1158**
    Timetables, **RAIL 981**
        Working timetables appendixes, **RAIL 1136**
See also GWR locomotives and rolling stock
    GWR/LMSR jt cttees
Brecon Forest Tramroad
    Miscellanea, **RAIL 1057**

Breconshire Railway and Canal Company
  (proposed)
    Prospectuses etc, **RAIL 1075**
Brentford and Isleworth Tramways
    Parliamentary papers, **RAIL 1066**
Bricklayer's Arms Extension Railway, **RAIL 66**
  (*managed by* London & Croydon R/SER jt cttee)
Bridgend Railway, **RAIL 67**
Bridgnorth, Wolverhampton and Staffordshire
  Railway
    Parliamentary papers, **RAIL 1066**
Bridgwater and Watchet Railway (proposed)
    Maps, **RAIL 1030**
    Parliamentary papers, **RAIL 1066**
Bridgwater Railway, **RAIL 68**
    Byelaws and regulations, **RAIL 1001**
    Parliamentary papers, **RAIL 1066**
    Share certificates, **RAIL 1158**
Bridport and Exeter *or* South Western and South
  Devon Coast Junction Railway (proposed)
    Prospectuses etc, **RAIL 1075**
Bridport Railway, **RAIL 69**
    Byelaws and regulations, **RAIL 1001**
    Miscellanea, **RAIL 1014**
    Parliamentary papers, **RAIL 1066; RAIL 1163**
    Prospectuses etc, **RAIL 1075; RAIL 1110**
    Railway and Canal Traffic Acts proceedings,
      RAIL 1038
    Reports and accounts, **RAIL 1110; RAIL 1116**
    Timetables, **RAIL 981**
See also GWR Secretary's papers
Brighton and Chichester Railway, **RAIL 70**
    Miscellanea, **RAIL 1005**
    Prospectuses etc, **RAIL 1075**
Brighton and Dyke Railway, **RAIL 1191**
    Miscellanea, **RAIL 1017**
    Prospectuses etc, **RAIL 1075**
    Share certificates, **RAIL 1158**
Brighton Corporation Tramways
    Reports and accounts, **RAIL 1114**
Brighton, Lewes and Hastings Railway, **RAIL 72**
Brighton, Shoreham and Steyning Railway
  (proposed)
    Prospectuses etc, **RAIL 1075**
Brighton, Uckfield and Tunbridge Wells Railway,
  RAIL 73
    Share certificates, **RAIL 1158**
Bristol and Birmingham Railway, **RAIL 74**
  (*includes records of* Bristol & Gloucester R)
    Miscellanea, **RAIL 1008**
    Rule books, **RAIL 1134**
    Timetables, **RAIL 981**
Bristol and Clifton Railway (proposed)
    Miscellanea, **RAIL 1057**
Bristol and English Channels Direct Junction
  Railway (proposed)
    Miscellanea, **RAIL 1014**

Bristol and Exeter Railway, **RAIL 75** (*includes
  records of working of* Bristol & Portishead Pier
  & R)
    Instructions to staff, **RAIL 1135**
    Joint committees with:
      GWR, **RAIL 238; RAIL 249**
        RAIL 79 (Bristol Harbour R)
        RAIL 725; RAIL 726 (W Cornwall R *q.v.*)
      S Devon R, **RAIL 249**
        RAIL 725; RAIL 726 (W Cornwall R *q.v.*)
    See also Bristol Jt Station Cttee; Cornwall R
    Maps, **RAIL 1030**
    Miscellanea, **RAIL 1008; RAIL 1014**
    Parliamentary papers, **RAIL 1066; RAIL 1163**
    Prospectus, **RAIL 1016**
    Reports and accounts, **RAIL 1016; RAIL 1110;
      RAIL 1116; RAIL 1117**
    Rule books, **RAIL 1134**
    Subscription contracts, **RAIL 1160**
    Timetables
      Public, **RAIL 905; RAIL 981**
      Working, **RAIL 906; RAIL 981**
    Welfare schemes, **RAIL 1115; RAIL 1174**
Bristol and Gloucester Railway (*formerly* Bristol &
  Gloucestershire R), **RAIL 76**
    Byelaws and regulations, **RAIL 1001**
    Miscellanea, **RAIL 1014**
    Rule books, **RAIL 1134**
    Subscription contracts, **RAIL 1160**
    Timetables, **RAIL 981**
See also Bristol & Birmingham R
Bristol and Liverpool Junction Railway (proposed)
    Miscellanea, **RAIL 1014**
Bristol and London and South Western Junction
  Railway (proposed)
    Miscellanea, **RAIL 1014**
    Parliamentary papers, **RAIL 1066**
Bristol and North Somerset Railway, **RAIL 77**
    Reports and accounts, **RAIL 1110; RAIL 1116**
See also GWR estates and rating
Bristol and Portishead Pier and Railway
    Miscellanea, **RAIL 1057**
    Parliamentary papers, **RAIL 1066**
    Reports and accounts, **RAIL 1110**
See also Bristol & Exeter R
Bristol and South Wales Junction Railway
    Reports and accounts, **RAIL 1116**
Bristol and South Wales Union Railway, **RAIL 78**
    Miscellanea, **RAIL 1057**
    Reports and accounts, **RAIL 1116**
Bristol Central Station and Railways (proposed)
    Parliamentary papers, **RAIL 1066**
Bristol Harbour Railway, **RAIL 79** (*includes minutes
  of jt cttee,* Bristol & Exeter R/GWR)
Bristol Joint Station Committee (Bristol &
  Exeter R/GWR/MR; *after 1876* GWR/MR),
    RAIL 80

Bristol, London and Southern Counties Railway
(proposed)
    Miscellanea, **RAIL 1057**
    Parliamentary papers, **RAIL 1066**
Bristol Northern and Western Railway (proposed)
    Share certificates, **RAIL 1158**
Bristol Port and Channel Docks and Railway
(proposed)
    Parliamentary papers, **RAIL 1066**
Bristol Port Extension Railways (proposed)
    Parliamentary papers, **RAIL 1066**
Bristol Port Railway and Pier Company (*includes*
    Clifton Extension R), **RAIL 81**
    Parliamentary papers, **RAIL 1066**
    Reports and accounts, **RAIL 1110**
See also GWR estates and rating
Bristol Tramways and Carriage Company
    Reports and accounts, **RAIL 1114**
British and Irish Grand Junction Railway
(proposed)
    Prospectuses etc, **RAIL 1075**
British Rail Engineering Ltd, **AN 112**
British Rail Hovercraft Ltd, **AN 179**
British Rail Property Board, Headquarters files,
  AN 169
British Railways
    Anglia Region
      Timetables, **RAIL 988**
    Chief Civil Engineer, **AN 129**
    Chief Executive (Railways) files, **AN 156**
    Chief Mechanical and Electrical Engineer,
      AN 120
    Chief Operating Manager, **AN 106**
    Eastern Region
      Accountant, **AN 27**
      Chief Regional Officer, **AN 26**
      Civil Engineer, **AN 28**
      Excursions, **AN 25**
      Labour and staff matters, **RAIL 1025**
      Locomotives and rolling stock, **RAIL 394**
      Mileage diagrams, **RAIL 798**
      Miscellanea, **RAIL 1005; RAIL 1006;**
        RAIL 1014; RAIL 1057
      Private siding agreements, **AN 138**
      Reports, **AN 92**
      Signalling plans and track diagrams,
        AN 23
      Stores Superintendent, **AN 24**
      Timetables
        Public, **RAIL 908**
        Working, **RAIL 909**
      Traffic agreements, **AN 138**
      Traffic notices, **AN 29; AN 140**
    See also GNR
      LNER deeds, contracts etc; locomotives and
        rolling stock; miscellanea
      MSLR

Fares annuals, **AN 130**
    International, **AN 135**
Financial departments, **AN 121**
Horse records, **AN 35** (*includes records of*
  L&YR, LNWR, LMSR, MR)
Hotels and catering, **AN 109** (*includes*
  records of:
    GWR; London & Birmingham R; LNER;
      LNWR; LBSCR; LMSR; MR; SER; SECR; SR)
    Locomotives and rolling stock, **AN 7**
      (*includes records of* LMSR *and* SR)
See also GWR locomotives and rolling stock
London Midland Area Board, **AN 116**
London Midland Region
    Civil Engineer, **AN 37**
    Closure of lines, **AN 155**
    General Manager's files, **AN 172**
    Horses, **AN 35**
    Labour and staff matters, **RAIL 1025**
    Maps, **RAIL 1030**
    Marine, **AN 39**
    Miscellanea, **RAIL 1005; RAIL 1007; RAIL**
      1021; RAIL 1057
    Reports, **AN 95**
    Research Department engineering reports,
      RAIL 792
    Signalling plans and track diagrams, **AN 93**
    Stations, **AN 31** (plans, drawings,
      photographs)
    Timetables
      Public, **RAIL 911**
      Working, **RAIL 912**
      Cheshire lines, **RAIL 925**
    Traders' ledger credit agreements, **RAIL 1165**
    Traffic notices, **AN 32; AN 38**
See also Cheshire Lines Cttee timetables
  MR
Marine
    Irish ferries timetables, **RAIL 910**
    Shipping circulars, **AN 137** (*includes*
      Sealink)
    Shipping timetables, **RAIL 915**
Miscellanea, **RAIL 1005; RAIL 1020**
North Eastern Area Board, **AN 117**
North Eastern Region
    Circulars, **RAIL 393**
    Labour and staff matters, **RAIL 1025**
    Line closures, **AN 168**
    Maps, **RAIL 1030**
    Minutes, **AN 105**
    Miscellanea, **RAIL 1005; RAIL 1006**
    Reports, **AN 92**
    Timetables: public, **RAIL 913**
      working, **RAIL 914**
See also LNER miscellanea
  NER
  N Sunderland R

British Railways (continued)
Passenger instruction manuals, **AN 133**
Passenger train service planning, **AN 102**
Photographs, **AN 14**
Posters, **AN 14**
Publicity, **AN 14** (photographs); **AN 17**
(holiday guides); **AN 90** (brochures); **AN 91**
(special events); **AN 111** (Public Relations
and Publicity Department)
Rates and charges, **AN 87**
Research Department reports:
Chemical Research Division, **AN 148**
Chemical Services, Assistant Director,
AN 149
Chemistry Division, **AN 149**
Chief of Research, **AN 146**
Electrical Research Division, **AN 147**;
AN 150
Engineering Division, **AN 139**
Metallurgy Division, **AN 152**
Operational Research Division, **AN 142**
Physics Division, **AN 145**
Research Planning, Director, **AN 146**
Scientific Services Division, **AN 149**
Vehicle and Track Division, **AN 143**
Royal trains and events, **AN 9**; **AN 10**
Rule books, **AN 94**
Scottish Region
Labour and staff matters, **RAIL 1025**
Miscellanea, **RAIL 1005**; **RAIL 1007**
Timetables
Public, **RAIL 916**
Working, **RAIL 917**
Southern Area Board, **AN 103**
Southern Region
Agreements, contracts, conveyances, deeds,
AN 151
Accountant, **AN 81**
Chief Regional Officer's files, **AN 157**
Labour and staff matters, **RAIL 1025**
Line closures, **AN 177**
London Airport rail link, **AN 154**
Maps, **RAIL 1030**
Marine, **AN 44**
Metallurgy Division reports, **AN 152**
Miscellanea, **RAIL 1005**; **RAIL 1014**;
RAIL 1017; **RAIL 1057**
Reports, **AN 43**
Signalling plans and track diagrams, **AN 42**
Traffic notices, **AN 41**
Timetables
Continental, **RAIL 978**
Public, **RAIL 918**
Working, **RAIL 919**
See also LSWR
SR locomotives and rolling stock; minutes
and reports; miscellanea; shipping services

Station furniture and vending machines,
AN 15
Ticket examiners' handbooks, **AN 132**
Timetables
Continental, **RAIL 907** (*includes* SR cross-
channel)
Foreign, **RAIL 928**
Irish ferries, **RAIL 910**
Public, **RAIL 908** (Eastern Region)
RAIL 911 (London Midland Region)
RAIL 913 (North Eastern Region)
RAIL 915 (National passenger)
RAIL 916 (Scottish Region)
RAIL 918 (Southern Region)
RAIL 920 (Western Region)
Working, **RAIL 988** (Anglia Region)
RAIL 909 (Eastern Region)
RAIL 912 (London Midland Region)
RAIL 914 (North Eastern Region)
RAIL 917 (Scottish Region)
RAIL 919 (Southern Region)
RAIL 921 (Western Region)
Traders' ledger credit agreements, **RAIL 1165**
Traffic censuses and surveys, **AN 82**
Training and education, **AN 110**
Travel agents' manuals, **AN 134**
Western Area Board, **AN 119**
Western Region
Brentford Dock barge invoices, **AN 45**
Bristol District diary, **AN 125**
Chief Mechanical and Electrical Engineer,
AN 47
Civil Engineer, **AN 51**
Contract documents, **RAIL 1190**
Excursions, **AN 53**
Maps, **RAIL 1030**
Miscellanea, **RAIL 1005**; **RAIL 1057**
Sidings agreements, **RAIL 1167**
Signalling plans and track diagrams, **AN 46**
Station plans and drawings, **AN 48** (*includes
records of* GWR)
Timetables
Public, **RAIL 920**
Working, **RAIL 921**
Traffic notices, **AN 52**; **AN 141**
See also Fishguard & Rosslare Rys & Harbours Co
GWR locomotives and rolling stock
Irish & English Traffic Conference
LMSR miscellanea; statistics
Llynvi & Ogmore R
British Railways Board
Annual reports and accounts, **AN 19**
British Rail Engineering Ltd (BREL), **AN 112**
Byelaws and regulations, **RAIL 1001**
Directories, **AN 22**
Freightliners Ltd, **AN 115**
GWR 150th anniversary celebrations, **AN 131**

Inter-regional committees, **AN 40**
Labour and staff matters, **RAIL 1025**
Manuals, **AN 22**
Marketing
   Services sector, **AN 176**
   Survey reports, **AN 173**
Members' papers, **AN 18**
Minutes, **AN 167**
National route code catalogue, **AN 159**
Policy Unit, **AN 170**
Privatization Studies Group, **AN 175**
Reports, **AN 16**
Retail circulars, **AN 153**
Review of railway field organization, **AN 124**
Sidings agreements, **RAIL 1167**
Statistics, **AN 20**
Technical reports, **AN 101**
British Railway Stockholders Union
   Reports and accounts, **RAIL 1116**
British Transport Commission
   Annual reports and accounts, **AN 11**
   Byelaws and regulations, **RAIL 1001**
   Chief Secretary's office, **AN 13** *includes records*
   of or about:
      Bicslade Tramway
      Derwent Valley Light R
      Easingwold R
      E Kent Light R
      Easton & Church Hope R
      Forth Bridge R
      GWR
      Kent & E Sussex R
      King's Lynn Docks & R
      Liverpool (Overhead) Electric R
      LMSR
      LTE
      N Sunderland Lt R
      Shropshire & Montgomeryshire Lt R
   Commercial and operating agreements, **AN 5**
   Minutes and papers, **AN 85**
   Miscellanea, **RAIL 1005; RAIL 1007;**
      RAIL 1057
   Parliamentary papers, **RAIL 1163**
   Pension scheme, **RAIL 1174**
   Press notices, **AN 79**
   Railway Executive
      Chief Regional Officers' meetings, **AN 99**
      Labour and staff matters, **RAIL 1025**
      Members' papers, **AN 6**
      Minutes and papers, **AN 4**
      Reports, **AN 8; AN 88**
      Shipping, **AN 83**
      Traders' ledger credit agreements,
         RAIL 1165
   Railways Staff Conference, **AN 98**
   Records and Relics Committee, **AN 104**
   Road services

Carter Paterson & Co, **RAIL 1130**
Hay's Wharf Cartage Co, **RAIL 1131**
Pickfords & Hay's Wharf Shipping &
   Forwarding Co, **RAIL 1132**
Pickfords Ltd, **RAIL 1133**
Seal registers, **AN 127**
Sidings agreements, **RAIL 1167**
Standing Conference on Co-ordination of
   Inland Transport, **AN 56**
Statistics, **AN 12**
Traders' ledger credit agreements,
   RAIL 1165
Transport Tribunal proceedings, **AN 80**
See also Llanelly & Mynydd Mawr R
   SR motor bus companies
British Transport Commission and British
   Railways Board
   Design Panel
      Files, **AN 160**
      Manuals, **AN 162**
      Reports, **AN 163**
   Industrial Relations Department, **AN 171**
   Personnel Department, **RAIL 174**
British Transport Historical Records Office, **AN
104** (administrative records)
British Transport Staff College, Woking, **AN 178**
Briton Ferry Dock and Railway (Briton Ferry
   Floating Dock Company), **RAIL 82**
Brixton, Clapham and Balham Extension Railway
   (proposed)
      Parliamentary papers, **RAIL 1066**
Bromley Direct Railway, **RAIL 83**
      Parliamentary papers, **RAIL 1066**
Brompton and Piccadilly Circus Railway
      Parliamentary papers, **RAIL 1066**
See also Great Northern, Piccadilly & Brompton R
Bromyard and Hereford Railway (proposed)
      Parliamentary papers, **RAIL 1066**
Brough and Market Weighton Railway
   (proposed)
      Prospectuses etc, **RAIL 1076**
Broxburn Railway
      Share certificates, **RAIL 1158**
Brynmawr and Western Valleys Railway
      Parliamentary papers, **RAIL 1066**
Buckfastleigh, Totnes and South Devon Railway,
   RAIL 84
      Miscellanea, **RAIL 1020**
      Railway and Canal Traffic Acts proceedings,
         RAIL 1038
      Reports and accounts, **RAIL 1110**
      Timetables, **RAIL 981**
Buckingham and Brackley Junction Railway,
   RAIL 85
Buckinghamshire and Northamptonshire Union
   Railway (proposed)
      Parliamentary papers, **RAIL 1066**

Buckinghamshire and Oxford and Bletchley
  Junction Railway
    Miscellanea, **RAIL 1057**
    Subscription contracts, **RAIL 1160**
Buckinghamshire Railway, **RAIL 86**
    Miscellanea, **RAIL 1057**
    Parliamentary papers, **RAIL 1066**
    Prospectuses etc, **RAIL 1075**
    Reports and accounts, **RAIL 1116**
Buckley Railway, **RAIL 87**
    Railway and Canal Traffic Acts proceedings,
      RAIL 1038
    Reports and accounts, **RAIL 1110**
Budleigh Salterton Railway, **RAIL 88**
    Byelaws and regulations, **RAIL 1001**
Bullo Pill Railway
    Miscellanea, **RAIL 1005**
Burry Port and Gwendreath Valley Railway,
    RAIL 89 (*includes records of predecessor* Burry Port
    Co)
    Byelaws and regulations, **RAIL 1001**
    Miscellanea, **RAIL 1014; RAIL 1057**
    Parliamentary papers, **RAIL 1066**
    Railway and Canal Traffic Acts proceedings,
      RAIL 1038
    Reports and accounts, **RAIL 1110;**
      RAIL 1116
    Rule books, **RAIL 1134**
    Timetables, **RAIL 981**
Burry Port Company *see* Burry Port & Gwendreath
    Valley R
Burscough and Southport Railway *see* L&YR/E
    Lancashire R jt cttee
Burton and Ashby Light Railway
    Parliamentary papers, **RAIL 1066**
See also LMSR Solicitor's records
    MR
Burton-upon-Trent and Nottingham Railway
    (proposed)
    Parliamentary papers, **RAIL 1066**
Bury and Tottington District Railway, **RAIL 90**
    Parliamentary papers, **RAIL 1066**
Bury St Edmunds and Thetford Railway
    Reports and accounts, **RAIL 1116**
Busby Railway
    Reports and accounts, **RAIL 1116**
Bute Docks Company
    Byelaws and regulations, **RAIL 1001** (*includes
      records of* GWR); **RAIL 1003**
    Parliamentary papers, **RAIL 1066** (*includes
      company's railways*)
See also Cardiff R
Buxton Chapel en le Frith and Sheffield Railway
    (proposed)
    Parliamentary papers, **RAIL 1066**
Caithness Railway
    Prospectuses etc, **RAIL 1075**

Caledonian and Dumbartonshire Junction Railway
    Reports and accounts, **RAIL 1116; RAIL 1117**
    Share certificates, **RAIL 1158**
Caledonian and Scottish Central Railway
    (proposed)
    Parliamentary papers, **RAIL 1066**
Caledonian Railway
    Instructions to staff, **RAIL 1135**
    Joint committees with:
      LNWR
        Carlisle goods traffic, **RAIL 98; RAIL 410;**
          RAIL 421
        Portpatrick & Wigtownshire Jt R,
          RAIL 421
        W Coast Conference, **RAIL 410; RAIL 727**
      GSWR
        Carlisle goods traffic, **RAIL 98; RAIL 410;**
          RAIL 421
        Portpatrick & Wigtownshire Jt R,
          RAIL 421
      MR
        Carlisle goods traffic, **RAIL 98; RAIL 410;**
          RAIL 421
        Portpatrick & Wigtownshire Jt R,
          RAIL 421
    See also Carlisle Citadel Station Cttee
    Labour and staff matters, **RAIL 1025**
    Law cases and arbitration, **RAIL 1027**
    Maps, **RAIL 1030**
    Miscellanea, **RAIL 1008; RAIL 1014;**
      RAIL 1015; RAIL 1057
    Parliamentary papers, **RAIL 1066**
    Prospectuses etc, **RAIL 1075**
    Railway and Canal Traffic Acts proceedings,
      RAIL 1038
    Railway Rates Tribunal proceedings,
      RAIL 1101
    Reports and accounts, **RAIL 1110; RAIL 1116;**
      RAIL 1117
    Rule books, **RAIL 1134**
    Savings Bank, reports and accounts,
      RAIL 1116
      Rules, **RAIL 1174**
    Share certificates, **RAIL 1158**
    Superannuation schemes, **RAIL 1174**
    Timetables, **RAIL 922; RAIL 981**
      Working timetables appendixes, **RAIL 1136**
    Welfare schemes, **RAIL 1174**
See also Irish & English Traffic Conference
    LMSR amalgamation
Caledonian, West Cumberland and Furness
    Railway (proposed)
    Prospectuses etc, **RAIL 1075**
Callander and Oban Railway
    Parliamentary papers, **RAIL 1066**
    Railway and Canal Traffic Acts proceedings,
      RAIL 1038

Reports and accounts, **RAIL 1116; RAIL 1117**
Share certificates, **RAIL 1158**
See also LMSR amalgamation
Callington Light Railway, **RAIL 799** (*includes records of* GWR)
Calne Railway, **RAIL 91**
    Railway and Canal Traffic Acts proceedings, **RAIL 1038**
    Reports and accounts, **RAIL 1110; RAIL 1116**
Campbeltown and Machrihanish Light Railway
    Reports and accounts, **RAIL 1116**
Camborne and Redruth Tramway
    Parliamentary papers, **RAIL 1068**
Cambrian Railways, **RAIL 92**
    Instructions to staff, **RAIL 1135**
    Labour and staff matters, **RAIL 1025**
    Law cases and arbitration, **RAIL 1027**
    Miscellanea, **RAIL 1008; RAIL 1014; RAIL 1020; RAIL 1057**
    Parliamentary papers, **RAIL 1066**
    Parliamentary plans, **RAIL 1071**
    Railway and Canal Traffic Acts proceedings, **RAIL 1038**
    Reports and accounts, **RAIL 1110; RAIL 1116; RAIL 1117**
    Rule books, **RAIL 1134**
    Timetables, **RAIL 923; RAIL 981**
      Working timetables appendixes, **RAIL 1136**
    Welfare fund accounts, **RAIL 1115**
See also GWR locomotives and rolling stock
    Irish & English Traffic Conference
    LMSR amalgamation
Cambridge and Lincoln Extension and Lincoln, York and Leeds Junction Railway, **RAIL 93**
Cambridge and Oxford Railway
    Subscription contracts, **RAIL 1160**
See also Royston & Hitchin R
Cambridge and York Railway (proposed) *see* GNR
Cannock Chase and Wolverhampton Railway
    Parliamentary papers, **RAIL 1066**
Cannock Mineral Railway, **RAIL 94**
    Reports and accounts, **RAIL 1110; RAIL 1116**
See also Derbyshire, Staffordshire & Worcestershire Jct R
Canterbury and Kent Coast Railway (proposed)
    Parliamentary papers, **RAIL 1066**
Canterbury and Whitstable Railway
    Miscellanea, **RAIL 1157**
Canvey Deep Water Wharf and Railway (proposed)
    Parliamentary papers, **RAIL 1066**
Cardiff and Caerphilly Railway (proposed)
    Miscellanea, **RAIL 1057**
Cardiff and Monmouthshire Valleys Railway (proposed)
    Parliamentary papers, **RAIL 1066**

Cardiff and Ogmore Valley Railway, **RAIL 95**
    Miscellanea, **RAIL 1057**
    Reports and accounts, **RAIL 1110; RAIL 1116**
Cardiff, Caerphilly and Aber Valley Railway (proposed)
    Miscellanea, **RAIL 1057**
Cardiff Corporation Tramways
    Reports and accounts, **RAIL 1114**
Cardiff, Penarth and Barry Junction Railways, **RAIL 96**
    Parliamentary papers, **RAIL 1066**
    Prospectus, **RAIL 1110**
    Reports and accounts, **RAIL 1110**
Cardiff Railway, **RAIL 97** (*includes records of predecessor* Bute Docks Co *q.v.*)
    Law cases and arbitration, **RAIL 1027**
    Maps, **RAIL 1030**
    Miscellanea, **RAIL 1014; RAIL 1057**
    Parliamentary papers, **RAIL 1066**
    Reports and accounts, **RAIL 1110; RAIL 1116; RAIL 1117**
    Rule books, **RAIL 1134**
    Working timetables appendixes, **RAIL 1136**
Carlisle and Eskdale Railway (proposed)
    Prospectuses etc, **RAIL 1076**
Carlisle and Hawick Railway (proposed)
    Prospectus, **RAIL 1116**
Carlisle and Silloth Bay Railway and Dock Company
    Parliamentary papers, **RAIL 1067; RAIL 1163**
    Reports and accounts, **RAIL 1116; RAIL 1117**
    Share certificates, **RAIL 1158**
Carlisle Citadel Station Committee (Cal R/LNWR) **RAIL 98; RAIL 410; RAIL 421** (*these include records of* Carlisle goods traffic committee, Cal R/GSWR/LNWR/MR)
    Law cases and arbitration, **RAIL 1027**
    Parliamentary papers, **RAIL 1066**
    Rule books, **RAIL 1134**
See also LMSR miscellanea
Carmarthen and Cardigan Railway, **RAIL 99** (*includes records of* GWR)
    Byelaws and regulations, **RAIL 1001**
    Law cases and arbitration, **RAIL 1027**
    Parliamentary papers, **RAIL 1066; RAIL 1163**
    Prospectus, **RAIL 1110**
    Reports and accounts, **RAIL 1110; RAIL 1116**
    Timetables, **RAIL 981**
See also GWR estates and rating
Carmarthenshire Railway or Tramroad, **RAIL 100** (*taken over, 1875, by* Llanelly & Mynydd Mawr R *q.v.*)
Carnarvon and Llanberis Railway, **RAIL 101**
    Reports and accounts, **RAIL 1116**
See also LNWR

Carnarvonshire Railway, **RAIL 102**
  Reports and accounts, **RAIL 1116**
  Rule books, **RAIL 1134**
See also LNWR
Carrickfergus and Larne Railway
  Reports and accounts, **RAIL 1116**
Carshalton, Sutton and Wimbledon Railway
  (proposed)
  Parliamentary papers, **RAIL 1066**
Carter Paterson and Company Ltd *see* BTC road
  services; GWR road services; LNER
  road services; LMSR road services; SR road
  services
Castlederg and Victoria Bridge Tramway
  Railway and Canal Traffic Acts proceedings,
    RAIL 1038
See also Irish & English Traffic Conference
Castle-Douglas and Dumfries Railway
  Reports and accounts, **RAIL 1116; RAIL 1117**
Caterham and Godstone Valley Railway
  (proposed)
  Parliamentary papers, **RAIL 1066**
Caterham Railway
  Timetables, **RAIL 981**
Cathcart District Railway
  Reports and accounts, **RAIL 1116**
  Share certificates, **RAIL 1158**
See also LMSR amalgamation
Cawood, Wistow and Selby Light Railway,
  RAIL 103
Cavan and Leitrim Light Railway (*formerly* Cavan,
  Leitrim & Roscommon Lt R & Tramway Co)
  Prospectus, **RAIL 1116**
  Railway and Canal Traffic Acts proceedings,
    RAIL 1038
  Reports and accounts, **RAIL 1110; RAIL 1116;
    RAIL 1117**
  Timetables, **RAIL 941**
See also Irish & English Traffic Conference
Central Cornwall Railway
  Parliamentary papers, **RAIL 1066**
Central Essex Light Railway
  Miscellanea, **RAIL 1057**
Central Kent Railway (proposed)
  Prospectuses etc, **RAIL 1075**
Central London Railway
  Labour and staff matters, **RAIL 1025**
  Miscellanea, **RAIL 1020; RAIL 1021;
    RAIL 1057**
  Parliamentary papers, **RAIL 1066**
  Parliamentary plans, **RAIL 1071**
  Pension fund, **RAIL 1174**
  Prospectuses etc, **RAIL 1075; RAIL 1076**
  Reports and accounts, **RAIL 1110; RAIL 1116;
    RAIL 1117**
  Rule books, **RAIL 1134**
  Sidings agreements, **RAIL 1167**

See also Underground Electric Rys Co
Central Metropolitan Railway (proposed)
  Parliamentary plans, **RAIL 1071**
Central Norfolk Railway (proposed)
  Parliamentary papers, **RAIL 1066**
Central of England Railway (proposed)
  Prospectuses etc, **RAIL 1075**
Central Wages Board
  Labour and staff matters, **RAIL 1025;
    RAIL 1026**
Central Wales and Carmarthen Junction Railway,
  RAIL 104 (*includes records of predecessor* Swansea
  & Carmarthen Rys)
  Byelaws and regulations, **RAIL 1001**
  Joint committee *see* Vale of Towy R Jt Cttee
  Miscellanea, **RAIL 1015**
  Parliamentary papers, **RAIL 1066**
  Railway Rates Tribunal proceedings,
    RAIL 1101
  Reports and accounts, **RAIL 1110; RAIL 1116**
Central Wales Extension Railway
  Reports and accounts, **RAIL 1116**
Central Wales Railway
  Miscellanea, **RAIL 1057**
  Prospectuses etc, **RAIL 1075**
  Reports and accounts, **RAIL 1116**
Central Wilts Light Railway (proposed)
  Miscellanea, **RAIL 1057**
Channel Bridge and Railway Company (proposed)
  Parliamentary papers, **RAIL 1066**
Channel Tunnel, **RAIL 779** (*includes records of*
  Channel Tunnel Co 1872 and 1887; SER; SR;
  Submarine Continental R)
  Parliamentary papers, **RAIL 1066**
Channel Tunnel Company
  Reports and accounts, **RAIL 1116; RAIL 1117**
Channel Tunnel Railway (proposed)
  Parliamentary papers, **RAIL 1066**
Chard and Taunton Railway, **RAIL 105**
Chard Railway, **RAIL 106**
  Parliamentary papers, **RAIL 1163**
Charing Cross and Euston Railway (proposed)
  Parliamentary plans, **RAIL 1071**
Charing Cross, Euston and Hampstead Railway
  Maps, **RAIL 1030**
  Parliamentary papers, **RAIL 1066**
  Reports and accounts, **RAIL 1110;
    RAIL 1116**
See also London Electric Rys
  Underground Electric Railways Co
Charing Cross, Hammersmith and District Electric
  Railway (proposed)
  Parliamentary papers, **RAIL 1066**
Charing Cross Railway, **RAIL 107**
  Law cases and arbitration, **RAIL 1027**
  Prospectuses etc, **RAIL 1075** (*as* London
    Bridge & Charing Cross R)

Reports and accounts, **RAIL 1116**
See also SR miscellanea
Charnwood Forest Railway, **RAIL 108**
    Miscellanea, **RAIL 1057**
    Reports and accounts, **RAIL 1116**
    Share certificates, **RAIL 1158**
See also LMSR amalgamation; miscellanea
Chatham and Brompton Tramways
    Parliamentary papers, **RAIL 1066**
Chatham and Canterbury Local Railway (proposed)
    Parliamentary contract, **RAIL 1163**
Chatham Loop Railway (proposed)
    Parliamentary papers, **RAIL 1066**
Cheadle Railway
    Timetables, **RAIL 981**
See also N Staffordshire R
Cheesewring Railway
    Miscellanea, **RAIL 1057**
Cheltenham and Great Western Union Railway, **RAIL 109**
    Maps, **RAIL 1030**
    Miscellanea, **RAIL 1008; RAIL 1014**
    Parliamentary papers, **RAIL 1066**
See also GWR miscellanea Brunel collection
Cheltenham and Oxford Railway
    Maps, **RAIL 1014**
    Parliamentary papers, **RAIL 1066**
Cheltenham and Oxford and London and Birmingham Union Railway (proposed) (*also called* Cheltenham, Oxford & Tring R)
    Maps, **RAIL 1030**
    Miscellanea, **RAIL 1014; RAIL 1057**
Cheltenham and Oxford Union Railway (proposed)
    Parliamentary papers, **RAIL 1163**
Cheltenham and Swindon Railway (proposed)
    Prospectuses etc, **RAIL 1075**
Cheltenham Station Company (MSWJR/MR)
    Miscellanea, **RAIL 1057**
Cheshire Lines Committee (GCR/GNR/MSLR/MR; *after 1923* LMSR/LNER), **RAIL 110; RAIL 783**
    Instructions to staff, **RAIL 1135**
    Labour and staff matters, **RAIL 1025**
    Law cases and arbitration, **RAIL 1027**
    Maps, **RAIL 1030**
    Miscellanea, **RAIL 1008; RAIL 1057**
    Officers' meetings, **RAIL 236**
    Parliamentary papers, **RAIL 1066; RAIL 1163**
    Reports and accounts, **RAIL 1110; RAIL 1116; RAIL 1117**
    Rule books, **RAIL 1134**
    Timetables
        Public, **RAIL 924; RAIL 981**
        Working, **RAIL 925** (*includes records of* BR(LM), GNR/MS&LR Jt Lines, MR)
        Working timetables appendixes, **RAIL 1136**

Traders' ledger credit agreements, **RAIL 1165**
See also Irish & English Traffic Conference
    Southport & Cheshire Lines Extension R
Cheshire Midland Railway, **RAIL 111**
Chester and Birkenhead Railway, **RAIL 112**
    Joint committee *see* Chester Jt Station Cttee
    Maps, **RAIL 1030**
    Miscellanea, **RAIL 1057**
    Parliamentary papers, **RAIL 1066**
    Parliamentary plans, **RAIL 1071**
    Rule books, **RAIL 1134**
    Subscription contracts, **RAIL 1160**
Chester and Crewe Railway, **RAIL 776**
    Maps, **RAIL 1030**
    Parliamentary plans, **RAIL 1071**
Chester and Holyhead Railway, **RAIL 113; RAIL 410**
    Byelaws and regulations, **RAIL 1001**
    Joint committee *see* Chester Jt Station Cttee
    Maps, **RAIL 1030**
    Miscellanea, **RAIL 1008; RAIL 1057**
    Parliamentary papers, **RAIL 1066; RAIL 1163**
    Parliamentary plans, **RAIL 1071**
    Reports and accounts, **RAIL 1110; RAIL 1116; RAIL 1117**
    Rule books, **RAIL 1134**
    Timetables, **RAIL 981**
See also LNWR
Chester and West Cheshire Junction Railway
    Parliamentary papers, **RAIL 1066**
Chester and West Cheshire Railway (proposed)
    Parliamentary papers, **RAIL 1066**
Chester Joint Station Committee, **RAIL 114; RAIL 410**
    (Chester & Birkenhead R/Chester & Holyhead R/Shrewsbury & Chester R
        after 1847, Birkenhead, Lancashire & Cheshire Jct R/Chester & Holyhead R/Shrewsbury & Chester R
        after 1854, Birkenhead, L & C Jct R/Chester & Holyhead R/GWR
        after 1858, Birkenhead, L & C Jct R/GWR/LNWR
        after 1859, Birkenhead R/GWR/LNWR)
        after 1860, GWR/LNWR)
    Rule books, **RAIL 1134**
    Timetables, **RAIL 981**
Chichester and Midhurst Railway, **RAIL 115**
    Parliamentary papers, **RAIL 1066**
Chipstead Valley Railway, **RAIL 116**
    Parliamentary papers, **RAIL 1066**
    Share certificates, **RAIL 1158**
Churnet and Blythe Junction Railway (proposed)
    see Macclesfield & Lichfield R
Churnet Valley Railway
    Parliamentary plans, **RAIL 1071**

Cirencester and Fairford Railway (proposed)
  Miscellanea, **RAIL 1057**
City and Brixton Railway
  Parliamentary papers, **RAIL 1066**
City and Crystal Palace Railway (proposed)
  Parliamentary papers, **RAIL 1066**
City and North East Suburban Electric Railway
  (proposed)
  Parliamentary papers, **RAIL 1066**
City and Richmond Railway (proposed)
  Prospectuses etc, **RAIL 1075**
City and South London Railway (*formerly* City of
  London & Southwark Subway)
  Labour and staff matters, **RAIL 1025**
  Miscellanea, **RAIL 1018; RAIL 1020**
  Parliamentary papers, **RAIL 1066**
  Pension fund, **RAIL 1174**
  Prospectus, **RAIL 1116**
  Reports and accounts, **RAIL 1110; RAIL 1116;
    RAIL 1117**
  Rule books, **RAIL 1134**
See also Underground Electric Rys Co
City and West End Railway (proposed)
  Parliamentary papers, **RAIL 1066**
  Parliamentary plans, **RAIL 1071**
  Prospectuses etc, **RAIL 1075**
City, Kingston and Richmond Railway (proposed)
  Parliamentary papers, **RAIL 1066**
City of Dublin Junction Railway *see* Dublin &
  S Eastern R/GNR(I) jt cttees
City of Glasgow Union Railway
  Railway and Canal Traffic Acts proceedings,
    RAIL 1038
  Reports and accounts, **RAIL 1116; RAIL 1117**
  Share certificates, **RAIL 1158**
City of London and Richmond Railway (proposed)
  Parliamentary papers, **RAIL 1014**
City of London and Metropolitan Tramways
  Parliamentary papers, **RAIL 1068**
City of London and Southwark Subway Company
  see City & S London R
City of London, Thames and West End Railway
  (proposed)
  Prospectuses etc, **RAIL 1075**
City Railway (proposed)
  Prospectuses, **RAIL 1016; RAIL 1075**
City Terminus Hotel Company (*taken over by* SER)
  Prospectuses etc, **RAIL 1075**
Clapham and City Subway (proposed)
  Parliamentary papers, **RAIL 1066**
Clapham Junction and Paddington Railway
  (proposed)
  Parliamentary papers, **RAIL 1066**
Clara and Banagher Railway
  Reports and accounts, **RAIL 1116**
Clarence Railway, **RAIL 117**
  Miscellanea, **RAIL 1157**

Parliamentary papers, **RAIL 1067**
  Prospectuses etc, **RAIL 1075; RAIL 1076**
  Reports and accounts, **RAIL 1111**
  Share certificates, **RAIL 1159**
See also NER
  Stockton & Hartlepool R
Clay Cross Railway
  Parliamentary papers, **RAIL 1066**
Cleator and Furness Railway Committee
  (FR/Whitehaven, Cleator & Egremont R),
  RAIL 118
Cleator and Workington Junction Railway,
  RAIL 119 (*includes records of jt cttee with* FR)
  Byelaws and regulations, **RAIL 1001**
  Parliamentary papers, **RAIL 1066**
  Railway and Canal Traffic Acts proceedings,
    RAIL 1038
  Reports and accounts, **RAIL 1110; RAIL 1116;
    RAIL 1117**
  Rule books, **RAIL 1134**
  Share certificates, **RAIL 1158**
  Timetables, **RAIL 981**
See also LMSR amalgamation
Clee Hill Incline and Railway
  Rule book, **RAIL 1134**
Cleobury Mortimer and Ditton Priors Light
  Railway, **RAIL 120**
  Miscellanea, **RAIL 1057**
  Reports and accounts, **RAIL 1110**
  Timetables, **RAIL 981**
Clevedon and Portishead Railway (proposed)
  Parliamentary papers, **RAIL 1066**
Cleveland Extension Mineral Railway
  (proposed)
  Prospectuses etc, **RAIL 1076**
Cleveland Railway, **RAIL 121**
  Miscellanea, **RAIL 1157**
  Parliamentary papers, **RAIL 1067**
  Prospectuses etc, **RAIL 1076; RAIL 1116**
  Reports and accounts, **RAIL 1117**
  Share certificates, **RAIL 1159**
Clifton Extension Railway
  Maps, **RAIL 1030**
  Railway and Canal Traffic Acts proceedings,
    RAIL 1038
See also Bristol Port R
  GWR/MR jt cttees
Clogher Valley Railway (*formerly* Clogher Valley
  Tramway)
  Railway and Canal Traffic Acts proceedings,
    RAIL 1038
  Reports and accounts, **RAIL 1116**
See also Irish & English Traffic Conference
Clonmel, Lismore and Dungarvon Railway
  Reports and accounts, **RAIL 1116**
Clydesdale Railway Guaranteed Company
  Reports and accounts, **RAIL 1116**

Coal Owners Associated (London) Railway
(proposed)
    Parliamentary papers, **RAIL 1066**
Cockermouth and Workington Railway, **RAIL 122**
    Joint committee with:
        Cockermouth, Keswick & Penrith R,
            RAIL 122 (Cockermouth station)
    Parliamentary papers, **RAIL 1066**
    Reports and accounts, **RAIL 1116; RAIL 1117**
Cockermouth, Keswick and Penrith Railway,
    RAIL 123
    Joint committees with:
        LNWR
            RAIL 122; RAIL 123; RAIL 410; RAIL 421
            (Cockermouth station)
            RAIL 563 (Penrith jt station)
        S&DR
            RAIL 563 (Penrith jt station)
    Miscellanea, **RAIL 1015; RAIL 1021**
    Prospectuses etc, **RAIL 1075; RAIL 1076**
    Railway and Canal Traffic Acts proceedings,
        RAIL 1038
    Reports and accounts, **RAIL 1110; RAIL 1116;**
        RAIL 1117
    Rule books, **RAIL 1134**
    Share certificates, **RAIL 1158**
    Timetables, **RAIL 981**
See also LMSR amalgamation
Colchester, Stour Valley, Sudbury and Halstead
    Railway, **RAIL 124**
    Reports and accounts, **RAIL 1116**
Coleford, Monmouth, Usk and Pontypool Railway,
    RAIL 125
    Byelaws and regulations, **RAIL 1001**
    Miscellanea, **RAIL 1014**
    Prospectuses etc, **RAIL 1075; RAIL 1110**
    Reports and accounts, **RAIL 1110; RAIL 1116**
    Timetables, **RAIL 981**
See also GWR estates and rating
Coleford Railway, **RAIL 126**
    Parliamentary papers, **RAIL 1066**
    Reports and accounts, **RAIL 1110**
Coleorton Railway
    Parliamentary papers, **RAIL 1016; RAIL 1066**
Collingbourne and Avon Valley Railway
    (proposed)
    Miscellanea, **RAIL 1057**
Colne and Bradford Extension Railway
    (proposed), **RAIL 127**
Colne Valley and Halstead Railway, **RAIL 128**
    Byelaws and regulations, **RAIL 1001**
    Law cases and arbitration, **RAIL 1027**
    Miscellanea, **RAIL 1057**
    Parliamentary papers, **RAIL 1066**
    Railway and Canal Traffic Acts proceedings,
        RAIL 1038
    Reports and accounts, **RAIL 1110; RAIL 1116;**

    RAIL 1117
    Rule book, **RAIL 1134**
    Share certificates, **RAIL 1158**
Commercial Railway
    Miscellanea, **RAIL 1016; RAIL 1021**
    Prospectuses etc, **RAIL 1016; RAIL 1075**
See also London & Blackwall R
Coniston Railway, **RAIL 129**
    Reports and accounts, **RAIL 1116; RAIL 1117**
Conway and Llanrwst Railway, **RAIL 130**
Cooke's National Railway (proposed)
    Prospectuses etc, **RAIL 1075**
Coras Iompair Eireann (Irish national rys)
    Miscellanea, **RAIL 1020**
    Reports and accounts, **RAIL 1116**
    Timetables, **RAIL 928; RAIL 941**
See also Fishguard & Rosslare Rys & Harbours Co
    Irish & English Traffic Conference
Cork and Bandon Railway
    Parliamentary papers, **RAIL 1163**
    Reports and accounts, **RAIL 1116; RAIL 1117**
Cork and Kinsale Junction Railway
    Prospectuses etc, **RAIL 1076**
    Reports and accounts, **RAIL 1116**
Cork and Limerick Direct Railway
    Reports and accounts, **RAIL 1116**
Cork and Macroom Direct Railway
    Railway and Canal Traffic Acts proceedings,
        RAIL 1038
    Reports and accounts, **RAIL 1110; RAIL 1116**
    Timetables, **RAIL 941**
Cork and Macroom Railway
    Reports and accounts, **RAIL 1116**
Cork and Muskerry Light Railway
    Railway and Canal Traffic Acts proceedings,
        RAIL 1038
Cork and Passage Railway
    Reports and accounts, **RAIL 1117**
Cork and Youghal Railway
    Parliamentary papers, **RAIL 1163**
    Reports and accounts, **RAIL 1116; RAIL 1117**
Cork, Bandon and South Coast Railway
    Railway and Canal Traffic Acts proceedings,
        RAIL 1038
    Reports and accounts, **RAIL 1110; RAIL 1116;**
        RAIL 1117
    Timetables, **RAIL 941**
See also Bantry Extension R
    Cork City Railways
    Irish & English Traffic Conference
Cork, Blackrock and Passage Railway
    Railway and Canal Traffic Acts proceedings,
        RAIL 1038
    Reports and accounts, **RAIL 1110; RAIL 1116;**
        RAIL 1117
    Timetables, **RAIL 941**
See also Irish & English Traffic Conference

Cork City Railways, **RAIL 131** (*run by* GWR, Cork, Bandon & S Coast R and Cork business interests. *These are* GWR *records*)
    Miscellanea, **RAIL 1057**
    Parliamentary papers, **RAIL 1066**
    Reports and accounts, **RAIL 1110**
Cork Junction Railways
    Miscellanea, **RAIL 1057**
    Parliamentary papers, **RAIL 1066**
Cork Link Railways (proposed)
    Parliamentary papers, **RAIL 1066**
Cork, Midleton and Youghal Railway
    Parliamentary papers, **RAIL 1163**
Cornwall and Devon Central Railway (proposed)
    Miscellanea, **RAIL 1057**
Cornwall Central Railway (proposed)
    Miscellanea, **RAIL 1014; RAIL 1057**
Cornwall Minerals Railway, **RAIL 133**
    Byelaws and regulations, **RAIL 1001**
    Joint committee with GWR, **RAIL 132**
    Miscellanea, **RAIL 1008; RAIL 1057**
    Railway and Canal Traffic Acts proceedings, **RAIL 1038**
    Reports and accounts, **RAIL 1110; RAIL 1116; RAIL 1117**
See also GWR Secretary's papers
    Newquay & Cornwall Jct R
Cornwall Railway, **RAIL 134** (*includes records of jt management cttee* Bristol & Exeter R/Cornwall R/GWR/S Devon R), **RAIL 630**
    Byelaws and regulations, **RAIL 1001**
    Joint committee:
        Plymouth jt station (GWR/S Devon R), **RAIL 568**
    Miscellanea, **RAIL 1008; RAIL 1014; RAIL 1020; RAIL 1057**
    Parliamentary papers, **RAIL 1066; RAIL 1163**
    Prospectuses etc, **RAIL 1075**
    Reports and accounts, **RAIL 1110; RAIL 1116; RAIL 1117**
    Rule books, **RAIL 1134**
    Timetables, **RAIL 981**
See also GWR correspondence and papers; miscellanea
    S Devon R
Corris Railway, **RAIL 135**
    Railway and Canal Traffic Acts proceedings, **RAIL 1038**
    Reports and accounts, **RAIL 1110; RAIL 1116; RAIL 1117**
Corwen and Bala Railway, **RAIL 136**
    Miscellanea, **RAIL 1057**
    Railway and Canal Traffic Acts proceedings, **RAIL 1038**
    Reports and accounts, **RAIL 1110; RAIL 1116**
See also GWR estates and rating

County Donegal Railways Joint Committee (GNR(I)/MR), **RAIL 137**
    Reports and accounts, **RAIL 1116**
See also LMSR secretarial papers
Coventry and Arley Railway (proposed)
    Parliamentary papers, **RAIL 1066**
Coventry and Leicester Junction Railway (proposed), **RAIL 138**
    Prospectuses etc, **RAIL 1075**
Coventry Central Station and Southam Junction Railway (proposed)
    Parliamentary papers, **RAIL 1066**
Coventry, Nuneaton, Birmingham and Leicester Railway, **RAIL 139**
    Miscellanea, **RAIL 1057**
    Subscription contracts, **RAIL 1160**
Cowbridge and Aberthaw Railway, **RAIL 140**
    Reports and accounts, **RAIL 1110**
Cowbridge Railway, **RAIL 141**
    Miscellanea, **RAIL 1014; RAIL 1057**
    Prospectus, **RAIL 1110**
    Reports and accounts, **RAIL 1110**
Cowes and Newport Railway, **RAIL 142**
    Joint committees with:
        Isle of Wight (Newport Jct) R, **RAIL 591** (Newport jt stn)
        Ryde & Newport R, **RAIL 591** (general; Newport jt stn)
    Reports and accounts, **RAIL 1110; RAIL 1116; RAIL 1117**
See also Isle of Wight Central R
Cranbrook and Paddock Wood Railway, **RAIL 143**
    Parliamentary papers, **RAIL 1066**
Crieff Junction Railway
    Reports and accounts, **RAIL 1116**
Cromford and High Peak Railway
    Byelaws and regulations, **RAIL 1001**
    Parliamentary papers, **RAIL 1163**
    Reports and accounts, **RAIL 1116**
    Rule books, **RAIL 1134**
See also LNWR
Crowhurst, Sidley and Bexhill Railway, **RAIL 145**
Croydon and Crystal Palace Railway (proposed)
    Parliamentary papers, **RAIL 1066**
Croydon and District Electric Tramway
    Parliamentary papers, **RAIL 1068**
Croydon and Kingston Junction Railway (proposed)
    Parliamentary papers, **RAIL 1066**
Croydon and Norwood Tramways
    Parliamentary papers, **RAIL 1066**
Croydon Central Station and Railways (proposed)
    Parliamentary papers, **RAIL 1066**
Croydon County Borough Tramways
    Reports and accounts, **RAIL 1114**
Croydon Direct Railway (proposed)
    Parliamentary papers, **RAIL 1066**

Croydon, Merstham and Godstone Iron Road
Photographs (*20th century*), **RAIL 1017**
Share certificates, **RAIL 1158**
Croydon, Mitcham and Kingston Railway
(proposed)
Parliamentary papers, **RAIL 1066**
Croydon, Norwood, Dulwich and London
Railway (proposed)
Parliamentary papers, **RAIL 1066**
Croydon, Oxted and East Grinstead Railway
Joint committee (LBSCR/SER), **RAIL 414**
Parliamentary papers, **RAIL 1066**
Crystal Palace and East London High Level
Junction Railway (proposed)
Parliamentary papers, **RAIL 1066**
Crystal Palace and South Eastern Junction
Railway (proposed)
Parliamentary papers, **RAIL 1066**
Crystal Palace and South London Junction
Railway, **RAIL 146**
Parliamentary papers, **RAIL 1066**
Reports and accounts, **RAIL 1116**
Crystal Palace, Anerley and Gipsy Hill Tramways
(proposed)
Parliamentary papers, **RAIL 1066**
Crystal Palace (High Level), Beulah and
Beckenham Railway (proposed)
Parliamentary papers, **RAIL 1066**
Crystal Palace High Level Railway (proposed)
Parliamentary papers, **RAIL 1066**
Crystal Palace New Railway (proposed)
Parliamentary papers, **RAIL 1066**
Crystal Palace Railway (proposed)
Parliamentary papers, **RAIL 1066**
Crystal Palace South Eastern and Metropolitan
Railway (proposed)
Parliamentary papers, **RAIL 1066**
Culm Valley Light Railway, **RAIL 147**
Prospectuses etc, **RAIL 1075**
Reports and accounts, **RAIL 1110**
Darenth Valley Tramway (proposed)
Parliamentary papers, **RAIL 1066**
Dare Valley Railway, **RAIL 148**
Reports and accounts, **RAIL 1110**
Darlington and Barnard Castle Railway, **RAIL 149**
Parliamentary papers, **RAIL 1067; RAIL 1163**
Prospectuses etc, **RAIL 1021; RAIL 1076**
Reports and accounts, **RAIL 1111; RAIL 1116;
RAIL 1117**
Subscription contracts, **RAIL 1161**
Share certificates, **RAIL 1159**
Timetables, **RAIL 981**
Darlington Street Railroad Company
Miscellanea, **RAIL 1021**
Dartmouth and Torbay Railway
Prospectuses, **RAIL 1014; RAIL 1110**
Reports and accounts, **RAIL 1110**

Deal and Dover Railway *see* Dover & Deal R
Deal, Walmer and Addisham Junction Railway
(proposed)
Parliamentary papers, **RAIL 1066**
Deal, Walmer and Dover Railway (proposed)
Parliamentary papers, **RAIL 1066**
Dean Forest and Gloucester Railway (proposed)
Prospectuses etc, **RAIL 1075**
See also Gloucester & Dean Forest R
Dean Forest, Monmouth, Usk and Pontypool
Railway (proposed)
Parliamentary papers, **RAIL 1163**
Prospectus, **RAIL 1014**
Dearne District Light Railways
Parliamentary papers, **RAIL 1066**
Dearne Valley Light Railways (proposed)
Parliamentary papers, **RAIL 1066**
Dearne Valley Railway, **RAIL 150; RAIL 410**
Law cases and arbitration, **RAIL 1027**
Maps, **RAIL 1030**
Parliamentary papers, **RAIL 1066**
Reports and accounts, **RAIL 1110; RAIL 1116**
See also LMSR amalgamation
LNWR
Dearness Valley Railway, **RAIL 151**
Parliamentary papers, **RAIL 1163**
Share certificates, **RAIL 1158**
Dee and Birkenhead Committee *see* N Wales &
Liverpool R Cttee
Dee and Mersey Junction Railway (proposed)
Parliamentary papers, **RAIL 1066**
Deeside Railway (Great North of Scotland
Railway)
Reports and accounts, **RAIL 1116; RAIL 1117**
Timetables, **RAIL 981**
Denbigh, Ruthin and Corwen Railway, **RAIL 152;
RAIL 410**
Byelaws and regulations, **RAIL 1001**
Parliamentary papers, **RAIL 1066**
Reports and accounts, **RAIL 1110;
RAIL 1116**
See also LNWR
Denbighshire Railway (proposed)
Parliamentary papers, **RAIL 1066**
Deptford Pier Junction Railway
Parliamentary papers, **RAIL 1016**
Derbyshire, Staffordshire and Worcestershire
Junction Railway (*after 1855 called* Cannock
Mineral R *q.v.*), **RAIL 153**
Map, **RAIL 1153**
Parliamentary papers, **RAIL 1163**
Share certificates, **RAIL 1158**
Derwent Valley Light Railway
Prospectuses etc, **RAIL 1075**
Reports and accounts, **RAIL 1111; RAIL 1116;
RAIL 1117**
See also BTC Chief Secretary's Office

De Trafford Light Railway
  Parliamentary papers, **RAIL 1066**
Devil's Bridge Railway (proposed)
  Miscellanea, **RAIL 1057**
Devon Central Railway (proposed)
  Miscellanea, **RAIL 1057**
Devon and Cornwall Central Railway
  Parliamentary papers, **RAIL 1066**
Devon and Cornwall Railway, **RAIL 154**
  Law cases and arbitration, **RAIL 1027**
  Parliamentary papers, **RAIL 1066**
  Reports and accounts, **RAIL 1116**
  Share certificates, **RAIL 1158**
Devon and Dorset Railway (proposed)
  Miscellanea, **RAIL 1014**
  Parliamentary papers, **RAIL 1066; RAIL 1163**
Devon and Somerset Railway, **RAIL 155**
  GWR miscellanea, **RAIL 1014**
  Parliamentary papers, **RAIL 1066**
  Railway and Canal Traffic Acts proceedings,
    RAIL 1038
  Reports and accounts, **RAIL 1110; RAIL 1116;
    RAIL 1117**
See also GWR estates and rating
Devon (North) and Somerset Railway (proposed)
  GWR miscellanea, **RAIL 1014**
Devon Valley Railway (*Scotland*)
  Share certificates, **RAIL 1158**
Dewsbury, Birstal, Somersal and Bradford Railway
  (proposed)
  Prospectuses etc, **RAIL 1075**
Didcot, Newbury and Southampton Railway,
  RAIL 156 (*until 1883* Didcot, Newbury &
  Southampton Jct R)
  Law cases and arbitration, **RAIL 1027**
  Miscellanea, **RAIL 1057**
  Parliamentary papers, **RAIL 1066**
  Prospectuses etc, **RAIL 1014; RAIL 1075;
    RAIL 1116**
  Railway and Canal Traffic Acts proceedings,
    RAIL 1038
  Reports and accounts, **RAIL 1110; RAIL 1116;
    RAIL 1117**
  Timetables, **RAIL 981**
See also GWR estates and rating
Dingwall and Skye Railway
  Parliamentary plans, **RAIL 1071**
Direct Birmingham, Oxford, Reading and Brighton
  Railway (proposed)
  Prospectuses etc, **RAIL 1075**
Direct City South Union Atmospheric Railway
  (proposed)
  Prospectuses etc, **RAIL 1075**
Direct London and Brighton Railway (proposed)
  Prospectuses etc, **RAIL 1075**
Direct London and Exeter Railway (proposed)
  Prospectuses etc, **RAIL 1075**

Direct London and Portsmouth Railway, **RAIL 157**
  Share certificates, **RAIL 1158**
Direct Manchester and Milford Railway
  (proposed)
  Parliamentary papers, **RAIL 1163**
Direct Northern Railway (proposed) *see* GNR
Direct Western Railway (proposed)
  Maps, **RAIL 1030**
  Prospectuses etc, **RAIL 1075**
Disley and Hayfield Railway, **RAIL 158**
Donegal Railway
  Parliamentary papers, **RAIL 1066**
  Reports and accounts, **RAIL 1116**
See also Irish & English Traffic Conference
Donkey Express Company (satirical prospectus),
  RAIL 1075
Dore and Chinley Railway
  Parliamentary papers, **RAIL 1066**
  Prospectuses etc, **RAIL 1075**
Dorking, Brighton and Arundel Atmospheric
  Railway (proposed)
  Prospectuses etc, **RAIL 1075**
Dornoch Light Railway
  Reports and accounts, **RAIL 1116**
See also LMSR amalgamation
Dorset Central Railway, **RAIL 159**
  GWR miscellanea, **RAIL 1014**
  Reports and accounts, **RAIL 1110; RAIL 1116;
    RAIL 1117**
See also Somerset & Dorset R
Dover and Deal Railway (*originally called* Deal &
  Dover R)
  Parliamentary papers, **RAIL 1066**
Dover Corporation Tramways
  Parliamentary papers, **RAIL 1066**
Dover, Deal and Sandwich Railway (proposed)
  Parliamentary papers, **RAIL 1066**
Downham and Stoke Ferry Railway, **RAIL 160**
  Reports and accounts, **RAIL 1110**
Downpatrick, Dundrum and Newcastle Railway
  Reports and accounts, **RAIL 1116**
Drayton Junction Railway
  Miscellanea, **RAIL 1057**
  Parliamentary papers, **RAIL 1066**
Drogheda *or* Grand Northern Trunk Railway
  (proposed)
  Prospectuses etc, **RAIL 1075**
Dublin and Antrim Junction Railway
  Reports and accounts, **RAIL 1116**
Dublin and Belfast Junction Railway
  Reports and accounts, **RAIL 1116; RAIL 1117**
See also Irish & English Traffic Conference
Dublin and Bray Railway
  Reports and accounts, **RAIL 1116**
Dublin and Drogheda Railway
  Miscellanea, **RAIL 1057**
  Reports and accounts, **RAIL 1116; RAIL 1117**

See also Irish & English Traffic Conference
GWR miscellanea Brunel collection
Dublin and Kingstown Railway
    Parliamentary papers, **RAIL 1066**
    Reports and accounts, **RAIL 1116; RAIL 1117**
Dublin and Lucan Steam Tramway
    Railway and Canal Traffic Acts proceedings,
        RAIL 1038
Dublin and Meath Railway
    Reports and accounts, **RAIL 1116**
Dublin and South Eastern Railway
    Joint committee with:
        City of Dublin Steam Packet Co/GNR(I),
            RAIL 1117 (City of Dublin Jct Rys) reports
            and accounts
    Law cases and arbitration, **RAIL 1027**
    Reports and accounts, **RAIL 1110; RAIL 1116;**
        RAIL 1117
    Timetables, **RAIL 941**
See also Irish & English Traffic Conference
    LMSR amalgamation
Dublin and Wexford Railway (proposed)
    Parliamentary contract, **RAIL 1163**
Dublin and Wicklow Railway
    Reports and accounts, **RAIL 1116; RAIL 1117**
Dublin Junction Railway
    Prospectus, **RAIL 1116**
Dublin Metropolitan Railway
    Prospectus, **RAIL 1116**
Dublin Trunk Connecting Railway
    Prospectuses etc, **RAIL 1075**
Dublin, Wicklow and Wexford Railway
    Parliamentary papers, **RAIL 1066**
    Railway and Canal Traffic Acts proceedings,
        RAIL 1038
    Reports and accounts, **RAIL 1110; RAIL 1116;**
        RAIL 1117
See also Irish & English Traffic Conference
Dudley and Birmingham Junction Railway
    (proposed)
    Prospectuses etc, **RAIL 1075**
Dudley and Oldbury Junction Railway
    Parliamentary papers, **RAIL 1066**
Dudley, Stourbridge and Kingswinford Tramways
    Parliamentary papers, **RAIL 1066**
Duffryn, Llynvi and Porthcawl Railway, **RAIL 161**
    Miscellanea, **RAIL 1014**
    Reports and accounts, **RAIL 1110**
See also Llynvi Valley R
Dulas Valley Mineral Railway
    Miscellanea, **RAIL 1057**
    Prospectuses etc, **RAIL 1075**
    Reports and accounts, **RAIL 1116**
See also Neath & Brecon R
Dumbarton and Balloch Joint Line
    (LMSR/LNER)
    Reports and accounts, **RAIL 1116**

Dumfries, Lochmaben and Lockerby Junction
    Railway
    Reports and accounts, **RAIL 1116**
Dunblane, Doune and Callander Railway
    Reports and accounts, **RAIL 1116**
    Timetables, **RAIL 981**
Dundalk and Blackrock Railway
    Subscription contract, **RAIL 1163**
Dundalk and Enniskillen Railway
    Parliamentary papers, **RAIL 1163**
    Reports and accounts, **RAIL 1116; RAIL 1117**
Dundalk and Greenore Railway, **RAIL 162;**
    RAIL 410
    Byelaws and regulations, **RAIL 1001**
    Joint committee with:
        Newry & Greenore R, **RAIL 410** (Jt works
            cttee)
    Rule books, **RAIL 1134**
See also Dundalk, Newry & Greenore R
    LNWR
Dundalk, Enniskillen and Londonderry Railway
    Miscellanea, **RAIL 1007**
Dundalk, Newry and Greenore Railway, **RAIL 162**
    (*includes records of predecessor* Dundalk &
    Greenore R)
    Byelaws and regulations, **RAIL 1001**
    Railway and Canal Traffic Acts proceedings,
        RAIL 1038
    Reports and accounts, **RAIL 1110; RAIL 1116**
    Rule books, **RAIL 1134**
See also Irish & English Traffic Conference
    LNWR
Dundee and Arbroath Joint Line Committee
    (LMSR/LNER)
    Reports and accounts, **RAIL 1116**
Dundee and Arbroath Railway
    Reports and accounts, **RAIL 1116; RAIL 1117**
Dundee and Newtyle Railway
    Reports and accounts, **RAIL 1116**
    Share certificates, **RAIL 1158**
See also LMSR amalgamation
Dundee, and Perth Railway
    Prospectuses etc, **RAIL 1075**
Dundee, Perth and Aberdeen Railway Junction
    Company
    Reports and accounts, **RAIL 1116; RAIL 1117**
Dunfermline and Queensferry Railway
    Share certificates, **RAIL 1158**
Dunstable Railway, **RAIL 163**
    Miscellanea, **RAIL 1057**
Durham and Cleveland Union Railway
    (proposed)
    Miscellanea, **RAIL 1021**
    Parliamentary papers, **RAIL 1066; RAIL 1067**
Durham and Sunderland Railway, **RAIL 164**
    Prospectuses etc, **RAIL 1075**
    Reports and accounts, **RAIL 1111**

Durham Coast Railway (proposed)
    Parliamentary papers, **RAIL 1066**
Durham Junction Railway, **RAIL 165**
Dursley and Midland Junction Railway,
    RAIL 166
    Parliamentary papers, **RAIL 1163**
Dyserth and Newmarket Light Railway
    Parliamentary papers, **RAIL 1066**
See also LNWR
Ealing and Shepherd's Bush Railway
    Rule books, **RAIL 1134**
See also GWR estates and rating
Easingwold Railway, **RAIL 167**
    Miscellanea, **RAIL 1006**
    Parliamentary papers, **RAIL 1067**
    Prospectuses etc, **RAIL 1076**
    Reports and accounts, **RAIL 1111;**
        RAIL 1117
See also BTC Chief Secretary's Office
East and West India Dock Co *see* London &
    Blackwall R
East and West India Docks and Birmingham
    Junction Railway
    Parliamentary papers, **RAIL 1066; RAIL 1163**
    Parliamentary plans, **RAIL 1071**
    Reports and accounts, **RAIL 1110; RAIL 1116**
    Subscription contracts, **RAIL 1160**
See also N London R
East and West Junction Railway
    Joint committee with:
        Stratford-upon-Avon, Towcester & Midland
        Jct R, **RAIL 168**
            Instructions to staff, **RAIL 1135**
            Reports and accounts, **RAIL 1116**
            Timetables, **RAIL 981**
    Law cases and arbitration, **RAIL 1027**
    Miscellanea, **RAIL 1014; RAIL 1020;**
        RAIL 1057
    Parliamentary papers, **RAIL 1066**
    Prospectuses, etc, **RAIL 1075**
    Railway and Canal Traffic Acts proceedings,
        RAIL 1038
    Reports and accounts, **RAIL 1116**
    Timetables, **RAIL 981**
See also Stratford-upon-Avon & Midland Jct R
East and West of England Junction Railway
    (proposed)
    Miscellanea, **RAIL 1020**
    Prospectuses etc, **RAIL 1075**
East and West Wales Railway (proposed)
    Parliamentary papers, **RAIL 1066**
    Parliamentary plans, **RAIL 1071**
East and West Yorkshire Junction Railway,
    RAIL 169
    Reports and accounts, **RAIL 1116**
East and West Yorkshire Union Light Railways
    Parliamentary papers, **RAIL 1066**

East and West Yorkshire Union Railways, **RAIL 170**
    Law cases and arbitration, **RAIL 1027**
    Parliamentary papers, **RAIL 1066; RAIL 1067**
    Prospectuses etc, **RAIL 1075; RAIL 1076**
    Reports and accounts, **RAIL 1110; RAIL 1116;**
        RAIL 1117
    Share certificates, **RAIL 1158**
East Anglian Railways, **RAIL 171**
    Miscellanea, **RAIL 1021**
    Parliamentary papers, **RAIL 1163**
    Reports and accounts, **RAIL 1110; RAIL 1116;**
        RAIL 1117
    Timetables, **RAIL 981**
Eastbourne, Seaford and Newhaven Railway
    Parliamentary papers, **RAIL 1066**
East Coast (Railway Companies) Conference
    (GNR/NBR/NER), **RAIL 172**
    East Coast Route timetables, **RAIL 926**
    Instructions to staff, **RAIL 1135**
East Denbighshire Railway (proposed)
    Parliamentary papers, **RAIL 1066**
Eastern and Midlands Railway, **RAIL 184**
    Parliamentary papers, **RAIL 1066**
    Prospectuses etc, **RAIL 1075**
    Railway and Canal Traffic Acts proceedings,
        RAIL 1038
    Reports and accounts, **RAIL 1016; RAIL 1110;**
        RAIL 1116; RAIL 1117
    Rule books, **RAIL 1134**
    Share certificates, **RAIL 1158**
    Timetables, **RAIL 981**
See also Irish & English Traffic Conference
Eastern and Northern Counties Junction Railway
    (proposed)
    Prospectuses etc, **RAIL 1075**
Eastern Counties and East Suffolk Joint
    Committee, **RAIL 185**
Eastern Counties and Trent Valley Junction
    Railway (proposed)
    Prospectuses etc, **RAIL 1075**
Eastern Counties Railway, **RAIL 186**
    Byelaws and Regulations, **RAIL 1001;**
        RAIL 1003 (Lowestoft Harbour)
    Joint committees with:
        Eastern Union Railway, **RAIL 186**
        East Suffolk Railway, **RAIL 185**
        Norfolk Railway, **RAIL 186**
    Law cases and arbitration, **RAIL 1027**
    Miscellanea, **RAIL 1014; RAIL 1016; RAIL 1021**
    Parliamentary papers, **RAIL 1163**
    Prospectuses etc, **RAIL 1075; RAIL 1076**
    Provident Society, **RAIL 1174**
    Reports and accounts, **RAIL 1110; RAIL 1116;**
        RAIL 1117
    Rule books, **RAIL 1134**
    Subscription contracts, **RAIL 1160**
    Timetables, **RAIL 981**

See also East Suffolk R
    GER
    LTSR
    Waveney Valley R
    Wells & Fakenham R
Eastern Union and Hadleigh Junction Railway
    Reports and accounts, **RAIL 1110**
Eastern Union Railway, **RAIL 187** (*includes records of cttee running* Ipswich, Bury & Norwich R)
    Joint committee with:
        Eastern Counties R/Norfolk Railway, **RAIL 186**
        Miscellanea, **RAIL 1014; RAIL 1016; RAIL 1021**
    Prospectuses etc, **RAIL 1076**
    Reports and accounts, **RAIL 1110; RAIL 1116; RAIL 1117**
    Timetables, **RAIL 981**
See also Ipswich & Bury St Edmunds R
East Glamorgan Railway (proposed)
    Parliamentary papers, **RAIL 1066**
East Gloucestershire and Wiltshire Railway (proposed)
    Parliamentary papers, **RAIL 1066**
East Gloucestershire Railway, **RAIL 173; RAIL 1193**
    GWR miscellanea, **RAIL 1014**
    Parliamentary papers, **RAIL 1066**
    Prospectuses etc, **RAIL 1075**
    Reports and accounts, **RAIL 1110; RAIL 1116**
    Timetables, **RAIL 981**
See also GWR estates and rating; miscellanea
East Grinstead and London Railway (proposed)
    Parliamentary papers, **RAIL 1066**
East Grinstead, Groombridge and Tunbridge Wells Railway, **RAIL 174**
    Share certificates, **RAIL 1158**
East Grinstead Railway
    Parliamentary papers, **RAIL 1163**
    Reports and accounts, **RAIL 1116**
East Ham County Borough Tramways
    Reports and accounts, **RAIL 1114**
East Kent Light Railway, **RAIL 175**
    Reports and accounts, **RAIL 1116**
East Kent Railway
    Parliamentary papers, **RAIL 1066**
    Reports and accounts, **RAIL 1116**
    Timetables, **RAIL 981**
See also BTC Chief Secretary's Office
    LCDR
East Lancashire Railway, **RAIL 176** (*includes records of predecessor* Manchester, Bury & Rossendale R)
    Byelaws and regulations, **RAIL 1001**
    Joint committees with:

        Blackburn & Preston R, **RAIL 176**
        L&YR, **RAIL 176**
          Blackburn R, **RAIL 52**
          Burscough & Southport R, **RAIL 1001** (byelaws)
          Liverpool jt line station, **RAIL 981** (timetables)
          Byelaws and regulations, **RAIL 1001**
          Preston station, **RAIL 410**
        LNWR, **RAIL 410** (Preston station)
    Miscellanea, **RAIL 1008**
    Parliamentary papers, **RAIL 1066; RAIL 1163**
    Reports and accounts, **RAIL 1116; RAIL 1117**
    Rule books, **RAIL 1134**
    Timetables, **RAIL 981**
See also L&YR
East Lincolnshire Railway, **RAIL 177**
    Byelaws and regulations, **RAIL 1001** (*made by* GNR)
    Subscription contracts, **RAIL 1160**
    Share certificates, **RAIL 1158**
    Timetables, **RAIL 981**
See also GNR
East London Railway, **RAIL 178**
    Byelaws and regulations, **RAIL 1001**
    Joint committee (GER/LBSCR/LCDR/Met District R/Met R/SER; *after 1923* LNER/Met District/Met R/SR; *after 1933* LNER/LPTB/SR), **RAIL 179**
    Accounts, **RAIL 1110**
    Railway & Canal Traffic Acts proceedings, **RAIL 1038**
    Reports and accounts, **RAIL 1116; RAIL 1117**
    Law cases and arbitration, **RAIL 1027**
    Parliamentary papers, **RAIL 1066**
    Prospectuses etc, **RAIL 1075**
    Reports and accounts, **RAIL 1110; RAIL 1116; RAIL 1117**
    Timetables, **RAIL 927**
East Metropolitan Railways (proposed)
    Parliamentary papers, **RAIL 1066**
East Norfolk Railway, **RAIL 180**
    Parliamentary papers, **RAIL 1066**
    Prospectuses etc, **RAIL 1075**
    Reports and accounts, **RAIL 1110**
East of Fife Railway
    Parliamentary papers, **RAIL 1163**
    Share certificates, **RAIL 1158**
East of London and Crystal Palace Railway (proposed)
    Parliamentary papers, **RAIL 1066**
East of London, Crystal Palace and South Eastern Junction Railway (proposed)
    Parliamentary papers, **RAIL 1066**

Easton and Church Hope Railway, **RAIL 188**
   Instructions to staff of GWR and LSWR about
     working, **RAIL 1135**
   Maps, **RAIL 1030**
   Parliamentary papers, **RAIL 1066**
   Prospectuses etc, **RAIL 1075**
   Reports and accounts, **RAIL 1110;**
     RAIL 1116
  See also BTC Chief Secretary's Office
   GWR Secretary's papers; estates and rating
Easton Neston Mineral and Towcester, Roade and
  Olney Junction Railway
   Parliamentary papers, **RAIL 1066**
East Somerset Railway, **RAIL 181**
   GWR miscellanea, **RAIL 1014**
   Reports and accounts, **RAIL 1110; RAIL 1116**
   Timetables, **RAIL 981**
East Suffolk Railway, **RAIL 182** (Eastern Counties
  R *records*)
   Joint committee with:
     Eastern Counties R, **RAIL 185**
   Prospectuses etc, **RAIL 1076**
   Reports and accounts, **RAIL 1116; RAIL 1117**
East Sussex Light Railway
   Miscellanea, **RAIL 1057**
East Usk Junction Railway (proposed)
   Prospectuses etc, **RAIL 1075**
East Usk Railway, **RAIL 183**
   Parliamentary papers, **RAIL 1066**
   Reports and accounts, **RAIL 1110**
Ebbw Valley and Cardiff Junction Railway
  (proposed)
   Miscellanea, **RAIL 1057**
Eden Valley Railway, **RAIL 189** (*includes records of
  predecessor* Westmoreland R *and successors* S&DR
  and NER)
   Miscellanea, **RAIL 1157**
   Parliamentary papers, **RAIL 1067**
   Prospectuses etc, **RAIL 1076; RAIL 1076**
   Reports and accounts, **RAIL 1116; RAIL 1117**
   Share certificates, **RAIL 1159**
   Subscription contracts, **RAIL 1161**
Edgware and Hampstead Railway
   Parliamentary papers, **RAIL 1066**
Edgware, Highgate and London Railway,
  RAIL 190
   Parliamentary papers, **RAIL 1066**
   Reports and accounts, **RAIL 1116**
  See also GNR working plans & sections
Edgware Road and Victoria Railway (proposed)
   Parliamentary papers, **RAIL 1066**
Edinburgh and Bathgate Railway
   Reports and accounts, **RAIL 1116**
   Share certificates, **RAIL 1158**
Edinburgh and District Tramways
   Reports and accounts, **RAIL 1114**
Edinburgh and Glasgow Railway

   Miscellanea, **RAIL 1014**
   Parliamentary papers, **RAIL 1163**
   Prospectuses etc, **RAIL 1075**
   Reports and accounts, **RAIL 1111; RAIL 1116;**
     RAIL 1117
   Rule books, **RAIL 1134**
   Share certificates, **RAIL 1158**
   Timetables, **RAIL 981**
Edinburgh and Northern Railway
   Share certificates, **RAIL 1158**
Edinburgh City Tramways
   Reports and accounts, **RAIL 1114**
Edinburgh, Glasgow and Leith Railway
  (proposed)
   Miscellanea, **RAIL 1057**
Edinburgh, Leith and Glasgow Railway (proposed)
   Prospectuses etc, **RAIL 1075**
Edinburgh, Leith and Granton Railway
   Share certificates, **RAIL 1158**
Edinburgh, Leith and Newhaven Railway
   Share certificates, **RAIL 1158**
Edinburgh, Loanhead and Roslyn Railway
   Share certificates, **RAIL 1158**
Edinburgh, Perth and Dundee Railway
   Miscellanea, **RAIL 1020**
   Reports and accounts, **RAIL 1116; RAIL 1117**
   Rule books, **RAIL 1134**
   Share certificates, **RAIL 1158**
   Timetables, **RAIL 981**
Edinburgh Suburban and Southside Junction
  Railway
   Share certificates, **RAIL 1158**
Elham Valley Light Railway
   Parliamentary papers, **RAIL 1066**
Elham Valley Railway, **RAIL 191**
Ellesmere and Whitchurch Railway (proposed)
   Subscription contracts, **RAIL 1160**
Ellesmere, Ruabon and Shrewsbury Railway
  (proposed)
   Parliamentary papers, **RAIL 1066**
Ely and Bury St Edmunds Light Railway
   Parliamentary papers, **RAIL 1066**
Ely and Clydach Valleys Railway, **RAIL 192**
   Parliamentary papers, **RAIL 1066**
   Reports and accounts, **RAIL 1110**
Ely and Newmarket Railway, **RAIL 193**
   Parliamentary papers, **RAIL 1066**
   Reports and accounts, **RAIL 1110;**
     RAIL 1117
Ely and Ogmore Valley Junction Railway
  (proposed)
   Parliamentary papers, **RAIL 1066**
Ely and St Ives Railway, **RAIL 194** (*includes records
  of predecessor* Ely, Haddenham & Sutton R)
   Reports and accounts, **RAIL 1110**
Ely, Haddenham and Sutton Railway, **RAIL 194**
   Reports and accounts, **RAIL 1110**

Ely Tidal Harbour and Railway
  Miscellanea, **RAIL 1057**
  Subscription contracts, **RAIL 1160**
See also Penarth Harbour Dock & R
Ely Valley and Vale of Neath Junction Railway
  (proposed)
  Parliamentary papers, **RAIL 1066**
Ely Valley Railway, **RAIL 195**
  Miscellanea, **RAIL 1057**
  Railway and Canal Traffic Acts proceedings,
    RAIL 1038
  Reports and accounts, **RAIL 1110**
Ennerdale Railway (proposed)
  Map, **RAIL 1030**
  Parliamentary papers, **RAIL 1066**
Enniskillen, Bundoran and Sligo Railway
  Railway & Canal Traffic Acts proceedings,
    RAIL 1038
Epping Railways, **RAIL 196**
Epsom and Leatherhead Railway, **RAIL 197**
  (*includes records of* LBSCR/LSWR Jt Cttee)
  Parliamentary papers, **RAIL 1066**
  Prospectuses etc, **RAIL 1075**
  Reports and accounts, **RAIL 1116**
Epsom Downs Extension Railway,
    RAIL 198
  Parliamentary papers, **RAIL 1066**
  Share certificates, **RAIL 1158**
Erewash Valley Railway
  Parliamentary plans, **RAIL 1071**
Erith Urban District Council Tramways
  Reports and accounts, **RAIL 1114**
Esk Valley Railway
  Reports and accounts, **RAIL 1116**
  Share certificates, **RAIL 1158**
Essex and Suffolk Railway (proposed)
  Prospectuses etc, **RAIL 1075**
Euston, St Pancras and Charing Cross Railway
  (proposed)
  Parliamentary papers, **RAIL 1066**
Evercreech, Keinton Mandeville and Somerton
  Tramway Syndicate
  Miscellanea, **RAIL 1057**
Evesham and Redditch Railway, **RAIL 199**
  Miscellanea, **RAIL 1057**
  Parliamentary papers, **RAIL 1066**
  Railway and Canal Traffic Acts proceedings,
    RAIL 1038
Evesham, Redditch and Stratford-upon-Avon
  Junction Railway, **RAIL 777**
  Parliamentary papers, **RAIL 1066**
Exemouth Docks and Railway
  Railway and Canal Traffic Acts proceedings,
    RAIL 1038
Exe Valley Railway, **RAIL 200**
  Miscellanea, **RAIL 1057**
  Parliamentary papers, **RAIL 1066**

Exeter and Chagford Railway (proposed)
  Miscellanea, **RAIL 1057**
Exeter and Crediton Railway, **RAIL 201**
  Miscellanea, **RAIL 1014**
  Parliamentary papers, **RAIL 1066**
  Reports and accounts, **RAIL 1110; RAIL 1116**
  Subscription contracts, **RAIL 1160**
Exeter and Exmouth Railway
  Parliamentary papers, **RAIL 1163**
  Reports and accounts, **RAIL 1116**
See also S Devon R
Exeter and Great Western Junction Railway
  (proposed)
  Map, **RAIL 1014**
Exeter and South Western Junction Railway
  (proposed)
  Prospectuses etc, **RAIL 1075**
Exeter Great Western Railway (proposed),
    RAIL 202
Exeter, Plymouth and Devonport Railway
  (proposed)
  Prospectuses etc, **RAIL 1075**
Exeter Railway, **RAIL 203** (*includes records of*
  predecessors Teign Valley R *and* Exeter, Teign
  Valley & Chagford R)
  Law cases and arbitration, **RAIL 1027**
  Miscellanea, **RAIL 1057**
  Reports and accounts, **RAIL 1110**
Exeter, Teign Valley and Chagford Railway,
    RAIL 203
  Law cases and arbitration, **RAIL 1027**
  Miscellanea, **RAIL 1014; RAIL 1057**
  Prospectus, **RAIL 1110**
Eyemouth Railway
  Share certificates, **RAIL 1158**
Fairbourne Miniature Railway
  Miscellanea, **RAIL 1057**
Fairford and Cirencester Railway (proposed)
  Parliamentary papers, **RAIL 1066**
Fakenham and Melton Railway (proposed)
  Parliamentary papers, **RAIL 1066**
Falkirk to Greenock and Glasgow Railway
  (proposed) *see* Junction R
Faringdon Railway, **RAIL 204**
  Miscellanea, **RAIL 1057**
  Reports and accounts, **RAIL 1110**
Felixstowe, Ipswich and Midland Railway
  (proposed)
  Miscellanea, **RAIL 1057**
Felixstowe Railway and Dock Company (*formerly*
  Felixstowe R & Pier Co)
  Railway and Canal Traffic Acts proceedings,
    RAIL 1038
  Reports and accounts, **RAIL 1110**
Fermoy and Lismore Railway
  Railway and Canal Traffic Acts proceedings,
    RAIL 1038

Festiniog and Blaenau Railway, **RAIL 205**
    Prospectuses etc, **RAIL 1075**
    Reports and accounts, **RAIL 1110**
Festiniog Railway
    Miscellanea, **RAIL 1057**
    Railway and Canal Traffic Acts proceedings,
        RAIL 1038
    Reports and accounts, **RAIL 1110; RAIL 1116;
        RAIL 1117**
    Timetables, **RAIL 981**
Fife and Kinross Railway
    Share certificates, **RAIL 1158**
Finn Valley Railway
    Railway and Canal Traffic Acts proceedings,
        RAIL 1038
See also Irish & English Traffic Conference
Firbeck Light Railway (NER)
    Parliamentary papers, **RAIL 1066**
Fishguard and Rosslare Railways and Harbours
    Company, **RAIL 206** (*joint enterprise between*
    GWR *and* Great Southern & Western R of
    Ireland; *after 1925* GWR/Great Southern Rys;
    after 1944 GWR/Coras Iompair Eireann; *after*
    1948 BR(WR)/CIE)
    Miscellanea, **RAIL 1057**
    Parliamentary papers, **RAIL 1066**
    Reports and accounts, **RAIL 1110;
        RAIL 1116**
Fleetwood, Preston and West Riding Junction
    Railway, **RAIL 207**
    Parliamentary papers, **RAIL 1066**
    Reports and accounts, **RAIL 1116**
    Share certificates, **RAIL 1158**
    Timetables, **RAIL 981**
Flintshire Railway (proposed)
    Parliamentary papers, **RAIL 1066**
    Prospectuses etc, **RAIL 1075**
Folkestone, Sandgate and Hythe Tramways
    Parliamentary papers, **RAIL 1066; RAIL 1068**
Forcett Railway, **RAIL 208**
    Reports and accounts, **RAIL 1110; RAIL 1117**
Forest of Dean Central Railway, **RAIL 209**
    Miscellanea, **RAIL 1014; RAIL 1057**
    Reports and accounts, **RAIL 1110; RAIL 1116**
    Share certificates, **RAIL 1158**
    Subscription contracts, **RAIL 1160**
See also GWR Secretary's papers; estates and
    rating
Forest of Dean Railway, **RAIL 210**
Forest of Dean Tramroad
    Miscellanea, **RAIL 1005**
Formartine and Buchan Railway
    Reports and accounts, **RAIL 1116**
Forth and Clyde Junction Railway
    Reports and accounts, **RAIL 1110; RAIL 1116;
        RAIL 1117**
    Share certificates, **RAIL 1158**

Forth Bridge Railway
    Parliamentary papers, **RAIL 1066; RAIL 1067**
    Reports and accounts, **RAIL 1116; RAIL 1117**
    Share certificates, **RAIL 1158**
See also BTC Chief Secretary's Office
Foxdale Railway
    Reports and accounts, **RAIL 1116**
Freightliners Ltd, **AN 115**
Freshwater, Yarmouth and Newport Railway,
    RAIL 211
    Miscellanea, **RAIL 1017**
    Parliamentary papers, **RAIL 1066**
    Reports and accounts, **RAIL 1110; RAIL 1116**
    Share certificates, **RAIL 1158**
    Timetables, **RAIL 981**
Frome, Yeovil and Weymouth Railway (proposed)
    Prospectuses etc, **RAIL 1075**
Frosterley and Stanhope Railway, **RAIL 212**
Fulham and Walham Green Railway (proposed)
    Miscellanea, **RAIL 1057**
    Parliamentary papers, **RAIL 1066**
Fulham Railway
    Miscellanea, **RAIL 1057**
Furness Railway, **RAIL 214**
    Byelaws and regulations, **RAIL 1003**
        (Barrow Docks)
    Hotels, **RAIL 1022**
    Joint committees with:
        Cleator & Workington Jct R, **RAIL 119**
        LNWR, **RAIL 403; RAIL 410; RAIL 421**
            Railway and Canal Traffic Acts
                proceedings, **RAIL 1038**
            Rule books, **RAIL 1134**
            See also LMSR miscellanea
        MR, **RAIL 213** (Carnforth & Wennington
            line)
        Whitehaven, Cleator & Egremont R,
            RAIL 118 (Cleator & Furness R)
    Law cases and arbitration, **RAIL 1027**
    Miscellanea, **RAIL 1007; RAIL 1014;
        RAIL 1015; RAIL 1020; RAIL 1057**
    Parliamentary papers, **RAIL 1066; RAIL 1163**
    Parliamentary plans, **RAIL 1071**
    Railway and Canal Traffic Acts proceedings,
        RAIL 1038
    Reports and accounts, **RAIL 1110; RAIL 1116;
        RAIL 1117**
    Rule books, **RAIL 1134**
    Share certificates, **RAIL 1158**
    Timetables, **RAIL 981**
    Traders' ledger credit agreements, **RAIL 1165**
See also Irish & English Traffic Conference
    LMSR amalgamation
Galway and Belfast Junction Railway (proposed)
    Prospectuses etc, **RAIL 1075**
Galway and Clifden Railway
    Prospectus, **RAIL 1116**

Galway and Kilkenny Railway
    Prospectuses etc, **RAIL 1075**
Galway, Oughterard and Clifden Railway
    Prospectus, **RAIL 1116**
Garstang and Knott End Railway, **RAIL 215**
    Parliamentary papers, **RAIL 1066**
    Railway and Canal Traffic Acts proceedings,
        RAIL 1038
    Reports and accounts, **RAIL 1116**
See also Knott End R
        LMSR amalgamation
Garston and Liverpool Railway
    Byelaws and regulations, **RAIL 1001**
    Parliamentary papers, **RAIL 1066**
Garston and Liverpool Railway Committee
    (GNR/MS&LR; *after 1865* MR), **RAIL 216**
Garturk and Garion Railway (*later* Wishaw &
    Coltness R *q.v.*)
    Subscription contracts, **RAIL 1163**
General Metropolitan Terminus and Extension
    Railway (proposed)
    Prospectuses etc, **RAIL 1075**
General Terminus and Glasgow Harbour
    Railway
    Reports and accounts, **RAIL 1116; RAIL 1117**
Girvan and Portpatrick Junction Railway
    Parliamentary papers, **RAIL 1066**
    Reports and accounts, **RAIL 1116**
Glasgow and Milngavie Junction Railway
    Reports and accounts, **RAIL 1116**
Glasgow and Portpatrick Railway
    Reports and accounts, **RAIL 1116**
Glasgow and South Western Railway
    Joint committees with:
        Cal R/LNWR
            Carlisle goods traffic, **RAIL 98; RAIL 410;**
                RAIL 421
            Portpatrick & Wigtownshire Jt R,
                RAIL 421
        MR, **RAIL 486**
            Carlisle goods traffic, **RAIL 98; RAIL 410;**
                RAIL 421
    Law cases and arbitration, **RAIL 1027**
    Maps, **RAIL 1030**
    Miscellanea, **RAIL 1014; RAIL 1057**
    Parliamentary papers, **RAIL 1066; RAIL 1163**
    Railway and Canal Traffic Acts proceedings,
        RAIL 1038
    Reports and accounts, **RAIL 1110; RAIL 1116;**
        RAIL 1117
    Rule books, **RAIL 1134**
    Savings bank rules, **RAIL 1174**
    Share certificates, **RAIL 1158**
    Superannuation schemes, **RAIL 1174**
    Timetables, **RAIL 929; RAIL 981**
See also Irish & English Traffic Conference
    LMSR amalgamation

Glasgow, Bothwell, Hamilton and Coatbridge
    Railway
    Parliamentary papers, **RAIL 1066**
    Share certificates, **RAIL 1158**
Glasgow City and District Railway
    Share certificates, **RAIL 1158**
Glasgow Corporation Tramways
    Reports and accounts, **RAIL 1114**
Glasgow District Subway Company
    Reports and accounts, **RAIL 1116; RAIL 1117**
Glasgow, Dumbarton and Helensburgh Railway
    Parliamentary papers, **RAIL 1163**
    Reports and accounts, **RAIL 1116**
    Share certificates, **RAIL 1158**
    Timetables, **RAIL 981**
Glasgow, Dumfries and Carlisle Railway
    Reports and accounts, **RAIL 1110**
    Rule books, **RAIL 1134**
Glasgow, Paisley and Greenock Railway
    Prospectuses etc, **RAIL 1075**
Glasgow, Paisley, Kilmarnock and Ayr Railway
    Reports and accounts, **RAIL 1110**
    Rule books, **RAIL 1134**
    Timetables, **RAIL 981**
Glasgow Union Railway (proposed)
    Parliamentary papers, **RAIL 1066**
Glasgow, Yoker and Clydebank Railway
    Share certificates, **RAIL 1158**
Gloucester and Cheltenham Railway
    Miscellanea, **RAIL 1005; RAIL 1057**
See also GWR
    MR Gloucester & Cheltenham R
        abandonment
Gloucester and Dean Forest Railway, **RAIL 217**
    Prospectus (Dean Forest & Gloucester R),
        RAIL 1014
    Reports and accounts, **RAIL 1110; RAIL 1116;**
        RAIL 1117
See also Dean Forest & Gloucester R
Gloucester and Hereford Railway (proposed)
    Prospectuses etc, **RAIL 1075**
Gloucester and Ledbury Railway (proposed)
    Parliamentary papers, **RAIL 1066**
Gloucester, Ross and Hereford Railway (proposed)
    Prospectuses etc, **RAIL 1075**
Glyncorrwg, Rhondda and Swansea Junction
    Railway (proposed)
    Miscellanea, **RAIL 1057**
    Parliamentary papers, **RAIL 1066**
Glyn Valley Tramway
    Reports and accounts, **RAIL 1116**
    Timetables, **RAIL 981**
Golden Valley Railway, **RAIL 218**
    Miscellanea, **RAIL 1057**
    Parliamentary papers, **RAIL 1066**
    Prospectuses etc, **RAIL 1075; RAIL 1110;**
        RAIL 1116

Railway and Canal Traffic Acts proceedings, **RAIL 1038**
Reports and accounts, **RAIL 1110; RAIL 1116**
Goole and Doncaster and Sheffield and Manchester Junction Railway (proposed)
Prospectus, **RAIL 1151**
Goole and Marshland Light Railway, **RAIL 219**
See also Axholme Jt R Cttee
Goole, Epworth and Owston Railway (proposed)
Parliamentary papers, **RAIL 1066; RAIL 1067**
Gorsedda Junction and Portmadoc Railway
Miscellanea, **RAIL 1057**
Railway and Canal Traffic Acts proceedings, **RAIL 1038**
Gosforth and Ponteland Light Railway *see* NER
Goxlodge Waggonway
Miscellanea, **RAIL 1157**
Grand Eastern Counties Railway (proposed)
Prospectuses etc, **RAIL 1075**
Grand Eastern Union Railway (proposed)
Prospectuses etc, **RAIL 1076**
Grand Junction and Midlands Union Railway (proposed)
Prospectuses etc, **RAIL 1075**
Grand Junction Great Western and South Western Junction Railway (proposed)
Miscellanea, **RAIL 1020; RAIL 1153**
Grand Junction Railway, **RAIL 220** (*includes records of* LNWR)
Joint committee with:
Manchester & Leeds R/North Union R, **RAIL 220; RAIL 534**
Maps, **RAIL 1030**
Miscellanea, **RAIL 1008; RAIL 1015; RAIL 1152**
Parliamentary papers, **RAIL 1147**
Parliamentary plans, **RAIL 1071**
Prospectuses etc, **RAIL 1075**
Reports and accounts, **RAIL 1110**
Subscription contracts, **RAIL 1160**
Timetables, **RAIL 981**
Grand Northern Trunk Railway (proposed) *see* Drogheda R
Grand Southern Railroad (proposed)
Prospectuses etc, **RAIL 1075**
Gravesend and Northfleet Docks and Railways (proposed)
Parliamentary papers, **RAIL 1066**
Gravesend and Northfleet Electric Tramways
Reports and accounts, **RAIL 1114**
Gravesend Embankment Landing Stage and Railway (proposed)
Parliamentary papers, **RAIL 1066**
Gravesend Railway, **RAIL 221** (*includes records of* LCDR *and* SECR)
Parliamentary papers, **RAIL 1066**

Gravesend, Northfleet and London Chatham and Dover Railway (proposed)
Parliamentary papers, **RAIL 1066**
Great Central Railway, **RAIL 226** (*includes records of* LNER *and* MSLR)
Byelaws and regulations, **RAIL 1001**
Instructions to staff, **RAIL 1135**
Joint committees with:
GNR, **RAIL 462**
GWR
Byelaws and regulations, **RAIL 1001**
Map, **RAIL 1014**
Parliamentary plans, **RAIL 1071**
Reports and accounts, **RAIL 1110; RAIL 1116; RAIL 1117**
Rule books, **RAIL 1134**
Sidings agreements, **RAIL 1167**
Timetables, **RAIL 981**
RAIL 239 (Banbury Jct R)
H&BR
Reports and accounts, **RAIL 1110; RAIL 1111; RAIL 1116** (GCR/H&BR/MR Jt Cttee)
RAIL 225 (Braithwell Jct to Laughton Jct line)
Byelaws and regulations, **RAIL 1001**
RAIL 310 (Gowdell to Braithwell line)
LNWR, **RAIL 421**
Reports and accounts, **RAIL 1110**
RAIL 410, RAIL 421; RAIL 435 (Manchester London Rd Station)
RAIL 465 (Manchester S Jct & Altrincham line)
Reports and accounts, **RAIL 1116**
Timetables, **RAIL 930**
Met R
Reports and accounts, **RAIL 1110; RAIL 1116**
Rule books, **RAIL 1134**
Sidings agreements, **RAIL 1167**
RAIL 223 (Quainton Rd to Canfield Pl)
MR, **RAIL 224; RAIL 462**
Byelaws and regulations, **RAIL 1001**
Instructions to staff, **RAIL 1135**
Parliamentary papers, **RAIL 1163**
Reports and accounts, **RAIL 1110; RAIL 1111; RAIL 1116** (GCR/H & BR/MR Jt Cttee; GCR/MR Jt Cttee)
Traders' ledger credit agreements, **RAIL 1165**
RAIL 225 (Braithwell Jct to Laughton Jct line)
Byelaws and regulations, **RAIL 1001**
N Staffordshire R
Byelaws and regulations, **RAIL 1001**
Reports and accounts, **RAIL 1110; RAIL 1116**

RAIL 448 (Macclesfield, Bollington &
   Marple R)
      Byelaws and regulations, **RAIL 1001**
      Reports and accounts, **RAIL 1110**
   Wrexham, Mold & Connah's Quay R
      RAIL 535 (Dee & Birkenhead; N Wales &
         Liverpool R)
See also Cheshire Lines Cttee
   Humber Conference
   Nottingham Jt Station Cttee
   Oldham, Ashton-under-Lyne & Guide
      Bridge Jct R Oldham R Cttee
   Stalybridge Jt Station Cttee
   S Yorkshire Jt Line Cttee
   W Riding R Jt Cttee
Labour and staff matters, **RAIL 1025**
Law cases and arbitration, **RAIL 1027**
Maps, **RAIL 1030**
Miscellanea, **RAIL 1005; RAIL 1007;**
   RAIL 1016; RAIL 1020; RAIL 1151;
   RAIL 1057
Parliamentary papers, **RAIL 1066; RAIL 1163**
Parliamentary plans, **RAIL 1071**
Prospectuses etc, **RAIL 1075**
Reports and accounts, **RAIL 1110; RAIL 1116;**
   RAIL 1117
Rule books, **RAIL 1134**
Savings bank rules, **RAIL 1174**
Share certificates, **RAIL 1158**
Sidings agreements, **RAIL 1167**
Superannuation funds, **RAIL 1174**
Timetables, **RAIL 931; RAIL 981**
   Working timetables appendixes,
      RAIL 1136
   Traders' ledger credit agreements,
      RAIL 1165
   Welfare schemes, **RAIL 1115; RAIL 1174**
See also Humber Warehousing & Transport Co
   Irish & English Traffic Conference
   LNER deeds; contracts etc; locomotives and
      rolling stock; miscellanea
   LMSR amalgamation
   MSLR
Great Eastern Northern Junction Railway
   (proposed)
      Miscellanea, **RAIL 1057**
      Parliamentary papers, **RAIL 1066**
Great Eastern Railway, RAIL 227 (*includes records*
   of Eastern Counties R, LNER *and records of or*
   about Wisbech, Outwell & Upwell Tramway)
      Byelaws and regulations, **RAIL 1003**
         (Lowestoft Harbour)
      Instructions to staff, **RAIL 1135**
      Joint committees with:
         GNR, **RAIL 233; RAIL 393**
            Byelaws and regulations, **RAIL 1001;**
               RAIL 1003 (Fossdyke Navigation)

Reports and accounts, **RAIL 1110;**
   RAIL 1116
Rule books, **RAIL 1134**
L&YR
   RAIL 340 (proposed L&Y/GE jct line)
LNWR
   Reports and accounts, **RAIL 1116**
See also E London R
   Norfolk & Suffolk Rys Cttee
   Tottenham & Hampstead Jct R
Labour and staff matters, **RAIL 1025**
Law cases and arbitration, **RAIL 1027**
Maps, **RAIL 1030**
Miscellanea, **RAIL 1014; RAIL 1016;**
   RAIL 1020; RAIL 1057
Parliamentary papers, **RAIL 1066**
Railway and Canal Traffic Acts proceedings,
   RAIL 1038
Railway Rates Tribunal proceedings,
   RAIL 1101
Reports and accounts, **RAIL 1110; RAIL 1116;**
   RAIL 1117
Rule books, **RAIL 1134**
Savings bank, **RAIL 1174**
Share certificates, **RAIL 1158**
Superannuation schemes, **RAIL 1174**
Timetables
   Continental, **RAIL 932; RAIL 976**
   Public, **RAIL 933; RAIL 981**
   Working, **RAIL 933**
      Working timetables appendices,
         RAIL 1136
   E London R, **RAIL 927**
Traders' ledger credit agreements,
   RAIL 1165
Welfare schemes, **RAIL 1115; RAIL 1174**
See also Irish & English Traffic Conference
   LNER deeds contracts etc; locomotives and
      rolling stock; miscellanea
   LMSR amalgamation
   Norfolk R
Greater London Railway (proposed)
   Parliamentary papers, **RAIL 1066**
Great Grimsby and Sheffield Junction Railway,
   RAIL 228 (*includes records of* MSLR)
   Joint committee with:
      Sheffield & Lincolnshire Jct R, **RAIL 229**
   Maps, **RAIL 1030**
   Miscellanea, **RAIL 1151**
   Reports and accounts, **RAIL 1110**
Great Leinster and Munster Railway
   Prospectuses etc, **RAIL 1075**
Great Marlow Railway, **RAIL 230**
   Byelaws and regulations, **RAIL 1001**
   Prospectuses etc, **RAIL 1075**
   Railway and Canal Traffic Acts proceedings,
      RAIL 1038

Reports and accounts, **RAIL 1110**
See also GWR miscellanea
Great North and South Wales and Worcester
Railway (proposed)
Miscellanea, **RAIL 1057**
Prospectus, **RAIL 1014**
Great North British Railway (proposed)
Prospectuses etc, **RAIL 1075; RAIL 1076**
Great Northern and City Railway
Parliamentary papers, **RAIL 1066**
Prospectuses etc, **RAIL 1075; RAIL 1116**
Reports and accounts, **RAIL 1110; RAIL 1116;**
RAIL 1117
Great Northern and Strand Railway
Parliamentary papers, **RAIL 1066**
Great Northern and Western Railway
Reports and accounts, **RAIL 1116;**
RAIL 1117
Great Northern Kirkstead and Little Steeping
Light Railway
Parliamentary papers, **RAIL 1066**
Great Northern, Piccadilly and Brompton R
(*formerly* Brompton & Piccadilly Circus R)
Maps, **RAIL 1030**
Parliamentary papers, **RAIL 1066**
Reports and accounts, **RAIL 1110**
Rule books, **RAIL 1134**
See also London Electric Rys
Underground Electric Rys Co
Great Northern Railway, **RAIL 236** *includes records*
of or about:
BR(ER)
Cambridge & York R
Direct Northern R
E Lincolnshire R (rolling stock)
GWR (rolling stock)
Leeds, Dewsbury & Manchester R (rolling
stock)
LNER
London & York R
North Staffordshire R (rolling stock)
Tickhill Lt R
Byelaws and regulations, **RAIL 1001;**
RAIL 1003 (Canals)
Correspondence, **RAIL 783**
Instructions to staff, **RAIL 1135**
Joint committees correspondence, **RAIL 783**
Joint committees with:
GCR
Reports and accounts, **RAIL 1110**
GER, **RAIL 233; RAIL 393**
Byelaws and regulations, **RAIL 1001;**
RAIL 1003 (Fossdyke Navigation)
Reports and accounts, **RAIL 1110;**
RAIL 1116
Rule books, **RAIL 1134**
L&YR

Byelaws and regulations, **RAIL 1001**
RAIL 341 (joint stations)
Leeds & Thirsk R, **RAIL 354** (Leeds Central
station)
Leeds, Dewsbury & Manchester R,
RAIL 354 (Leeds Central station)
Leeds Northern R, **RAIL 354** (Leeds Central
station)
LNWR, **RAIL 234; RAIL 408; RAIL 410;**
RAIL 421
Byelaws and regulations, **RAIL 1001**
Reports and accounts, **RAIL 1110;**
RAIL 1116
RAIL 341; RAIL 410 (joint stations)
MSLR, **RAIL 235; RAIL 236** (Officers'
Conference); **RAIL 461**
Timetables, **RAIL 925**
RAIL 736 (W Riding & Grimsby R *and*
Wakefield station)
MR
Timetables, **RAIL 961; RAIL 981**
RAIL 236 (GNR/MR Jt Railway Officers'
Meeting)
RAIL 736 (Wakefield station)
NBR
Timetables, **RAIL 926** (East Coast Route)
NER
Timetables, **RAIL 926** (East Coast Route)
See also Cheshire Lines Committee
E Coast (Railway Companies) Conference
Garston & Liverpool R Cttee
Halifax & Ovenden Jt Cttee
Halifax High Level R Jt Cttee
Leeds Central Station
London & W Riding Association
Methley R Jt Cttee
Norfolk & Suffolk Jt Rys Cttee
Nottingham Jt Station Cttee
S Yorkshire Jt Line Cttee
W Riding R Jt Cttee
Labour and staff matters, **RAIL 1025**
Law cases and arbitration, **RAIL 1027**
Maps, **RAIL 1030**
Miscellanea, **RAIL 1007; RAIL 1008; RAIL 1014;**
RAIL 1016; RAIL 1020; RAIL 1057;
RAIL 1151; RAIL 1153; RAIL 1157
Notices, **RAIL 981**
Parliamentary papers, **RAIL 1066; RAIL 1163**
Prospectuses etc, **RAIL 1075**
Railway and Canal Traffic Acts proceedings,
RAIL 1038
Reports and accounts, **RAIL 1110; RAIL 1116;**
RAIL 1117
Rule books, **RAIL 1134**
Savings bank, **RAIL 1174**
Share certificates, **RAIL 1158; RAIL 1159**
Sidings agreements, **RAIL 1167**

Subscription contracts, **RAIL 1160**
Superannuation Fund, **RAIL 1174**
Surveyor and Estate Agent correspondence,
   RAIL 1189
Timetables, **RAIL 925** (GNR/MS&LR jt lines);
   RAIL 926 (East Coast Route, GNR/NER/
   NBR); **RAIL 935**; **RAIL 981**
     Working timetables appendixes, **RAIL 1136**
Traders' ledger credit agreements, **RAIL 1165**
Welfare fund accounts etc, **RAIL 1115;**
   RAIL 1174
Working plans and sections, **RAIL 796**
   (*includes records of* Edgware, Highgate &
   London R)
See also E Lincolnshire R
   Irish & English Traffic Conference
   LNER accountant; deeds contracts etc;
     locomotives and rolling stock; miscellanea
   LMSR amalgamation
Great Northern Railway (*Ireland*)
   Joint committees with:
     Dublin & South Eastern R/City of Dublin
      Steam Packet Co, **RAIL 1117** (City of
      Dublin Jct R, reports & accounts)
     MR, **RAIL 137** (County Donegal Rys)
   Miscellanea, **RAIL 1057**
   Parliamentary papers, **RAIL 1066**
   Railway and Canal Traffic Acts proceedings,
     RAIL 1038
   Reports and accounts, **RAIL 1110; RAIL 1116;**
     RAIL 1117
   Timetables, **RAIL 941**
     Working timetables appendixes, **RAIL 1136**
See also Irish & English Traffic Conference
Great North of England, Clarence and Hartlepool
   Junction Railway, **RAIL 231**
   Prospectuses etc, **RAIL 1076**
   Reports and accounts, **RAIL 1116**
Great North of England Railway, **RAIL 232**
   (*includes records of* NER; York & Newcastle R *and*
   York, Newcastle & Berwick R)
   Joint committees with:
     York & N Midland R;
      RAIL 232 (York station)
      RAIL 772 (lease and sale of GNoER)
   Miscellanea, **RAIL 1157**
   Parliamentary papers, **RAIL 1016; RAIL 1067**
   Prospectuses etc, **RAIL 1075; RAIL 1076**
   Rule books, **RAIL 1134**
   Share certificates, **RAIL 1159**
   Subscription contracts, **RAIL 1161**
   Timetables, **RAIL 981**
See also NER
Great North of Scotland Railway
   Maps, **RAIL 1030**
   Miscellanea, **RAIL 1016; RAIL 1057**
   Parliamentary papers, **RAIL 1163**

Railway and Canal Traffic Acts proceedings,
   RAIL 1038
Reports and accounts, **RAIL 1110; RAIL 1111;**
   RAIL 1116; RAIL 1117
Savings bank rules, **RAIL 1174**
Share certificates, **RAIL 1158**
Timetables, **RAIL 934; RAIL 981**
See also Deeside R
Great Southern and Western Railway
   Miscellanea, **RAIL 1014**
   Parliamentary papers, **RAIL 1066; RAIL 1163**
   Parliamentary plans, **RAIL 1071**
   Railway and Canal Traffic Acts proceedings,
     RAIL 1038
   Reports and accounts, **RAIL 1110; RAIL 1116;**
     RAIL 1117
   Rule books, **RAIL 1134**
   Timetables, **RAIL 941**
See also Fishguard & Rosslare Rys & Harbours Co
   Irish & English Traffic Conference
   LMSR amalgamation
Great Southern Railway(s)
   Reports and accounts, **RAIL 1110; RAIL 1116;**
     RAIL 1117
   Timetables, **RAIL 941**
     Working timetables appendixes, **RAIL 1136**
See also Fishguard & Rosslare Rys & Harbours Co
   Irish & English Traffic Conference
Great Western, Amersham and Aylesbury Railway
   (proposed)
     Parliamentary papers, **RAIL 1066**
Great Western and Brentford Railway, **RAIL 237**
   Parliamentary papers, **RAIL 1163**
   Reports and accounts, **RAIL 1110; RAIL 1116;**
     RAIL 1117
Great Western and City Junction Railway
   (proposed)
     Subscription contract, **RAIL 1163**
Great Western and Cornwall Junction Railway
   (proposed)
     Prospectuses etc, **RAIL 1075**
Great Western and Uxbridge Railway, **RAIL 247**
   (*includes records of* GWR)
Great Western and Wycombe Railway (*or*
   Wycombe R *q.v.*)
     Prospectuses etc, **RAIL 1075**
Great Western Railway
   Accidents, **RAIL 270**
   Accountant's records, **RAIL 272**
   Air services (GWR Air Services and Railway
     Air Services), **RAIL 253; RAIL 257;**
     RAIL 1014
   Birkenhead line, dispute with LNWR,
     RAIL 1194
   Bute Docks byelaws, **RAIL 1001**
   Byelaws and regulations, **RAIL 1001**
   Ceremonial, **RAIL 1009**

GWR (continued)
   Chief Mechanical Engineer's Department
      circulars, **RAIL 1182**
   Civil Engineer's records, **RAIL 273**
   Contract documents, **RAIL 1190**
   Correspondence and papers, **RAIL 257**
      (*including records of or about*: Cornwall R;
      Malmesbury R; Railway Air Services;
      Staines & W Drayton R)
   Deeds contracts etc, **RAIL 252**
   Estates and rating, **RAIL 274** *including records*
      of or about:
      Bala & Festiniog R
      Bristol & N Somerset R
      Bristol Port R & Pier Co
      Carmarthen & Cardigan R
      Coleford, Monmouth, Usk & Pontypool R
      Corwen & Bala R
      Devon & Somerset R
      Didcot, Newbury & Southampton R
      Ealing & Shepherd's Bush R
      E Gloucestershire R
      Easton & Church Hope R
      Forest of Dean Central R
      Hall's Tramway (Penar Branch)
      Kington & Eardisley R
      Ledbury & Gloucester line (Newent R *and*
         Ross & Ledbury R)
      Leominster & Kington R
      Liskeard & Looe R
      Llynvi & Ogmore R
      Milford R
      Much Wenlock & Severn Jct R
      Nantwich & Market Drayton R
      Rhondda & Swansea Bay R
      Rhymney R Jt Cttee
      Ross & Monmouth R
      Severn & Wye & Severn Bridge R
      Wellington & Severn Jct R
      Wenlock R
      W London Extension R
      Weymouth & Portland R
      Whitland & Cardigan Bay R
      Worcester, Bromyard & Leominster R
      Wye Valley R
   See also Rating of property
   Gloucester & Cheltenham R abandonment,
      RAIL 1184
   Hotels, **RAIL 1022**
   Instructions to staff, **RAIL 1135**
   Joint committees with:
      Bristol & Exeter R, **RAIL 238;**
         RAIL 249
         RAIL 79 (Bristol Harbour R)
         RAIL 80 (Bristol jt station)
         RAIL 134 (Cornwall R)
         RAIL 725; RAIL 726 (W Cornwall R *q.v.*)

Cornwall R
   RAIL 568 (Plymouth jt station)
Cornwall Minerals R, **RAIL 132**
GCR
   Byelaws and regulations, **RAIL 1001**
   Map, **RAIL 1014**
   Parliamentary plans, **RAIL 1071**
   Reports and accounts, **RAIL 1110;**
      RAIL 1116; RAIL 1117
   Rule books, **RAIL 1134**
   Sidings agreements, **RAIL 1167**
   Timetables, **RAIL 981**
   RAIL 239 (Banbury Jct R)
Llynvi & Ogmore R, **RAIL 381**
LNER
   RAIL 239 (Banbury Jct R)
   RAIL 250 (W London electrification)
   RAIL 390 (pooling; Standing Jt Cttee)
LNWR, **RAIL 404**
   Byelaws and regulations, **RAIL 1001**
   Labour and staff matters, **RAIL 1025**
   Railway and Canal Traffic Acts
      proceedings, **RAIL 1038**
   Rule books, **RAIL 1134**
   Working timetables appendixes,
      RAIL 1136
   RAIL 35 (Birkenhead R)
   RAIL 1038 (Railway and Canal Traffic
      Acts proceedings)
      Ludlow & Clee Hill R
      Pontypool & Talywain R
      Shrewsbury & Hereford R
      Shrewsbury & Welshpool R (*q.v.*)
      Tenbury R
   RAIL 617 (Shrewsbury & Hereford R)
   RAIL 690 (Tenbury R)
   RAIL 410 (W London Extension R)
   RAIL 759 (Wolverhampton High Level
      station)
See also LMSR miscellanea
LSWR, **RAIL 240; RAIL 258**
   RAIL 410 (W London Extension R)
See also Easton & Church Hope R
LMSR, **RAIL 416**
   Byelaws and regulations, **RAIL 1001**
   Reports and accounts, **RAIL 1110**
   RAIL 1005 (Avonmouth Lt R miscellanea)
   RAIL 402 (Brecon & Merthyr jt section)
   RAIL 241 (Midland section)
   RAIL 1116; RAIL 1117 (Severn & Wye &
      Severn Bridge R reports and accounts)
   RAIL 1136 (Severn & Wye R working
      timetable appendixes)
   RAIL 981 (Shrewsbury & Hereford Jt
      Line timetables)
   RAIL 390 (Standing Jt Cttee)
   RAIL 254 (Vale of Towy R)

LPTB
  RAIL 390 (Standing Jt Cttee)
  RAIL 250 (W London electrification)
Met R
  RAIL 1134 (W London R rule books)
MR, **RAIL 241**
  Byelaws and regulations, **RAIL 1001**
  Reports and accounts, **RAIL 1110**
  RAIL 81 (Clifton Extension R)
    Railway and Canal Traffic Acts
    proceedings, **RAIL 1038**
  RAIL 287 (Halesowen Railway)
  RAIL 603 (Severn & Wye & Severn Br R)
    Reports and accounts, **RAIL 1110**
  RAIL 1110 (Severn & Wye R & Canal
    Co reports and accounts)
  RAIL 1135 (Severn & Wye Jt R
    instructions to staff)
  RAIL 1136 (Severn & Wye R working
    timetable appendixes)
See also Estates and rating
  GWR/LMSR jt cttee
Monmouthshire R & Canal, **RAIL 250;**
  RAIL 499
Port Talbot R & Docks, **RAIL 242** (operation
  by GWR)
Rhondda & Swansea Bay R, **RAIL 243**
  (operation by GWR)
Rhymney R
  Byelaws and regulations, **RAIL 1001**
  Maps, **RAIL 1030**
  Reports and accounts, **RAIL 1110**
  RAIL 244 (Bargoed railways)
Shrewsbury & Birmingham R, **RAIL 283**
  (joint traffic)
Shrewsbury & Chester R, **RAIL 283** (joint
  traffic)
S Devon R, **RAIL 249**
  RAIL 568 (Plymouth jt station)
  RAIL 725; RAIL 726 (W Cornwall R *q.v.*)
SR, **RAIL 240; RAIL 245; RAIL 258**
  RAIL 390 (Standing Jt Cttee)
S Wales R, **RAIL 284**
Stratford-upon-Avon R, **RAIL 246**
  (operation by GWR)
Taff Vale R
  Railway and Canal Traffic Acts
    proceedings, **RAIL 1038**
Waterford & Limerick R, **RAIL 250** (Traffic)
W London R
  Rule books, **RAIL 1134**
W Midland R, **RAIL 248; RAIL 284**
  RAIL 617 (Shrewsbury & Hereford R)
See also Chester Jt Station Cttee
  Bristol Jt Station Cttee
  Cornwall R
  Hammersmith & City R Jt Cttee

  Hereford Jt Station Construction & Traffic
    Cttee
  Newport Street Jt Cttee
  Northern Alliance
  Shrewsbury Jt Station Cttee
  Shrewsbury & Wellington Jt Line Cttee
  Southern Association Conference
  Vale of Towy R Jt Cttee
  Wolverhampton Jt Cttees
  Wrexham & Minera R Jt Cttee
Labour and staff matters, **RAIL 1025**
Law cases and arbitration, **RAIL 1027**
Litigation against West Bromwich
  Improvement Commissioners, **RAIL 1199**
Locomotives and rolling stock:
  RAIL 254 *including records of or about*:
    Alexandra Dock R
    Barry R
    Brecon & Methyr Tydfil Jct R
    BR
    Cambrian Rys
    Llanelly & Mynydd Mawr R
    MSWJR
    Neath & Brecon R
    Port Talbot R & Docks Co
    Rhondda & Swansea Bay R
    Rhymney R
    Shrewsbury & Birmingham R
    Shrewsbury & Chester R
    Shropshire & Montgomeryshire Lt R
      (BR *records*)
    S Devon R
    S Wales Mineral R
    Swansea Harbour Trust
    Taff Vale R
    Vale of Neath R
    Vale of Towy R (*jt working with* LNWR
      and LMSR)
See also GNR
Management Board and committees, **RAIL 788**
Maps, **RAIL 1030**
Minutes and reports, **RAIL 250; RAIL 1016**
Miscellanea, **RAIL 1005; RAIL 1007; RAIL 1008;**
  RAIL 1014; RAIL 1015; RAIL 1020; RAIL 1057
  RAIL 253 *including records of or about*:
    Liskeard & Looe R
    London & Windsor R
    Mawddwy R
    MSWJR
    Moretonhampstead & S Devon R
    Neath & Brecon R
    Port Talbot R & Dock Co
    Princetown R
    Railway Air Services
    Rhondda & Swansea Bay R
    Ross & Monmouth R
    S Wales R

GWR (continued)
>   S Wales Mineral R
>   Teign Valley R
>   Van R
>   Watlington & Princes Risborough R
>   Welshpool & Llanfair R
>   Wrexham & Ellesmere R
>   *Also includes GWR records about railways*
>   *absorbed at the Grouping*
>   **RAIL 1149** I K Brunel Collection, *including*
>   *records of or about:*
>   Cheltenham & Great Western Union R
>   Dublin & Drogheda R
>   London & Brighton R
>   London & Southampton R
>   N Midland R
>   Oxford & Great Western Union R
>   S Devon R
>   S Wales R
>   Vale of Neath R
>   **RAIL 267** Special reports *including records of*
>   *or about:*
>   Avon & Gloucestershire R
>   Berks & Hants R
>   Birmingham & Oxford R
>   Cornwall R
>   E Gloucester R
>   Great Marlow R
>   Hammersmith & City R
>   Midland & Great Western Jct R
>   (proposed)
>   Midland & S Wales Jct R (proposed)
>   MSWJR
>   Pontypool, Caerleon & Newport R
>   Shepherd's Bush, Acton & Brentford R
>   (proposed)
>   W London Extension R
>   Whitland & Cardigan R
>   *Also includes GWR records about railways it*
>   *absorbed*
> Parliamentary
>   Acts, **RAIL 259; RAIL 260**
>   Bills, **RAIL 255; RAIL 280; RAIL 1196**
>   Opposition to LNWR Bills, **RAIL 1198**
>   Opposition to Wallasey Embankment Bill,
>   **RAIL 1202**
>   Papers, **RAIL 1066; RAIL 1067; RAIL 1163**
>   Plans, **RAIL 262; RAIL 1071**
> Petitions to directors, **RAIL 256**
> Prospectuses etc, **RAIL 1075; RAIL 1076;**
>   **RAIL 1110**
> Publications, **RAIL 268; RAIL 269**
> Railway and Canal Traffic Acts proceedings,
>   **RAIL 1038**
> Railway Rates Tribunal proceedings, **RAIL 1101**
> Rating of property, **RAIL 263** *see also* Estates &
>   rating

Refreshment rooms and catering, **RAIL 1181**
Reports and accounts, **RAIL 1110; RAIL 1116;**
>   **RAIL 1117**
Road services
>   Carter Paterson & Co, **RAIL 1130**
>   Hay's Wharf Cartage Co, **RAIL 1131**
>   Pickfords & Hay's Wharf Shipping &
>   Forwarding Co, **RAIL 1132**
>   Pickfords Ltd, **RAIL 1133**
Rolling stock *see* locomotives and rolling
>   stock
Royal events, **RAIL 1009; RAIL 1010**
Rule books, **RAIL 1134**
Savings bank rules, **RAIL 1174**
Secretary's papers, **RAIL 258** *including records*
>   *of or about:*
>   Bishops Castle R
>   Bridport R
>   Cornwall Mineral R
>   Easton & Church Hope R
>   Forest of Dean Central R
>   Hammersmith & City R
>   Helston R
>   Milford Docks Co
>   Milford Haven Docks & R
>   Potteries, Shrewsbury & N Wales R
>   Railway Clearing House
>   Railway Companies' Association
>   Ross & Monmouth R
>   Shrewsbury & Hereford R
>   Shropshire Rys
>   Tenbury & Bewdley R
>   W Cornwall R
>   W London Extension R
>   W London R
>   Weymouth & Portland R
Severn tunnel, **RAIL 265; RAIL 775**
Shares and shareholders, **RAIL 251**
Shipping services, **RAIL 281**
Sidings agreements, **RAIL 1167**
Signal and telegraph records, **RAIL 282**
Solicitor's records, **RAIL 275**
Staff, **RAIL 264**
Statistics, **RAIL 266**
Strikes and civil disturbances, **RAIL 786**
Suggestions and Inventions Committee,
>   **RAIL 787**
Superannuation schemes, **RAIL 1174**
Swindon
>   Mechanics Institution, **RAIL 276**
>   New Swindon Improvement Co, **RAIL 277**
>   New Swindon schools, **RAIL 278**
Timetables
>   Public, **RAIL 936; RAIL 981**
>   Working, **RAIL 271** (Train use, timekeeping
>   etc); **RAIL 937; RAIL 938**
>   Working timetable appendixes, **RAIL 1136**

Trains
    Notices, **RAIL 279**
    Passenger train loading, **RAIL 261;**
      RAIL 271
    Timekeeping, **RAIL 271**
    Welfare schemes, **RAIL 1115; RAIL 1174**
See also Birmingham & Oxford Jct R
    Birmingham, Wolverhampton & Dudley R
    BR hotels and catering
    BR(WR) station plans and drawings
    BTC Chief Secretary's Office
    Callington Lt R
    Carmarthen & Cardigan R
    Cork City R
    Fishguard & Rosslare Rys & Harbours Co
    Great Western & Uxbridge R
    Irish & English Traffic Conference
    Kington & Eardisley R
    Llanelly & Mynydd Mawr R
    Llynvi & Ogmore R
    Newport Street Jt Cttee
    Oxford & Rugby R
    Pontypool, Caerleon & Newport R
    Severn Tunnel R
    Vale of Neath R
    Wallingford & Watlington R
    W Cornwall R Jt Cttee
    Wilts, Somerset & Weymouth R
    Windsor & Ascot R
    Wycombe R
Great Western Southern and Eastern Counties
  Railway (proposed) (*also called* Ipswich and
  Southampton Railway)
    Prospectuses etc, **RAIL 1075**
Greenoch and Wemyss Bay Railway
    Reports and accounts, **RAIL 1116**
Greenwich and Gravesend Railway
  (proposed)
    Prospectuses etc, **RAIL 1075**
Greenwich and Woolwich Railway (proposed)
    Prospectuses etc, **RAIL 1075**
Greenwich Extension Railway (proposed)
    Parliamentary papers, **RAIL 1066**
Guildford, Kingston and London Railway
  (proposed)
    Parliamentary papers, **RAIL 1066**
Guiseley, Yeadon and Rawdon Railway
    Parliamentary papers, **RAIL 1066**
Gwendreath Valleys Railway, **RAIL 285**
    Miscellanea, **RAIL 1057**
    Railway and Canal Traffic Acts proceedings,
      RAIL 1038
    Reports and accounts, **RAIL 1110;**
      RAIL 1116
Hadlow Valley Railway (proposed)
    Parliamentary papers, **RAIL 1066**

Halehead and Widnes Canal Dock and Railway
  (proposed)
    Parliamentary papers, **RAIL 1066**
Halesowen and Bromsgrove Railway (*also known
  as* Halesowen & Bromsgrove Branch R)
    Parliamentary papers, **RAIL 1066**
    Prospectuses etc, **RAIL 1075**
See also Halesowen R
Halesowen Railway, **RAIL 286** (*includes records of
  predecessor* Halesowen & Bromsgrove R)
    Parliamentary papers, **RAIL 1066**
    Prospectuses etc, **RAIL 1075**
    Reports and accounts, **RAIL 1110;**
      RAIL 1116
    Timetables, **RAIL 981**
See also GWR/MR jt cttees
Halifax and Ovenden Joint Committee
  (GNR/L&YR/LNWR; *in 1922* GNR/LNWR;
  after 1923 LMSR/LNER) **RAIL 288; RAIL 410;**
  RAIL 783
    Reports and accounts, **RAIL 1110**
Halifax and Ovendon Junction Railway
    Reports and accounts, **RAIL 1116**
Halifax and Ovenden Railway
    Reports and accounts, **RAIL 1116**
Halifax High Level and North and South Junction
  Railway, **RAIL 289**
Halifax High Level Railway Joint Committee
  (GNR/L&YR, *in 1922* GNR/LNWR) **RAIL 290;**
  RAIL 783
Halifax, Huddersfield and Keighley Railway
  (proposed)
    Parliamentary papers, **RAIL 1066**
Halifax, Thornton and Keighley Railway
  (proposed)
    Parliamentary papers, **RAIL 1066**
Hall's Tramway *see* GWR estates and rating
Hampstead Junction Railway, **RAIL 291**
Hampstead, Midland, North Western and Charing
  Cross Junction Railway (proposed)
    Parliamentary plans, **RAIL 1071**
Hampstead, St Pancras and Charing Cross
  Railway (proposed)
    Parliamentary papers, **RAIL 1066**
Hammersmith and City Junction Railway
  (proposed)
    Parliamentary papers, **RAIL 1066**
    Prospectuses etc, **RAIL 1075**
Hammersmith and City Railway
    Miscellanea, **RAIL 1008; RAIL 1014**
    Reports and accounts, **RAIL 1110;**
      RAIL 1116
See also Hammersmith & City R Jt Cttee
    GWR Secretary's papers
Hammersmith, Fulham and Westminster Railway
  (proposed)
    Subscription contract, **RAIL 1163**

Hammersmith and City Railway Joint Committee
(GWR/Met R)
    Byelaws, **RAIL 1001**
    Reports and accounts, **RAIL 1110; RAIL 1116**
    Rule books, **RAIL 1134**
Harborne Railway, **RAIL 292**
    Byelaws and regulations, **RAIL 1001**
    Reports and accounts, **RAIL 1116**
    Share certificates, **RAIL 1158**
See also LMSR amalgamation
Harrow and District Railway (proposed)
    Parliamentary papers, **RAIL 1066**
Harrow and Stanmore Railway, **RAIL 293**
    Sidings agreements, **RAIL 1167**
Harrow and Uxbridge Railway
    Parliamentary papers, **RAIL 1066**
    Prospectuses etc, **RAIL 1075**
Harrow, Ealing and Willesden Railway (proposed)
    Parliamentary papers, **RAIL 1066**
Harrow Road and Paddington Tramways
    Parliamentary papers, **RAIL 1066**
Harrow, Uxbridge and High Wycombe Railway
    (proposed)
    Parliamentary papers, **RAIL 1066**
Hartlepool Dock and Railway, **RAIL 294** (*includes
    records of* NER)
    Byelaws and regulations, **RAIL 1003**
    Miscellanea, **RAIL 1157**
    Reports and accounts, **RAIL 1110; RAIL 1111;
        RAIL 1116**
    Share certificate, **RAIL 1159**
See also NER
Hartlepool Harbour and Railway (proposed)
    Prospectuses etc, **RAIL 1075; RAIL 1076**
Hartlepool Junction Railway *see* NER
Hartlepool Port Wet Docks and Railways
    (proposed)
    Prospectuses etc, **RAIL 1075**
Hartlepool Railway (proposed)
    Prospectuses etc, **RAIL 1075**
Harwich Railway (proposed)
    Subscription contracts, **RAIL 1160**
Hastings Harbour District Railway
    Parliamentary papers, **RAIL 1066**
    Prospectuses etc, **RAIL 1075**
Hastings Harbour Railway (proposed)
    Parliamentary papers, **RAIL 1066**
Hatfield and St Albans Railway, **RAIL 295**
    Reports and accounts, **RAIL 1116**
    Share certificates, **RAIL 1159**
Hatfield Moor Light Railway
    Parliamentary papers, **RAIL 1067**
Havant, Hambledon and Droxford Railway
    (proposed)
    Parliamentary papers, **RAIL 1066**
Hawes and Melmerby Railway, **RAIL 296**
    Prospectuses etc, **RAIL 1076**

Hayes and Farnborough Railway (proposed)
    Parliamentary papers, **RAIL 1066**
Hayling Bridge and Causeway Management
    Committee (*sold to* LBSCR, *1878*) **RAIL 297**
Hayling Railways, **RAIL 298** (*leased to* LBSCR,
    1874)
    Reports and accounts, **RAIL 1110; RAIL 1117**
Hay's Wharf Cartage Company Ltd *see* BTC road
    services; GWR road services; LNER road
    services; LMSR road services; SR road services
Heaton Lodge and Wortley Railway (proposed)
    Parliamentary papers, **RAIL 1066**
Heddon-on-the-Wall and Ryton Railway
    (proposed)
    Notice, **RAIL 1152**
Hedingham and Long Melford Light Railway
    (proposed)
    Miscellanea, **RAIL 1057**
Helston Railway, **RAIL 299**
    Miscellanea, **RAIL 1014; RAIL 1057**
    Prospectus, **RAIL 1110**
    Railway and Canal Traffic Acts proceedings,
        RAIL 1038
    Reports and accounts, **RAIL 1110**
See also GWR Secretary's papers
Hereford and Gloucester Railway (proposed)
    Prospectuses etc, **RAIL 1075**
Hereford and Kidderminster Railway (proposed)
    Prospectuses etc, **RAIL 1075**
Hereford, Hay and Brecon Railway, **RAIL 300**
    Miscellanea, **RAIL 1057**
    Parliamentary papers, **RAIL 1066**
    Reports and accounts, **RAIL 1116**
    Share certificates, **RAIL 1158**
Hereford Joint Station Construction and Traffic
    Committees (GWR/Shrewsbury & Hereford R;
    after 1867 GWR/LNWR), **RAIL 301**
See also LNWR/GWR Jt Cttee (**RAIL 404**)
Hereford, Ross and Gloucester Railway,
    RAIL 302
    Miscellanea, **RAIL 1057**
    Parliamentary papers, **RAIL 1163**
    Prospectuses etc, **RAIL 1075**
    Reports and accounts, **RAIL 1110; RAIL 1116;
        RAIL 1117**
    Timetables, **RAIL 981**
Hereford Tramway
    Miscellanea, **RAIL 1057**
Herne Bay and Faversham Railway *see* Kent Coast
    R
Hertford and Welwyn Junction Railway
    Reports and accounts, **RAIL 1116**
Hertford, Luton and Dunstable Railway
    Reports and accounts, **RAIL 1116**
Hexham and Allendale Railway, **RAIL 303**
    Reports and accounts, **RAIL 1111;
        RAIL 1116**

Highclere, Kingsclere and Basingstoke Light
    Railway (proposed)
        Miscellanea, **RAIL 1057**
Highland Railway
        Miscellanea, **RAIL 1057**
        Railway and Canal Traffic Acts proceedings,
            RAIL 1038
        Reports and accounts, **RAIL 1110; RAIL 1116;**
            RAIL 1117
        Rule books, **RAIL 1134**
        Savings bank rules, **RAIL 1174**
        Share certificates, **RAIL 1158**
        Timetables, **RAIL 939; RAIL 981**
            Working timetables appendixes, **RAIL 1136**
See also LMSR amalgamation
Holmwood, Cranleigh and Midhurst Railway
    (proposed)
        Miscellanea, **RAIL 1017**
Holyhead Railway or Tramway (proposed)
        Subscription contracts, **RAIL 1160**
Holywell Railway, **RAIL 304**
Horncastle and Kirkstead Railway *see* Horncastle
    R
Horncastle Railway, **RAIL 305** (*includes records of*
    predecessor Horncastle & Kirkstead R)
        Reports and accounts, **RAIL 1016; RAIL 1110**
        Share certificates, **RAIL 1158**
        Subscription contracts, **RAIL 1160**
Horsham and Guildford Direct Railway, **RAIL 306**
        Share certificates, **RAIL 1158**
Horsham, Dorking and Leatherhead Railway,
    RAIL 307
        Prospectuses etc, **RAIL 1075**
        Reports and accounts, **RAIL 1116**
Hounslow and Metropolitan Railway
        Miscellanea, **RAIL 1057**
        Parliamentary papers, **RAIL 1066**
        Railway and Canal Traffic Acts proceedings,
            RAIL 1038
Hove, Worthing and District Tramways
        Parliamentary papers, **RAIL 1068**
Hoylake and Birkenhead Rail and Tramway
    Company
        Parliamentary papers, **RAIL 1066**
        Reports and accounts, **RAIL 1110**
See also Seacombe, Hoylake & Deeside R
Hoylake Railway
        Parliamentary papers, **RAIL 1066**
        Reports and accounts, **RAIL 1116**
Huddersfield and Elland Railway (proposed)
        Parliamentary papers, **RAIL 1066**
Huddersfield and Halifax Railway (proposed)
        Parliamentary papers, **RAIL 1066**
Huddersfield and Manchester Railway and Canal
    Company, **RAIL 308** (*includes records of* LNWR)
        Miscellanea, **RAIL 1008**
        Parliamentary plans, **RAIL 1071**

        Share certificates, **RAIL 1158**
        Subscription contracts, **RAIL 1160**
Huddersfield and Sheffield Railway
        Prospectus, **RAIL 1151**
Huddersfield, Halifax and Bradford Railway
    (proposed)
        Parliamentary papers, **RAIL 1066**
Huddersfield Joint Station Committee
    (L&YR/LNWR) **RAIL 309; RAIL 410**
Huddersfield South and East Junction Railway
    (proposed)
        Parliamentary papers, **RAIL 1066**
Hull and Barnsley and West Riding Junction
    Railway and Dock Company *see* H&BR
Hull and Barnsley Junction Railway (proposed),
    RAIL 311 *see also* LMSR amalgamation
Hull and Barnsley Railway, RAIL 312 (*includes*
    records about S Yorkshire R). Hull & Barnsley R *is*
    the short title adopted in 1905. Before that the title
    was Hull & Barnsley & W Riding Jct R & Dock
    Co *although* Hull & Barnsley R *was often used*
    Byelaws and regulations, **RAIL 1003**
        (Docks)
    Instructions to staff, **RAIL 1135**
    Joint committees with:
        GCR
            Reports and accounts, **RAIL 1110;**
                RAIL 1111 RAIL 1116 (GCR/H&BR/
                MR)
            RAIL 225 (Braithwell Jct to Laughton Jct
                line)
                Byelaws and regulations, **RAIL 1001**
            RAIL 310 (Gowdell to Braithwell line)
        MR
            Reports and accounts, **RAIL 1110;**
                RAIL 1111 RAIL 1116 (GCR/H&BR/
                MR)
            RAIL 225 (Braithwell Jct to Laughton Jct
                line)
                Byelaws and regulations, **RAIL 1001**
        NER, **RAIL 525** (Hull Jt Dock)
    Law cases and arbitration, **RAIL 1027**
    Miscellanea, **RAIL 1005; RAIL 1020;**
        RAIL 1057
    Parliamentary papers, **RAIL 1066;**
        RAIL 1067
    Prospectuses etc, **RAIL 1075; RAIL 1076**
    Railway and Canal Traffic Acts proceedings,
        RAIL 1038
    Reports and accounts, **RAIL 1110; RAIL 1111;**
        RAIL 1116; RAIL 1117
    Rule books, **RAIL 1134**
    Savings bank, **RAIL 1174**
    Share certificates, **RAIL 1158; RAIL 1159**
    Timetables, **RAIL 940; RAIL 981**
See also Irish & English Traffic Conference
        LNER locomotives & rolling stock

Hull and Holderness Railway, **RAIL 313**
   Parliamentary papers, **RAIL 1163**
   Reports and accounts, **RAIL 1111; RAIL 1116; RAIL 1117**
   Rule books, **RAIL 1134**
Hull and Hornsea Railway, **RAIL 314**
   Prospectuses etc, **RAIL 1076**
   Reports and accounts, **RAIL 1111; RAIL 1116**
   Rule books, **RAIL 1134**
   Share certificates, **RAIL 1159**
   Timetables, **RAIL 981**
Hull and Lincoln Railway (proposed)
   Parliamentary papers, **RAIL 1066; RAIL 1067**
   Prospectuses etc, **RAIL 1075**
Hull and Market Weighton Railway (proposed)
   Prospectuses etc, **RAIL 1076**
Hull and North Western Junction Railway
   Parliamentary papers, **RAIL 1066; RAIL 1067**
Hull and Selby Railway, **RAIL 315**
   Miscellanea, **RAIL 1014; RAIL 1157**
   Prospectuses etc, **RAIL 1075**
   Reports and accounts, **RAIL 1016; RAIL 1111; RAIL 1116; RAIL 1117**
   Share certificates, **RAIL 1159**
   Timetables, **RAIL 981**
   See also Manchester Leeds & Hull Associated R (proposed)
Hull and South Yorkshire Extension Railway
   Parliamentary papers, **RAIL 1066**
Hull and West Riding Junction Railway (proposed)
   Prospectuses etc, **RAIL 1075**
Hull, Barnsley and West Riding Junction Railway and Dock Company *see* Hull & Barnsley R
Hull Corporation Tramways
   Parliamentary papers, **RAIL 1068**
Hull Joint Dock Committee *see* H&BR/NER Jt Cttee
Hull, Lincoln and Nottingham Railway (proposed)
   Prospectuses etc, **RAIL 1075**
Hull, Sheffield and Midland Direct Railway (proposed)
   Prospectuses etc, **RAIL 1075**
Hull South and West Junction Railway (proposed)
   Parliamentary papers, **RAIL 1066; RAIL 1067**
Hull South Bridge Company, **RAIL 316** (*company guaranteed by* NER. *Includes records of* NER *and* LNER)
   Reports and accounts, **RAIL 1110; RAIL 1111; RAIL 1116**
Humber Commercial Railway and Dock Company, **RAIL 317**
   Law cases and arbitration, **RAIL 1027**
   Maps, **RAIL 1030**
   Parliamentary papers, **RAIL 1066; RAIL 1067**
   Prospectuses etc, **RAIL 1075**
   Reports and accounts, **RAIL 1110**
   Share certificates, **RAIL 1158**

Humber Conference (LNWR/L&YR/MS&LR (GCR *after 1897*)/NER) **RAIL 318; RAIL 410**
Humber Warehousing and Transport Company, **RAIL 319** (*Company guaranteed by* GCR *and, after 1923*, LNER)
Hundred of Hoo Extension Railway (proposed)
   Parliamentary papers, **RAIL 1066**
Hundred of Hoo Railway, **RAIL 320**
Hundred of Manhood and Selsey Tramways
   Reports and accounts, **RAIL 1116; RAIL 1117**
Hunslet Railway
   Parliamentary papers, **RAIL 1066; RAIL 1067**
Hunstanton and West Norfolk Railway, **RAIL 321**
Hylton, Southwick and Monkwearmouth Railway, **RAIL 322**
   Reports and accounts, **RAIL 1111**
   Share certificates, **RAIL 1159**
Hythe and Sandgate Railway, **RAIL 323**
Idle and Shipley Railway, **RAIL 324**
   Parliamentary papers, **RAIL 1066**
Ilford Urban District Council Tramways
   Reports and accounts, **RAIL 1114**
Ilfracombe Railway, **RAIL 325**
   Parliamentary papers, **RAIL 1066**
   Share certificates, **RAIL 1158**
Industrial Court
   Labour and staff matters, **RAIL 1025; RAIL 1026**
International Railway Congress Association
   Bulletins, **RAIL 1024**
   Proceedings, **RAIL 1023**
   Sixteenth session, London, 1954, **AN 128**
Inverness and Aberdeen Junction Railway
   Reports and accounts, **RAIL 1116; RAIL 1117**
   Share certificates, **RAIL 1158**
Inverness and Nairn Railway
   Reports and accounts, **RAIL 1116; RAIL 1117**
Inverness and Perth Junction Railway
   Prospectus, **RAIL 1075; RAIL 1116**
   Reports and accounts, **RAIL 1116**
Inverury and Old Meldrum Railway
   Parliamentary papers, **RAIL 1163**
Ipstones Mineral Branch Railway (proposed)
   Subscription contract, **RAIL 1163**
Ipswich and Bury St Edmunds Railway (*from 1846 called* Ipswich, Bury & Norwich R), **RAIL 326** (*includes records of successor* Eastern Union R)
   Reports and accounts, **RAIL 1110**
   See also Eastern Union R
Ipswich and Southampton Railway (proposed) *see* Great Western Southern & Eastern Counties R
Ipswich and Yarmouth Coast Railway (proposed)
   Prospectuses etc, **RAIL 1075**
Ipswich, Bury and Norwich Railway *see* Eastern Union R; Ipswich & Bury St Edmunds R
Irish and British Traffic Conference *see* Irish & English Traffic Conference

Irish and English Goods Traffic Conference *see*
  Irish & English Traffic Conference
Irish and English Live Stock Traffic Conference *see*
  Irish & English Traffic Conference
Irish and English Traffic Conference, **RAIL 327** *see*
  also RCH Cttees, **RAIL 1080**
    Includes records of:
    Belfast Traffic Conference *see also* RCH
      Cttees, **RAIL 1080**
    Belfast Traffic Meeting
    Irish & British Traffic Conference
    Irish & English Goods Traffic Conference *see*
      also RCH Cttees, **RAIL 1080**
    Irish & English Live Stock Traffic
      Conference *see also* RCH Cttees,
        RAIL 1080
    Scottish & Irish Traffic Conference
    Many railway companies and nationalized
    transport bodies in Britain and Ireland took
    part, including pre-group companies, the four
    grouped railways, and BR. They are not listed
    here but cross-references to this series will be
    found in the entries for the companies
    concerned.
Irish Metropolitan Junction Railway (proposed)
  Prospectuses etc, **RAIL 1075**
Irish North Western Railway
  Reports and accounts, **RAIL 1116;**
    RAIL 1117
See also Irish & English Traffic Conference
Irish Railway Clearing House
  Distance book, **RAIL 1089**
  Minutes, **RAIL 1075**
  Miscellanea, **RAIL 1057**
  Regulations, **RAIL 1092**
See also Irish & English Traffic Conference
  RCH
Irish South Eastern Railway
  Reports and accounts, **RAIL 1116; RAIL 1117**
Isle of Axholme Light Railway *see* Axholme Jt R
  Cttee; NER
Isle of Man Railway
  Miscellanea, **RAIL 1020; RAIL 1057**
  Prospectus, **RAIL 1075**
  Reports and accounts, **RAIL 1116; RAIL 1117**
Isle of Wight and Ryde Pier Railway
  (LSWR/LBSCR)
  Law cases and arbitration, **RAIL 1027**
  Parliamentary papers, **RAIL 1066**
Isle of Wight Central Railway, **RAIL 328** (*includes*
  records of Cowes & Newport R; Isle of Wight R;
  Ryde & Newport R *and* SR)
  Byelaws and regulations, **RAIL 1001**
  Miscellanea, **RAIL 1017**
  Reports and accounts, **RAIL 1110; RAIL 1116;**
    RAIL 1117
  Rule books, **RAIL 1134**

Timetables, **RAIL 981**
  Working timetables appendixes, **RAIL 1136**
Isle of Wight (Newport Junction) Railway,
  RAIL 329
  Joint committee with;
    Cowes & Newport R/Ryde & Newport R,
      RAIL 591 (Newport jt station)
  Reports and accounts, **RAIL 1110; RAIL 1116;**
    RAIL 1117
Isle of Wight Railway, **RAIL 330**
  Miscellanea, **RAIL 1057**
  Parliamentary papers, **RAIL 1163**
  Reports and accounts, **RAIL 1110; RAIL 1116;**
    RAIL 1117
  Rule books, **RAIL 1134**
  Timetables, **RAIL 981**
See also Isle of Wight Central Railway
Islington and Euston Railway (proposed)
  Parliamentary papers, **RAIL 1066**
Jedburgh Railway
  Parliamentary papers, **RAIL 1163**
  Prospectuses etc, **RAIL 1076**
  Reports and accounts, **RAIL 1116**
  Share certificates, **RAIL 1158**
Jersey Eastern Railway
  Reports and accounts, **RAIL 1116**
  Timetables, **RAIL 928**
Jersey Railways and Tramways
  Reports and accounts, **RAIL 1116**
  Timetables, **RAIL 928**
Joint Railways and City Terminus Railway
  (proposed)
  Prospectuses etc, **RAIL 1075**
Junction Railway (proposed) (Falkirk to Garnkirk
  and Glasgow Railway)
  Prospectuses etc, **RAIL 1075**
Kanturk and Newmarket Railway
  Railway and Canal Traffic Acts proceedings,
    RAIL 1038
Kearney Tube *see* N & S Shields R
Keighley and Worth Valley Railway, **RAIL 331**
  Share certificates, **RAIL 1158**
Keighley Corporation Tramways
  Reports and accounts, **RAIL 1114**
Keith and Dufftown Railway
  Reports and accounts, **RAIL 1116**
Kelvedon, Coggeshall and Halstead Light Railway
  (proposed)
  Miscellanea, **RAIL 1057**
Kelvedon, Tiptree and Tollesbury Light Railway
  Miscellanea, **RAIL 1057**
  Parliamentary papers, **RAIL 1066**
Kelvin Valley Railway
  Share certificates, **RAIL 1158**
Kendal and Windermere Railway
  Reports and accounts, **RAIL 1116;**
    RAIL 1117

Kensington Station and North-West and South
   London Junction Railway
      Maps, **RAIL 1014; RAIL 1030**
Kent and East Sussex Light Railway, **RAIL 332**
   (*includes records of predecessor* Rother Valley Lt R)
      Miscellanea, **RAIL 1057**
      Reports and accounts, **RAIL 1116; RAIL 1117**
See also BTC Chief Secretary's Office
Kent Coast Railway, **RAIL 333** (*including records of
   predecessors* Herne Bay & Faversham R and
   Margate R)
      Reports and accounts, **RAIL 1116**
Kent Railway (proposed)
      Share certificates, **RAIL 1158**
Kettering and Thrapstone Railway *see* LNWR
Kettering, Thrapstone and Huntingdon Railway
      Law cases and arbitration, **RAIL 1027**
      Reports and accounts, **RAIL 1116**
Kew, Turnham Green and Hammersmith Railway
   (proposed)
      Parliamentary papers, **RAIL 1066**
Kidderminster and Leominster Junction Railway
   (proposed)
      Prospectuses etc, **RAIL 1075**
Kidderminster and Stourport Electric Tramway
      Parliamentary papers, **RAIL 1066; RAIL 1068**
Killarney Junction Railway
      Reports and accounts, **RAIL 1116; RAIL 1117**
Killin Railway
      Reports and accounts, **RAIL 1116**
See also LMSR amalgamation
Kilsyth and Bonnybridge Railway
      Reports and accounts, **RAIL 1110**
Kingsbridge and Salcombe Railway, **RAIL 335**
      Prospectus, **RAIL 1014**
Kingsbridge and South Devon Railway (proposed)
      Prospectuses etc, **RAIL 1075**
Kingsbridge Railway
      Miscellanea, **RAIL 1057**
King's Lynn Docks and Railway (*also known as*
   King's Lynn Dock Co), **RAIL 334**
      Reports and accounts, **RAIL 1112; RAIL 1116;
      RAIL 1117**
See also BTC Chief Secretary's Office
Kingston and London Railway
      Parliamentary papers, **RAIL 1066**
Kingston-upon-Hull City Tramways
      Reports and accounts, **RAIL 1114**
Kingstown and Kingsbridge Junction Railway
      Prospectus, **RAIL 1116**
Kington and Eardisley Railway, **RAIL 336** (*includes
   records of* GWR)
      Miscellanea, **RAIL 1008; RAIL 1014**
      Parliamentary papers, **RAIL 1066**
      Railway and Canal Traffic Acts proceedings,
      RAIL 1038
      Reports and accounts, **RAIL 1110; RAIL 1116**

      Timetables, **RAIL 981**
      See also GWR estates and rating
Kington Railway (or Tramway)
      Miscellanea, **RAIL 1014; RAIL 1057**
Kinross-shire Railway
      Reports and accounts, **RAIL 1116**
      Share certificates, **RAIL 1158**
Kirkcaldy and District Railway
      Parliamentary papers, **RAIL 1066**
      Prospectus, **RAIL 1116**
      Share certificates, **RAIL 1158**
Kirkcudbright Railway
      Parliamentary papers, **RAIL 1066**
Kirkstead and Little Steeping Light Railway
   (proposed)
      Parliamentary papers, **RAIL 1066**
King's Cross, Charing Cross and Waterloo Subway
   (proposed)
      Parliamentary plans, **RAIL 1071**
Kings Road Railway (proposed)
      Parliamentary papers, **RAIL 1066**
Kington R
      Share certificate, **RAIL 1014**
Knaresbrough and Pately Bridge Railway
   (proposed)
      Prospectuses etc, **RAIL 1076**
Knighton Railway
      Reports and accounts, **RAIL 1116**
      Timetables, **RAIL 981**
Knott End Railway (*successor to* Garstang & Knott
   End R *q.v.*), **RAIL 337**
      Parliamentary papers, **RAIL 1066**
      Prospectus, **RAIL 1116**
      Reports and accounts, **RAIL 1116;
      RAIL 1117**
      Share certificates, **RAIL 1158**
      Timetables, **RAIL 981**
See also LMSR amalgamation
Lambourn Valley Railway, **RAIL 338**
      Byelaws and regulations, **RAIL 1001**
      Miscellanea, **RAIL 1057**
      Reports and accounts, **RAIL 1110**
Lambourne, Wantage and Didcot Light Railway
   (proposed)
      Miscellanea, **RAIL 1057**
Lampeter, Aberayron and New Quay Light
   Railway, **RAIL 339**
      Miscellanea, **RAIL 1057**
      Prospectuses etc, **RAIL 1075; RAIL 1110**
      Reports and accounts, **RAIL 1110**
Lanarkshire and Ayrshire Railway
      Reports and accounts, **RAIL 1116**
      Share certificates, **RAIL 1158**
See also LMSR amalgamation
Lancashire and North Yorkshire R
   (proposed)
      Share certificates, **RAIL 1158**

Lancashire and Yorkshire Railway, **RAIL 343**
includes records of:
Ashton, Stalybridge & Liverpool Jct R
East Lancashire R
Manchester & Leeds R
Manchester & Southport R
Sheffield, Rotherham, Barnsley, Wakefield,
Huddersfield & Goole R
Byelaws and regulations, **RAIL 1001**
Deeds, contracts etc, **RAIL 795** (*includes records
of* LMSR)
Instructions to staff, **RAIL 1135**
Joint committees with
E Lancashire R, **RAIL 176**
RAIL 52 (Blackburn Railway)
RAIL 1001 (Burscough & Southport R
byelaws)
RAIL 981 (Liverpool jt line station,
timetables)
Byelaws and regulations, **RAIL 1001**
RAIL 410 (Preston station)
GER, **RAIL 340** (proposed L&Y/GE
junction line)
GNR
Byelaws and regulations, **RAIL 1001**
RAIL 290 (Halifax High Level)
RAIL 341 (Jt stations)
RAIL 413 (London & W Riding
Association)
Lancashire Union Rys, **RAIL 342; RAIL 410**
Liverpool, Crosby & Southport R, **RAIL 372**
LNWR, **RAIL 405; RAIL 421**
Byelaws and regulations, **RAIL 1001**
Parliamentary papers, **RAIL 1163**
Rule books, **RAIL 1134**
RAIL 623 (Jt stations)
RAIL 342; RAIL 410 (Lancashire Union
Rys)
Railway and Canal Traffic Acts
proceedings, **RAIL 1038**
RAIL 410 (Leeds jt station)
RAIL 410 (North Union R)
Railway and Canal Traffic Acts
proceedings, **RAIL 1038**
RAIL 410 (Preston & Wyre R)
Railway & Canal Traffic Acts
proceedings, **RAIL 1038**
Timetables, **RAIL 981**
RAIL 410 (Preston station)
RAIL 1038 (Ribble Branch, Railway &
Canal Traffic Acts proceedings)
See also LMSR miscellanea
NER
Byelaws and regulations, **RAIL 1001**
RAIL 13 (Axholme Jt R)
RAIL 526 (Isle of Axholme and Goole &
Marshland Lt Rys)

See also Huddersfield Jt Station Cttee
Humber Conference
Leeds Central Station
London & W Riding Association
Methley R Jt Cttee
Normanton Jt Station Cttee
Preston & Longridge R Jt Cttee
S Yorkshire Jt Line Cttee
Labour and staff matters, **RAIL 1025**
Law cases and arbitration, **RAIL 1027**
Maps, **RAIL 1030**
Miscellanea, **RAIL 1005; RAIL 1007;
RAIL 1008; RAIL 1014; RAIL 1015;
RAIL 1020; RAIL 1057**
Parliamentary papers, **RAIL 1066; RAIL 1067;
RAIL 1147; RAIL 1163**
Railway & Canal Traffic Acts proceedings,
RAIL 1038
Reports and accounts, **RAIL 1110; RAIL 1116;
RAIL 1117**
Rule books, **RAIL 1134**
Savings bank rules, **RAIL 1174**
Share certificates, **RAIL 1158**
Superannuation schemes, **RAIL 1174**
Timetables, **RAIL 942; RAIL 981**
Working timetables appendixes, **RAIL 1136**
Traders' ledger credit agreements, **RAIL 1165**
Welfare schemes, **RAIL 1174**
See also BR horse records
Irish & English Traffic Conference
LMSR amalgamation; solicitor's records
Manchester Bolton & Bury Canal Navigation
& R
Lancashire, Derbyshire and East Coast Railway,
RAIL 344
Maps, **RAIL 1030**
Miscellanea, **RAIL 1021**
Parliamentary papers, **RAIL 1066; RAIL 1163**
Prospectuses etc, **RAIL 1075**
Reports and accounts, **RAIL 1110; RAIL 1116;
RAIL 1117**
Timetables, **RAIL 981**
Working timetables appendixes, **RAIL 1136**
Traders' ledger credit agreements, **RAIL 1165**
Lancashire Union Railways, **RAIL 345**
Byelaws and regulations, **RAIL 1001**
Joint committee with:
L&YR/LNWR, **RAIL 342; RAIL 410**
Parliamentary papers, **RAIL 1066; RAIL 1067**
Reports and accounts, **RAIL 1116**
Lancaster and Carlisle Railway, **RAIL 346** (*includes
records of* LNWR); **RAIL 410**
Joint committee *see* Tebay Jt Station Cttee
Miscellanea, **RAIL 1008**
Parliamentary papers, **RAIL 1067**
Parliamentary plans, **RAIL 1071**
Prospectuses etc, **RAIL 1075**

Reports and accounts, **RAIL 1110**; **RAIL 1116**; **RAIL 1117**
  Subscription contracts, **RAIL 1160**
  Timetables, **RAIL 981**
See also LNWR
  Manchester, Buxton, Matlock & Midlands Jct R
Lancaster and Preston Junction Railway, **RAIL 347**
  Miscellanea, **RAIL 1014**
  Prospectuses etc, **RAIL 1075**
  Reports and accounts, **RAIL 1116**; **RAIL 1117**
  Subscription contracts, **RAIL 1160**
  Timetables, **RAIL 981**
Larne and Stranraer Steamboat Company
  Reports and accounts, **RAIL 1116**
Larne and Stranraer Steamship Joint Committee (Belfast & Northern Counties R/Portpatrick & Wigtownshire R)
  Reports and accounts, **RAIL 1116**
Lastingham and Rosedale Light Railway
  Miscellanea, **RAIL 1006**
Latimer Road and Acton Railway
  Miscellanea, **RAIL 1005**; **RAIL 1057**
  Parliamentary papers, **RAIL 1066**
  Prospectuses etc, **RAIL 1075**
  Reports and accounts, **RAIL 1110**
Lauder Light Railway
  Reports and accounts, **RAIL 1110**
Launceston and South Devon Railway, **RAIL 348**
  Prospectus, **RAIL 1014**
  Reports and accounts, **RAIL 1116**
Leadburn, Linton and Dolphinton Railway
  Reports and accounts, **RAIL 1116**
  Share certificates, **RAIL 1158**
Leamington, Warwick and Stratford-upon-Avon Railway (proposed), **RAIL 1197**
  Subscription contract, **RAIL 1163**
Leatherhead and Dorking Railway (proposed)
  Parliamentary papers, **RAIL 1066**
Leeds and Bradford Railway, **RAIL 350**
  Subscription contracts, **RAIL 1160**
Leeds and Selby Railway, **RAIL 351** (*includes records of* NER *and* York & N Midland R)
  Miscellanea, **RAIL 1015**; **RAIL 1016**; **RAIL 1153**; **RAIL 1157**
  Prospectuses etc, **RAIL 1075**
  Reports and accounts, **RAIL 1014**
  Timetables, **RAIL 981**
Leeds and Thirsk Railway
  Joint committee *see* Leeds Central Station
  Miscellanea, **RAIL 1005**
  Prospectuses etc, **RAIL 1076**
  Reports and accounts, **RAIL 1110**
  Share certificates, **RAIL 1159**
  Timetables, **RAIL 981** (freight)
See also Leeds Northern R

Leeds and York Railway (proposed)
  Prospectuses etc, **RAIL 1076**
Leeds, Bradford and Halifax Junction Railway, **RAIL 352**
  Parliamentary papers, **RAIL 1066**; **RAIL 1163**
  Reports and accounts, **RAIL 1116**; **RAIL 1117**
  Timetables, **RAIL 981**
Leeds, Castleford and Pontefract Junction Railway, **RAIL 353** (*includes records of* NER)
  Reports and accounts, **RAIL 1110**
Leeds Central Station, **RAIL 354**; **RAIL 410**
  Constituted by GNR, Leeds & Thirsk R, Leeds, Dewsbury & Manchester *and* Manchester & Leeds R. *After amalgamations in 1840s & 1850s run jointly by* GNR/L&YR/LNWR/NER
Leeds City Tramways
  Reports and accounts, **RAIL 1114**
Leeds, Dewsbury and Manchester Railway, **RAIL 355** (*includes records of* LNWR)
  Joint committee *see* Leeds Central Station
  Miscellanea, **RAIL 1153**
  Parliamentary plans, **RAIL 1071**
See also GNR
Leeds New Joint Station Committee (LNWR/NER; *after 1923* LNER/LMS), **RAIL 356**; **RAIL 410**; **RAIL 421**; **RAIL 417**
  Reports and accounts, **RAIL 1110**; **RAIL 1116** (LMSR/LNER)
See also LMSR miscellanea
Leeds Northern Railway, **RAIL 357** (*includes records of predecessor* Leeds & Thirsk R *and of* NER)
  Joint committees with:
    York & N Midland R/York Newcastle & Berwick R, **RAIL 773**
    See also Leeds Central Station
  Miscellanea, **RAIL 1021**; **RAIL 1157**
  Parliamentary papers, **RAIL 1066**
  Reports and accounts, **RAIL 1110**; **RAIL 1111**; **RAIL 1116**
  Rule books, **RAIL 1134**
  Timetables, **RAIL 981**
See also NER
Leeds, Pontefract and Sheffield Junction Railway (proposed)
  Parliamentary papers, **RAIL 1066**; **RAIL 1067**
  Miscellanea, **RAIL 1057**
Leeds Suburban Railway (proposed)
  Parliamentary papers, **RAIL 1067**
Leek and Manifold Valley Light Railway, **RAIL 358**
  Miscellanea, **RAIL 1007**
  Reports and accounts, **RAIL 1110**; **RAIL 1116**
See also LMSR amalgamation
  N Staffordshire R
Leek, Caldon Low and Hartington Light Railways *see* N Staffordshire R

Lee-on-the-Solent Light Railway, **RAIL 349**
Leicester and Bedford Railway (proposed)
    Miscellanea, **RAIL 1153**
Leicester and Swannington Railway, **RAIL 359**
    (*includes records of* MR)
Leicester and Tamworth Junction Railway
    (proposed), **RAIL 361**
        Miscellanea, **RAIL 1057**
        Subscription contracts, **RAIL 1160**
Leicester City Tramways
    Reports and accounts, **RAIL 1114**
Leicester, Tamworth, Coventry, Birmingham and
    Trent Valley Junction Railway (proposed),
    RAIL 360
        Miscellanea, **RAIL 1057**
        Prospectuses etc, **RAIL 1075**
Leicester, Tamworth, Coventry, Birmingham and
    Trent Valley Railway
        Miscellanea, **RAIL 1057**
Leigh and South Central Lancashire Railway
    (proposed)
        Parliamentary papers, **RAIL 1066**
Leighton Buzzard Light Railway
    Reports and accounts, **RAIL 1116**
Leominster and Bromyard Railway, **RAIL 362**
    Parliamentary plans, **RAIL 1071**
    Reports and accounts, **RAIL 1110**
Leominster and Kington Railway, **RAIL 363**
    Miscellanea, **RAIL 1014**
    Railway and Canal Traffic Acts proceedings,
        RAIL 1038
    Reports and accounts, **RAIL 1110; RAIL 1116**
    Timetables, **RAIL 981**
See also GWR estates and rating
Leslie Railway
    Parliamentary papers, **RAIL 1163**
    Share certificates, **RAIL 1158**
Leven and East of Fife Railway
    Reports and accounts, **RAIL 1116**
Leven Railway
    Share certificates, **RAIL 1158**
Lewes and East Grinstead Railway, **RAIL 364**
    Parliamentary papers, **RAIL 1066**
See also LBSCR
Lewes and Uckfield Railway, **RAIL 365**
    Reports and accounts, **RAIL 1116**
Leyton Urban District Council Tramways
    Reports and accounts, **RAIL 1114**
Limavady and Dungiven Railway
    Railway and Canal Traffic Acts proceedings,
        RAIL 1038
Limerick and Castle-Connell and Extension to
    Killaloe Railway
        Reports and accounts, **RAIL 1116**
Limerick and Castle-Connell Railway
    Parliamentary papers, **RAIL 1163**
    Reports and accounts, **RAIL 1116**

Limerick and Ennis Railway
    Reports and accounts, **RAIL 1116**
Limerick and Foynes Railway
    Reports and accounts, **RAIL 1116**
Limerick and Kerry Railway
    Reports and accounts, **RAIL 1110; RAIL 1116**
Limerick, Castle-Connell and Killaloe Railway
    Reports and accounts, **RAIL 1116**
Limerick, Ennis and Killaloe Junction Railway
    Parliamentary papers, **RAIL 1163**
Lincoln and Skegness Railway (proposed)
    Parliamentary papers, **RAIL 1066**
Liskeard and Caradon Railway, **RAIL 366**
    Miscellanea, **RAIL 1005; RAIL 1014;**
        RAIL 1057
    Parliamentary papers, **RAIL 1066**
    Railway and Canal Traffic Acts proceedings,
        RAIL 1038
    Reports and accounts, **RAIL 1110**
    Rule books, **RAIL 1134**
Liskeard and Looe Railway (*formerly* Liskeard &
    Looe Union Canal Co), **RAIL 367**
    Miscellanea, **RAIL 1005; RAIL 1014;**
        RAIL 1020; RAIL 1057
    Parliamentary papers, **RAIL 1066**
    Railway and Canal Traffic Acts proceedings,
        RAIL 1038
    Reports and accounts, **RAIL 1110**
    Timetables, **RAIL 981**
See also GWR estates and rating; miscellanea
Listowel and Ballybunion Railway
    Railway and Canal Traffic Acts proceedings,
        RAIL 1038
Liverpool and Bury Railway, **RAIL 368** (*includes*
    records of predecessor Bolton, Wigan & Liverpool R)
    Parliamentary papers, **RAIL 1147**
Liverpool and Chester Railway (proposed),
    RAIL 369
Liverpool and Lancashire Northern Railway
    (proposed) *see* Liverpool & Leeds R
Liverpool and Leeds Railway (proposed),
    RAIL 370 (*briefly known as* Liverpool &
    Lancashire Northern R)
Liverpool and Manchester Railway, **RAIL 371**
    Maps, **RAIL 1030**
    Miscellanea, **RAIL 1007; RAIL 1008;**
        RAIL 1015; RAIL 1057
    Parliamentary papers, **RAIL 1066**
    Parliamentary plans, **RAIL 1071**
    Prospectus, **RAIL 1110**
    Reports and accounts, **RAIL 1110**
    Rule books, **RAIL 1134**
    Share certificates, **RAIL 1158**
    Subscription contracts, **RAIL 1160**
    Timetables, **RAIL 981**
Liverpool Corporation Tramways
    Reports and accounts, **RAIL 1114**

Liverpool, Crosby and Southport Railway,
   RAIL 372 (*includes records of jt cttee with* L&YR)
      Miscellanea, **RAIL 1008**
      Parliamentary plans, **RAIL 1071**
      Reports and accounts, **RAIL 1116**
      Subscription contracts, **RAIL 1160**
Liverpool, Manchester and Newcastle Junction
   Railway
      Map, **RAIL 1152**
      Miscellanea, **RAIL 1157**
      Reports and accounts, **RAIL 1111; RAIL 1116**
      Share certificates, **RAIL 1159**
Liverpool New Cattle Market and Railways
   (Liverpool Cattle Market Co)
      Parliamentary papers, **RAIL 1066**
Liverpool, Ormskirk and Preston Railway,
   RAIL 373
Liverpool (Overhead) Electric Railway, **RAIL 778**
      Reports and accounts, **RAIL 1116; RAIL 1117**
      Working timetables appendixes, **RAIL 1136**
See also BTC Chief Secretary's Office
Liverpool, St Helens and South Lancashire
   Railway, **RAIL 374** (*includes records of predecessor*
   St Helens & Wigan Jct R)
      Parliamentary papers, **RAIL 1066**
      Reports and accounts, **RAIL 1110**
Liverpool, Southport and Preston Junction
   Railway, **RAIL 375**
      Railway and Canal Traffic Acts proceedings,
         RAIL 1038
      Reports and accounts, **RAIL 1116; RAIL 1117**
Liverpool Tramways
      Parliamentary papers, **RAIL 1068**
Lizard Light Railway
      Miscellanea, **RAIL 1057**
Llanelly and Llandilo Railway
      Timetables, **RAIL 981**
Llanelly and Llandilo Railway and Dock Company
   (proposed)
      Prospectuses etc, **RAIL 1075**
Llanelly and Mynydd Mawr Railway, **RAIL 376**
   (*includes records of* GWR *and* BTC)
      Miscellanea, **RAIL 1057**
      Railway and Canal Traffic Acts proceedings,
         RAIL 1038
See also Carmarthenshire R or Tramroad
   GWR locomotives and rolling stock
Llanelly and Pontardulais Railway (proposed)
      Miscellanea, **RAIL 1057**
      Parliamentary papers, **RAIL 1066**
Llanelly Harbour and Pontardulais Railway
   (proposed)
      Parliamentary papers, **RAIL 1066**
Llanelly Railway and Dock Company, **RAIL 377**
      Byelaws and regulations, **RAIL 1001**
      Joint committee *see* Vale of Towy R Jt Cttee
      Law cases and arbitration, **RAIL 1027**

Parliamentary papers, **RAIL 1066; RAIL 1163**
Prospectuses etc, **RAIL 1075**
Reports and accounts, **RAIL 1110; RAIL 1116;**
   RAIL 1117
Timetables, **RAIL 981**
Llanfihangel Tramway
      Miscellanea, **RAIL 1057**
Llanfoist Tramway
      Miscellanea, **RAIL 1057**
Llanfyllin and Llangynog Railway
      Parliamentary plans, **RAIL 1071**
Llanfyllin Railway (proposed)
      Parliamentary plans, **RAIL 1071**
Llangammarch and Neath and Brecon Railway
      Miscellanea, **RAIL 1057**
Llangollen and Corwen Railway, **RAIL 378**
      Railway and Canal Traffic Acts proceedings,
         RAIL 1038
      Reports and accounts, **RAIL 1110; RAIL 1116**
Llanidloes and Newtown Railway, **RAIL 379**
      Miscellanea, **RAIL 1008**
      Parliamentary papers, **RAIL 1066; RAIL 1163**
      Reports and accounts, **RAIL 1116**
Llantrissant and Taff Vale Junction Railway,
   RAIL 380
      Parliamentary papers, **RAIL 1066**
      Prospectus, **RAIL 1110**
      Reports and accounts, **RAIL 1110; RAIL 1116**
Llynvi and Ogmore Railway, **RAIL 382** (*includes
   records of* GWR *and* BR)
      Joint committee with GWR, **RAIL 381**
      Maps, **RAIL 1030**
      Miscellanea, **RAIL 1014; RAIL 1057**
      Reports and accounts, **RAIL 1110; RAIL 1116**
See also GWR estates and rating
Llynvi and Tonddu Railway
      Reports and accounts, **RAIL 1110**
Llynvi Valley Railway, **RAIL 383** (*includes records
   relating to* Duffryn, Llynvi & Porthcawl R)
      Miscellanea, **RAIL 1014**
      Parliamentary papers, **RAIL 1163**
      Reports and accounts, **RAIL 1110; RAIL 1116;**
         RAIL 1117
London and Aylesbury Railway
      Parliamentary papers, **RAIL 1066**
London and Birmingham Railway, **RAIL 384**
   (*includes records of* London, Coventry &
   Birmingham R (proposed) *and* LNWR)
      Byelaws and regulations, **RAIL 1001**
      Maps, **RAIL 1030**
      Miscellanea, **RAIL 1007; RAIL 1008;**
         RAIL 1015; RAIL 1016; RAIL 1057;
         RAIL 1153
      Parliamentary papers, **RAIL 1066**
      Parliamentary plans, **RAIL 1071**
      Prospectuses etc, **RAIL 1075**
      Reports and accounts, **RAIL 1110**

Share certificates and dividend warrants,
RAIL 1158
Subscription contracts, **RAIL 1160**
Timetables, **RAIL 981**
See also BR hotels and catering
LNWR
Trent Valley R
Warwick & Leamington Union R
London and Blackwall Railway, **RAIL 385** (*includes
some records of predecessor* Commercial R *q.v. and*
East & W India Dock Co)
Miscellanea, **RAIL 1021**
Parliamentary papers, **RAIL 1066; RAIL 1163**
Parliamentary plans, **RAIL 1071**
Prospectuses etc, **RAIL 1075**
Reports and accounts, **RAIL 1110; RAIL 1116;
RAIL 1117**
Rule books, **RAIL 1134**
Share certificates, **RAIL 1158**
See also LTSR
London and Brighton Railway, **RAIL 386** (*includes
records of the* LBSCR)
Byelaws and regulations, **RAIL 1001**
Joint committees with:
London & Croydon R
RAIL 71 (committee of amalgamation)
RAIL 386 (London Bridge station; jt
locomotive committee)
South Eastern R
RAIL 386 (London Bridge station; jt
locomotive committee)
Miscellanea, **RAIL 1016; RAIL 1017;
RAIL 1153**
Parliamentary papers, **RAIL 1066**
Prospectuses etc, **RAIL 1075; RAIL 1076**
Reports and accounts, **RAIL 1110; RAIL 1117**
Timetables, **RAIL 981**
See also GWR miscellanea Brunel collection
London and Chatham and Chatham and
Portsmouth Junction Railway (proposed),
RAIL 387 (*Project taken over by* London &
Croydon R *in 1844*)
London and Croydon Railway, **RAIL 388**
Byelaws and regulations, **RAIL 1001**
Joint committees with:
London & Brighton R
RAIL 71 (committee of amalgamation)
RAIL 386 (London Bridge station; jt
locomotive committee)
South Eastern Railway
RAIL 66 (Bricklayers' Arms Extension R)
RAIL 386 (London Bridge station;
jt locomotive committee)
Miscellanea, **RAIL 1006; RAIL 1008; RAIL 1017**
Parliamentary papers, **RAIL 1066**
Reports and accounts, **RAIL 1110**
Timetables, **RAIL 981**

See also London & Chatham & Chatham &
Portsmouth Jct R (proposed)
London and Dover Railway
Parliamentary papers, **RAIL 1066**
Prospectuses etc, **RAIL 1075**
Timetables, **RAIL 981**
London and Eastbourne Railway (proposed)
Parliamentary papers, **RAIL 1066**
London and Greenwich Railway, **RAIL 389**
Prospectuses etc, **RAIL 1075**
Reports and accounts, **RAIL 1116**
London and Mid-Western Railway (proposed),
RAIL 1183
Map, **RAIL 1014**
Parliamentary papers, **RAIL 1163**
London and North Eastern Railway
Absorption of subsidiary companies
(grouping), **RAIL 390**
Accountant, **RAIL 400** (*includes records of*
GNR)
Air services, **RAIL 390; RAIL 393**
Byelaws and regulations, **RAIL 1001;
RAIL 1003** (Canals and docks)
Correspondence and papers, **RAIL 396**
Deeds contracts etc, **RAIL 392** (*includes records
of* BR(ER), GCR, GER, GNR, NER)
Housing organizations, **RAIL 1058**
Instructions to staff, **RAIL 1135**
Joint committees with:
GWR
RAIL 239 (Banbury Jct R)
RAIL 250 (W London electrification)
RAIL 390 (pooling; Standing Jt Cttee)
LMSR, **RAIL 417; RAIL 421**
Byelaws and regulations, **RAIL 1001**
Locomotives and traffic, **RAIL 390**
Pooling, **RAIL 390**
Reports and accounts, **RAIL 1116** *includes*:
Aberdeen Jt Station Cttee
Dumbarton & Balloch line
Dundee & Arbroath line
Leeds New Station Cttee
Perth General Station Cttee
Perth Station Hotel & Refreshment
Rooms
Princes Dock Branch Jt Line Cttee
Road services, **RAIL 390**
Rule books, **RAIL 1134**
RAIL 224; RAIL 225 (Braithwell Jct to
Laughton Jct Line)
RAIL 222 (GCR/LNWR Jt Cttee)
RAIL 224 (GCR/MR Jt Cttee)
RAIL 234 (GNR/LNWR Jt Cttee)
RAIL 448 (Macclesfield, Bollington &
Marple R)
RAIL 390; RAIL 465 (Manchester S Jct &
Altrincham R)

LNER (continued)
        RAIL 551 (Oldham, Ashton-under-Lyne & Guide Bridge Jct R)
        RAIL 224 (Sheffield & Midland Cttee)
        RAIL 390 (Standing Jt Cttee)
        RAIL 421 (Tebay Jt Station Cttee)
        See also Macclesfield, Bollington & Marple R
    LPTB
        Timetables, **RAIL 984**
        RAIL 250 (W London electrification)
        RAIL 390 (Standing Jt Cttee)
    Met R
        Byelaws and regulations, **RAIL 1001**
        Rule books, **RAIL 1134**
        RAIL 1110 (Watford Committee reports and accounts)
    SR
        RAIL 390 (Standing Jt Cttee)
    See also Axholme Jt R Cttee
    Cheshire Lines Cttee
    E London R
    Halifax & Ovenden Jt Cttee
    Leeds New Station Cttee
    LMSR miscellanea
    Methley R Jt Cttee
    Mid-Nottinghamshire Jt Ctte
    Norfolk & Suffolk Jt Rys Cttee
    Normanton Jt Station Cttee
    Otley & Ilkley Jt Line Cttee
    S Yorkshire Jt Line Cttee
    Tottenham & Hampstead Jct R
  Labour and staff matters, **RAIL 1025**
  Law cases and arbitration, **RAIL 1027**
  Locomotives and rolling stock, **RAIL 394** (*includes records of or about* BR(E), GCR, GER, GNR, H&BR, M&GNJR, NER)
  Maps, **RAIL 1030**
  Mileage diagrams, **RAIL 798**
  Minutes and reports, **RAIL 390** *including*:
    Manchester S Jct & Altrincham R
    N Sunderland R
    Railway Air Services
    Sand Hutton Lt R
    Seaforth & Sefton Jct R
  Miscellanea, **RAIL 393** (*includes records of* BR(E), BR(NE), GCR, GER, GNR, NER); **RAIL 1005; RAIL 1006; RAIL 1008; RAIL 1014; RAIL 1015; RAIL 1016; RAIL 1020; RAIL 1021; RAIL 1057; RAIL 1058**
  N & S Shields Lt R (Kearney Tube), **RAIL 780**
  North Eastern Area
    Deeds etc, **RAIL 794**
  N Sunderland R, **RAIL 533; RAIL 390**
  Parliamentary
    Acts, **RAIL 1062; RAIL 1063; RAIL 1064; RAIL 1065**
    Bills, **RAIL 395; 1066; 1067; 1069**
    Papers, **RAIL 1066; RAIL 1067**
  Publications and publicity, **RAIL 399; RAIL 981**
  Railway Rates Tribunal proceedings, **RAIL 1101**
  Reports and accounts, **RAIL 1110; RAIL 1116; RAIL 1117**
  Road services
    Carter Paterson & Co, **RAIL 1130**
    Hay's Wharf Cartage Co, **RAIL 1131**
    Pickfords & Hay's Wharf Shipping & Forwarding Co, **RAIL 1132**
    Pickfords Ltd, **RAIL 1133**
  Rolling stock, **RAIL 394**
  Rule books, **RAIL 1134**
  Sand Hutton Lt R, **RAIL 390**
  Savings banks, **RAIL 1174**
  Shares and shareholders, **RAIL 391**
  Share certificates, **RAIL 1158**
  Shipping services, **RAIL 390**
  Sidings agreements, **RAIL 1167**
  Staff, **RAIL 397**
    Instructions and guidance, **RAIL 1178**
    Pension societies, **RAIL 390**
  Statistics, **RAIL 398**
  Stockholders Association reports and accounts, **RAIL 1116**
  Strikes and civil disturbances, **RAIL 789**
  Superannuation schemes, **RAIL 1174**
  Timetables
    Public, **RAIL 943; RAIL 981**
    Working, **RAIL 944**
      appendixes, **RAIL 1136**
  Traders' ledger credit agreements, **RAIL 1165**
  Train notices, **RAIL 401** (*includes records of* NER)
  Welfare schemes, **RAIL 1174**
  See also BR hotels and catering;
    GCR
    GER
    GNR
    Hull South Bridge Co
    Irish & English Traffic Conference
    MSLR
    NER
    S&DR
London and North Western Railway, RAIL 410
  includes records of or about:
    Ashton,Stalybridge & Liverpool Jct R
    Bedford & Cambridge R
    Birmingham, Wolverhampton & Stour Valley R
    Carnarvon & Llanberis R
    Carnarvonshire R
    Chester & Holyhead R
    Cromford & High Peak R
    Dearne Valley R
    Denbigh, Ruthin & Corwen R

Dundalk & Greenore R
Dundalk, Newry & Greenore R
Dyserth & Newmarket Light R
Kettering & Thrapstone R
Lancaster & Carlisle R
London & Birmingham R
LMSR
Merthyr, Tredegar & Abergavenny R
N & S Western Jct R
North London R
Shropshire Union Rys & Canal Co
Sirhowy R
S Leicestershire R
S London R (proposed)
Stockport, Disley & Whaley Bridge R
Vale of Clwyd R
Waterford & Limerick R
Whitehaven, Cleator & Egremont R
Byelaws and regulations, **RAIL 1001**
Deeds, contracts, etc, **RAIL 791**
Guarantee Fund, **RAIL 410**
Instructions to staff, **RAIL 1135**
Insurance Society, reports and accounts,
    RAIL 1116
Joint committees with:
    Birkenhead, Lancashire & Cheshire Jct R
        RAIL 35 (Birkenhead R)
    Brecon & Merthyr R
        RAIL 402; RAIL 410; RAIL 421
            Rule books, **RAIL 1134**
    Cal R
        RAIL 410; RAIL 421 (Carlisle goods
            traffic)
        RAIL 421 (Portpatrick & Wigtownshire Jt
            R)
        RAIL 410; RAIL 727 (W Coast
            Conference)
    Central Wales & Carmarthen Jct R
        RAIL 410 (Vale of Towy R)
    Cockermouth, Keswick & Penrith R
        RAIL 122; RAIL 123; RAIL 410; RAIL 421
            (Cockermouth jt station)
        RAIL 563 (Penrith jt station)
    E Lancashire R, **RAIL 410** (Preston station)
    Furness R, **RAIL 403; RAIL 410; RAIL 421**
        Rule books, **RAIL 1134**
        Railway & Canal Traffic Acts
            proceedings, **RAIL 1038**
See also LMSR miscellanea
GSWR
    RAIL 98; RAIL 410; RAIL 421 (Carlisle
        goods traffic)
    RAIL 421 (Portpatrick & Wigtownshire Jt
        R)
GCR
    Reports and accounts, **RAIL 421;**
        RAIL 1110

RAIL 410; RAIL 421; RAIL 435
    (Manchester London Rd station)
RAIL 465 (Manchester S Jct & Altrincham
    line)
    Reports and accounts, **RAIL 1116**
    Timetables, **RAIL 930**
See also LMSR miscellanea
GER, **RAIL 1116** (reports & accounts)
GNR, **RAIL 234; RAIL 408; RAIL 410;**
    RAIL 421
    Byelaws and regulations,
        RAIL 1001
    Reports and accounts, **RAIL 1110;**
        RAIL 1116
    RAIL 410 (Halifax High Level)
    RAIL 341; RAIL 410 (Jt stations)
See also LMSR miscellanea
GWR, **RAIL 404**
    Byelaws and regulations, **RAIL 1001**
    Labour and staff matters, **RAIL 1025**
    Railway and Canal Traffic Acts
        proceedings, **RAIL 1038** *includes*:
            Ludlow & Clee Hill R
            Pontypool & Talywain R
            Shrewsbury & Hereford R
            Tenbury R
    Rule books, **RAIL 1134**
    Working timetables appendixes,
        RAIL 1136
    RAIL 35 (Birkenhead R)
    RAIL 617 (Shrewsbury & Hereford R)
    RAIL 690 (Tenbury R)
    RAIL 410 (W London Extension R)
    RAIL 759 (Wolverhampton High Level
        station)
See also LMSR miscellanea
L&YR
    Byelaws and regulations, **RAIL 1001**
    Parliamentary papers, **RAIL 1163**
    Rule books, **RAIL 1134**
    RAIL 623 (Jt stations)
    RAIL 342; RAIL 410 (Lancashire Union
        Rys)
    Railway & Canal Traffic Acts
        proceedings, **RAIL 1038**
    RAIL 410 (Leeds jt station)
    RAIL 410 (North Union R)
    Railway & Canal Traffic Acts
        proceedings, **RAIL 1038**
    RAIL 410 (Preston & Wyre R)
    Railway & Canal Traffic Acts
        proceedings, **RAIL 1038**
    Timetables, **RAIL 981**
    RAIL 410 (Preston station)
    RAIL 1038 (Ribble Branch, Railway &
        Canal Traffic Acts proceedings)
See also LMSR miscellanea

LNWR (continued)
    Llanelly R & Dock Co, **RAIL 410; RAIL 706**
      (Vale of Towy R)
    LSWR, **RAIL 410** (W London Extension R)
    LBSCR, **RAIL 410** (W London Extension R)
    London Electric Rys, **RAIL 410** (Jt stock)
    MSLR, **RAIL 408; RAIL 409**
      RAIL 410; RAIL 421; RAIL 435
        (Manchester London Rd station)
      RAIL 410; RAIL 464; RAIL 465
        (Manchester S Jct & Altrincham R)
      RAIL 410; RAIL 551 (Oldham, Ashton-
        under-Lyne & Guide Bridge Jct R)
      RAIL 464 (Warrington & Stockport)
    MR, **RAIL 406; RAIL 409; RAIL 421**
      Rule books, **RAIL 1134**
      RAIL 98; RAIL 410; RAIL 421 (Carlisle
        goods traffic)
      RAIL 410 (N & S Western Jct R)
      RAIL 421 (Portpatrick & Wigtownshire
        Jt R)
    See also LMSR miscellanea
    NER
      RAIL 410 (Axholme Jt R)
      RAIL 356; RAIL 410; RAIL 417; RAIL 421
        (Leeds New station)
      RAIL 410 (Methley R)
    North London R
      RAIL 521; RAIL 410 (N & S Western
        Jct R)
    North Staffordshire R, **RAIL 449**
      (Macclesfield jt station)
    North Western & Charing Cross R,
      RAIL 410
    Rhymney R, **RAIL 407**
    See also LMSR miscellanea
    Shrewsbury & Birmingham R
      RAIL 759 (Wolverhampton High Level
        station)
        Rule books, **RAIL 1134**
    Shropshire Union Rys & Canal Co
      Amalgamated Board, **RAIL 623**
      Parliamentary plans, **RAIL 1071**
    SER
      RAIL 410 (N Western & Charing Cross R)
    S&DR
      RAIL 563 (Penrith jt station)
      RAIL 686 (Tebay station)
    W Midland R
      RAIL 617 (Shrewsbury & Hereford R)
    See also Ashby & Nuneaton Jt Cttee
    Carlisle Citadel Station Cttee
    Chester Jt Station Cttee
    Halifax & Ovenden Jt Cttee
    Hereford Jt Station Construction & Traffic
      Cttee
    Humber Conference

    Huddersfield Jt Station Cttee
    Leeds Central Station
    London & W Riding Association
    Normanton Jt Station Cttee
    Northern Alliance
    Oldham, Ashton-under-Lyne & Guide
      Bridge Jct R, Oldham R Cttee
    Preston & Longridge Jt Cttee
    Shrewsbury & Wellington Jt Line Cttee
    Shrewsbury Jt Station Cttee
    Southern Association Conference
    South Yorkshire Jt Lines Cttee
    Stalybridge Jt Station Cttee
    Tebay Jt Station Cttee
    Vale of Towy R Jt Cttee
    Wrexham & Minera R Jt Cttee
Labour and staff matters, **RAIL 1025**
Law cases and arbitration, **RAIL 1027**
Maps, **RAIL 1030**
Miscellanea, **RAIL 1005; RAIL 1007;**
    RAIL 1008; RAIL 1014; RAIL 1015;
    RAIL 1020; RAIL 1057
Opposition to Wallasey Embankment Bill,
    RAIL 1202
Parliamentary papers, **RAIL 1066; RAIL 1147;**
    RAIL 1163
Parliamentary plans, **RAIL 1071**
Prospectuses etc, **RAIL 1075**
Provident and Pension Society, **RAIL 1116;**
    RAIL 1174
Railway and Canal Traffic Acts proceedings,
    RAIL 1038
Railway Rates Tribunal proceedings,**RAIL 1101**
Reports and accounts, **RAIL 1110; RAIL 1116;**
    RAIL 1117
Rule books, **RAIL 1134**
Savings Bank reports and accounts, **RAIL 1117**
    Rules, **RAIL 1174**
Share certificates and dividend warrants,
    RAIL 1158
Sidings agreements, **RAIL 1167**
Superannuation schemes, **RAIL 1174**
Timetables
    Public, **RAIL 945; RAIL 981**
    Working, **RAIL 946**
      appendixes, **RAIL 1136**
Traders' ledger credit agreements, **RAIL 1165**
Welfare schemes, **RAIL 1115; RAIL 1174**
See also Birmingham, Wolverhampton & Stour
    Valley R
    BR horse records
    BR hotels and catering
    Grand Junction R
    Huddersfield & Manchester R & Canal Co
    Irish & English Traffic Conference
    Lancaster & Carlisle R
    Leeds, Dewsbury & Manchester R

London & Birmingham R
LMSR amalgamation, correspondence and
  papers, minutes and reports, shares and
  shareholders
Manchester & Birmingham R
Manchester, Buxton, Matlock & Midlands Jct R
Shropshire Union Railway & Canal Co.
Stockport, Disley & Whaley Bridge R
Vale of Clwyd R
London and North Western Railway and
  Buckinghamshire Railways (proposed)
  Parliamentary papers, **RAIL 1163**
London and Southampton Railway, **RAIL 412**
  (*includes records of* LSWR)
  Parliamentary papers, **RAIL 1066**
  Prospectuses etc, **RAIL 1075**
  Reports and accounts, **RAIL 1110**
  Timetables, **RAIL 981**
See also GWR miscellanea Brunel collection
London and South Wales Railway (proposed)
  Miscellanea, **RAIL 1057**
London and South Western Railway, RAIL 411
  (*includes records of* BR(S), SR)
  Byelaws and regulations, **RAIL 1001**
  Engine Drivers Firemen Locomotive and
    Electrical Engineering Departments
      Friendly Society *see* SR
      Pension Society *see* SR
  Instructions to staff, **RAIL 1135**
  Joint committees with:
    GWR, **RAIL 240; RAIL 258**
      RAIL 410 (W London Extension R)
    See also Easton & Church Hope R
    LNWR, **RAIL 410** (W London Extension R)
    LBSCR
      RAIL 197 (Epsom & Leatherhead R)
      RAIL 410 (W London Extension R)
      RAIL 414 (Epsom & Leatherhead R;
        Portsmouth R; Portsmouth, Southsea &
        Ryde Jt Rlys & Steam Packets; Tooting,
        Merton & Wimbledon R)
    See also Isle of Wight & Ryde Pier R
    Somerset & Dorset Jt Line Cttee
  Labour and staff matters, **RAIL 1025**
  Law cases and arbitration, **RAIL 1027**
  Maps, **RAIL 1030**
  Miscellanea, **RAIL 1005; RAIL 1008;**
    RAIL 1014; RAIL 1017; RAIL 1020;
    RAIL 1057
  New Provident and Sick Benefit Society *see* SR
  Parliamentary papers, **RAIL 1066; RAIL 1163**
  Parliamentary plans, **RAIL 1071**
  Prospectuses etc, **RAIL 1075**
  Railway and Canal Traffic Acts proceedings,
    RAIL 1038
  Reports and accounts, **RAIL 1110; RAIL 1116;**
    RAIL 1117

Savings bank, **RAIL 1174** (rules) *see also* SR
Superannuation Fund Association,
  RAIL 1174
  see also SR
Timetables
  Continental, **RAIL 976**
  Public, **RAIL 947; RAIL 981**
  Working, **RAIL 948**
    appendixes, **RAIL 1136**
Welfare records, **RAIL 1174**
See also Bentley & Bordon Lt R
  London & Southampton R
  N Devon & Cornwall Jct Lt R
  SR locomotives and rolling stock; minutes and
    reports; miscellanea
  Stonehouse Pool Improvement Co
London and Suburban Traction Company *holding
  company for:*
    London United Tramways
    Metropolitan Electric Tramways
    S Metropolitan Electric Tramways &
      Lighting Co
  Reports and accounts, **RAIL 1114**
London and West Riding Association
  (L&YR/LNWR/GNR/MR/NER), **RAIL 413**
London and Windsor Railway (proposed),
  RAIL 989
  Parliamentary plans, **RAIL 1071**
  Prospectus, **RAIL 1016**
See also GWR miscellanea
London and Worcester and Rugby and Oxford
  Railway (proposed) *see* London, Worcester & S
  Staffordshire R
London and York and Direct Northern Railways
  Joint Board *see* GNR
London and York Railway (proposed) *see* GNR
  Miscellanea, **RAIL 1153**
London, Beaconsfield and High Wycombe Railway
  (proposed)
  Parliamentary papers, **RAIL 1066**
London Bridge and Charing Cross Railway
  (proposed)
  Parliamentary papers, **RAIL 1066**
  Prospectuses etc, **RAIL 1075**
See also Charing Cross R
London, Brighton and South Coast Railway,
  RAIL 414 (*includes records of or about* Lewes &
  E Grinstead R; W Sussex Jct R)
  Byelaws and regulations, **RAIL 1001**
  Deeds, contracts etc, **RAIL 797**
  Instructions to staff, **RAIL 1135**
  Joint committees with:
    GWR, **RAIL 410** (W London Extension R)
    LNWR, **RAIL 410** (W London Extension R)
    LSWR
      RAIL 197 (Epsom & Leatherhead R)
      RAIL 410 (W London Extension R)

LBSCR (continued)
    RAIL 414 (Epsom & Leatherhead R;
        Portsmouth R; Portsmouth, Southsea &
        Ryde Jt Rys & Steam Packets; Tooting,
        Merton & Wimbledon R)
    SER
    RAIL 414 (Croydon & Oxted line)
    RAIL 760 (Woodside & S Croydon)
  See also E London R
    Isle of Wight & Ryde Pier Co
  Labour and staff matters, **RAIL 1025**
  Law cases and arbitration, **RAIL 1027**
  Maps, **RAIL 1030**
  Miscellanea, **RAIL 1005; RAIL 1014;**
    RAIL 1017; RAIL 1020; RAIL 1057
  Parliamentary papers, **RAIL 1066; RAIL 1163**
  Pension Fund reports and accounts,
    RAIL 1117 *see also* SR
  Prospectuses etc, **RAIL 1075**
  Provident Society reports and accounts,
    RAIL 1117
  Railway and Canal Traffic Acts proceedings,
    RAIL 1038
  Reports and accounts, **RAIL 1110; RAIL 1116;**
    RAIL 1117
  Rule books, **RAIL 1134**
  Savings bank rules, **RAIL 1174**
  Superannuation schemes, **RAIL 1174**
  Timetables
    Continental, **RAIL 949**
    Public, **RAIL 950; RAIL 981**
    Tourist, **RAIL 952**
    Working, **RAIL 951**
      appendixes, **RAIL 1136**
    E London R, **RAIL 927**
  Traders' ledger credit agreements, **RAIL 1165**
  Welfare fund accounts etc, **RAIL 1115;**
    RAIL 1174
See also BR hotels and catering
    Hayling Bridge & Causeway Management Cttee
    Hayling R
    London & Brighton R
    Newhaven and Seaford Sea Defence
      Commissioners
    Newhaven Harbour Co
London, Bristol and South Wales Direct Railway
  (proposed)
    GWR miscellanea, **RAIL 1014**
London, Bucks and East Gloucester Railway
  (proposed)
    Parliamentary papers, **RAIL 1066**
London, Camberwell and Dulwich Tramways
    Parliamentary papers, **RAIL 1066**
London Central Electric Railway (proposed)
    Parliamentary plans, **RAIL 1071**
London Central Subway Railway (proposed)
    Parliamentary papers, **RAIL 1066**

    Parliamentary plans, **RAIL 1071**
London (City) and Finsbury (Borough)
  Improvements and Railway City Terminus and
  Stations (proposed)
    Subscription contract, **RAIL 1163**
London, Chatham and Dover Railway, **RAIL 415**
  (*includes records of predecessor* E Kent R)
  Instructions to staff, **RAIL 1135**
  Joint committees *see* E London R
    Sittingbourne & Sheerness & LCDR Jt Cttee
  Law cases and arbitration, **RAIL 1027**
  Miscellanea, **RAIL 1008; RAIL 1014;**
    RAIL 1017
  Parliamentary papers, **RAIL 1066**
  Prospectuses etc, **RAIL 1075**
  Railway & Canal Traffic Acts proceedings,
    RAIL 1038
  Reports and accounts, **RAIL 1110; RAIL 1116;**
    RAIL 1117
  Rule books, **RAIL 1134**
  Savings bank **RAIL 1174** (rules) *see also* SR
  Timetables
    Continental, **RAIL 953**
    Public, **RAIL 954; RAIL 981**
    Working, **RAIL 955**
      appendixes, **RAIL 1136**
    E London R, **RAIL 927**
  Welfare schemes, **RAIL 1174**
See also Gravesend R
    SECR
London, Chatham and North Kent Railway
  (proposed)
    Prospectuses etc, **RAIL 1075**
See also North Kent R (Vignoles')
London County Council Tramways
    Miscellanea, **RAIL 1057**
    Parliamentary papers, **RAIL 1066; RAIL 1068**
    Reports and accounts, **RAIL 1114**
    Rule books, **RAIL 1134**
London County Tramways (proposed)
    Parliamentary papers, **RAIL 1066**
London, Coventry and Birmingham Railway
  (proposed) *see* London & Birmingham R
London, Deptford and Greenwich Tramways
    Law cases and arbitration, **RAIL 1027**
    Parliamentary papers, **RAIL 1066**
Londonderry and Coleraine Railway
    Reports and accounts, **RAIL 1116; RAIL 1117**
    Share certificates, **RAIL 1158**
Londonderry and Enniskillen Railway
    Reports and accounts, **RAIL 1116; RAIL 1117**
    Timetables, **RAIL 941**
Londonderry and Lough Swilly Railway
    Railway and Canal Traffic Acts proceedings,
      RAIL 1038
    Reports and accounts, **RAIL 1116**
See also Irish & English Traffic Conference

Londonderry Railway (Seaham to Sunderland)
  Railway and Canal Traffic Acts proceedings,
    RAIL 1038
  Timetable, **RAIL 981**
London Electric Transport Finance Corporation
  Reports and accounts, **RAIL 1116**
London Electric Railways (*division of* Underground
  Electric Rys Co of London *controlling* Baker St &
  Waterloo R, Charing Cross, Euston &
  Hampstead R, *and* Great Northern, Piccadilly &
  Brompton R)
    Labour and staff matters, **RAIL 1025**
    LER/LNWR jt stock, **RAIL 410**
    Miscellanea, **RAIL 1020**
    Parliamentary papers, **RAIL 1066**
    Pension fund, **RAIL 1174**
    Reports and accounts, **RAIL 1110; RAIL 1116;**
      RAIL 1117
    Rule books, **RAIL 1134**
    Timetables, **RAIL 984**
London, Essex and Kent Coast Junction Railway
  Parliamentary papers, **RAIL 1066**
London Grand Junction Railway (proposed)
  Prospectus, **RAIL 1016**
London, Lewes and Brighton Railway
  Parliamentary papers, **RAIL 1066**
London, Midland and Scottish Railway
  Air services, **RAIL 253; RAIL 425**
  Amalgamation (under Railways Act 1921),
    RAIL 427 (*includes papers about railway
    companies amalgamated into the LMSR. They
    are not listed individually here but are cross-
    referred to this series from their own index
    entries*)
  Byelaws and regulations, **RAIL 1001;**
    RAIL 1003 (Holyhead Harbours)
  Civil Engineer's records, **RAIL 430**
  Correspondence and papers, **RAIL 424**
    (*includes records of* Wolverhampton &
    Cannock Chase Lt R *and* LNWR agreements
    with Irish Rys)
  Deeds, contracts etc, **RAIL 420**
  Hotels, **RAIL 1022**
  Instructions to staff, **RAIL 1135**
  Joint committees with:
    GWR
      Byelaws and regulations, **RAIL 1001**
      Reports and accounts, **RAIL 1110**
      RAIL 1005 (Avonmouth Lt R miscellanea)
      RAIL 402 (Brecon & Merthyr jt section)
      RAIL 241 (Midland section)
      RAIL 1116; RAIL 1117 (Severn & Wye &
        Severn Bridge R reports and accounts)
      RAIL 1136 (Severn & Wye R working
        timetable appendixes)
      RAIL 981 (Shrewsbury & Hereford Jt
        Line timetables)

    RAIL 390 (Standing Jt Cttee)
    RAIL 254 (Vale of Towy R)
  LNER, **RAIL 417; RAIL 421**
    Byelaws and regulations, **RAIL 1001**
    Locomotives and traffic, **RAIL 390**
    Pooling, **RAIL 390**
    Reports and accounts, **RAIL 1116** *includes*:
      Aberdeen Jt Station Cttee
      Dumbarton & Balloch line
      Dundee & Arbroath line
      Leeds New Station Cttee
      Perth General Station Cttee
      Perth Station Hotel and Refreshment
        Rooms
      Princes Dock Branch Jt Line Cttee
    Road services, **RAIL 390**
    Rule books, **RAIL 1134**
    RAIL 224; RAIL 225 (Braithwell Jct to
      Laughton Jct Line)
    RAIL 222 (GCR/LNWR Jt Cttee)
    RAIL 224 (GCR/MR Jt Cttee)
    RAIL 234 (GNR/LNWR Jt Cttee)
    RAIL 448 (Macclesfield, Bollington &
      Marple R)
    RAIL 390; RAIL 465 (Manchester S Jct &
      Altrincham R)
    RAIL 551 (Oldham, Ashton-under-Lyne
      & Guide Bridge Jct R)
    RAIL 224 (Sheffield & Midland Cttee)
    RAIL 390 (Standing Jt Cttee)
    RAIL 421 (Tebay Jt Station Cttee)
  See also Macclesfield, Bollington & Marple R
  LPTB
    RAIL 390 (Standing Jt Cttee)
  SR
    RAIL 390 (Standing Jt Cttee)
  See also Axholme Jt R Cttee
    Cheshire Lines Cttee
    Halifax & Ovenden Jt Cttee
    Leeds New Jt Station Cttee
    Methley R Jt Cttee
    Mid-Nottinghamshire Jt Cttee
    Norfolk & Suffolk Jt Rys Cttee
    Normanton Jt Station Cttee
    Otley & Ilkley Jt Line Cttee
    Somerset & Dorset Jt Line Cttee
    S Yorkshire Jt Line Cttee
    Tottenham & Hampstead Jct R
  Labour and staff matters, **RAIL 1025**
  Law cases and arbitration, **RAIL 1027**
  Locomotives, **RAIL 422**
  Maps, **RAIL 1030**
  Minutes and reports, **RAIL 418** (*includes
    records of* LNWR)
  Miscellanea, **RAIL 1005; RAIL 1007;**
    RAIL 1014; RAIL 1015; RAIL 1020;
    RAIL 1021; RAIL 1057

LMSR (continued)
    RAIL 421 *includes records of or about:*
        BR
        Charnwood Forest R
        Manchester South Jct & Altrincham R
        N & S Western Jct R
        N London R
        Shropshire Union Rys & Canal Co
    and joint committees:
        Brecon & Merthyr R
        Carlisle Citadel station
        Carlisle goods traffic
        Cockermouth station
        GCR/LNWR
        GNR/LNWR
        GWR/LNWR
        L&YR/LNWR
        Leeds New station
        LNWR/Furness R
        LNWR/MR
        LNWR/Rhymney R
        LMSR/LNER Jt lines
        Manchester London Road station
        Portpatrick & Wigtownshire Jt R
        Stalybridge station
        Tebay jt station
    Northern Counties Committee, **RAIL 542**
        Reports and accounts, **RAIL 1116**
        Timetables, **RAIL 941**
    See also Irish & English Traffic Conference
        Northern Counties R Committee
    Parliamentary
        Bills, **RAIL 423**
        Railways Act 1921 papers, **RAIL 427**
        Papers, **RAIL 1066; RAIL 1163**
    Publications, **RAIL 429**
    Railway Rates Tribunal proceedings, **RAIL 1101**
    Record Office files, **RAIL 1007**
    Reports and accounts, **RAIL 1110; RAIL 1116; RAIL 1117**
    Research Department engineering reports, **RAIL 792**
    Road services
        Carter Paterson & Co, **RAIL 1130**
        Hay's Wharf Cartage Co, **RAIL 1131**
        Pickfords & Hay's Wharf Shipping & Forwarding Co, **RAIL 1132**
        Pickfords Ltd, **RAIL 1133**
    Rolling stock, **RAIL 422**
    Royal events, **RAIL 1010**
    Rule books, **RAIL 1134**
    Secretarial papers, **RAIL 425** (*includes records about* County Donegal Rys)
    Shares and shareholders, **RAIL 419** (*includes records of* LNWR)
    Share certificates and dividend warrants, **RAIL 1158**

    Shipping services, **RAIL 433; RAIL 425**
    Sidings agreements, **RAIL 1167**
    Solicitor's records, **RAIL 431** (*includes records of or about* Avonmouth Lt R; Burton & Ashby Lt R; L&YR; MR; Wolverhampton & Cannock Chase R)
    Staff, **RAIL 426**
    Statistics, **RAIL 428** (*includes records of* BR)
    Superannuation schemes, **RAIL 1174**
    Timetables
        Public, **RAIL 956**
        Working, **RAIL 957**
            appendixes, **RAIL 1136**
        Northern Counties Committee, **RAIL 941**
            Working timetables appendixes, **RAIL 1136**
    Traders' ledger credit agreements, **RAIL 1165**
    Train notices, **RAIL 432**
    Welfare schemes, **RAIL 1115; RAIL 1174**
See also BR horse records; hotels and catering; locomotive and rolling stock records
        BTC Chief Secretary's Office
        L&YR, deeds, contracts etc
        LNWR
        LTSR
        MR
London, Newbury and Bath Direct Railway (proposed)
    GWR miscellanea, **RAIL 1014**
London Omnibus Tramway (proposed)
    Prospectuses etc, **RAIL 1078**
London Outer Circle Railway (proposed)
    Parliamentary papers, **RAIL 1066**
London, Oxford and Cheltenham Railway (proposed), **RAIL 434**
    Parliamentary papers, **RAIL 1066**
    Prospectuses etc, **RAIL 1075**
    Subscription contracts, **RAIL 1160**
London Passenger Transport Board
    Instructions to staff, **RAIL 1135**
    Joint committees with:
        GWR
            RAIL 250 (W London electrification)
            RAIL 390 (Standing Jt Cttee)
        LNER
            Timetables, **RAIL 984**
            RAIL 250 (W London electrification)
            RAIL 390 (Standing Jt Cttee)
        LMSR
            RAIL 390 (Standing Jt Cttee)
        SR
            RAIL 390 (Standing Jt Cttee)
    See also E London R
    Labour and staff matters, **RAIL 1025**
    Law cases and arbitration, **RAIL 1027**
    Miscellanea, **RAIL 1020**
    Parliamentary papers, **RAIL 1066**

Railway Rates Tribunal proceedings,
    RAIL 1101
Reports and accounts, **RAIL 1110; RAIL 1116;**
    RAIL 1117
Sidings agreements, **RAIL 1167**
Timetables, **RAIL 984; RAIL 1136**
Welfare records, **RAIL 1174**
London, Reigate and Brighton Railway (proposed)
    Parliamentary papers, **RAIL 1066**
London Road Station, Manchester, Joint
    Committee (LNWR/MSLR; *after 1897*
    LNWR/GCR), **RAIL 435; RAIL 410**
See also LMSR miscellanea
London, Salisbury and Yeovil Junction Railway
    (proposed), **RAIL 436**
London, Salisbury, Exeter, Plymouth and
    Falmouth Railway (proposed)
    Prospectuses etc, **RAIL 1075**
London Southern Tramways
    Parliamentary papers, **RAIL 1066**
London Street Tramways
    Parliamentary papers, **RAIL 1066**
London, Tilbury and Dartford and Kent Coast
    Junction Railway (proposed)
    Parliamentary papers, **RAIL 1066**
London, Tilbury and Southend Extension Railway
    (*shareholders in this line were incorporated as*
    London, Tilbury & Southend R *in 1852*)
    Reports and accounts, **RAIL 1116; RAIL 1117**
London, Tilbury and Southend Railway, **RAIL 437**
    (*includes records of original jt cttee* Eastern
    Counties R/London & Blackwall R; LMSR; MR)
    Instructions to staff, **RAIL 1135**
    Joint committees with:
      Met District R
        Instructions to staff, **RAIL 1135**
        RAIL 1110; RAIL 1116 (Whitechapel &
        Bow R reports and accounts)
      MR, **RAIL 696** (Tottenham & Forest Gate R)
    Law cases and arbitration, **RAIL 1027**
    Miscellanea, **RAIL 1020**
    Parliamentary papers, **RAIL 1066; RAIL 1163**
    Railway and Canal Traffic Acts proceedings,
      RAIL 1038
    Reports and accounts, **RAIL 1110; RAIL 1116;**
      RAIL 1117
    Rule books, **RAIL 1134**
    Share certificates, **RAIL 1158**
    Timetables, **RAIL 981**
    Traders' ledger credit agreements,
      RAIL 1165
See also London, Tilbury & Southend Extension R
London, Tilbury, Dartford and Kent Coast Junction
    Railway (proposed)
    Parliamentary papers, **RAIL 1066**
London Tramways
    Miscellanea, **RAIL 1057**

Parliamentary papers, **RAIL 1066**
London Transport Executive
    Labour and staff matters, **RAIL 1025**
    Miscellanea, **RAIL 1005; RAIL 1018**
    Timetables, **RAIL 984**
    Welfare records, **RAIL 1174**
See also BTC Chief Secretary's Office
London United Electric Railways (proposed)
    Parliamentary papers, **RAIL 1066**
London United Tramways
    Law cases and arbitration, **RAIL 1027**
    Parliamentary papers, **RAIL 1068**
    Reports and accounts, **RAIL 1114**
See also London & Suburban Traction Co
London Universal Railway (proposed)
    Prospectuses etc, **RAIL 1075**
London, Walthamstow and Epping Forest Railway
    Maps, **RAIL 1030**
    Parliamentary papers, **RAIL 1066**
London, Worcester and South Staffordshire
    Railway (proposed), **RAIL 438** (*formerly* London
    and Worcester & Rugby & Oxford R)
London, Worcester and South Wales Railway
    Miscellanea, **RAIL 1057**
    Parliamentary papers, **RAIL 1066**
Looe Railway
    Timetables, **RAIL 981**
Loose Valley Railway
    Parliamentary papers, **RAIL 1066**
Lostock Hall Light Railway (proposed)
    Parliamentary papers, **RAIL 1066**
Lostock Light Railway (proposed)
    Parliamentary papers, **RAIL 1066**
Lostwithiel and Fowey Railway, **RAIL 1176**
    Miscellanea, **RAIL 1057**
    Parliamentary papers, **RAIL 1066**
    Reports and accounts, **RAIL 1116**
Loughborough and Sheepshed Railway
    Parliamentary papers, **RAIL 1066**
Loughrea and Attymon Light Railway
    Railway and Canal Traffic Acts proceedings,
      RAIL 1038
Louth and East Coast Railway, **RAIL 439** (*includes
    records about* Sutton & Willoughby R)
    Prospectuses etc, **RAIL 1075**
Louth and Lincoln Railway, **RAIL 440**
    Prospectuses etc, **RAIL 1075; RAIL 1116**
Lower Thames Tunnel Railways (proposed)
    Maps, **RAIL 1030**
Lowestoft Railway and Harbour Company,
    RAIL 441
    Reports and accounts, **RAIL 1116**
Ludgershall and Tidworth Railway
    Miscellanea, **RAIL 1057**
Ludlow and Clee Hill Railway, **RAIL 442**
    Reports and accounts, **RAIL 1116**
See also GWR/LNWR jt cttees

Luton, Dunstable and Welwyn Junction Railway
  Parliamentary papers, **RAIL 1163**
  Prospectuses etc, **RAIL 1075**
  Reports and accounts, **RAIL 1116**
  Sidings agreements, **RAIL 1167**
Lydd Railway, **RAIL 443**
  Parliamentary papers, **RAIL 1066**
Lydney and Millbrook Railway *see* Severn & Wye
  R & Canal Co
Lymington Railway, **RAIL 1192**
  Reports and accounts, **RAIL 1116**
Lynmouth and Minehead Light Railway
  (proposed)
  Maps, **RAIL 1030**
Lynn and Fakenham Railway
  Parliamentary papers, **RAIL 1066**
  Reports and accounts, **RAIL 1110; RAIL 1116**
See also Irish & English Traffic Conference
  M&GNJR Jt Cttee
Lynn and Hunstanton Railway, **RAIL 444**
Lynn and Sutton Bridge Railway, **RAIL 445**
  Prospectuses etc, **RAIL 1075**
Lynton and Barnstaple Railway, **RAIL 446**
  Miscellanea, **RAIL 1057**
  Reports and accounts, **RAIL 1110; RAIL 1116**
  Timetables, **RAIL 981**
See also SR deeds etc
Macclesfield and Knutsford Railway, **RAIL 447**
  (*includes records of predecessor* Macclesfield,
  Knutsford & Warrington R)
Macclesfield and Lichfield Railway *or* Churnet and
  Blythe Junction Railway (proposed)
  Prospectuses etc, **RAIL 1076**
Macclesfield, Bollington and Marple Railway,
  RAIL 448 (*includes records of jt cttees* GCR/N
  Staffordshire R; LMSR/LNER)
  Reports and accounts, **RAIL 1110**
See also GCR/N Staffordshire R Jt Cttee
Macclesfield Joint Station Committee (LNWR/N
  Staffordshire R), **RAIL 449**
  Railway and Canal Traffic Acts proceedings,
  RAIL 1038
Macclesfield, Knutsford and Warrington Railway
  see Macclesfield & Knutsford R
Maenclochog Railway (*probably* Narberth &
  Maenclochog R)
  Timetables, **RAIL 981**
Maidenhead and Guildford Railway (proposed)
  Miscellanea, **RAIL 1057**
Maidstone and Ashford Railway, **RAIL 450**
Maidstone, Rochester and Gravesend Railway
  (proposed)
  Prospectuses etc, **RAIL 1075**
Maldon, Witham and Braintree Railway, **RAIL 451**
Malmesbury Railway, **RAIL 452**
  Reports and accounts, **RAIL 1110**
See also GWR correspondence and papers

Malton and Driffield Junction Railway, **RAIL 453**
  (*includes records of* NER)
  Prospectuses etc, **RAIL 1075; RAIL 1076**
  Reports and accounts, **RAIL 1111; RAIL 1116**
See also NER
Manchester and Birmingham Railway, **RAIL 454**
  (*includes records of* LNWR)
  Maps, **RAIL 1030**
  Miscellanea, **RAIL 1008**
  Parliamentary plans, **RAIL 1071**
Manchester and Bolton Railway
  Timetables, **RAIL 981**
Manchester and Cheshire Junction Railway
  (proposed)
  Miscellanea, **RAIL 1016**
  Prospectuses etc, **RAIL 1075**
Manchester and Leeds Railway, **RAIL 1175**
  Byelaws and regulations, **RAIL 1001**
  Joint committees with:
    Grand Junction R/North Union R,
    RAIL 220; RAIL 534
    See also Leeds Central Station
  Miscellanea, **RAIL 1008; RAIL 1016;**
    RAIL 1020
  Parliamentary plans, **RAIL 1071**
  Prospectuses etc, **RAIL 1075**
  Reports and accounts, **RAIL 1110**
  Rule books, **RAIL 1134**
  Subscription contracts, **RAIL 1160**
  Timetables, **RAIL 981**
See also L&YR
  Manchester, Bolton & Bury Canal Navigation
    & R
  Manchester, Leeds & Hull Associated R
    (proposed)
  Sheffield, Rotherham, Barnsley, Wakefield,
    Huddersfield & Goole R
Manchester and Lincoln Railway *see* MSLR
Manchester and Lincoln Union Railway and Canal
  Company
  Joint committee *see* Sheffield & Lincolnshire
    Jct R and M&LUR&C Co Jt Cttee
  Miscellanea, **RAIL 1153**
  Subscription contracts, **RAIL 1160**
Manchester and Liverpool Electric Express
  Railway
  Parliamentary papers, **RAIL 1066**
Manchester and Liverpool, Swansea and Milford
  Haven Junction Railway (proposed)
  Miscellanea, **RAIL 1057**
  Prospectuses etc, **RAIL 1075**
Manchester and Milford Haven Junction Railway
  (proposed)
  Subscription contract, **RAIL 1163**
Manchester and Milford Railway, **RAIL 456**
  Byelaws and regulations, **RAIL 1001**
  Friendly Society reports, **RAIL 1174**

Joint Committee with Pembroke & Tenby R,
RAIL 455
Map, **RAIL 1014**
Parliamentary papers, **RAIL 1066**
Prospectuses etc, **RAIL 1075; RAIL 1110**
Railway and Canal Traffic Acts proceedings,
RAIL 1038
Reports and accounts, **RAIL 1110; RAIL 1116;**
RAIL 1117
Rule books, **RAIL 1134**
Timetables, **RAIL 981**
Manchester and Sheffield Railway
Parliamentary plans, **RAIL 1071**
Manchester and Southampton Railway (proposed)
Prospectuses etc, **RAIL 1075**
Manchester and Southport Railway, **RAIL 457**
Parliamentary papers, **RAIL 1163**
See also L&YR
Manchester, Bolton and Bury Canal Navigation
and Railway, **RAIL 458** (*includes records of*
Manchester & Leeds R; L&YR)
Miscellanea, **RAIL 1014**
Parliamentary papers, **RAIL 1147**
Timetables, **RAIL 981**
Manchester, Bury and Rossendale Railway,
RAIL 176
Prospectuses etc, **RAIL 1075**
See also E Lancashire R
Manchester, Buxton, Matlock and Midlands
Junction Railway, **RAIL 459** (*includes records of*
predecessor Mansfield & Buxton R *and* Lancaster
& Carlisle R; LNWR)
Prospectuses etc, **RAIL 1075; RAIL 1076**
Reports and accounts, **RAIL 1110;**
RAIL 1116
Subscription contracts, **RAIL 1160**
Manchester Corporation Tramways
Reports and accounts, **RAIL 1114**
Manchester, Leeds and Hull Associated Railway
(proposed) (*temporary union of* Hull & Selby R
and Manchester & Leeds R), **RAIL 460**
Manchester, Midland and Great Grimsby Junction
Railway (proposed)
Prospectuses etc, **RAIL 1076**
Manchester, Sheffield and Lincolnshire Railway,
RAIL 463 (*includes records of* BR(ER), GCR,
LNER, Manchester & Lincoln R)
Byelaws and regulations, **RAIL 1003** (Canals
and docks)
Instructions to staff, **RAIL 1135**
Joint committees with:
GNR, **RAIL 235; RAIL 236** (Officers'
Conference)**; RAIL 461**
Timetables, **RAIL 925**
RAIL 736 (W Riding & Grimsby R *and*
Wakefield station)
LNWR, **RAIL 408; RAIL 409**

RAIL 410; RAIL 421; RAIL 435
(Manchester London Rd station)
RAIL 410; RAIL 464; RAIL 465
(Manchester S Jct & Altrincham R)
RAIL 410; RAIL 551 (Oldham, Ashton-
under-Lyne & Guide Bridge Jct R)
RAIL 410; RAIL 421; RAIL 661
(Stalybridge station)
RAIL 464 (Warrington & Stockport)
MR
Byelaws and regulations, **RAIL 1001**
RAIL 216 (Garston Liverpool R)
RAIL 1066 (Sheffield & Midland Cttee
Parliamentary papers)
Reports and accounts, **RAIL 1110**
RAIL 736 (Wakefield station)
S Yorkshire R & River Dun Co
RAIL 736 (Wakefield station)
Warrington & Stockport R
RAIL 464 (Manchester, S Jct &
Altrincham & Stockport Jct)
W Riding & Grimsby R
RAIL 736 (Wakefield station)
Wrexham, Mold & Connah's Quay R
RAIL 535 (Wirral Rys; Dee & Birkenhead
later N Wales & Liverpool R Cttee)
See also Cheshire Lines Cttee
Humber Conference
Nottingham Jt Station Cttee
Law cases and arbitration, **RAIL 1027**
Maps, **RAIL 1030**
Miscellanea, **RAIL 1007; RAIL 1008;**
RAIL 1014; RAIL 1016; RAIL 1021;
RAIL 1057; RAIL 1151; RAIL 1152
Parliamentary papers, **RAIL 1066;**
RAIL 1163
Parliamentary plans, **RAIL 1071**
Prospectuses etc, **RAIL 1075**
Railway & Canal Traffic Acts proceedings,
RAIL 1038
Reports and accounts, **RAIL 1110; RAIL 1116;**
RAIL 1117
Rule books, **RAIL 1134**
Savings bank rules, **RAIL 1174**
Share certificates, **RAIL 1158; RAIL 1159**
Subscription contracts, **RAIL 1160**
Timetables, **RAIL 958; RAIL 981**
Traders' ledger credit agreements,
RAIL 1165
Welfare schemes, **RAIL 1115; RAIL 1174**
See also GCR
Great Grimsby & Sheffield Jct R
Irish & English Traffic Conference
Sheffield, Ashton-under-Lyne & Manchester R
Manchester, Sheffield and Midland Junction
Railway (proposed)
Miscellanea, **RAIL 1153**

Manchester, Southampton and Poole Railway
  (proposed)
    Miscellanea, **RAIL 1153**
Manchester South Junction and Altrincham
  Railway, **RAIL 465** (*includes records of jt cttees*
  LNWR/MSLR; LNWR/GCR; LMSR/LNER)
    Byelaws and regulations, **RAIL 1001**
    Joint committee LNWR/MSLR/Warrington
      and Stockport R, **RAIL 464**
    Law cases and arbitration, **RAIL 1027**
    Maps, **RAIL 1030**
    Miscellanea, **RAIL 1008**; **RAIL 1020**;
      RAIL 1151
    Parliamentary papers, **RAIL 1066**
    Parliamentary plans, **RAIL 1071**
    Reports and accounts, **RAIL 1110**; **RAIL 1116**
    Rule books, **RAIL 1134**
    Subscription contracts, **RAIL 1160**
    Timetables, **RAIL 981**
See also LNER minutes and reports
  LMSR miscellanea
Manchester South Union Railway, **RAIL 466**
    Prospectuses etc, **RAIL 1075**
Mansfield and Buxton Railway *see* Manchester,
  Buxton, Matlock & Midlands Jct R
Mansfield and Pinxton Railway, **RAIL 467**
Mansfield and Retford Railway (proposed)
    Parliamentary papers, **RAIL 1066**
Mansfield Railway, **RAIL 468**
    Parliamentary papers, **RAIL 1066**
    Prospectuses etc, **RAIL 1075**
    Reports and accounts, **RAIL 1116**
    Share certificates, **RAIL 1158**
Manx Electric Railway
    Miscellanea, **RAIL 1057**
    Reports and accounts, **RAIL 1116**
Manx Northern Railway
    Miscellanea, **RAIL 1057**
    Reports and accounts, **RAIL 1116**;
      RAIL 1117
Marble Arch, Regent Circus and City Subway
  (proposed)
    Parliamentary plans, **RAIL 1071**
Margate Railway *see* Kent Coast R
Margate Tramways (proposed)
    Parliamentary papers, **RAIL 1066**
Market Deeping Railway (proposed)
    Miscellanea, **RAIL 1057**
Market Drayton and Madeley Railway
    Prospectuses etc, **RAIL 1075**
See also Nantwich and Market Drayton R
Market Harborough, Melton Mowbray and
  Nottingham Railway (proposed)
    Parliamentary papers, **RAIL 1066**
Marlborough and Grafton Railway, **RAIL 469**
    Miscellanea, **RAIL 1057**
    Parliamentary papers, **RAIL 1066**

Marlborough Railway, **RAIL 470**
    Railway and Canal Traffic Acts proceedings,
      RAIL 1038
    Reports and accounts, **RAIL 1110**
Marple New Mills and Hayfield Junction Railway,
  RAIL 471
Maryport and Carlisle Railway, **RAIL 472**
    Miscellanea, **RAIL 1008**; **RAIL 1014**;
      RAIL 1057
    Parliamentary papers, **RAIL 1066**; **RAIL 1163**
    Railway and Canal Traffic Acts proceedings,
      RAIL 1038
    Reports and accounts, **RAIL 1110**; **RAIL 1116**;
      RAIL 1117
    Rule books, **RAIL 1134**
    Share certificates, **RAIL 1158**
    Timetables, **RAIL 981**
    Working timetables appendixes, **RAIL 1136**
See also LMSR amalgamation
  Newcastle-upon-Tyne & Carlisle R
Maryport, Caldbeck and Hesket-new-Market
  Railway (proposed)
    Prospectuses etc, **RAIL 1075**
Mawddwy Railway, **RAIL 473**
    Miscellanea, **RAIL 1014**; **RAIL 1057**
    Railway and Canal Traffic Acts proceedings,
      RAIL 1038
    Reports and accounts, **RAIL 1110**; **RAIL 1116**
See also GWR miscellanea
Maybole and Girvan Railway
    Parliamentary papers, **RAIL 1066**
Melin-Griffith Tramway
    Miscellanea, **RAIL 1057**
Mellis and Eye Railway
    Railway and Canal Traffic Acts proceedings,
      RAIL 1038
    Reports and accounts, **RAIL 1110**
Melton Mowbray and Market Harborough
  Railway (proposed)
    Prospectuses etc, **RAIL 1075**
Meon Valley Railway (proposed)
    Parliamentary papers, **RAIL 1066**
Merionethshire Railway, **RAIL 1195**
    Reports and accounts, **RAIL 1116**
Merrybent and Darlington Railway, **RAIL 474**
    Miscellanea, **RAIL 1021**
    Reports and accounts, **RAIL 1116**
Mersey Docks and Harbour Board
    Byelaws and regulations, **RAIL 1003**
      (Birkenhead Dock Rys)
    Reports and accounts, **RAIL 1116**; **RAIL 1117**
Mersey Railway, **RAIL 475** *includes records of*
  predecessor Mersey Pneumatic R)
    Joint committee with Wirral R, **RAIL 475**;
      RAIL 756 (Birkenhead Pk station)
    Maps, **RAIL 1030**
    Parliamentary papers, **RAIL 1066**

Prospectuses etc, **RAIL 1075; RAIL 1116**
Railway and Canal Traffic Acts proceedings,
    RAIL 1038
Reports and accounts, **RAIL 1110; RAIL 1116;**
    RAIL 1117
Share certificates, **RAIL 1158**
Timetables, **RAIL 981**
    Working timetables appendixes, **RAIL 1136**
Merthyr, Tredegar and Abergavenny Railway,
    RAIL 476; RAIL 410
    Prospectuses etc, **RAIL 1075**
    Reports and accounts, **RAIL 1116; RAIL 1117**
See also LNWR
Merthyr Tydfil and Cardiff Railway (proposed)
    Miscellanea, **RAIL 1014**
    Parliamentary papers, **RAIL 1016; RAIL 1066**
    Prospectuses etc, **RAIL 1075**
Methley Railway Joint Committee (GNR/L&YR/
    NER; *in 1922* GNR/LNWR/NER; *from 1923*
    LMSR/LNER), **RAIL 410; RAIL 477; RAIL 783**
    Byelaws and regulations, **RAIL 1001**
    Reports and accounts, **RAIL 1110; RAIL 1111;**
        RAIL 1116; RAIL 1117
Metropolitan and Regents Circus Railway
    (proposed)
    Parliamentary papers, **RAIL 1066**
    Parliamentary plans, **RAIL 1071**
Metropolitan and St John's Wood Railway
    Parliamentary papers, **RAIL 1066**
    Prospectuses etc, **RAIL 1076**
    Reports and accounts, **RAIL 1110; RAIL 1116**
Metropolitan and South Western Junction Railway
    Parliamentary papers, **RAIL 1066**
Metropolitan District Railway
    Instructions to staff, **RAIL 1135**
    Joint committees *see* E London R; Whitechapel
        & Bow R Jt Cttee
    Labour and staff matters, **RAIL 1025**
    Law cases and arbitration, **RAIL 1027**
    Maps, **RAIL 1030**
    Miscellanea, **RAIL 1005; RAIL 1018;**
        RAIL 1020; RAIL 1057
    Parliamentary papers, **RAIL 1066**
    Pension fund, **RAIL 1174**
    Prospectuses etc, **RAIL 1075**
    Railway and Canal Traffic Acts proceedings,
        RAIL 1038
    Reports and accounts, **RAIL 1110; RAIL 1116;**
        RAIL 1117
    Rule books, **RAIL 1134**
    Timetables, **RAIL 960; RAIL 981**
        E London R, **RAIL 927**
        Working timetables appendixes, **RAIL 1136**
See also Underground Electric Rys Co
Metropolitan Electric Tramways
    Parliamentary papers, **RAIL 1068**
    Reports and accounts, **RAIL 1114**

See also London & Suburban Traction Co
Metropolitan General Grand Junction Railway
    (proposed)
    Prospectuses etc, **RAIL 1075**
Metropolitan Grand Union Railway (proposed)
    Parliamentary papers, **RAIL 1066**
Metropolitan Inner Circle Completion Railway
    Parliamentary papers, **RAIL 1066**
Metropolitan Outer Circle Railway
    Miscellanea, **RAIL 1057**
    Parliamentary papers, **RAIL 1066**
Metropolitan Railway
    Byelaws and regulations, **RAIL 1001**
    Instructions to staff, **RAIL 1135**
    Joint committee with:
        GCR
            Reports and accounts, **RAIL 1110;**
                RAIL 1116
            Rule books, **RAIL 1134**
            Sidings agreements, **RAIL 1167**
            RAIL 223 (Quainton Rd to Canfield Pl)
        GWR, **RAIL 1134** (W London R rule books)
        LNER
            Byelaws and regulations, **RAIL 1001**
            Reports and accounts, **RAIL 1116**
            Rule books, **RAIL 1134**
            RAIL 1110 (Watford Cttee reports and
                accounts)
        W London R
            Rule books, **RAIL 1134**
    See also E London R
        Hammersmith & City R Jt Cttee
    Law cases and arbitration, **RAIL 1027**
    Maps, **RAIL 1030**
    Miscellanea, **RAIL 1005; RAIL 1007;**
        RAIL 1008; RAIL 1020; RAIL 1057
    Parliamentary papers, **RAIL 1066; RAIL 1163**
    Prospectuses etc, **RAIL 1075**
    Railway and Canal Traffic Acts proceedings,
        RAIL 1038
    Reports and accounts, **RAIL 1110; RAIL 1116;**
        RAIL 1117
    Rule books, **RAIL 1134**
    Savings bank rules, **RAIL 1174**
    Superannuation schemes, **RAIL 1174**
    Timetables, **RAIL 959; RAIL 981**
        E London R, **RAIL 927**
    Welfare fund accounts, **RAIL 1115;**
        RAIL 1174
Metropolitan Railway Suspension Bridge
    (proposed)
    Prospectuses etc, **RAIL 1075**
Michelstown and Fermoy Light Railway
    Railway and Canal Traffic Acts proceedings,
        RAIL 1038
Mid-Devon Light Railway
    Miscellanea, **RAIL 1057**

Mid-Eastern and Great Northern Junction
  Railways (proposed)
    Prospectuses etc, **RAIL 1075**
Middlesbrough and Guisborough Railway,
  RAIL 483
    Miscellanea, **RAIL 1157**
    Parliamentary papers, **RAIL 1163**
    Prospectuses etc, **RAIL 1075; RAIL 1076**
    Reports and accounts, **RAIL 1111; RAIL 1116**
    Share certificates, **RAIL 1159**
    Subscription contracts, **RAIL 1161**
Middlesbrough and Redcar Railway, **RAIL 484**
  (*includes records of* NER)
    Byelaws and regulations, **RAIL 1001**
    Miscellanea, **RAIL 1021; RAIL 1157**
    Prospectuses etc, **RAIL 1076**
    Reports and accounts, **RAIL 1111; RAIL 1116**
    Share certificates, **RAIL 1158; RAIL 1159**
    Timetables, **RAIL 981**
Middlesex and Surrey Grand Junction Railway
  (proposed)
    Prospectuses etc, **RAIL 1075**
Mid-Hants Railway
    Parliamentary papers, **RAIL 1066**
Mid-Kent and North-Kent Junction Railway
    Parliamentary papers, **RAIL 1163**
Mid-Kent (Bromley and St Mary Cray) Railway,
  RAIL 478
    Parliamentary papers, **RAIL 1066**
    Reports and accounts, **RAIL 1116**
Mid-Kent Railway
    Reports and accounts, **RAIL 1116**
Midland and Eastern Railway, **RAIL 485**
    Share certificates, **RAIL 1158**
Midland and Great Northern Railways Joint
  Committee (*known as* Midland & Great
  Northern Joint R: GNR/MR; *after 1923*
  LNER/LMSR), **RAIL 487** (*includes records of*
  Lynn and Fakenham R); **RAIL 783** (GNR
  correspondence)
    Instructions to staff, **RAIL 1135**
    Labour and staff matters, **RAIL 1025**
    Maps, **RAIL 1030**
    Miscellanea, **RAIL 1020**
    Parliamentary papers, **RAIL 1066**
    Reports and accounts, **RAIL 1110; RAIL 1116**
    Rule books, **RAIL 1134**
    Timetables, **RAIL 961**
      Working timetables appendixes, **RAIL 1136**
See also GNR
    Irish and English Traffic Conference
    LNER locomotives & rolling stock
Midland and Great Western Junction Railway
  (proposed) *see* GWR miscellanea special reports
Midland and South Eastern Junction Railway
  (proposed)
    Prospectuses etc, **RAIL 1075**

Midland and South Wales Junction Railway
  (proposed) *see* GWR miscellanea special reports
Midland and South Western Junction Railway,
  RAIL 489
    Instructions to staff, **RAIL 1135**
    Miscellanea, **RAIL 1014; RAIL 1057**
    Parliamentary papers, **RAIL 1066**
    Prospectus, **RAIL 1116**
    Railway & Canal Traffic Acts proceedings,
      RAIL 1038
    Reports and accounts, **RAIL 1110; RAIL 1116;
      RAIL 1117**
    Timetables, **RAIL 981**
See also Cheltenham Station Co
    GWR locomotives and rolling stock;
      miscellanea
Midland and Staffordshire Railway (proposed)
    Parliamentary papers, **RAIL 1066**
Midland, Birmingham, Wolverhampton and
  Milford Railway (proposed)
    Parliamentary papers, **RAIL 1066**
Midland Counties Coalfields Railway (proposed)
    Parliamentary papers, **RAIL 1066**
Midland Counties and Shannon Junction Railway
    Reports and accounts, **RAIL 1116; RAIL 1117**
Midland Counties Railway, **RAIL 490**
    Dividend warrants, **RAIL 1158**
    Miscellanea, **RAIL 1007; RAIL 1008;
      RAIL 1015; RAIL 1016; RAIL 1057;
      RAIL 1157**
    Prospectuses etc, **RAIL 1075; RAIL 1076**
    Reports and accounts, **RAIL 1110**
    Subscription contracts, **RAIL 1160**
    Timetables, **RAIL 981**
See also MR
Midland Great Western Railway
    Parliamentary papers, **RAIL 1066**
    Railway and Canal Traffic Acts proceedings,
      RAIL 1038
    Reports and accounts, **RAIL 1110; RAIL 1116;
      RAIL 1117**
    Timetables, **RAIL 941**
See also Irish & English Traffic Conference
    LMSR amalgamation
Midland Railway, RAIL 491 (*includes records of or
  about* BR(LM); Burton & Ashby Lt R; Midland
  Counties R; LMSR Solicitor's records)
    Byelaws and regulations, **RAIL 1001**
    Deeds, contracts etc, **RAIL 793**
    Gloucester & Cheltenham R abandonment,
      RAIL 1184
    Hotels, **RAIL 1022**
    Instructions to staff, **RAIL 1135**
    Joint committees with:
      Cal R
        RAIL 98; RAIL 410; RAIL 421 (Carlisle
          goods traffic)

RAIL 421 (Portpatrick & Wigtownshire
Jt R)
Furness R, **RAIL 213** (Carnforth &
Wennington line)
GSWR, **RAIL 486**
RAIL 98; **RAIL 410**; **RAIL 421** (Carlisle
goods traffic)
RAIL 421 (Portpatrick & Wigtownshire
Jt R)
GCR, **RAIL 224**; **RAIL 462**
Byelaws and regulations, **RAIL 1001**
Instructions to staff, **RAIL 1135**
Parliamentary papers, **RAIL 1163**
Reports and accounts, **RAIL 1110**;
RAIL 1111
RAIL 1116 (GCR/H&BR/MR)
Traders' ledger credit agreements,
RAIL 1165
RAIL 225 (Braithwell Jct to Laughton
Jct line)
Byelaws and regulations, **RAIL 1001**
GNR
RAIL 236 (GNR/MR Jt Railway Officers'
Meeting)
RAIL 736 (Wakefield station)
Timetables, **RAIL 961**; **RAIL 981**
GNR(I)
RAIL 137 (County Donegal R)
GWR, **RAIL 241**
Byelaws and regulations, **RAIL 1001**
Reports and accounts, **RAIL 1110**
RAIL 81 (Clifton Extension R)
Railway and Canal Traffic Acts
proceedings, **RAIL 1038**
RAIL 287 (Halesowen Railway)
RAIL 603 (Severn & Wye & Severn Br R)
Reports and accounts, **RAIL 1110**
RAIL 1110 (Severn & Wye R & Canal Co,
reports & accounts)
RAIL 1135 (Severn & Wye Jt R,
instructions to staff)
RAIL 1136 (Severn & Wye R, working
timetables appendixes)
See also GWR estates and rating
GWR/LMSR Jt Cttees
H&BR
Reports and accounts, **RAIL 1110**;
RAIL 1111; **RAIL 1116** (GCR/H&BR/
MR)
RAIL 225 (Braithwell Jct to Laughton
Jct line)
Byelaws and regulations, **RAIL 1001**
LNWR, **RAIL 406**; **RAIL 409**; **RAIL 421**
Rule books, **RAIL 1134**
RAIL 98; **RAIL 410**; **RAIL 421** (Carlisle
goods traffic)
RAIL 410 (N & S Western Jct R)

RAIL 421 (Portpatrick & Wigtownshire
Jt R)
See also LMSR miscellanea
LTSR
RAIL 696 (Tottenham & Forest Gate R)
MSLR, **RAIL 224**; **RAIL 462**
Byelaws and regulations, **RAIL 1001**
RAIL 1066 (Sheffield & Midland Cttee)
Parliamentary papers; reports and
accounts, **RAIL 1110**
RAIL 736 (Wakefield station)
NER, Miscellanea, **RAIL 1057**
N London R
RAIL 521; **RAIL 410** (N & S Western
Jct R)
S Yorkshire R & River Dun Co
RAIL 736 (Wakefield station)
West Riding & Grimsby R
RAIL 736 (Wakefield station)
See also Ashby & Nuneaton Jt Cttee
Bristol Jt Station Cttee
Cheshire Lines Cttee
Garston & Liverpool R Cttee
London & W Riding Association
Norfolk & Suffolk Jt Rys Cttee
Normanton Jt Station Cttee
Otley & Ilkley Jt Line Cttee
Somerset & Dorset Jt Line Cttee
S Yorkshire Jt Lines Cttee
Swinton & Knottingley Jt R
Tottenham & Hampstead Jct R
Labour and staff matters, **RAIL 1025**
Law cases and arbitration, **RAIL 1027**
Maps, **RAIL 1030**
Miscellanea, **RAIL 1005**; **RAIL 1006**;
RAIL 1007; **RAIL 1008**; **RAIL 1014**;
RAIL 1015; **RAIL 1020**; **RAIL 1021**;
RAIL 1057
Northern Counties Committee, **RAIL 542**
Law cases and arbitration, **RAIL 1027**
Timetables, **RAIL 941**
See also Irish & English Traffic Conference
Northern Counties R Cttee
Parliamentary papers, **RAIL 1066**; **RAIL 1067**;
RAIL 1147; **RAIL 1163**
Parliamentary plans, **RAIL 1071**
Prospectuses etc, **RAIL 1075**
Railway and Canal Traffic Acts proceedings,
RAIL 1038
Reports and accounts, **RAIL 1110**; **RAIL 1116**;
RAIL 1117
Rule books, **RAIL 1134**
Savings bank rules, **RAIL 1174**
Share certificates and dividend warrants,
RAIL 1158
Sidings agreements, **RAIL 1167**
Subscription contracts, **RAIL 1160**

MR (continued)
> Superannuation schemes, **RAIL 1174**
> Timetables
>> Public, **RAIL 962; RAIL 981**
>> Working, **RAIL 925; RAIL 963; RAIL 981**
>>> appendixes, **RAIL 1136**
> *See also* Cheshire Lines Cttee timetables
> Traders' ledger credit agreements,
>> **RAIL 1165**
> Welfare schemes, **RAIL 1194**
See also, BR horse records; hotels and catering
> Cheltenham Station Co
> Irish & English Traffic Conference
> Leicester & Swannington R
> LMSR amalgamation; Solicitor's records
> LTSR
> Tottenham & Forest Gate R
Midland Wagon Company
> Reports and accounts, **RAIL 1116**
Mid-London Electric Railway (proposed)
> Parliamentary plans, **RAIL 1071**
Mid-Nottinghamshire Joint Railways Committee
> (LMSR/LNER)
>> Miscellanea, **RAIL 1057**
>> Parliamentary papers, **RAIL 1066**
Mid-Suffolk Light Railway, **RAIL 479**
> Reports and accounts, **RAIL 1116**
> Timetables, **RAIL 981**
Mid-Sussex and Midhurst Junction Railway,
> **RAIL 480**
> Reports and accounts, **RAIL 1116**
Mid-Sussex Railway, **RAIL 481**
> Reports and accounts, **RAIL 1116**
Mid-Wales Railway, **RAIL 482**
> Byelaws and regulations, **RAIL 1001**
> Miscellanea, **RAIL 1014; RAIL 1057**
> Parliamentary papers, **RAIL 1066**
> Prospectuses etc, **RAIL 1075; RAIL 1110**
> Reports and accounts, **RAIL 1110; RAIL 1116;**
>> **RAIL 1117**
> Subscription contracts, **RAIL 1160**
> Timetables, **RAIL 981**
Milford Docks Company *see* GWR Secretary's
> papers
Milford Haven Docks and Railway *see* GWR
> Secretary's papers
Milford Haven Railway and Estate Company
> Prospectuses etc, **RAIL 1075; RAIL 1076**
Milford Junction Railway (*later* Milford R)
> Subscription contracts, **RAIL 1163**
Milford Railway, **RAIL 492**
> Prospectus, **RAIL 1110**
> Railway and Canal Traffic Acts proceedings,
>> **RAIL 1038**
> Reports and accounts, **RAIL 1110**
See also GWR estates and rating
> Milford Jct R

Minehead Railway, **RAIL 493** (*includes records of
> predecessor* Watchet & Minehead R)
> Railway and Canal Traffic Acts proceedings,
>> **RAIL 1038**
Minster and Ramsgate Junction Railway (proposed)
> Parliamentary papers, **RAIL 1066**
Minsterley Mineral Railway (*later* Snailbeach R)
> Miscellanea, **RAIL 1014**
Mitcheldean Road and Forest of Dean Junction
> Railway, **RAIL 494**
> Reports and accounts, **RAIL 1110**
Mold and Denbigh Junction Railway, **RAIL 495**
> Byelaws and regulations, **RAIL 1001**
> Parliamentary papers, **RAIL 1066**
> Reports and accounts, **RAIL 1110; RAIL 1116**
> Share certificates, **RAIL 1158**
See also LMSR amalgamation
Mold and Treiddyn Railway (proposed)
> Parliamentary plans, **RAIL 1071**
Mold Railway, **RAIL 496**
> Parliamentary plans, **RAIL 1071**
Monkland Railways
> Reports and accounts, **RAIL 1116; RAIL 1117**
> Share certificates, **RAIL 1158**
Monmouth and Hereford Railway, **RAIL 497**
> Miscellanea, **RAIL 1057**
Monmouth Railway, **RAIL 498**
> Miscellanea, **RAIL 1005; RAIL 1014**
Monmouth, Ross and Gloucester Railway
> (proposed)
> Miscellanea, **RAIL 1014**
Monmouthshire Railway and Canal Company,
> **RAIL 500** (*includes records about* Newport &
> Pontypool R)
> Instructions to staff, **RAIL 1135**
> Joint committee with:
>> GWR, **RAIL 499; RAIL 250**
> Miscellanea, **RAIL 1008; RAIL 1014; RAIL 1057**
> Parliamentary papers, **RAIL 1066; RAIL 1163**
> Prospectuses etc, **RAIL 1075**
> Provident Society, **RAIL 1174**
> Reports and accounts, **RAIL 1110; RAIL 1116;**
>> **RAIL 1117**
> Rule books, **RAIL 1134**
> Share certificates, **RAIL 1158**
> Timetables, **RAIL 981**
Montgomeryshire Railway (proposed)
> Bill, **RAIL 1147**
Montrose and Bervie Railway
> Reports and accounts, **RAIL 1116**
> Share certificates, **RAIL 1158**
Morecambe Harbour and Railway
> Subscription contract, **RAIL 1160**
Moretonhampstead and South Devon Railway,
> **RAIL 501**
> Miscellanea, **RAIL 1057**
> Prospectus, **RAIL 1014**

See also GWR miscellanea
Morayshire and Perthshire Direct Junction
   Railway (proposed)
      Prospectuses etc, **RAIL 1075**
Morayshire Railway
      Reports and accounts, **RAIL 1116; RAIL 1117**
Mountain Ash Tramways (proposed)
      Parliamentary papers, **RAIL 1068**
Mowddwy Railway *see* Mawddwy R
Much Wenlock and Severn Junction Railway,
   RAIL 502
      Parliamentary papers, **RAIL 1066**
      Prospectuses etc, **RAIL 1075**
      Railway and Canal Traffic Acts proceedings,
         RAIL 1038
      Reports and accounts, **RAIL 1110**
See also GWR estates and rating
Much Wenlock, Craven Arms and Coalbrookdale
   Railway (proposed)
      Prospectuses etc, **RAIL 1075**
See also Wenlock R
Muirkirk, Mauchline and Dalmellington Railway
      Parliamentary papers, **RAIL 1066**
Mullingar, Kells and Drogheda Railway
   (proposed)
      Parliamentary papers, **RAIL 1066**
Mumbles Railway and Pier Company
      Miscellanea, **RAIL 1057**
      Parliamentary papers, **RAIL 1066**
      Reports and accounts, **RAIL 1116**
Muswell Hill and Alexandra Palace Railway,
   RAIL 503
      Law cases and arbitration, **RAIL 1027**
      Reports and accounts, **RAIL 1110**
Nantwich and Market Drayton Railway, **RAIL 504**
   (*includes records under original title* Market
   Drayton & Madeley R)
      Prospectuses etc, **RAIL 1075**
      Railway and Canal Traffic Acts proceedings,
         RAIL 1038
      Reports and accounts, **RAIL 1110; RAIL 1116**
See also GWR estates and rating
Narberth & Maenclochog Railway *see*
   Maenclochog R
Nationalized Industries Computer Committee,
   AN 113
National Union of Railwaymen
      Labour and staff matters, **RAIL 1025;**
         RAIL 1026
National Wages Board, **RAIL 1025; RAIL 1026**
Neath and Brecon Railway, **RAIL 505** (*includes*
   records of predecessor Dulas Valley Mineral R)
      Law cases and arbitration, **RAIL 1027**
      Miscellanea, **RAIL 1005; RAIL 1008;**
         RAIL 1014; RAIL 1057
      Parliamentary papers, **RAIL 1066**
      Prospectus, **RAIL 1110**

Railway and Canal Traffic Acts proceedings,
   RAIL 1038
Reports and accounts, **RAIL 1110; RAIL 1116;**
   RAIL 1117
Timetables, **RAIL 981**
See also GWR locomotives and rolling stock;
   miscellanea
Irish & English Traffic Conference
Neath, Pontardawe and Brun-aman Railway
      Parliamentary papers, **RAIL 1066**
Neath, Pontardawe and Brynmawr Railway
   (proposed)
      Parliamentary papers, **RAIL 1066**
Nettlebridge Valley Railway
      Miscellanea, **RAIL 1057**
      Parliamentary papers, **RAIL 1066**
Newark and Melton Mowbray and Leicester
   Railway (proposed)
      Parliamentary papers, **RAIL 1066**
Newbury, Basingstoke, London and Southampton
   Railway (proposed)
      GWR miscellanea, **RAIL 1014**
      Prospectuses etc, **RAIL 1075**
Newcastle and Berwick Railway, **RAIL 506**
      Miscellanea, **RAIL 1152; RAIL 1157**
      Reports and accounts, **RAIL 1110**
      Share certificate, **RAIL 1159**
      Timetables, **RAIL 981**
See also GNoER
   NER
   York, Newcastle & Berwick R
Newcastle and Darlington Junction Railway
      Miscellanea, **RAIL 1152; RAIL 1157**
      Reports and accounts, **RAIL 1110**
      Timetables, **RAIL 981**
See also York, Newcastle & Berwick R
Newcastle and London Railway (proposed)
      Miscellanea, **RAIL 1021**
Newcastle and North Shields Railway
      Miscellanea, **RAIL 1016; RAIL 1157**
Newcastle, Derwent and Weardale Railway
   (proposed), **RAIL 508**
      Miscellanea, **RAIL 1021**
      Parliamentary papers, **RAIL 1067**
      Prospectuses etc, **RAIL 1075; RAIL 1076**
Newcastle-upon-Tyne and Carlisle Railway,
   RAIL 509 (*includes records of* Maryport & Carlisle
   R; NER)
      Miscellanea, **RAIL 1008; RAIL 1014;**
         RAIL 1016; RAIL 1020; RAIL 1021;
         RAIL 1157
      Parliamentary papers, **RAIL 1066; RAIL 1067**
      Prospectuses etc, **RAIL 1075; RAIL 1076**
      Reports and accounts, **RAIL 1110; RAIL 1111;**
         RAIL 1116; RAIL 1117
      Rule books, **RAIL 1134**
      Share certificates, **RAIL 1159**

Timetables, **RAIL 981**
Newcastle-upon-Tyne and Derwent Railway
(proposed)
Prospectus, **RAIL 1021**
Newcastle-upon-Tyne and Derwent Valley
Railway (proposed)
Prospectuses etc, **RAIL 1075; RAIL 1076**
Newcastle-upon-Tyne and North Shields Railway,
RAIL 507
Miscellanea, **RAIL 1157**
Parliamentary papers, **RAIL 1016**
Prospectuses etc, **RAIL 1075**
Share certificate, **RAIL 1159**
Newcastle-upon-Tyne City Tramways
Reports and accounts, **RAIL 1114**
Newcastle-upon-Tyne Corporation Tramways
Parliamentary papers, **RAIL 1068**
Newcastle-upon-Tyne, North Shields and
Tynemouth Railway (proposed)
Miscellanea, **RAIL 1157**
Prospectuses etc, **RAIL 1075; RAIL 1076**
New Cross and Waterloo Railway (proposed)
Parliamentary papers, **RAIL 1066**
Newent Railway, **RAIL 510**
Parliamentary papers, **RAIL 1066**
Railway and Canal Traffic Acts proceedings,
RAIL 1038
Reports and accounts, **RAIL 1110**
See also GWR estates and rating, Ledbury &
Gloucester line
Newhaven and Seaford Sea Defence
Commissioners **RAIL 511** (*dividend guaranteed by*
LBSCR *which was represented on the Commission*)
Newhaven Harbour Company (*some directors were
appointed by* LBSCR)
Reports and accounts, **RAIL 1116; RAIL 1117**
Newmarket Railway, **RAIL 512**
Reports and accounts, **RAIL 1116**
Newport, Abergavenny and Hereford Railway,
RAIL 513
Parliamentary papers, **RAIL 1066;
RAIL 1163**
Prospectuses etc, **RAIL 1075**
Reports and accounts, **RAIL 1110; RAIL 1116;
RAIL 1117**
Newport and Pontypool Railway *see*
Monmouthshire R & Canal Co
Newport and Nantyglo Railway (proposed)
Prospectuses etc, **RAIL 1075**
Newport and Ryde Direct Railway
Parliamentary papers, **RAIL 1066**
Newport Dock Company *see* Alexandra (Newport
& S Wales) Docks & R
Newport, Godshill and St Lawrence Railway,
RAIL 514
Reports and accounts, **RAIL 1116**
Timetables, **RAIL 981**

Newport Pagnell Railway
Reports and accounts, **RAIL 1116**
Siding agreements, **RAIL 1167**
Newport Railway (*Scotland*)
Share certificates, **RAIL 1158**
Newport (Monmouthshire) Tramways
Prospectuses etc, **RAIL 1075**
Newport Street Joint Committee
(GWR/Corporation of Newport *for street
improvement*), **RAIL 515**
Newquay and Cornwall Junction Railway,
RAIL 516 (*includes records of* Cornwall Minerals
R)
Prospectuses etc, **RAIL 1075; RAIL 1110**
Reports and accounts, **RAIL 1110; RAIL 1116**
Newry and Armagh Railway
Reports and accounts, **RAIL 1116; RAIL 1117**
See also Irish & English Traffic Conference
Newry and Enniskillen Railway
Parliamentary papers, **RAIL 1163**
Reports and accounts, **RAIL 1116; RAIL 1117**
Newry and Greenore Railway
Joint committee with:
Dundalk & Greenore R, **RAIL 410** (Joint
works)
Newry, Warrenpoint and Rostrevor Railway
Reports and accounts, **RAIL 1116**
See also Irish & English Traffic Conference
Newton and Warrington Railway (proposed)
Parliamentary plans, **RAIL 1071**
Newtown and Machynlleth Railway, **RAIL 517**
Parliamentary papers, **RAIL 1066**
Prospectus, **RAIL 1110**
Reports and accounts, **RAIL 1110; RAIL 1116**
Rule books, **RAIL 1134**
Subscription contracts, **RAIL 1160**
Newtown and Oswestry Railway (proposed)
Parliamentary papers, **RAIL 1163**
See also Oswestry & Newtown R
Nine Elms to Deptford Railway (proposed)
Prospectuses etc, **RAIL 1075**
Nine Mile Point Railway (proposed)
Parliamentary papers, **RAIL 1066**
Norfolk and Suffolk Joint Railways Committee
(GER/GNR/MR; *after 1923* LMSR/LNER),
RAIL 518; RAIL 783
Reports and accounts, **RAIL 1110;
RAIL 1116**
Timetables, **RAIL 981**
See also GNR
Norfolk Central Railway (proposed)
Miscellanea, **RAIL 1020**
Norfolk Railway, **RAIL 519** (*includes records of*
GER)
Joint committee with:
Eastern Counties R/Eastern Union R,
RAIL 186

Miscellanea, **RAIL 1021**
Reports and accounts, **RAIL 1116; RAIL 1117**
Timetables, **RAIL 981**
Normanton Joint Station Committee
(L&YR/MR/York & N Midland R; *after 1854*
L&YR/MR/NER; *in 1922* LNWR; MR/NER;
after 1923 LMSR/LNER), **RAIL 520**
 RAIL 410 (LNWR/MR/NER)
Northampton and Banbury Junction Railway,
 RAIL 538
Parliamentary papers, **RAIL 1066**
Railway and Canal Traffic Acts proceedings,
 RAIL 1038
Reports and accounts, **RAIL 1116; RAIL 1117**
Northampton and Banbury Railway, **RAIL 539**
Prospectuses etc, **RAIL 1075**
Subscription contracts, **RAIL 1160**
Northampton and Leicester Railway *or* South
Midland Railway (proposed)
Prospectuses etc, **RAIL 1075**
Northampton and Peterborough Railway
(proposed)
Parliamentary papers, **RAIL 1066**
Northampton, Banbury and Cheltenham Railway
(proposed), **RAIL 540**
North and East Riding Junction Railway
(proposed)
Miscellanea, **RAIL 1153**
North and South Gravesend Tunnel Railway
(proposed)
Parliamentary papers, **RAIL 1066**
North and South Junction Railway (proposed)
Prospectuses etc, **RAIL 1075**
North and South Shields Light Railway (Kearney
Tube), **RAIL 780** (LNER *records*)
North and South Staffordshire Junction Railway
(proposed)
Prospectus, **RAIL 1116**
North and South Wales Railway (proposed)
Prospectuses etc, **RAIL 1075**
North and South Western Hampstead and City
Railway (proposed)
Miscellanea, **RAIL 1057**
Prospectus, **RAIL 1116**
Share certificates, **RAIL 1158**
Subscription contracts, **RAIL 1160;
RAIL 1163**
North and South Western Junction Railway,
 RAIL 521
Byelaws and regulations, **RAIL 1001**
Joint committee (LNWR/MR/N London R),
 RAIL 421; RAIL 521
Parliamentary papers, **RAIL 1066; RAIL 1163**
Parliamentary plans, **RAIL 1071**
Reports and accounts, **RAIL 1110; RAIL 1116;
RAIL 1117**
Share certificates, **RAIL 1158**

See also LMSR amalgamation; miscellanea
LNWR
North and South Wiltshire Railway
Maps, **RAIL 1030**
Parliamentary papers, **RAIL 1066**
North British Arbroath and Montrose Railway
Share certificates, **RAIL 1158**
North British Hawick and Carlisle Junction
Railway (proposed)
Reports and accounts, **RAIL 1117**
North British Railway
Hotels, **RAIL 1022**
Instructions to staff, **RAIL 1135**
Joint committee *see* E Coast (Railway Cos')
Conference
Labour and staff matters, **RAIL 1025**
Law cases and arbitration, **RAIL 1027**
Maps, **RAIL 1030**
Miscellanea, **RAIL 1007; RAIL 1014;
RAIL 1021; RAIL 1057; RAIL 1157**
Parliamentary papers, **RAIL 1066; RAIL 1163**
Railway and Canal Traffic Acts proceedings,
 RAIL 1038
Reports and accounts, **RAIL 1110; RAIL 1116;
RAIL 1117**
Rule books, **RAIL 1134**
Savings bank rules, **RAIL 1174**
Share certificates, **RAIL 1158**
Superannuation schemes, **RAIL 1174**
Timetables
Public, **RAIL 926** (East Coast Route);
 RAIL 966; RAIL 981
Working, **RAIL 965**
appendixes, **RAIL 1136**
Welfare schemes, **RAIL 1115; RAIL 1174**
See also Irish & English Traffic Conference
North Cheshire Railway (proposed)
Prospectuses etc, **RAIL 1076**
North Cornwall Railway, **RAIL 522**
Miscellanea, **RAIL 1057**
Parliamentary papers, **RAIL 1066**
Reports and accounts, **RAIL 1110**
North Devon and Cornwall Junction Light
Railway, **RAIL 523** (*includes records of* LSWR;
Torrington & Okehampton Lt R, *later* N Devon
Direct R)
Reports and accounts, **RAIL 1110; RAIL 1116**
North Devon and Somerset Railway (proposed)
Parliamentary papers, **RAIL 1066**
North Devon Direct R *see* N Devon & Cornwall
Lt R
North Devon Railway and Dock Company,
 RAIL 524 (*includes records of predecessor* Taw Vale
R & Dock Co)
GWR miscellanea, **RAIL 1014**
Parliamentary papers, **RAIL 1066**
Reports and accounts, **RAIL 1116; RAIL 1117**

North Eastern and North Western Junction
  Railway (proposed)
    Prospectuses etc, **RAIL 1076**
North Eastern Railway, **RAIL 527** *includes records*
  of or about:
    BR(NE)
    Clarence R
    Gosforth & Ponteland Lt R
    GNoER
    Hartlepool Dock & R
    Hartlepool Jct R
    Isle of Axholme Lt R
    Leeds Northern R
    LNER
    Malton & Driffield Jct R
    Newcastle & Berwick R
    N Holderness Lt R
    Sand Hutton Lt R;
    Whitby, Redcar & Middlesbrough Union R;
    York & N Midland R
    York, Newcastle & Berwick R
    Byelaws and regulations, **RAIL 1001;**
      RAIL 1003 (Docks)
    Deeds, etc, **RAIL 794**
    Instructions to staff, **RAIL 1135**
    Joint committees with:
      H&BR, **RAIL 525** (Hull Jt Dock)
      L&YR
        Byelaws and regulations, **RAIL 1001**
        RAIL 13 (Axholme Jt R)
        RAIL 526 (Isle of Axholme and Goole &
          Marshland Lt Rys)
      LNWR
        RAIL 410 (Axholme Jt R)
        RAIL 356; RAIL 410; RAIL 417; RAIL 421
          (Leeds New station)
        RAIL 410; RAIL 421; RAIL 686 (Tebay
          station)
      MR
        Miscellanea, **RAIL 1057**
      S&DR
        RAIL 47 (Bishop Auckland Station)
    See also E Coast (Railway Cos')
      Conference
      Humber Conference
      Leeds Central Station
      London & W Riding Association
      Methley R Jt Cttee
      Normanton Jt Station Cttee
      Otley & Ilkley Jt Line Cttee
      S Yorkshire Jt Line Cttee
      Swinton & Knottingley Jt R
    Labour and staff matters, **RAIL 1025**
    Law cases and arbitration, **RAIL 1027**
    Maps, **RAIL 1030**
    Miscellanea, **RAIL 1006; RAIL 1008;**
      RAIL 1014; RAIL 1016; RAIL 1020;
      RAIL 1021; RAIL 1057; RAIL 1152;
      RAIL 1155; RAIL 1157
    Parliamentary papers, **RAIL 1066; RAIL 1067**
    Prospectuses etc, **RAIL 1075**
    Railway and Canal Traffic Acts proceedings,
      RAIL 1038
    Reports and accounts, **RAIL 1110; RAIL 1111;**
      RAIL 1116; RAIL 1117
    Rule books, **RAIL 1134**
    Savings bank, **RAIL 1174**
    Share certificates, **RAIL 1159**
    Superannuation schemes, **RAIL 1174**
    Timetables
      Public, **RAIL 926** (East Coast Route);
        RAIL 967; RAIL 981
      Working, **RAIL 968**
        appendixes, **RAIL 1136**
  See also Eden Valley R
    Firbeck Lt R
    GNoER
    Hartlepool Dock & R
    Hull S Bridge Co
    Irish & English Traffic Conference
    Leeds & Selby R
    Leeds, Castleford & Pontefract Jct R
    Leeds Northern R
    LNER locomotives & rolling stock;
      miscellanea; train notices
    LMSR amalgamation
    Malton & Driffield Jct R
    Middlesbrough & Redcar R
    Newcastle-upon-Tyne & Carlisle R
    Pontop & S Shields R
    S Durham & Lancashire Union R
    Stockton & Darlington R
    W Hartlepool Harbour & R
North Eastern Railway and Hull and Barnsley and
  West Riding Junction Railway and Dock
  Company Joint Committee (Hull Joint Dock
  Committee), **RAIL 525**
North East London Railway
    Parliamentary papers, **RAIL 1066**
Northern Alliance (GWR/LNWR/OWWR/S
  Staffordshire R), **RAIL 250; RAIL 410**
Northern and Eastern Railway, **RAIL 541**
    Parliamentary papers, **RAIL 1016**
    Prospectuses etc, **RAIL 1075**
    Reports and accounts, **RAIL 1111; RAIL 1116**
    Timetables, **RAIL 981**
Northern and Southern Railways Metropolitan
  Junction (proposed)
    Reports and accounts, **RAIL 1116**
Northern Counties Railway Committee
  (*management of former* Belfast & Northern
  Counties R *by* MR *and, after 1923* LMSR),
  RAIL 542
    Law cases and arbitration, **RAIL 1027**

Reports and accounts, **RAIL 1116**
Timetables (LMSR), **RAIL 941**
See also Irish & English Traffic Conference
Northern Counties Union Railway, **RAIL 543**
(*includes records about proposed* York & Carlisle R
and Yorkshire & Glasgow R)
Reports and accounts, **RAIL 1116; RAIL 1117**
Share certificates, **RAIL 1159**
Northern Ireland Railways
Timetables, **RAIL 928**
Northern Ireland Transport Board
Timetables, **RAIL 941**
Northern Junction Railway (proposed)
Parliamentary papers, **RAIL 1066**
Northern Railway
Reports and accounts, **RAIL 1116**
North Holderness Light Railway *see* NER
Northumberland Central Railway
Reports and accounts, **RAIL 1116**
North Kent Extension Railway
Parliamentary papers, **RAIL 1066**
North Kent Railway
Miscellanea, **RAIL 1153**
North Kent Railway (proposed) *Vignoles' line, also
called* London, Chatham & N Kent R
Parliamentary papers, **RAIL 1066**
Northleach and Witney Railway (proposed)
Parliamentary papers, **RAIL 1066; RAIL 1185**
North Lindsay Light Railways, **RAIL 528**
North London Railway, **RAIL 529** (*includes records
of predecessor* E&W India Docks & Birmingham
Jct R); **RAIL 410**
Byelaws and regulations, **RAIL 1001**
Instructions to staff, **RAIL 1135**
Joint committee with:
LNWR/MR, **RAIL 521; RAIL 410**
(N & S Western Jct R)
Labour and staff matters, **RAIL 1025**
Law cases and arbitration, **RAIL 1027**
Miscellanea, **RAIL 1008; RAIL 1014;
RAIL 1015**
Parliamentary papers, **RAIL 1066**
Railway and Canal Traffic Acts proceedings,
RAIL 1038
Reports and accounts, **RAIL 1110; RAIL 1116;
RAIL 1117**
Rule books, **RAIL 1134**
Share certificates, **RAIL 1158**
Sidings agreements, **RAIL 1167**
Timetables, **RAIL 981**
Working timetables appendixes,
RAIL 1136
See also LNWR
LMSR amalgamation; miscellanea
North Metropolitan Railway (*promoted as*
Bayswater, Paddington & Holborn Bridge R)
Subscription contract, **RAIL 1160**

North Metropolitan Railway and Canal Company
Miscellanea, **RAIL 1057**
Reports and accounts, **RAIL 1110**
North Metropolitan Tramways
Reports and accounts, **RAIL 1114**
North Midland Railway, **RAIL 530**
Miscellanea, **RAIL 1008; RAIL 1020;
RAIL 1021; RAIL 1153; RAIL 1157**
Parliamentary papers, **RAIL 1066**
Prospectuses etc, **RAIL 1075**
Reports and accounts, **RAIL 1110**
Rule books, **RAIL 1134**
Subscription contracts, **RAIL 1160**
Timetables, **RAIL 981**
See also GWR miscellanea Brunel collection
North Monkland Railway
Share certificates, **RAIL 1158**
North of England Union Railway (proposed)
Parliamentary papers, **RAIL 1066**
Prospectuses etc, **RAIL 1075; RAIL 1076**
North Pembrokeshire and Fishguard Railway,
RAIL 531 (*includes records of predecessor*
Rosebush & Fishguard R)
Parliamentary papers, **RAIL 1066**
Reports and accounts, **RAIL 1110**
North Staffordshire Railway, RAIL 532 (*includes
records of* Leek, Caldon Low and Hartington Lt
Rys; Cheadle R; Leek & Manifold Valley Lt R;
Waterhouses & Hulme End Lt R)
Bill, **RAIL 1147**
Dividend warrants, **RAIL 1158**
Instructions to staff, **RAIL 1135**
Joint committees with:
GCR
Byelaws and regulations, **RAIL 1001**
Reports and accounts, **RAIL 1110**
RAIL 448 (Macclesfield, Bollington &
Marple R)
Byelaws and regulations, **RAIL 1001**
Reports and accounts, **RAIL 1110**
LNWR, **RAIL 449** (Macclesfield jt station)
Law cases and arbitration, **RAIL 1027**
Maps, **RAIL 1030**
Miscellanea, **RAIL 1005; RAIL 1007;
RAIL 1015; RAIL 1057; RAIL 1151**
Parliamentary papers, **RAIL 1066; RAIL 1163**
Parliamentary plans, **RAIL 1071**
Railway and Canal Traffic Acts proceedings,
RAIL 1038
Reports and accounts, **RAIL 1110; RAIL 1116;
RAIL 1117**
Rule books, **RAIL 1134**
Savings bank rules, **RAIL 1174**
Share certificates, **RAIL 1158**
Timetables
Public, **RAIL 969; RAIL 981**
Working, **RAIL 970**

Traders' ledger credit agreements, **RAIL 1165**
Welfare funds, **RAIL 1174**
See also GNR
    Irish & English Traffic Conference
    LMSR amalgamation
North Sunderland Railway, **RAIL 533** (*includes records of* BR(NE), LNER)
    Prospectuses etc, **RAIL 1076**
    Reports and accounts, **RAIL 1111; RAIL 1117**
    Share certificates, **RAIL 1159**
    Timetables, **RAIL 981**
See also BTC Chief Secretary's Office
    LNER minutes and reports
Northumberland and Lancashire Junction Railway (proposed)
    Prospectuses etc, **RAIL 1076**
Northumberland Central Railway
    Share certificates, **RAIL 1158**
Northumberland Railway (proposed)
    Prospectuses etc, **RAIL 1076**
North Union Railway, **RAIL 534** (*includes records of predecessors* Preston & Wigan R *and* Wigan Branch R)
    Dividend warrants, **RAIL 1158**
    Joint committee with:
        Grand Jct R/Manchester & Leeds R, **RAIL 220; RAIL 534**
    Miscellanea, **RAIL 1008**
    Prospectuses etc, **RAIL 1075**
    Rule books, **RAIL 1134**
    Subscription contracts, **RAIL 1160**
North Wales and Liverpool Railway Committee *formerly* Wirral Rys Cttee *and* Dee Birkenhead Cttee (MSLR/Wrexham Mold & Connah's Quay R; *after 1897* GCR/WM&CQR), **RAIL 535**
    Miscellanea, **RAIL 1151**
North Wales Mineral Railway
    Parliamentary plans, **RAIL 1071**
    Prospectus, **RAIL 1110**
See also Shrewsbury & Chester R
North Wales Narrow Gauge Railways
    Parliamentary papers, **RAIL 1066**
    Railway and Canal Traffic Acts proceedings, **RAIL 1038**
    Reports and accounts, **RAIL 1116**
North West Central Railway
    Parliamentary papers, **RAIL 1066**
North West London Railway
    Parliamentary papers, **RAIL 1066**
North Western and Charing Cross Railway
    Joint committee LNWR/SER, **RAIL 410**
    Parliamentary plans, **RAIL 1071**
    Prospectuses etc, **RAIL 1075**
North Western and Ealing Railway (proposed)
    Parliamentary papers, **RAIL 1066**

North Western Railway, **RAIL 536**
    Maps, **RAIL 1030**
    Prospectuses etc, **RAIL 1076**
    Reports and accounts, **RAIL 1116; RAIL 1117**
    Subscription contracts, **RAIL 1160**
North Yorkshire and Cleveland Railway, **RAIL 537**
    Miscellanea, **RAIL 1157**
    Parliamentary papers, **RAIL 1163**
    Prospectuses etc, **RAIL 1076**
    Reports and accounts, **RAIL 1111; RAIL 1116; RAIL 1117**
Norwich and Spalding Railway, **RAIL 544**
    Miscellanea, **RAIL 1016**
    Parliamentary papers, **RAIL 1066; RAIL 1163**
    Subscription contracts, **RAIL 1163**
Nottingham and Grantham Railway and Canal Company (*formerly* Ambergate, Nottingham & Boston & Eastern Jct R & Canal Co *q.v.*), **RAIL 545**
    Reports and accounts, **RAIL 1110; RAIL 1116; RAIL 1117**
Nottingham and Mansfield Railway (proposed)
    Parliamentary plans, **RAIL 1071**
Nottingham and Retford Railway
    Parliamentary papers, **RAIL 1066**
Nottingham City Tramways
    Reports and accounts, **RAIL 1114**
Nottingham Joint Station Committee (GNR/MS&LR; *after 1897* GNR/GCR), **RAIL 546; RAIL 783**
    Reports and accounts, **RAIL 1110**
Nottingham Suburban Railway, **RAIL 547**
Nottingham, Vale of Belvoir and Grantham Railway (proposed), **RAIL 548**
Nuneaton and Hinckley Railway
    Parliamentary plans, **RAIL 1071**
Oakwood Railway
    Miscellanea, **RAIL 1057**
Oakwood Tramroad
    Miscellanea, **RAIL 1057**
Ogmore Valley Railways, **RAIL 549**
    Miscellanea, **RAIL 1057**
    Parliamentary papers, **RAIL 1066**
    Prospectuses etc, **RAIL 1075**
    Reports and accounts, **RAIL 1110; RAIL 1116**
Okehampton and Bideford Railway (proposed)
    Prospectuses etc, **RAIL 1075**
Okehampton Railway
    Parliamentary papers, **RAIL 1066**
Oldbury Railway, **RAIL 550**
    Railway and Canal Traffic Acts proceedings, **RAIL 1038**
    Reports and accounts, **RAIL 1110; RAIL 1116**
Oldham, Ashton-under-Lyne and Guide Bridge Junction Railway, **RAIL 551** (*Oldham Railway Committee* LNWR/MSLR; *after 1897* LNWR/GCR; *after 1923* LMSR/LNER), **RAIL 410; RAIL 551**

Parliamentary plans, **RAIL 1071**
Reports and accounts, **RAIL 1110;**
   RAIL 1116
Rule books, **RAIL 1134**
Subscription contracts, **RAIL 1160**
Timetables, **RAIL 981**
Oswestry and Llangynog Railway
   Promotion papers, **RAIL 1147**
Oswestry and Newtown Railway, **RAIL 552** (*before incorporation known as* Newtown & Oswestry R *and* Oswestry Welchpool & Newtown R)
   Land, **RAIL 1147**
   Miscellanea, **RAIL 1057**
   Parliamentary papers, **RAIL 1066**
   Reports and accounts, **RAIL 1110;**
      RAIL 1116
   Subscription contracts, **RAIL 1160; RAIL 1163**
Oswestry, Ellesmere and Whitchurch Railway,
   RAIL 553
   Miscellanea, **RAIL 1057**
   Parliamentary papers, **RAIL 1066**
   Parliamentary plans, **RAIL 1071**
   Reports and accounts, **RAIL 1116**
Oswestry, Shrewsbury and Ellesmere Railway
   (proposed)
   Parliamentary papers, **RAIL 1066**
Oswestry, Welchpool and Newtown Railway
   (proposed) *see* Oswestry & Newtown R
Otley and Ilkley Joint Line Committee (MR/NER,
   after 1923 LMSR/LNER), **RAIL 554**
   Byelaws and regulations, **RAIL 1001**
   Miscellanea, **RAIL 1057**
Oxford and Aylesbury Tramroad
   Timetables, **RAIL 981**
Oxford and Bletchley Junction Railway, **RAIL 555**
Oxford and Great Western Union Railway
   (proposed) *see* Oxford R; GWR miscellanea
   Brunel collection
Oxford and Rugby Railway, **RAIL 556** (*includes records of* GWR)
   Parliamentary papers, **RAIL 1066**
Oxford and Salisbury Direct Railway (proposed)
   GWR miscellanea, **RAIL 1014**
Oxford Railway, **RAIL 557** (*includes records of proposed* Oxford & Great Western Union R)
Oxford, Southampton, Gosport and Portsmouth
   Railway (proposed)
   Prospectuses etc, **RAIL 1075**
Oxford, Thame, High Wycombe and Uxbridge
   Junction Railway (proposed)
   Miscellanea, **RAIL 1057**
   Prospectuses etc, **RAIL 1075**
Oxford Street and City Railway (proposed)
   Parliamentary plans, **RAIL 1071**
Oxford, Witney, Cheltenham and Gloucester
   Independent Railway (proposed)
   Parliamentary papers, **RAIL 1158**

Oxford, Worcester and Wolverhampton Railway,
   RAIL 558 (*including records of successor* W
Midland R)
   Joint committees *see*:
      Northern Alliance
      Southern Association Conference
      Wolverhampton Jt Cttees
   Law cases and arbitration, **RAIL 1027**
   Maps, **RAIL 1030**
   Miscellanea, **RAIL 1007; RAIL 1014**
   Oxford to Brentford line, **RAIL 784**
   Parliamentary papers, **RAIL 1066; RAIL 1163**
   Parliamentary plans, **RAIL 1071**
   Prospectuses etc, **RAIL 1075**
   Reports and accounts, **RAIL 1110; RAIL 1116;**
      RAIL 1117
   Rule books, **RAIL 1134**
   Share certificate, **RAIL 1159**
   Timetables, **RAIL 981**
See also Stratford & Moreton R
Oxted and Groombridge Railway
   Parliamentary papers, **RAIL 1066**
Oystermouth Tramroad
   Miscellanea, **RAIL 1057**
Painswick Railway
   Miscellanea, **RAIL 1057**
Peckham and East Dulwich Tramways
   Parliamentary papers, **RAIL 1066**
Peebles Railway
   Reports and accounts, **RAIL 1116; RAIL 1117**
   Share certificates, **RAIL 1158**
Pembroke and Tenby Railway, **RAIL 559**
   Joint committee with Manchester & Milford R,
      RAIL 455
   Parliamentary papers, **RAIL 1066**
   Railway and Canal Traffic Acts proceedings,
      RAIL 1038
   Reports and accounts, **RAIL 1110; RAIL 1116;**
      RAIL 1117
   Rule books, **RAIL 1134**
   Timetables, **RAIL 981**
Penarth and Cardiff Light Railway (proposed)
   Parliamentary papers, **RAIL 1066**
Penarth Extension Railway, **RAIL 560**
   Railway & Canal Traffic Acts proceedings,
      RAIL 1038
   Reports and accounts, **RAIL 1110; RAIL 1117**
Penarth Harbour Dock and Railway, **RAIL 561**
   (*includes records of predecessor* Ely Tidal Harbour
& R)
   Byelaws and regulations, **RAIL 1001**
     (Taff Vale R)
   Joint committee with Taff Vale R, **RAIL 562**
   Miscellanea, **RAIL 1057**
   Parliamentary papers, **RAIL 1066;**
      RAIL 1147
   Prospectuses etc, **RAIL 1075**

Reports and accounts, **RAIL 1110; RAIL 1116; RAIL 1117**

Rule books, **RAIL 1134**

Penicuik Railway

Share certificates, **RAIL 1158**

Penllwyn Railway

Parliamentary papers, **RAIL 1066**

Penrith Joint Station Committee (Cockermouth, Keswick & Penrith R/LNWR/S&DR), **RAIL 563**

Perth and Dunkeld Railway

Reports and accounts, **RAIL 1116**

Perth General Station Committee (LMSR/LNER)

Reports and accounts, **RAIL 1116**

Perth Station Hotel and Refreshment Rooms (LMSR/LNER)

Reports and accounts, **RAIL 1116**

Peterborough, Wisbech and Sutton Railway, **RAIL 564**

Parliamentary plans, **RAIL 1071**

Reports and accounts, **RAIL 1116**

Petersfield Railway, **RAIL 565**

Pewsey and Salisbury Light Railway

Miscellanea, **RAIL 1057**

Parliamentary papers, **RAIL 1066**

Pewsey, Salisbury and Southampton Railway (proposed)

Miscellanea, **RAIL 1057**

Parliamentary papers, **RAIL 1066**

Piccadilly and City Railway (proposed)

Parliamentary papers, **RAIL 1066**

Piccadilly, City and North East London Railway (proposed)

Parliamentary papers, **RAIL 1066**

Pickfords Ltd *see* BTC road services; GWR road services; LNER road services; LMSR road services; SR road services

Pinner Railway (proposed)

Parliamentary papers, **RAIL 1066**

Pirbright, Aldershot and Farnham Railway (proposed)

Parliamentary papers, **RAIL 1066**

Plymouth and Dartmoor Railway, **RAIL 566**

Miscellanea, **RAIL 1017; RAIL 1057**

Parliamentary papers, **RAIL 1066**

Prospectuses etc, **RAIL 1075**

Reports and accounts, **RAIL 1110; RAIL 1116; RAIL 1117**

Plymouth, Devonport and Exeter Railway (proposed)

Prospectus, **RAIL 1110**

Plymouth, Devonport and South Western Junction Railway, **RAIL 567**

Law cases and arbitration, **RAIL 1027**

Miscellanea, **RAIL 1014**

Parliamentary papers, **RAIL 1066**

Prospectuses etc, **RAIL 1075**

Reports and accounts, **RAIL 1116; RAIL 1117**

Plymouth Joint Station Committee (Cornwall R/S Devon R; *after 1878* Cornwall R/GWR), **RAIL 568**

Plymouth, Tavistock and Okehampton and North Devon Railway (proposed)

Subscription contract, **RAIL 1163**

Pontardawe and Brynmawr Railway

Miscellanea, **RAIL 1057**

Pontefract, Doncaster, Worksop and Mansfield Junction Railway (proposed)

Miscellanea, **RAIL 1153**

Pontop and South Shields Railway, **RAIL 569** (*includes records of predecessor* Stanhope & Tyne R *and successor* NER)

Miscellanea, **RAIL 1021**

Pontypool and Talywain Railway *see* GWR/LNWR jt cttees

Pontypool, Caerleon and Newport Railway, **RAIL 570** (*includes records of* GWR)

Parliamentary papers, **RAIL 1066**

Reports and accounts, **RAIL 1110**

See also GWR miscellanea special reports

Pontypridd, Caerphilly and Newport Railway, **RAIL 571**

Miscellanea, **RAIL 1057**

Parliamentary papers, **RAIL 1066**

Railway and Canal Traffic Acts proceedings, **RAIL 1038**

Reports and accounts, **RAIL 1110**

Timetables, **RAIL 981**

Pontypridd Urban District Council Tramways

Parliamentary papers, **RAIL 1068**

Poole and Bournemouth Railway, **RAIL 572**

Poplar and Canning Town Railway (proposed)

Maps, **RAIL 1030**

Portadown and Dungannon Railway

Reports and accounts, **RAIL 1116**

Port Carlisle Dock and Railway

Parliamentary plans, **RAIL 1071**

Reports and accounts, **RAIL 1116; RAIL 1117**

Share certificates, **RAIL 1158**

Portland Railway

Miscellanea, **RAIL 1057**

Portmadoc, Beddgelert and South Snowdon Railway (proposed)

Parliamentary papers, **RAIL 1066**

Portmadoc, Croesor and Beddgelert Tram Railway

Prospectuses etc, **RAIL 1075**

Railway and Canal Traffic Acts proceedings, **RAIL 1038**

Portpatrick and Wigtownshire Joint Railway (Cal R/GSWR/LNWR/MR), **RAIL 421**

Joint committee with:

Belfast & Northern Counties R, **RAIL 1116** (Larne & Stranraer Steamboat Co reports and accounts)

Parliamentary papers, **RAIL 1066**

Reports and accounts, **RAIL 1116**
Share certificates, **RAIL 1158**
See also LMSR amalgamation; miscellanea
Portpatrick Railway
Reports and accounts, **RAIL 1116**
Portsea Railway (proposed)
Miscellanea, **RAIL 1017**
Portsmouth, Basingstoke and Godalming Railway
(proposed)
Parliamentary papers, **RAIL 1066**
Port Wrexham Harbour and Railway (proposed)
Prospectuses etc, **RAIL 1075**
Portsmouth City Tramways
Reports and accounts, **RAIL 1114**
Portsmouth Junction Railway (proposed)
Prospectuses etc, **RAIL 1075**
Portsmouth Railway, **RAIL 575**
Parliamentary papers, **RAIL 1066; RAIL 1163**
Reports and accounts, **RAIL 1116; RAIL 1117**
Portsmouth Waterside Extension Railway
(proposed)
Miscellanea, **RAIL 1017**
Port Talbot and Rhondda Railway (proposed)
Miscellanea, **RAIL 1057**
Port Talbot Company, **RAIL 573**
Port Talbot Railway and Docks Company,
RAIL 574
Byelaws and regulations, **RAIL 1001**
Joint committee with:
GWR, **RAIL 242** (operation by GWR)
Labour and staff matters, **RAIL 1025**
Miscellanea, **RAIL 1057**
Parliamentary papers, **RAIL 1066**
Prospectuses etc, **RAIL 1075**
Reports and accounts, **RAIL 1110; RAIL 1116;
RAIL 1117**
Timetables, **RAIL 981**
See also GWR miscellanea; locomotives and
rolling stock
Post Office (London) Railway
Miscellanea, **RAIL 1057**
Parliamentary papers, **RAIL 1066**
Potteries Junction Railway (proposed)
Parliamentary papers, **RAIL 1066; RAIL 1180**
Potteries, Shrewsbury and North Wales Railway
Correspondence, **RAIL 1147**
Miscellanea, **RAIL 1057**
Reports and accounts, **RAIL 1116**
See also GWR Secretary's papers
Preseley and Newport Railway (proposed)
GWR miscellanea, **RAIL 1014**
Preston and Blackburn Tramways (proposed)
Parliamentary papers, **RAIL 1066**
Preston and Horwich Tramways (proposed)
Parliamentary papers, **RAIL 1066**
Preston and Longridge Railway
Prospectuses etc, **RAIL 1075**

Preston and Longridge Railway Joint Committee
(L&YR/LNWR), **RAIL 576; RAIL 410**
Byelaws and regulations, **RAIL 1001**
Prospectuses etc, **RAIL 1075**
Railway and Canal Traffic Acts proceedings,
RAIL 1038
Preston and Lytham Tramways and Tramroad
(proposed)
Parliamentary papers, **RAIL 1066**
Preston and Lytham Railway (proposed)
Prospectuses etc, **RAIL 1075**
Preston and Wigan Railway
Subscription contracts, **RAIL 1160**
See also North Union R
Preston and Wyre Railway Harbour and Dock
Company, **RAIL 577** (*includes records of
predecessors* Preston & Wyre R & Harbour Co *and*
Preston & Wyre Dock Co)
Byelaws and regulations, **RAIL 1001**
Miscellanea, **RAIL 1015**
Prospectuses etc, **RAIL 1075**
Timetables, **RAIL 981**
See also L&YR/LNWR jt cttees
Preston, Chorley and Horwich Tramways
Parliamentary papers, **RAIL 1066**
Preston, Longton and Southport Railway
(proposed)
Parliamentary papers, **RAIL 1066**
Princes Dock Branch Joint Line Committee
(LMSR/LNER)
Reports and accounts, **RAIL 1116**
Princetown Railway, **RAIL 578**
Miscellanea, **RAIL 1057**
Railway and Canal Traffic Acts proceedings,
RAIL 1038
Reports and accounts, **RAIL 1110**
See also GWR miscellanea
Provincial Tramways
Reports and accounts, **RAIL 1114**
Pullman Car Company
Law cases and arbitration, **RAIL 1027**
Reports and accounts, **RAIL 1116; RAIL 1117**
Superannuation scheme, **RAIL 1174**
Purton Pill Railway (proposed)
Miscellanea, **RAIL 1014**
Pwylleli and Nevin Light Railway (proposed)
Miscellanea, **RAIL 1005**
Pwylleli, Nevin and Port Dinlleyn Light Railway
(proposed)
Miscellanea, **RAIL 1005**
Pye Bridge and Mansfield Railway (proposed)
Parliamentary plans, **RAIL 1071**
Radstock and Keynsham Railway (proposed)
Parliamentary papers, **RAIL 1066**
Radstock, Wrington and Congresbury Junction
Railway
Parliamentary papers, **RAIL 1066**

Railway Air Services (*Airline operated by* GWR, LMSR, LNER, SR and Imperial Airways)
Miscellanea, **RAIL 1020**
Photographs, press cuttings, instructions, **RAIL 253**
Timetables, **RAIL 981**
See also GWR air services; correspondence and papers; miscellanea
LNER air services
LMSR air services
Railway Assessment Authority
Miscellanea, **RAIL 1007**
Railway Benevolent Institution, **RAIL 1166**
Reports of meetings, **RAIL 1075**
Rules, **RAIL 1174**
Railway Clerks' Association
Labour and staff matters, **RAIL 1025**
Railway Clearing House
Coaching arrangements, **RAIL 1093**
Committee minutes and reports, **RAIL 410; RAIL 1075; RAIL 1080; RAIL 1081**
Conference minutes and reports, **RAIL 1080; RAIL 1081**
Deeds, agreements, plans, **RAIL 1084**
Distance books, **RAIL 1089** (*includes record of* Irish Railway Clearing House)
Financial records, **RAIL 1075**
Instructions to staff, **RAIL 1135**
Junction diagrams, **RAIL 1082**
Law reports, **RAIL 1094**
Maps and plans, **RAIL 1032**
Membership covenants, **RAIL 1097**
Miscellanea, **RAIL 1008; RAIL 1021; RAIL 1057; RAIL 1085; RAIL 1086**
Orders, **RAIL 1095**
Parliamentary papers, **RAIL 1066**
Regulations and classification of goods, **RAIL 1091; RAIL 1092** (*includes* Irish Railway Clearing House regulations)
Reports and accounts, **RAIL 1117**
Rule books, **RAIL 1134**
Staff records, **RAIL 1096**
Station handbooks, **RAIL 1087**
See also GWR Secretary's papers
Irish & English Traffic Conference
Railway Clearing System Superannuation Fund Association/Corporation, **RAIL 1174**
Reports and accounts, **RAIL 1116**
Railway Companies' Association
Minutes and reports, **RAIL 1098; RAIL 1099**
Miscellanea, **RAIL 1100** (*includes records of* SR)
Railway and Canal Traffic Acts proceedings, **RAIL 1038**
Reports and accounts, **RAIL 1116; RAIL 1117**
See also GWR Secretary's papers
Railway Executive *see* BTC

Railway Executive Committee (1914–1919), **AN 1**
Instructions to staff, **RAIL 1135**
Labour and staff matters, **RAIL 1025; RAIL 1026**
Miscellanea, **RAIL 1057**
Railway Executive Committee (1939–1947)
Files, **AN 2**
Instructions to staff, **RAIL 1135**
Minutes and reports, **AN 3**
Miscellanea, **RAIL 1057**
Railway Finance Corporation
Reports and accounts, **RAIL 1114; RAIL 1116**
Railway Investment Company
Reports and accounts, **RAIL 1116**
Railway Officers and Servants Railway Provident Society and Railway Orphan Fund, **RAIL 1174**
Railway Officers and Servants Sick Fund, **RAIL 1174**
Railway Passengers Assurance Company
Reports and accounts, **RAIL 1117**
Railway Rates Tribunal, proceedings, **RAIL 1101**
Railway Reform League
Reports and accounts, **RAIL 1116**
Railways Athletic Association
Reports and accounts, **RAIL 1116**
Railway Servants Orphanage
Concert programmes, **RAIL 1174**
Railway Shopmen's National Council
Labour and staff matters, **RAIL 1025; RAIL 1026**
Railway Staff Conference, **RAIL 1026**
Railway Staff Joint Council, **RAIL 1026**
Railway Staff National Council, **RAIL 1026**
Railway Staff National Tribunal, **RAIL 1025; RAIL 1026**
Railways Staff Conference, **RAIL 1025; RAIL 1135; RAIL 1172**
Railway Students Association, **RAIL 1107**
Reports and accounts, **RAIL 1117**
Welfare fund accounts, **RAIL 1115**
Ramsey and Somersham Junction Railway
Railway and Canal Traffic Acts proceedings, **RAIL 1038**
Reports and accounts, **RAIL 1110**
Ramsgate, Deal and Dover Railway (proposed)
Parliamentary papers, **RAIL 1066**
Ramsgate, Deal and Minster Railway (proposed)
Parliamentary papers, **RAIL 1066**
Rathkeale and Newcastle Junction Railway
Reports and accounts, **RAIL 1110; RAIL 1116**
Ravenglass and Eskdale Railway
Railway and Canal Traffic Acts proceedings, **RAIL 1038**
Reading and Reigate Atmospheric Railway (proposed)
Prospectuses etc, **RAIL 1075**

Reading Corporation Tramways
    Reports and accounts, **RAIL 1114**
Reading, Guildford and Reigate Railway,
    RAIL 579
    Miscellanea, **RAIL 1014**
    Reports and accounts, **RAIL 1116**
Rea Valley line (proposed)
    Prospectuses etc, **RAIL 1075**
Redcar Railway (proposed)
    Prospectuses etc, **RAIL 1076**
Redditch Railway, **RAIL 580**
    Prospectuses etc, **RAIL 1075**
    Reports and accounts, **RAIL 1116**
    Timetables, **RAIL 981**
Redruth and Chasewater Railway
    Miscellanea, **RAIL 1014**
    Parliamentary papers, **RAIL 1163**
    Railway and Canal Traffic Acts proceedings,
        RAIL 1038
    Rule books, **RAIL 1134**
Regents Canal, City and Docks Railway
    Miscellanea, **RAIL 1057**
    Parliamentary papers, **RAIL 1066**
    Parliamentary plans, **RAIL 1071**
Regents Canal Railway (proposed)
    Prospectuses etc, **RAIL 1075; RAIL 1076**
Retired Railway Officers' Society, **RAIL 1156**
Rhondda and Bristol Channel Railway (proposed)
    Miscellanea, **RAIL 1057**
Rhondda and Swansea Bay Railway, **RAIL 581**
    Joint committee with:
        GWR, **RAIL 243** (operation by GWR)
    Labour and staff matters, **RAIL 1025**
    Miscellanea, **RAIL 1020; RAIL 1057**
    Parliamentary papers, **RAIL 1066**
    Prospectuses, **RAIL 1014; RAIL 1110**
    Railway and Canal Traffic Acts proceedings,
        RAIL 1038
    Reports and accounts, **RAIL 1110; RAIL 1116;
        RAIL 1117**
    Rule books, **RAIL 1134**
    Timetables, **RAIL 981**
    See also GWR estates and rating; locomotives
        and rolling stock; miscellanea
Rhondda Tramways
    Law cases and arbitration, **RAIL 1027**
Rhondda Urban District Council Tramways
    Parliamentary papers, **RAIL 1068**
Rhondda Valley and Hirwain Junction Railway,
    RAIL 582
    Miscellanea, **RAIL 1057**
    Reports and accounts, **RAIL 1110**
Rhymney Railway, **RAIL 583**
    Byelaws and regulations, **RAIL 1001**
    Instructions to staff, **RAIL 1135**
    Joint committees with:
        GWR, **RAIL 244** (Bargoed railways)

    Byelaws and regulations, **RAIL 1001**
        Maps, **RAIL 1030**
    LNWR, **RAIL 407; RAIL 421**
    See also GWR estates and rating
    Labour and staff matters, **RAIL 1025**
    Law cases and arbitration, **RAIL 1027**
    Maps, **RAIL 1030**
    Miscellanea, **RAIL 1008; RAIL 1014;
        RAIL 1020; RAIL 1057**
    Parliamentary papers, **RAIL 1066; RAIL 1067;
        RAIL 1163**
    Prospectuses etc, **RAIL 1075; RAIL 1110**
    Railway and Canal Traffic Acts proceedings,
        RAIL 1038
    Reports and accounts, **RAIL 1110; RAIL 1116;
        RAIL 1117**
    Rule books, **RAIL 1134**
    Subscription contracts, **RAIL 1160**
    Timetables, **RAIL 981**
        Working timetables appendixes, **RAIL 1136**
See also GWR locomotives and rolling stock
Richmond Railway, **RAIL 584**
Rickmansworth, Amersham and Chesham Railway
    Parliamentary papers, **RAIL 1066**
    Reports and accounts, **RAIL 1116**
Ringwood, Christchurch and Bournemouth
    Railway, **RAIL 585**
Romney, Hythe and Dymchurch Railway
    Miscellanea, **RAIL 1005**
Rosebush and Fishguard Railway
    Prospectuses etc, **RAIL 1075**
See also N Pembrokeshire & Fishguard R
Rosebush, Fishguard and Geodic Railway
    (proposed)
    Miscellanea, **RAIL 1057**
Ross and Ledbury Railway, **RAIL 586**
    Parliamentary papers, **RAIL 1066**
    Railway and Canal Traffic Acts proceedings,
        RAIL 1038
    Reports and accounts, **RAIL 1110**
See also GWR estates and rating, Ledbury &
    Gloucester line
Ross and Monmouth Railway, **RAIL 587**
    Railway and Canal Traffic Acts proceedings,
        RAIL 1038
    Reports and accounts, **RAIL 1110; RAIL 1116**
See also GWR estates and rating; miscellanea;
    Secretary's papers
Rotherham and Bawtry Railway
    Parliamentary papers, **RAIL 1066**
Rotherham, Blythe and Sutton Railway
    Parliamentary papers, **RAIL 1066**
Rotherham County Borough Tramways
    Reports and accounts, **RAIL 1114**
Rotherham, Maltby and Laughton Railway
    Miscellanea, **RAIL 1057**
    Parliamentary papers, **RAIL 1066**

Rother Valley Light Railway
    Miscellanea, **RAIL 1057**
    Parliamentary papers, **RAIL 1066**
See also Kent & E Sussex Lt R
Rowrah and Kelton Fell Railway
    Railway and Canal Traffic Acts proceedings,
      RAIL 1038
Royal Arsenal Railways
    Rule books, **RAIL 1134**
Royal Grand Junction Railway (proposed)
    Prospectuses etc, **RAIL 1075**
Royston and Hitchin Railway, **RAIL 588** (*includes*
    records of predecessor Cambridge & Oxford R)
    Reports and accounts, **RAIL 1110; RAIL 1116**
    Subscription contracts, **RAIL 1160**
Rugby and Leamington Railway, **RAIL 589**
    (*includes records of proposed* Rugby, Leamington &
    Warwick R)
Rugby and Stamford Railway (proposed)
    Miscellanea, **RAIL 1008**
    Parliamentary plans, **RAIL 1071**
Rugby, Leamington and Warwick Railway
    (proposed) *see* Rugby & Leamington R
Rumney Railway, **RAIL 590**
    Miscellanea, **RAIL 1014**
    Parliamentary papers, **RAIL 1066**
    Timetables, **RAIL 981** (freight)
Ryde and Newport Railway, **RAIL 591**
    Joint committees with:
        Cowes & Newport R, **RAIL 591** (general;
        Newport jt station)
        Isle of Wight (Newport Jct) R, **RAIL 591**
        (Newport jt station)
    Reports and accounts, **RAIL 1116; RAIL 1117**
See also Isle of Wight Central R
Ryde Pier Company (*absorbed by* SR), **RAIL 592**
    Reports and accounts, **RAIL 1110**
St Andrews Railway
    Reports and accounts, **RAIL 1116**
    Share certificates, **RAIL 1158**
St George's Harbour Railway (proposed)
    Prospectuses etc, **RAIL 1075**
St Helens and Great Sankey Junction Railway
    (proposed)
    Parliamentary papers, **RAIL 1066**
St Helens and Runcorn Gap Railway *see* St Helens
    Canal & R
St Helens and Wigan Junction Railway
    Parliamentary papers, **RAIL 1066**
See also Liverpool, St Helens & S Lancashire R
St Helens Canal and Railway, **RAIL 593** (*includes*
    records of predecessor St Helens & Runcorn Gap R)
    Parliamentary papers, **RAIL 1066; RAIL 1067;**
      RAIL 1163
    Reports and accounts, **RAIL 1116; RAIL 1117**
St Ives and West Cornwall Junction Railway
    Subscription contract, **RAIL 1163**

St Johns Chapel Railway (proposed)
    Parliamentary papers, **RAIL 1067**
St Just (Falmouth) Ocean Wharves and Railway
    Parliamentary papers, **RAIL 1066**
Salisbury and Dorset Junction Railway, **RAIL 594**
Salisbury and Dorsetshire Junction Railway
    (proposed)
    Prospectuses etc, **RAIL 1075**
Salisbury and Yeovil Railway, **RAIL 595**
    Parliamentary papers, **RAIL 1066; RAIL 1163**
    Reports and accounts, **RAIL 1116; RAIL 1117**
Salisbury Railway and Market House Company
    Reports and accounts, **RAIL 1116**
Sand Hutton Light Railway *see* LNER minutes and
    reports
    NER
Scarborough and Whitby Railway, **RAIL 596**
    Law cases and arbitration, **RAIL 1027**
    Miscellanea, **RAIL 1157**
    Prospectuses etc, **RAIL 1076; RAIL 1116**
    Railway and Canal Traffic Acts, proceedings,
      RAIL 1038
    Reports and accounts, **RAIL 1111**
Scarborough, Bridlington and West Riding
    Junction Railways, **RAIL 597**
    Law cases and arbitration, **RAIL 1027**
    Parliamentary papers, **RAIL 1066;**
      RAIL 1067
    Reports and accounts, **RAIL 1110**
Scotswood, Newburn and Wylam Railway,
    RAIL 598 (*includes records of predecessor*
    Scotswood, Newburn & Wylam R & Dock Co)
    Reports and accounts, **RAIL 1110**
Scotswood, Newburn and Wylam Railway and
    Dock Company
    Prospectuses etc, **RAIL 1076**
    Reports and accounts, **RAIL 1110**
    Share certificates, **RAIL 1159**
Scottish and Irish Traffic Conference *see* Irish &
    English Traffic Conference
Scottish Central Railway
    Parliamentary papers, **RAIL 1066**
    Reports and accounts, **RAIL 1110; RAIL 1116;**
      RAIL 1117
    Timetables, **RAIL 981**
Scottish Midland Junction Railway
    Maps, **RAIL 1030**
    Reports and accounts, **RAIL 1116;**
      RAIL 1117
Scottish North Eastern Railway
    Parliamentary papers, **RAIL 1066**
    Reports and accounts, **RAIL 1110; RAIL 1116;**
      RAIL 1117
    Share certificates, **RAIL 1158**
Scottish Railway Stockholders Protection
    Association
    Reports and accounts, **RAIL 1116**

Seacombe, Hoylake and Deeside Railway,
  RAIL 599 (*includes records of predecessor*
  Hoylake & Birkenhead Rail & Tramway Co *q.v.*)
    Miscellanea, **RAIL 1057**
    Parliamentary papers, **RAIL 1066**
    Reports and accounts, **RAIL 1110; RAIL 1116**
Seaforth and Sefton Junction Railway, **RAIL 600**
    Maps, **RAIL 1030**
    Parliamentary papers, **RAIL 1066**
See also LNER minutes and reports
Sealink *see* BR marine
Seaton and Beer Railway, **RAIL 601**
Seghill Railway
    Timetable, **RAIL 1006**
Selkirk and Galashiels Railway
    Reports and accounts, **RAIL 1116**
    Share certificates, **RAIL 1158**
Sevenoaks, Maidstone and Tunbridge and South
  Eastern Railway Junction Railway (proposed)
    Parliamentary papers, **RAIL 1066**
Sevenoaks, Maidstone and Tunbridge Railway,
  RAIL 602 (*including records of predecessor*
  Sevenoaks R)
    Parliamentary papers, **RAIL 1066**
    Reports and accounts, **RAIL 1116**
Severn and Wye and Severn Bridge Railway,
  RAIL 603 (*includes records of jt cttee* GWR/MR)
    Law cases and arbitration, **RAIL 1027**
    Maps, **RAIL 1030**
    Miscellanea, **RAIL 1014; RAIL 1020**
    Parliamentary papers, **RAIL 1066**
    Railway and Canal Traffic Acts proceedings,
      RAIL 1038
    Reports and accounts, **RAIL 1110; RAIL 1116;**
      RAIL 1117
    Rule books, **RAIL 1134**
See also GWR estates and rating
    GWR/MR jt cttees
Severn and Wye Railway and Canal Company,
  RAIL 604 (*includes records of predecessor* Lydney
  & Millbrook R)
    Miscellanea, **RAIL 1008; RAIL 1014**
    Parliamentary papers, **RAIL 1066; RAIL 1163**
    Reports and accounts, **RAIL 1110; RAIL 1116**
See also GWR jt cttees
Severn Bridge and Forest of Dean Central Railway
    Parliamentary papers, **RAIL 1066**
Severn Bridge Railway, **RAIL 605**
    Miscellanea, **RAIL 1014**
    Parliamentary papers, **RAIL 1066**
    Reports and accounts, **RAIL 1110**
Severn Junction Railway
    Parliamentary papers, **RAIL 1066**
Severn Tunnel Railway, **RAIL 775** (*includes records
  of* GWR)
Severn Valley Railway, **RAIL 606**
    Parliamentary papers, **RAIL 1163**

Prospectuses etc, **RAIL 1075**
    Reports and accounts, **RAIL 1110; RAIL 1116**
Shareholders' guides and manuals:
    Bradshaw's, **RAIL 1140**
    Slaughter's Railway Intelligence, **RAIL 1142**
    Tuck's, etc, **RAIL 1144**
Sheffield and Chesterfield Junction Railway
  (proposed)
    Miscellanea, **RAIL 1153**
Sheffield and Goole Railway (proposed)
    Prospectus, **RAIL 1151**
Sheffield and Humber Railway (proposed)
    Miscellanea, **RAIL 1153**
    Prospectuses etc, **RAIL 1075**
Sheffield and Lincolnshire Junction Railway,
  RAIL 607
    Joint committee with:
      Great Grimsby & Sheffield Jct R, **RAIL 229**
    Maps, **RAIL 1030**
    Miscellanea, **RAIL 1153**
    Prospectus, **RAIL 1151**
Sheffield and Lincolnshire Junction Railway and
  Manchester and Lincoln Union Railway and
  Canal Companies Joint Committee, **RAIL 608**
Sheffield and Manchester Railway
    Miscellanea, **RAIL 1151**
    Parliamentary papers, **RAIL 1016**
    Prospectus, **RAIL 1151**
Sheffield and Rotherham Railway, **RAIL 609**
    Miscellanea, **RAIL 1015; RAIL 1153**
    Parliamentary papers, **RAIL 1066;**
      RAIL 1067
    Prospectus, **RAIL 1016**
    Rule books, **RAIL 1134**
    Subscription contracts, **RAIL 1160**
Sheffield, Ashton-under-Lyne and Manchester
  Railway, **RAIL 610** (*includes records of* MSLR)
    Maps, **RAIL 1030**
    Miscellanea, **RAIL 1008; RAIL 1151;**
      RAIL 1153
    Prospectuses etc, **RAIL 1075; RAIL 1076;**
      RAIL 1151
    Reports and accounts, **RAIL 1110**
    Share certificate, **RAIL 1159**
    Timetables, **RAIL 981**
Sheffield, Buxton, Leek, Potteries and Crewe
  Railway (proposed)
    Prospectuses etc, **RAIL 1075**
Sheffield Central Station and District Railway
  (proposed)
    Miscellanea, **RAIL 1021**
Sheffield, Chapeltown and Elsecar Junction
  Railway (proposed)
    Miscellanea, **RAIL 1057**
Sheffield, Chesterfield and Staffordshire Railway
  (proposed)
    Parliamentary papers, **RAIL 1066**

Sheffield Corporation Tramways
  Reports and accounts, **RAIL 1114**
Sheffield District Railway, **RAIL 611**
  Byelaws and regulations, **RAIL 1001**
  Parliamentary papers, **RAIL 1066**
  Prospectuses etc, **RAIL 1075**
  Reports and accounts, **RAIL 1110; RAIL 1116;
    RAIL 1117**
  Timetables, **RAIL 981**
    Working timetables appendixes, **RAIL 1136**
Sheffield, Rotherham and Bawtry Railway
  (proposed)
    Parliamentary papers, **RAIL 1066; RAIL 1067**
Sheffield, Rotherham, Barnsley, Wakefield,
  Huddersfield and Goole Railway, **RAIL 612**
  (*Northern portion was leased to* Manchester &
  Leeds R, *Southern portion to* S Yorkshire,
  Doncaster & Goole R *later* S Yorkshire R & River
  Dun Co)
    Reports and accounts, **RAIL 1116**
See also L&YR
Sheffield Union Railway (proposed)
  Prospectus, **RAIL 1151**
Sheffield, Wortley, Silkston and Wakefield Railway
  (proposed)
    Prospectuses etc, **RAIL 1076**
Shepherd's Bush, Acton and Brentford Railway
  (proposed) *see* GWR miscellanea; special reports
Shireoaks Laughton and Maltby Railway,
  RAIL 613
    Parliamentary papers, **RAIL 1066; RAIL 1067**
Shoreham, Horsham and Dorking Railway
  (proposed)
    Parliamentary papers, **RAIL 1066**
    Prospectuses etc, **RAIL 1075**
Shortlands and Nunhead Railway, **RAIL 614**
  Parliamentary papers, **RAIL 1066**
Shortlands, Knockholt and Otford Railway
  (proposed)
    Parliamentary papers, **RAIL 1066**
Shrewsbury and Aberystwyth Railway (proposed)
  Prospectus etc, **RAIL 1110; RAIL 1116**
Shrewsbury and Birmingham Railway, **RAIL 615**
  (*includes records of predecessors* Shrewsbury &
  Wolverhampton R *and* Shrewsbury,
  Wolverhampton, Dudley & Birmingham R)
    Joint committees with:
      GWR
        RAIL 283 (joint traffic)
      Shrewsbury & Chester R
        RAIL 283 (jt traffic)
        RAIL 759 (through traffic)
    See also Shrewsbury & Wellington Jt Line Cttee
      Shrewsbury Jt Station Cttee
      Wolverhampton Jt Cttees
    Miscellanea, **RAIL 1057**
    Parliamentary plans, **RAIL 1071**

  Prospectuses etc, **RAIL 1075**
  Reports and accounts, **RAIL 1110; RAIL 1116**
  Rule books, **RAIL 1134**
  Share certificates, **RAIL 1158**
  Timetables, **RAIL 981**
  See also GWR locomotives and rolling stock
Shrewsbury and Chester Railway, **RAIL 616**
  (*includes records of constituents* Shrewsbury,
  Oswestry & Chester Jct R *and* N Wales
  Mineral R)
    Joint committees with:
      GWR, **RAIL 283** (joint traffic)
      Oxford, Worcester & Wolverhampton R
        RAIL 759 (Wolverhampton through
          traffic)
      Shrewsbury & Birmingham R
        RAIL 238 (jt traffic)
        RAIL 759 (through traffic)
    See also Chester Jt Station Cttee
      Shrewsbury Jt Station Cttee
    Maps, **RAIL 1030**
    Miscellanea, **RAIL 1014; RAIL 1057**
    Reports and accounts, **RAIL 1110;
      RAIL 1116**
    Timetables, **RAIL 981**
See also GWR locomotives and rolling stock
Shrewsbury and Hereford Railway (including jt
  cttee GWR/LNWR/W Midland R; *after 1863*
  GWR/LNWR; *after 1923* GWR/LMSR),
  RAIL 617
    Joint committee *see* Shrewsbury Jt Station
      Cttee
    Miscellanea, **RAIL 1057**
    Parliamentary papers, **RAIL 1066**
    Reports and accounts, **RAIL 1014; RAIL 1110;
      RAIL 1116; RAIL 1117**
    Rule books, **RAIL 1134**
    Share certificates, **RAIL 1158**
    Subscription contracts, **RAIL 1160**
    Timetables, **RAIL 981** (jt cttees)
See also GWR/LMS jt cttees
  GWR/LNWR jt cttees
  GWR Secretary's papers
Shrewsbury and North Wales Railway
  Miscellanea, **RAIL 1057**
  Parliamentary papers etc, **RAIL 1147**
Shrewsbury and Potteries Junction Railway
  Miscellanea, **RAIL 1057**
  Parliamentary papers, **RAIL 1066;
    RAIL 1147**
Shrewsbury and Trent Valley Union Railway
  (proposed)
    Subscription contracts, **RAIL 1160**
Shrewsbury and Wellington Joint Line Committee
  (Shrewsbury & Birmingham R/Shropshire
  Union R & Canal Co), **RAIL 618** (*also includes
  records of* Shrewsbury Jt Station Cttee *q.v.*).

By amalgamation both these cttees became
GWR/LNWR); **RAIL 410**
    Railway and Canal Traffic Acts proceedings,
      RAIL 1038
    Rule books, **RAIL 1134**
Shrewsbury and Welshpool Railway
    Miscellanea, (GWR/LNWR jt),
      RAIL 1014
    Reports and accounts, **RAIL 1110**
See also GWR/LNWR jt cttees
Shrewsbury and Wolverhampton Railway
    (proposed)
    GWR miscellanea, **RAIL 1014**
See also Shrewsbury & Birmingham R
Shrewsbury, Ironbridge and Bridgenorth Railway
    (proposed)
    Subscription contract, **RAIL 1163**
Shrewsbury Joint Station Committee (Shrewsbury
    & Birmingham R/Shrewsbury & Chester
    R/Shrewsbury & Hereford R/Shropshire Union
    R & Canal Co; *after 1854* GWR/S&HR/SUR&C
    Co), **RAIL 618; RAIL 619**
    Miscellanea, **RAIL 1057**
    Railway and Canal Traffic Acts proceedings,
      RAIL 1038
    Rule books, **RAIL 1134**
Shrewsbury, Oswestry and Chester Junction
    Railway
    Parliamentary plans, **RAIL 1071**
See also Shrewsbury & Chester R
Shrewsbury, Oswestry and Ellesmere Railway
    (proposed)
    Bill, **RAIL 1147**
    Parliamentary plans, **RAIL 1071**
    Subscription contracts, **RAIL 1160**
Shrewsbury, Wolverhampton, Dudley and
    Birmingham Railway *see* Shrewsbury &
    Birmingham R
Shrewsbury, Wolverhampton and South
    Staffordshire Junction Railway, **RAIL 620**
    Miscellanea, **RAIL 1057**
Shropshire and Montgomeryshire Light Railway,
    RAIL 621
    Miscellanea, **RAIL 1008; RAIL 1020;**
      RAIL 1057
    Reports and accounts, **RAIL 1116**
See also BTC Chief Secretary's Office
    GWR locomotives and rolling stock
Shropshire Railways, **RAIL 622**
    Miscellanea, **RAIL 1057**
    Parliamentary papers, **RAIL 1066**
    Parliamentary plans, **RAIL 1071**
    Prospectuses etc, **RAIL 1075**
    Reports and accounts, **RAIL 1116**
See also GWR Secretary's papers
Shropshire Union Railways and Canal Company,
    RAIL 623 (*includes records of* L&YR/LNWR

jt stations; W London Extension R); **RAIL 410;
RAIL 421**
    Byelaws and regulations, **RAIL 1001**
    Dividend warrants, **RAIL 1158**
    Joint committees with
      LNWR
        Parliamentary plans, **RAIL 1071**
        RAIL 623 (Amalgamated Board)
      Shrewsbury & Birmingham R
        RAIL 618 (Shrewsbury & Wellington line)
    See also Shrewsbury Jt Station Cttee
    Miscellanea, **RAIL 1015**
    Parliamentary papers, **RAIL 1163**
    Parliamentary plans, **RAIL 1071**
    Prospectuses etc, **RAIL 1075**
    Reports and accounts, **RAIL 1110; RAIL 1116;**
      RAIL 1117
    Rule books, **RAIL 1134**
    Subscription contracts, **RAIL 1160**
    Timetables, **RAIL 981**
    Traders' ledger credit agreements, **RAIL 1165**
See also LNWR
    LMSR amalgamation; miscellanea
Sidmouth Railway
    Byelaws and regulations, **RAIL 1001**
Silloth Railway and Dock Company (proposed)
    Parliamentary papers, **RAIL 1067**
Sirhowy Railway, **RAIL 624; RAIL 410**
    Byelaws and regulations, **RAIL 1001**
    Law cases and arbitration, **RAIL 1027**
    Miscellanea, **RAIL 1014; RAIL 1057**
    Reports and accounts, **RAIL 1110; RAIL 1116**
    Timetables, **RAIL 981**
See also LNWR
Sittingbourne and Maidstone Railway (proposed)
    Parliamentary papers, **RAIL 1066**
Sittingbourne and Sheerness and London
    Chatham and Dover Railways Joint
    Committee, **RAIL 625**
Sittingbourne and Sheerness Railway
    Reports and accounts, **RAIL 1116**
Skipton and Ilkley Railway (proposed)
    Parliamentary papers, **RAIL 1066**
Skipton and Kettlewell Railway
    Parliamentary papers, **RAIL 1066; RAIL 1067**
Skipton, Wharfdale and Leyburn Junction Railway
    (proposed)
    Parliamentary papers, **RAIL 1066**
Slaughter, M. S. *see* Shareholders' guides and
    manuals
Sligo and Shannon Junction Railway (proposed)
    Prospectuses etc, **RAIL 1075**
Sligo, Leitrim and Northern Counties Railway
    Railway and Canal Traffic Acts proceedings,
      RAIL 1038
    Reports and accounts, **RAIL 1116; RAIL 1117**
See also Irish & English Traffic Conference

Snailbeach District Railway
  Railway & Canal Traffic Acts proceedings,
    RAIL 1038
Snailbeach Railway *see* Minsterley Mineral R
Solway Junction Railway
  Parliamentary papers, **RAIL 1066**
  Reports and accounts, **RAIL 1116; RAIL 1117**
See also LMSR amalgamation
Solway Railway (Caledonian Guaranteed)
  (proposed)
  Share certificates, **RAIL 1158**
Somerset and Dorset Joint Line Committee
  (LSWR/MR; *after 1923* LMSR/SR *sometimes
  called* Somerset Jt Cttee), **RAIL 626; RAIL 421**
    Byelaws and regulations, **RAIL 1001**
    Gradient diagrams, **RAIL 1030**
    Instructions to staff, **RAIL 1135**
    Reports and accounts, **RAIL 1110; RAIL 1116**
    Timetables, **RAIL 972; RAIL 981**
      Working timetables appendixes, **RAIL 1136**
See also Somerset & Dorset R
Somerset and Dorset Railway, **RAIL 627** (*includes
  records of* Dorset Central R; Somerset & Dorset Jt
  Cttee)
    Dividend warrants, **RAIL 1158**
    Parliamentary papers, **RAIL 1066**
    Prospectuses etc, **RAIL 1075**
    Reports and accounts, **RAIL 1110; RAIL 1116;
      RAIL 1117**
    Rule books, **RAIL 1134**
    Timetables, **RAIL 972**
Somerset Central Railway, **RAIL 628**
    Parliamentary papers, **RAIL 1163**
    Reports and accounts, **RAIL 1110; RAIL 1116;
      RAIL 1117**
Somerset Joint Committee *see* Somerset & Dorset Jt
  Line Cttee
Somerset, Keinton Mandeville and Castle Carey
  Tramway
    Miscellanea, **RAIL 1057**
Somersetshire Tramways
    Miscellanea, **RAIL 1057**
Somersetshire Midland Railway (proposed)
    GWR miscellanea, **RAIL 1014**
Southampton and Andover, Basingstoke and
  Salisbury Railway (proposed)
    Subscription contract, **RAIL 1163**
Southampton and Dorchester Railway, **RAIL 644**
    Miscellanea, **RAIL 1014**
Southampton and Winchester Great Western
  Junction Railway
    Miscellanea, **RAIL 1057**
    Parliamentary papers, **RAIL 1066**
Southampton County Borough Tramways
    Reports and accounts, **RAIL 1114**
Southampton Tramways
    Parliamentary papers, **RAIL 1068**

South Clare Railways
    Reports and accounts, **RAIL 1116**
South Devon and Somerset Railway (proposed)
    Parliamentary papers, **RAIL 1066**
South Devon and Tavistock Railway, **RAIL 629**
    Parliamentary papers, **RAIL 1163**
    Reports and accounts, **RAIL 1116**
South Devon, Cornwall and West Cornwall
  Railways, **RAIL 630**
    Timetables, **RAIL 981**
South Devon Railway, **RAIL 631** (*includes records of*
  Cornwall R; Exeter & Exmouth R; W Cornwall
  R); **RAIL 630**
    Joint committees with:
      Bristol & Exeter R, **RAIL 249**
        RAIL 725; RAIL 726 (W Cornwall R *q.v.*)
      Cornwall Railway
        RAIL 568 (Plymouth jt station)
      GWR, **RAIL 249**
        RAIL 568 (Plymouth jt station)
        RAIL 725; RAIL 726 (W Cornwall R *q.v.*)
See also Cornwall R
    Law cases and arbitration, **RAIL 1027**
    Miscellanea, **RAIL 1008; RAIL 1014;
      RAIL 1020; RAIL 1057**
    Parliamentary papers, **RAIL 1066**
    Prospectuses etc, **RAIL 1075; RAIL 1110**
    Reports and accounts, **RAIL 1110; RAIL 1116;
      RAIL 1117**
    Rule books, **RAIL 1134**
    Timetables, **RAIL 981**
See also GWR locomotives and rolling stock;
  miscellanea Brunel collection
South Durham and Lancashire Union Railway,
  RAIL 634 (*includes records of* S&DR; NER)
    Joint committee *see* Tebay Jt Station Cttee
    Law cases and arbitration, **RAIL 1027**
    Miscellanea, **RAIL 1006; RAIL 1021;
      RAIL 1157**
    Parliamentary papers, **RAIL 1067**
    Prospectuses etc, **RAIL 1075; RAIL 1076**
    Reports and accounts, **RAIL 1116; RAIL 1117**
    Share certificates, **RAIL 1159**
    Subscription contracts, **RAIL 1163**
South Durham Railway (proposed)
    Miscellanea, **RAIL 1016**
    Parliamentary papers, **RAIL 1067**
**South Eastern and Chatham Railways Managing
  Committee** (*formed 1899, ran the SER and LCDR
  as a single railway, usually referred to as the
  S Eastern & Chatham R*), **RAIL 633** (*includes
  records of* LCDR; SER; SR)
    Byelaws and regulations, **RAIL 1001**
    Instructions to staff, **RAIL 1135**
    Labour and staff matters, **RAIL 1025**
    Law cases and arbitration, **RAIL 1027**
    Maps, **RAIL 1030**

Miscellanea, **RAIL 1007; RAIL 1014;
RAIL 1017**
Parliamentary papers, **RAIL 1066**
Pension funds *see* SR
Reports and accounts, **RAIL 1110; RAIL 1116;
RAIL 1117**
Rule books, **RAIL 1134**
Servants' Sick and Benefit Society *see* SR
Superannuation funds, **RAIL 1174**
Timetables
Continental, **RAIL 973**
Public, **RAIL 974**
Working, **RAIL 975**
appendixes, **RAIL 1136**
Welfare schemes, **RAIL 1174**
See also BR hotels and catering
Gravesend R
SER
SR locomotives and rolling stock; miscellanea
South Eastern, Brighton, Lewes and Newhaven
Railway, **RAIL 634**
Prospectuses etc, **RAIL 1075**
South Eastern Metropolitan Tramways
Parliamentary papers, **RAIL 1066**
South Eastern Railway, RAIL 635 (*includes records*
of SECR; SR)
Byelaws and regulations, **RAIL 1001**
Hotels, **RAIL 1022**
Instructions to staff, **RAIL 1135**
Joint Committees with:
London & Brighton R
RAIL 386 (London Bridge station;
jt locomotive cttee)
London & Croydon R
RAIL 386 (London Bridge station;
jt locomotive cttee)
LNWR, **RAIL 410** (N Western & Charing
Cross R)
LBSCR, **RAIL 414** (Croydon & Oxted line)
N Western & Charing Cross R, **RAIL 410**
See also E London R
Law cases and arbitration, **RAIL 1027**
Miscellanea, **RAIL 1008; RAIL 1014;
RAIL 1016; RAIL 1017; RAIL 1057**
Parliamentary papers, **RAIL 1066; RAIL 1163**
Prospectuses etc, **RAIL 1075; RAIL 1076**
Railway and Canal Traffic Acts proceedings,
RAIL 1038
Reports and accounts, **RAIL 1110; RAIL 1116;
RAIL 1117**
Rule books, **RAIL 1134**
Savings bank, **RAIL 1174** (rules) *see also* SR
Timetables
Continental, **RAIL 976**
E London R, **RAIL 927**
Public, **RAIL 977; RAIL 981**
Working, **RAIL 977**

Welfare funds, **RAIL 1115; RAIL 1174**
See also BR hotels and catering
Channel Tunnel
City Terminus Hotel Co
SECR
SR miscellanea
South East Metropolitan Tramways
Parliamentary papers, **RAIL 1066**
Southend-on-Sea and Colchester Light Railway
Parliamentary papers, **RAIL 1066**
Southend-on-Sea and District Light Railway
Miscellanea, **RAIL 1057**
Southern Association Conference
(GWR/LNWR/OWWR/S Staffordshire R),
RAIL 250; RAIL 410
Southern Railway
Accountant's records, **RAIL 654**
Brighton Section Athletic Club reports and
accounts, **RAIL 1117**
Brunswick House Institute and Club reports
and accounts, **RAIL 1116**
Byelaws and regulations, **RAIL 1001;
RAIL 1003** (Brading Harbour)
Deeds, contracts etc, **RAIL 647** (*includes records*
about Lynton & Barnstaple R)
Eastern Section Athletic Association reports
and accounts, **RAIL 1117**
Employees' Supplementary Pension Society
reports and accounts, **RAIL 1116; RAIL 1117**
Engineering Society, Eastleigh, reports and
accounts, **RAIL 1116**
Institute reports and accounts, **RAIL 1116;
RAIL 1117**
Instructions to staff, **RAIL 1135**
Joint committees with:
GWR, **RAIL 240; RAIL 245; RAIL 258
RAIL 390** (Standing Jt Cttee)
LNER, **RAIL 390** (Standing Jt Cttee)
LMSR, **RAIL 390** (Standing Jt Cttee)
LPTB, **RAIL 390** (Standing Jt Cttee)
See also E London R
Somerset & Dorset Jt Line Cttee
Labour and staff matters, **RAIL 1025**
Law cases and arbitration, **RAIL 1027**
Locomotives and rolling stock, **RAIL 649**
(*includes records of* BR(SR); LSWR; SECR)
LBSCR Pension Fund reports and accounts,
RAIL 1116; RAIL 1117
LBSC Section Supplementary Fund for
Assisting Annuitants reports and accounts,
RAIL 1117
LCDR Savings Bank reports and accounts,
RAIL 1116; RAIL 1117
LSWR Co's Engine Drivers Firemen
Locomotive and Electrical Engineering
Departments Pension Society reports and
accounts, **RAIL 1116; RAIL 1117**

SR (continued)
LSWR Friendly Society reports and accounts,
RAIL 1116; RAIL 1117
LSWR New Provident and Sick Benefit
Society reports and accounts, **RAIL 1117**
LSWR Savings Bank reports and accounts,
RAIL 1117
LSWR Superannuation Fund Association
reports and accounts, **RAIL 1117**
Minutes and reports, **RAIL 645** (*includes
records of* BR(SR); LSWR)
Miscellanea, **RAIL 648** (*includes records of*
BR(SR); Charing Cross R; LSWR; SECR;
SER)**; RAIL 1005; RAIL 1014; RAIL 1017;
RAIL 1020; RAIL 1057**
Motor bus companies, **RAIL 650** (*includes
records of* BTC)
Parliamentary papers, **RAIL 1066**
Publications, **RAIL 652; RAIL 653**
Railway Rates Tribunal proceedings,
RAIL 1101
Reports and accounts, **RAIL 1110; RAIL 1116;
RAIL 1117**
Rifle Club (Eastleigh) reports and accounts,
RAIL 1116
Road services
Carter Paterson & Co, **RAIL 1130**
Hay's Wharf Cartage Co, **RAIL 1131**
Pickfords & Hay's Wharf Shipping &
Forwarding Co, **RAIL 1132**
Pickfords Ltd, **RAIL 1133**
Rolling stock, **RAIL 649**
Rule books, **RAIL 1134**
Savings Bank reports and accounts, **RAIL 1117**
Servants' Orphanage reports and accounts,
RAIL 1117
Shares and shareholders, **RAIL 646**
Shipping services, **RAIL 655** (*includes records of*
BR(SR))
Southampton Docks reports and accounts,
RAIL 1117
Southampton Docks and Marine Sports Club
reports and accounts, **RAIL 1117**
SECR Cos' Servants' Sick and Benefit Society
reports and accounts, **RAIL 1116; RAIL 1117**
SECR Pension Fund reports and accounts,
RAIL 1117
SEC Section Enginemen and Motormen's
Pension Fund Society reports and accounts,
RAIL 1117
SER Provident Savings Bank reports and
accounts, **RAIL 1116; RAIL 1117**
Southern Section Provident Society reports
and accounts, **RAIL 1117**
South Western Section Clerical Staff Provident
Death Fund reports and accounts,
RAIL 1117

Sports Club (Raynes Park) reports and
accounts, **RAIL 1116; RAIL 1117**
Staff, **RAIL 651**
Superannuation Fund reports and accounts,
RAIL 1116
Superannuation schemes, **RAIL 1174**
Temperence Society reports and accounts,
RAIL 1117
Timetables
Continental, **RAIL 978**
Public, **RAIL 979**
Working, **RAIL 980**
appendixes, **RAIL 1136**
See also BR timetables continental
Welfare fund accounts, **RAIL 1115**
Western Section Provident and Sick Benefit
Society reports and accounts, **RAIL 1116**
Western Section Sports Club reports and
accounts, **RAIL 1117**
See also BR hotels and catering; locomotive and
rolling stock records
Channel Tunnel
Irish & English Traffic Conference
Isle of Wight Central R
LSWR
LMSR amalgamation
Railway Companies Association miscellanea
Ryde Pier Co
SER
SECR
Southern Railway (*Ireland*)
Reports and accounts, **RAIL 1110; RAIL 1116**
South Hampshire Railway and Pier Company
(*authorized by* Swindon, Marlborough &
Andover R *Acts. Originally known as* Totton &
Lepe line *or* Stone Point R)
Miscellanea, **RAIL 1057**
South Hams (Devon) Railway (proposed)
Prospectuses etc, **RAIL 1075**
South Hams Railway
Miscellanea, **RAIL 1057**
South Lancashire Tramways (proposed)
Parliamentary papers, **RAIL 1068**
South Lancashire Railway and Dock
Parliamentary papers, **RAIL 1066**
South Leicestershire Railway, **RAIL 636; RAIL 410**
Reports and accounts, **RAIL 1116**
See also LNWR
South London Tramways
Parliamentary papers, **RAIL 1066; RAIL 1068**
South London Railway (proposed)
Parliamentary papers, **RAIL 1066**
See also LNWR
South Metropolitan Electric Tramways and
Lighting Co Ltd
Reports and accounts, **RAIL 1114**
See also London & Suburban Traction Co

South Midland and Southampton Junction
Railway (proposed)
Miscellanea, **RAIL 1057**
South Midland Counties Railway (proposed)
Prospectuses etc, **RAIL 1075**
South Midland *or* Northampton and Leicester
Railway (proposed)
Prospectuses etc, **RAIL 1075**
South Midland Railway (proposed), **RAIL 637**
Miscellanea, **RAIL 1057**
Subscription contracts, **RAIL 1160**
Southport and Cheshire Lines Extension Railway,
RAIL 656 (*worked by* CLC)
Parliamentary papers, **RAIL 1066**
Prospectuses etc, **RAIL 1075**
Reports and accounts, **RAIL 1116**
Share certificates, **RAIL 1158**
Southport and Euxton Junction Railway
(proposed)
Prospectuses etc, **RAIL 1075**
South Shields, Sunderland and District Tramways
(proposed)
Parliamentary papers, **RAIL 1068**
South Staffordshire and Birmingham District
Steam Tramways
Parliamentary papers, **RAIL 1068**
South Staffordshire and Central Wales, Cradley
Heath and Dudley Railway (proposed)
Prospectuses etc, **RAIL 1075**
South Staffordshire and London Railway
(proposed)
Parliamentary papers etc, **RAIL 1147**
South Staffordshire Railway, **RAIL 638**
Joint committees *see* Northern Alliance;
Southern Association Conference
Parliamentary papers, **RAIL 1147; RAIL 1163**
Parliamentary plans, **RAIL 1071**
Reports and accounts, **RAIL 1110; RAIL 1116;
RAIL 1117**
Timetables, **RAIL 981**
South Wales and Bristol Direct Railway (proposed)
Parliamentary papers, **RAIL 1066**
South Wales and Great Western Direct Railway
Miscellanea, **RAIL 1057**
Parliamentary papers, **RAIL 1066**
South Wales and Northamptonshire Junction
Railway (proposed)
Prospectuses etc, **RAIL 1075**
South Wales and Severn Bridge Railway
(proposed)
Miscellanea, **RAIL 1014; RAIL 1057**
South Wales and Southampton Railway
(proposed)
Miscellanea, **RAIL 1014**
South Wales Mineral Railway, **RAIL 639**
Miscellanea, **RAIL 1057**
Parliamentary papers, **RAIL 1066; RAIL 1163**

Prospectus, **RAIL 1116**
Railway & Canal Traffic Acts proceedings,
RAIL 1038
Reports and accounts, **RAIL 1110; RAIL 1116**
See also GWR locomotives and rolling stock;
miscellanea
South Wales Railway, **RAIL 640**
Joint committee with:
GWR/W Midland R, **RAIL 284**
Miscellanea, **RAIL 1014; RAIL 1057**
Parliamentary papers, **RAIL 1163**
Prospectuses etc, **RAIL 1075; RAIL 1110**
Provident Society, **RAIL 1174**
Reports and accounts, **RAIL 1110; RAIL 1116;
RAIL 1117**
Rule books, **RAIL 1134**
Share certificate, **RAIL 1159**
Timetables, **RAIL 981**
See also GWR miscellanea
Southwark and Deptford Tramways
Parliamentary papers, **RAIL 1066**
South Western and Isle of Wight Railway
Miscellanea, **RAIL 1057**
Parliamentary papers, **RAIL 1066**
South Western and South Devon Coast Junction
Railway (proposed) *see* Bridport & Exeter R
South Western Midland and Eastern Counties
Grand Union Railway (proposed)
Prospectuses etc, **RAIL 1075**
South Western Railway (proposed)
Prospectuses etc, **RAIL 1075**
Southwold Railway
Miscellanea, **RAIL 1020; RAIL 1021**
Railway and Canal Traffic Acts proceedings,
RAIL 1038
Reports and accounts, **RAIL 1110; RAIL 1116**
Timetables, **RAIL 981**
South Yorkshire, Coal Railway and Canal and
Goole and Doncaster Railway *see* S Yorkshire R
& River Dun Co
South Yorkshire, Doncaster and Goole Railway
Parliamentary papers, **RAIL 1066**
See also Sheffield, Rotherham, Barnsley, Wakefield,
Huddersfield & Goole R *and* S Yorkshire R &
River Dun Co
South Yorkshire Joint Line Committee
(GCR/GNR/L&YR/MR/NER; *in 1922* LNWR
replaced L&YR; *after 1923* LMSR/LNER),
**RAIL 390; RAIL 410; RAIL 417; RAIL 641;
RAIL 783**
Byelaws and regulations, **RAIL 1001**
Instructions to staff, **RAIL 1135**
Miscellanea, **RAIL 1057**
Parliamentary papers, **RAIL 1066**
Parliamentary plans, **RAIL 1071**
Reports and accounts, **RAIL 1110; RAIL 1116;
RAIL 1117**

See also GNR
South Yorkshire Junction Railway, **RAIL 642**,
    Parliamentary papers, **RAIL 1066; RAIL 1067**
    Reports and accounts, **RAIL 1110**
See also H&BR
South Yorkshire Railway and River Dun Company,
    RAIL 643 (*includes records of predecessors* S
    Yorkshire Coal R & Canal & Goole & Doncaster
    R *and* S Yorkshire Doncaster & Goole R)
    Joint committee with:
        MSLR/MR/W Riding & Grimsby R, **RAIL
          736** (Wakefield station)
    Parliamentary papers, **RAIL 1066; RAIL 1067;**
        RAIL 1163
    Reports and accounts, **RAIL 1116; RAIL 1117**
See also Sheffield, Rotherham, Barnsley, Wakefield,
    Huddersfield & Goole R
Spalding and Bourn Railway, **RAIL 657**
    Parliamentary papers, **RAIL 1066**
    Prospectuses etc, **RAIL 1075**
Spalding, Bourn and Stamford Junction Railway
    (proposed)
    Subscription contract, **RAIL 1163**
Spilsby and Firsby Railway, **RAIL 658**
Stafford and Uttoxeter Railway
    Miscellanea, **RAIL 1007**
    Parliamentary papers, **RAIL 1066**
    Prospectuses etc, **RAIL 1075**
Staines and West Drayton Railway, **RAIL 659**
    Miscellanea, **RAIL 1005**
    Parliamentary papers, **RAIL 1066**
    Prospectuses etc, **RAIL 1075; RAIL 1110**
    Railway & Canal Traffic Acts proceedings,
        RAIL 1038
    Reports and accounts, **RAIL 1110**
See also GWR correspondence and papers
Staines, Chertsey and Wokingham Railway
    (proposed)
    Parliamentary papers, **RAIL 1066**
Staines, Wokingham and Woking Railway,
    RAIL 660 (*known before incorporation as* Staines
    Wokingham & Woking Jct R)
    Parliamentary papers, **RAIL 1163**
    Reports and accounts, **RAIL 1116**
Stalybridge Joint Station Committee
    (LNWR/MSLR; *after 1897* LNWR/GCR),
    RAIL 661; RAIL 410; RAIL 421
See also LMSR miscellanea
Stamford and Essendine Railway, **RAIL 662**
    Parliamentary papers, **RAIL 1163**
    Reports and accounts, **RAIL 1116**
Stanhope and Tyne Railroad, **RAIL 663**
    Miscellanea, **RAIL 1157**
    Rule books, **RAIL 1134**
    Share certificates, **RAIL 1159**
See also Pontop & S Shields R
Stert and Westbury Railway

Miscellanea, **RAIL 1057**
Stirling and Dunfermline Railway
    Reports and accounts, **RAIL 1116**
    Share certificates, **RAIL 1158**
Stock Conversion and Investment Trust (*company
    managing railway stock*)
    Prospectus, **RAIL 1116**
    Reports and accounts, **RAIL 1116**
Stockport and Manchester Railway (proposed)
    Prospectuses etc, **RAIL 1075**
Stockport and Woodley Junction Railway,
    RAIL 664
Stockport, Disley and Whaley Bridge Railway,
    RAIL 665 (*includes records of LNWR*); **RAIL 410**
    Parliamentary papers, **RAIL 1163**
    Reports and accounts, **RAIL 1116; RAIL 1117**
See also LNWR
Stockport, Timperley and Altrincham Junction
    Railway, **RAIL 666**
    Prospectuses etc, **RAIL 1075**
Stockton and Cleveland Union Railway (proposed)
    Prospectuses etc, **RAIL 1076**
Stockton and Darlington Railway, **RAIL 667**
    (*includes records of LNER; NER*)
    Byelaws and regulations, **RAIL 1003** (River
        Tees)
    Joint committees with:
        Cockermouth, Keswick & Penrith R,
          RAIL 563 (Penrith jt station)
        LNWR
          RAIL 536 (Penrith jt station)
          RAIL 686 (Tebay station)
        NER, **RAIL 47** (Bishop Auckland Station)
    Law cases and arbitration, **RAIL 1027**
    Miscellanea, **RAIL 1016; RAIL 1021;**
        RAIL 1057; RAIL 1157
    Parliamentary papers, **RAIL 1066; RAIL 1067;**
        RAIL 1163
    Prospectuses etc, **RAIL 1075; RAIL 1076**
    Reports and accounts, **RAIL 1111; RAIL 1116;**
        RAIL 1117
    Rule books, **RAIL 1134**
    Share certificates, **RAIL 1159**
    Subscription contracts, **RAIL 1161**
    Timetables, **RAIL 981**
See also Eden Valley R
    S Durham & Lancashire Union R
Stockton and Hartlepool Railway, **RAIL 668**
    (*includes records of jt board meetings with*
    Clarence R)
    Miscellanea, **RAIL 1157**
    Prospectuses etc, **RAIL 1076**
    Reports and accounts, **RAIL 1111;**
        RAIL 1116
    Share certificates, **RAIL 1159**
Stockton and Stokesley Railway (proposed)
    Prospectuses etc, **RAIL 1075; RAIL 1076**

Stockton, Clarence and Hartlepool Union Railway
and Dock (proposed)
Prospectuses etc, **RAIL 1076**
Stokes Bay Railway and Pier Company, **RAIL 669**
Reports and accounts, **RAIL 1116**
Subscription contract, **RAIL 1163**
Stokesley and Tees Railway (proposed)
Prospectuses etc, **RAIL 1076**
Stone, Darenth and Swanley Tramroads and
Thames Jetty (proposed)
Parliamentary papers, **RAIL 1066**
Stonehouse and Nailsworth Railway
Parliamentary papers, **RAIL 1066**
Stonehouse Pool Improvement Company
(*transferred to LSWR, 1909*), **RAIL 670**
Reports and accounts, **RAIL 1116; RAIL 1117**
Stone Point Railway *see* S Hampshire R & Pier Co
Stottesden, Kinlet and Billingsley Light Railway
Miscellanea, **RAIL 1057**
Stourbridge Railway, **RAIL 671**
Parliamentary plans, **RAIL 1071**
Reports and accounts, **RAIL 1110; RAIL 1116**
Share certificates, **RAIL 1158**
Subscription contracts, **RAIL 1160**
Stour Valley Railway (proposed)
Parliamentary plans, **RAIL 1071**
Strabane and Letterkenny Railway, **RAIL 672**
Reports and accounts, **RAIL 1116**
Strabane, Raphoe and Convoy Railway (proposed)
Parliamentary papers, **RAIL 1066**
Stratford and Moreton Railway, **RAIL 673**
(*includes records of* Oxford, Worcester &
Wolverhampton R)
Miscellanea, **RAIL 1014**
Stratford and Salford Railway (proposed)
Miscellanea, **RAIL 1057**
Stratford-upon-Avon and Midland Junction
Railway, **RAIL 674** (*includes records of predecessors*
E & W Jct R *and* Stratford-upon-Avon, Towcester
& Midland Jct R)
Maps, **RAIL 1030**
Parliamentary papers, **RAIL 1163**
Reports and accounts, **RAIL 1110; RAIL 1116;
RAIL 1117**
Rule books, **RAIL 1134**
Share certificates and dividend warrants,
RAIL 1158
Sidings agreements, **RAIL 1167**
Timetables, **RAIL 981; RAIL 982**
Working timetables appendixes, **RAIL 1136**
Traders' ledger credit agreements,
RAIL 1165
See also LMSR amalgamation
Stratford-upon-Avon Railway, **RAIL 675**
Byelaws and regulations, **RAIL 1001**
Joint committee with:
GWR, **RAIL 246** (operation by GWR)

Reports and accounts, **RAIL 1110; RAIL 1116**
Stratford-upon-Avon, Towcester and Midland
Junction Railway
Joint committee with:
E & W Jct Railway, **RAIL 168**
Instructions to staff, **RAIL 1135**
Reports and accounts, **RAIL 1116**
Timetables, **RAIL 981**
Maps, **RAIL 1030**
Parliamentary papers, **RAIL 1066**
Reports and accounts, **RAIL 1116**
Timetables, **RAIL 981**
See also Stratford-upon-Avon & Midland Jct R
Strathendrick and Aberfoyle Railway
Share certificates, **RAIL 1158**
Stroud and Painswick Light Railway
Miscellanea, **RAIL 1057**
Stroud and Severn Rail Road (proposed)
Miscellanea, **RAIL 1019**
Stroud District and Cheltenham Tramways
Parliamentary papers, **RAIL 1068**
Submarine Continental Railway *see* Channel
Tunnel
Sunningdale and Cambridgetown Railway
Reports and accounts, **RAIL 1116**
Surrey and Sussex Junction Railway, **RAIL 676**
Parliamentary papers, **RAIL 1066**
Subscription contracts, **RAIL 1160**
Sutton and London and South Western Junction
Railway (proposed)
Parliamentary papers, **RAIL 1066**
Sutton and Willoughby Railway, **RAIL 677**
Parliamentary papers, **RAIL 1066**
See also Louth & E Coast R
Sutton, Rotherham and Barnsley Railway
(proposed)
Parliamentary papers, **RAIL 1066**
Swanage Railway
Reports and accounts, **RAIL 1116; RAIL 1117**
Swansea and Carmarthen Railways
Parliamentary papers, **RAIL 1066**
See also Central Wales & Carmarthen Jct R
Swansea and Clydach Railway (proposed)
Parliamentary papers, **RAIL 1066**
Swansea and Mumbles Railway
Miscellanea, **RAIL 1014; RAIL 1057**
Parliamentary papers, **RAIL 1066**
Reports and accounts, **RAIL 1116; RAIL 1117**
Swansea and Neath Railway, **RAIL 678**
Miscellanea, **RAIL 1057**
Parliamentary papers, **RAIL 1066**
Prospectuses etc, **RAIL 1075**
Swansea Docks and Mineral Valleys Railway
(proposed)
Parliamentary papers, **RAIL 1163**
Parliamentary plans, **RAIL 1071**
Subscription contracts, **RAIL 1160**

Swansea Harbour Trust
    Instructions to staff about railway working,
      RAIL 1135
    Reports and accounts, **RAIL 1116; RAIL 1117**
See also GWR locomotives and rolling stock
Swansea Improvements and Tramways Company
    Miscellanea, **RAIL 1057**
    Reports and accounts, **RAIL 1116**
Swansea, Oystermouth and Mumbles Railway
    Miscellanea, **RAIL 1057**
Swansea Union Railway (proposed)
    Parliamentary papers, **RAIL 1066**
Swansea Vale and Neath and Brecon Junction
    Railway, **RAIL 790**
    Miscellanea, **RAIL 1057**
    Parliamentary papers, **RAIL 1066**
    Reports and accounts, **RAIL 1110; RAIL 1116**
Swansea Vale Railway, **RAIL 679**
    Law cases and arbitration, **RAIL 1027**
    Maps, **RAIL 1030**
    Parliamentary papers, **RAIL 1066; RAIL 1163**
    Reports and accounts, **RAIL 1116**
Swansea Valley Railway, **RAIL 680**
Swindon and Cheltenham Extension Railway,
    RAIL 681
    Maps, **RAIL 1030**
    Miscellanea, **RAIL 1014; RAIL 1057**
    Parliamentary papers, **RAIL 1066**
    Prospectuses etc, **RAIL 1075**
    Reports and accounts, **RAIL 1110; RAIL 1116**
Swindon and Highworth Railway, **RAIL 682**
    Miscellanea, **RAIL 1057**
    Reports and accounts, **RAIL 1110**
    Share certificates, **RAIL 1158**
Swindon, Marlborough and Andover Railway,
    RAIL 683
    Law cases and arbitration, **RAIL 1027**
    Miscellanea, **RAIL 1014; RAIL 1057**
    Parliamentary papers, **RAIL 1066**
    Reports and accounts, **RAIL 1110; RAIL 1116**
    Rule books, **RAIL 1134**
    Timetables, **RAIL 981**
See also South Hampshire R & Pier Co
Swinton and Knottingley Joint Railway
    (MR/NER), **RAIL 488** (*includes records of*
    Brackenhill Lt R)
    Byelaws and regulations, **RAIL 1001**
    Maps, **RAIL 1030**
    Rule books, **RAIL 1134**
    Parliamentary papers, **RAIL 1066; RAIL 1067**
Sydenham and Farnborough Railway (proposed)
    Parliamentary papers, **RAIL 1066**
Symington, Biggar and Broughton Railway
    Reports and accounts, **RAIL 1116**
Syston and Peterborough Railway (proposed)
    Parliamentary plans, **RAIL 1071**
Taff and Bargoed Junction Railway (proposed)

Parliamentary papers, **RAIL 1066**
Taff Vale, Great Western and Merthyr Junction
    Railway (proposed)
    Miscellanea, **RAIL 1057**
Taff Vale Railway, **RAIL 684**
    Byelaws and regulations, **RAIL 1001**
    Instructions to staff, **RAIL 1135**
    Joint committees with:
      GWR, Railway and Canal Traffic Acts
        proceedings, **RAIL 1038**
      Penarth Harbour Dock & R, **RAIL 562**
    Labour and staff matters, **RAIL 1025**
    Law cases and arbitration, **RAIL 1027**
    Maps, **RAIL 1030**
    Miscellanea, **RAIL 1005; RAIL 1008;**
      RAIL 1014; RAIL 1020; RAIL 1057
    Parliamentary papers, **RAIL 1066; RAIL 1067**
    Railway and Canal Traffic Acts proceedings,
      RAIL 1038
    Reports and accounts, **RAIL 1110; RAIL 1116;**
      RAIL 1117
    Rule books, **RAIL 1134**
    Share certificates, **RAIL 1158**
    Subscription contracts, **RAIL 1160**
    Timetables, **RAIL 981**
      Working timetables appendixes, **RAIL 1136**
    Welfare fund accounts, **RAIL 1115**
See also GWR locomotives and rolling stock
    Irish & English Traffic Conference
    Penarth Harbour Dock & R byelaws and
      regulations
Talyllyn Railway
    Railway and Canal Traffic Acts proceedings,
      RAIL 1038
    Timetables, **RAIL 981**
Tanat Valley Light Railway, **RAIL 685**
    Miscellanea, **RAIL 1057**
    Reports and accounts, **RAIL 1110**
Tavistock and Gunnislake Railway (proposed)
    Parliamentary papers, **RAIL 1066**
Taw Vale Railway and Dock Co
    Parliamentary papers, **RAIL 1163**
See also N Devon R & Dock Co
Tebay Joint Station Committee (*successively*
    Lancaster & Carlisle R/S Durham & Lancashire
    Union R; LNWR/S Durham & LUR;
    LNWR/S&DR; LNWR/NER; LMSR/LNER),
    RAIL 686; RAIL 410; RAIL 421
See also LMSR miscellanea
Tees and Weardale Railway (proposed)
    Parliamentary papers, **RAIL 1067**
Tees Valley Railway, **RAIL 687**
    Prospectuses etc, **RAIL 1076**
    Reports and accounts, **RAIL 1111; RAIL 1116**
    Timetables, **RAIL 981**
Tees, Weardale and Tyne Junction Railroad
    (proposed)

Prospectus, **RAIL 1016**
Teign Valley Railway, **RAIL 688**
    Miscellanea, **RAIL 1057**
    Parliamentary papers, **RAIL 1066**
    Prospectuses, **RAIL 1014**
    Railway and Canal Traffic Acts proceedings,
      RAIL 1038
    Reports and accounts, **RAIL 1110**
See also Exeter R
    GWR miscellanea
Teme Valley Railway
    Miscellanea, **RAIL 1057**
Tenbury and Bewdley Railway, **RAIL 689**
    Miscellanea, **RAIL 1014; RAIL 1057**
    Reports and accounts, **RAIL 1110; RAIL 1116**
See also GWR Secretary's papers
Tenbury Railway, **RAIL 690** (*includes records of jt*
   cttee GWR/LNWR)
    Miscellanea, **RAIL 1057**
    Reports and accounts, **RAIL 1116**
    Timetables, **RAIL 981**
See also GWR/LNWR jt cttees
Tendring Hundred Railway, **RAIL 691**
    Reports and accounts, **RAIL 1116**
Tenterden Railway, **RAIL 692**
    Parliamentary papers, **RAIL 1066**
Thames Deep-Water Dock Railway (proposed)
    Parliamentary papers, **RAIL 1066**
Thames Deep Water Wharf and Railways
   (proposed)
    Parliamentary papers, **RAIL 1066**
Thames Embankment and Railway (proposed)
    Subscription contract, **RAIL 1163**
Thames Ocean Wharf and Railway (proposed)
    Parliamentary papers, **RAIL 1066**
Thames Haven Dock and Railway
    Prospectuses etc, **RAIL 1075**
    Reports and accounts, **RAIL 1116**
Thames Haven Railway (proposed)
    Prospectuses etc, **RAIL 1075**
Thames Valley Railway, **RAIL 693**
Thetford and Watton Railway, **RAIL 694**
    Miscellanea, **RAIL 1016**
    Reports and accounts, **RAIL 1116**
    Timetables, **RAIL 981**
Throckley Waggonway
    Miscellanea, **RAIL 1157**
Tickhill Light Railway
    Parliamentary papers, **RAIL 1066**
See also GNR
Tilbury and Gravesend Tunnel Junction Railway
   (proposed)
    Parliamentary papers, **RAIL 1066**
Timetables, *see entries under company names. Note*
   that **RAIL 981** *is a miscellaneous series of timetables*
   and guides relating to road and sea, as well as rail,
   services. Bus companies and shipping companies

referred to in **RAIL 981** *are not noted here but the*
   series has been included in the entry for each railway
   company clearly represented in it. **RAIL 981** *has a*
   wide spread of dates, from 1840 onwards. Bradshaw's
   and other general timetables and guides will be found
   in **RAIL 900–904**
Timoleague and Courtmacsherry Extension Light
   Railway
    Railway and Canal Traffic Acts proceedings,
      RAIL 1038
Tiverton and North Devon Railway, **RAIL 695**
    Prospectus, **RAIL 1110**
    Railway and Canal Traffic Acts proceedings,
      RAIL 1038
    Reports and accounts, **RAIL 1110**
Tooting, Balham and Brixton Railway
   (proposed)
    Parliamentary papers, **RAIL 1066**
Tooting, Merton and Wimbledon Railway *see*
   LSWR/LBSCR jt cttees
Torbay and Brixham Railway
    Miscellanea, **RAIL 1057**
    Reports and accounts, **RAIL 1110**
Torrington and Okehampton Railway *see* N Devon
   & Cornwall Jct Lt R
Totnes, Paignton and Torquay Direct Railway
    Miscellanea, **RAIL 1057**
Tottenham and Forest Gate Railway, **RAIL 696**
   (*includes records of* MR *and jt cttee* LTSR/MR)
    Parliamentary papers, **RAIL 1066**
    Reports and accounts, **RAIL 1110**
    Share certificates, **RAIL 1158**
    Timetables, **RAIL 981**
See also LMSR amalgamation
Tottenham and Hampstead Junction Railway,
   RAIL 697 (*includes records of jt cttee* GER/MR;
   after 1923 LMSR/LNER)
    Instructions to staff (GER/MR), **RAIL 1135**
    Law cases and arbitration (GER/MR),
      RAIL 1027
    Miscellanea, **RAIL 1057**
    Parliamentary papers, **RAIL 1066**
    Railway and Canal Traffic Acts proceedings,
      RAIL 1038
    Reports and accounts, **RAIL 1110; RAIL 1116**
    (co and jt cttee)
Totton and Lepe Line *see* S Hampshire R & Pier Co
Towcester and Buckingham Railway
    Parliamentary papers, **RAIL 1066**
Trafford Park Dock and Railway (proposed)
    Parliamentary papers, **RAIL 1066**
Tralee and Dingle Light Railway
    Railway and Canal Traffic Acts proceedings,
      RAIL 1038
See also Irish & English Traffic Conference
Tralee and Fenit Railway
    Reports and accounts, **RAIL 1116**

Tralee and Killarney Railway
  Reports and accounts, **RAIL 1116**
Tranmere Dock and Railway (proposed)
  Parliamentary papers, **RAIL 1066**
Transport Users Consultative Committees, **AN 56**
Treferig Valley Railway
  Reports and accounts, **RAIL 1110**
Trent, Ancholme and Grimsby Railway, **RAIL 698**
  Law cases and arbitration, **RAIL 1027**
  Reports and accounts, **RAIL 1116**
Trent Valley, Midlands and Grand Junction
  Railway
  Parliamentary plans, **RAIL 1071**
  Subscription contracts, **RAIL 1160**
Trent Valley Railway, **RAIL 699** (*includes records of*
  London & Birmingham R)
  Miscellanea, **RAIL 1008; RAIL 1014**
  Reports and accounts, **RAIL 1110**
Tring and Reigate Railway (proposed)
  Prospectuses etc, **RAIL 1075**
Tring, Cambridge and Newmarket Railway
  (proposed)
  Prospectuses etc, **RAIL 1075**
Truro and Newquay Junction Railway (proposed)
  Parliamentary papers, **RAIL 1066**
Truro and Newquay Railway (proposed)
  Parliamentary papers, **RAIL 1066**
Tuck, H. *see* Shareholders' guides and manuals
Tunbridge Wells and Eastbourne Railway
  Parliamentary papers, **RAIL 1066**
Tunstall Railway (proposed)
  Parliamentary papers, **RAIL 1066**
Twrch and Tawe Valleys Railway (proposed)
  Miscellanea, **RAIL 1057**
  Parliamentary papers, **RAIL 1066**
Tynemouth Docks and Morpeth and Shields Direct
  Railway (proposed)
  Subscription contract, **RAIL 1163**
Tyneside Tramways and Tramroads
  Parliamentary papers, **RAIL 1068; RAIL 1069**
  Reports and accounts, **RAIL 1117**
Ulster Transport Authority
  Miscellanea, **RAIL 1005**
  Timetables, **RAIL 941**
See also Irish & English Traffic Conference
Ulster Railway
  Parliamentary papers, **RAIL 1163**
  Reports and accounts, **RAIL 1116; RAIL 1117**
  Timetables, **RAIL 941**
See also Irish & English Traffic Conference
Ulverstone and Lancaster Railway, **RAIL 700**
  Miscellanea, **RAIL 1021**
  Parliamentary plans, **RAIL 1071**
  Reports and accounts, **RAIL 1116; RAIL 1117**
  Subscription contracts, **RAIL 1160**
Underground Electric Railways Company of
  London *This company controlled the* Met District

R, Central London R, City and S London R *and*
  London Electric Rys
  Instructions to staff, **RAIL 1135**
  Miscellanea, **RAIL 1057**
  Reports and accounts, **RAIL 1110; RAIL 1116;
    RAIL 1117**
  Timetables, **RAIL 983**
    Working timetables appendixes, **RAIL 1136**
Upsall, Normanby and Ormesby Railway
  (proposed)
  Parliamentary papers, **RAIL 1067**
Usk and Towey Railway
  Parliamentary papers, **RAIL 1066**
Usk Valley Railway
  Miscellanea, **RAIL 1057**
  Parliamentary papers, **RAIL 1066**
Uxbridge and Rickmansworth Railway, **RAIL 701**
  Miscellanea, **RAIL 1057**
  Parliamentary papers, **RAIL 1066**
  Reports and accounts, **RAIL 1116**
Vale of Clwyd Railway, **RAIL 410**
  Byelaws and regulations, **RAIL 1001**
  Miscellanea, **RAIL 1057**
  Parliamentary plans, **RAIL 1071**
  Prospectuses etc, **RAIL 1075**
  Reports and accounts, **RAIL 1116; RAIL 1117**
See also LNWR
Vale of Crickhowell Railway
  Parliamentary papers, **RAIL 1066**
Vale of Glamorgan Railway, **RAIL 702**
  Miscellanea, **RAIL 1057**
  Parliamentary papers, **RAIL 1066**
  Prospectuses etc, **RAIL 1075**
  Reports and accounts, **RAIL 1110; RAIL 1117**
Vale of Llangollen Railway, **RAIL 703**
  Railway and Canal Traffic Acts proceedings,
    RAIL 1038
  Reports and accounts, **RAIL 1110;
    RAIL 1116**
Vale of Neath Railway, **RAIL 704** (*includes records of*
  GWR)
  Miscellanea, **RAIL 1057**
  Parliamentary papers, **RAIL 1066**
  Reports and accounts, **RAIL 1014; RAIL 1110;
    RAIL 1116; RAIL 1117**
  Subscription contracts, **RAIL 1163**
  Timetables, **RAIL 981**
See also GWR locomotives and rolling stock;
  miscellanea Brunel collection
Vale of Rheidol Light Railway, **RAIL 705**
  Miscellanea, **RAIL 1057**
  Reports and accounts, **RAIL 1110; RAIL 1116;
    RAIL 1117**
  Share certificates, **RAIL 1158**
Vale of Towy Railway
  Reports and accounts, **RAIL 1116**
  Timetables, **RAIL 981**

Vale of Towy Railway Joint Committee (Central Wales Rys/Llanelly R & Dock Co; LNWR/ Llanelly R&D Co), **RAIL 706; RAIL 410** (LNWR/GWR)
    Byelaws and regulations, **RAIL 1001**
    Miscellanea, **RAIL 1057**
    Railway and Canal Traffic Acts proceedings, **RAIL 1038**
    Reports and accounts, **RAIL 1110**
    Rule books, **RAIL 1134**
    Timetables, **RAIL 981**
See also GWR locomotives and rolling stock GWR/LMSR jt cttees
Van Railway
    Miscellanea, **RAIL 1014**
    Railway and Canal Traffic Acts proceedings, **RAIL 1038**
    Reports and accounts, **RAIL 1116**
See also GWR miscellanea
Victoria Station and North Western and Great Western Junction Railway (proposed)
    Parliamentary plans, **RAIL 1071**
Victoria Station and Pimlico Railway, **RAIL 707**
    Miscellanea, **RAIL 1005**
    Parliamentary papers, **RAIL 1066**
    Reports and accounts, **RAIL 1110; RAIL 1116; RAIL 1117**
    Subscription contracts, **RAIL 1160**
Wainfleet and Firsby Railway
    Miscellanea, **RAIL 1057**
Wallasey County Borough Tramways
    Reports and accounts, **RAIL 1114**
Wallingford and Watlington Railway, **RAIL 708** (*includes records of* GWR)
    Miscellanea, **RAIL 1057**
    Reports and accounts, **RAIL 1110**
Walsall County Borough Tramways
    Reports and accounts, **RAIL 1114**
Walthamstow, Clapton and City Railway (proposed)
    Prospectuses etc, **RAIL 1075**
Walthamstow Urban District Council Tramways
    Reports and accounts, **RAIL 1114**
Wansbeck Railway
    Reports and accounts, **RAIL 1116**
Wantage Tramway
    Miscellanea, **RAIL 1005**
Ware, Hadham and Buntingford Railway, **RAIL 709**
    Reports and accounts, **RAIL 1116**
Warrington and Altrincham Junction Railway
    Parliamentary papers, **RAIL 1163**
    Reports and accounts, **RAIL 1116**
See also Warrington & Stockport R
Warrington and Newton Extension Railway (proposed)
    Parliamentary papers, **RAIL 1016**

Warrington and Stockport Railway, **RAIL 710** (*includes records of predecessor* Warrington & Altrincham Jct R)
    Joint committee with:
        LNWR/MSLR, **RAIL 464** (Manchester S Jct & Altrincham R & Warrington & Stockport)
    Prospectuses etc, **RAIL 1075**
    Reports and accounts, **RAIL 1116**
Warrington Corporation Tramways
    Parliamentary papers, **RAIL 1068**
Warrington, Knutsford, Macclesfield and Buxton Railway
    Reports and accounts, **RAIL 1116**
Warwick and Leamington Union Railway, **RAIL 711** (*includes records of* London & Birmingham R)
    Prospectuses etc, **RAIL 1075**
Warwickshire and London Railway (proposed), **RAIL 712**
    Share certificates, **RAIL 1158**
    Subscription contracts, **RAIL 1160**
Watchet and Minehead Railway
    Maps, **RAIL 1030**
See also Minehead R
Waterford and Central Ireland Railway
    Parliamentary papers, **RAIL 1066**
    Railway and Canal Traffic Acts proceedings, **RAIL 1038**
    Reports and accounts, **RAIL 1110; RAIL 1116**
Waterford and Kilkenny Railway
    Reports and accounts, **RAIL 1116; RAIL 1117**
Waterford and Limerick Railway
    Joint committee with GWR, **RAIL 250** (Traffic)
    Miscellanea, **RAIL 1057**
    Railway and Canal Traffic Acts proceedings, **RAIL 1038**
    Reports and accounts, **RAIL 1110; RAIL 1116; RAIL 1117**
See also Irish & English Traffic Conference LNWR
Waterford and Tramore Railway
    Railway and Canal Traffic Acts proceedings, **RAIL 1038**
    Reports and accounts, **RAIL 1116; RAIL 1117**
Waterford, Dungarvon and Lismore Railway
    Railway and Canal Traffic Acts proceedings, **RAIL 1038**
    Reports and accounts, **RAIL 1110; RAIL 1116**
Waterford, Limerick and Western Railway
    Law cases and arbitration, **RAIL 1027**
    Miscellanea, **RAIL 1014**
    Parliamentary papers, **RAIL 1066**
    Reports and accounts, **RAIL 1116; RAIL 1117**
See also Irish & English Traffic Conference

Waterford, Wexford, Wicklow and Dublin
Railway
  Prospectuses etc, **RAIL 1075**
Waterloo and City Railway, **RAIL 713**
  Byelaws and regulations, **RAIL 1001**
  Maps, **RAIL 1030**
  Miscellanea, **RAIL 1057**
  Parliamentary papers, **RAIL 1066**
  Prospectuses etc, **RAIL 1075; RAIL 1110**
  Reports and accounts, **RAIL 1110**
Waterloo and Whitehall Railway
  Prospectuses etc, **RAIL 1075; RAIL 1076**
  Reports and accounts, **RAIL 1116**
Waterhouses and Hulme End Light Railway
  see N Staffordshire R
Watford and Edgware Junction Railway
  Parliamentary papers, **RAIL 1066**
Watford and Edgware Railway
  Maps, **RAIL 1030**
Watford and Rickmansworth Railway
  Byelaws and regulations, **RAIL 1001**
  Reports and accounts, **RAIL 1116**
Watford, Edgware and London Railway
  Parliamentary papers, **RAIL 1066**
Watford, Rickmansworth and Uxbridge Railway
  (proposed)
  Prospectuses etc, **RAIL 1075**
Watlington and Princes Risborough Railway,
  RAIL 785
  Accounting records, **RAIL 253**
  Miscellanea, **RAIL 1057**
  Reports and accounts, **RAIL 1110; RAIL 1116**
See also GWR miscellanea
Watton and Swaffham Railway, **RAIL 714**
  Reports and accounts, **RAIL 1116**
Waveney Valley Railway, **RAIL 715** (Eastern
  Counties R *records*)
  Parliamentary papers, **RAIL 1163**
  Reports and accounts, **RAIL 1116; RAIL 1117**
Wear and Derwent Junction Railway, **RAIL 716**
  (*includes records of* Wear Valley R)
  Timetables, **RAIL 981**
Weardale Extension Railway
  Prospectuses etc, **RAIL 1076**
Wear Valley Extension Railway, **RAIL 717**
  Parliamentary papers, **RAIL 1067**
Wear Valley Railway, **RAIL 718**
  Miscellanea, **RAIL 1021; RAIL 1157**
  Parliamentary papers, **RAIL 1067**
  Prospectuses etc, **RAIL 1076**
  Reports and accounts, **RAIL 1111; RAIL 1116**
  Share certificate, **RAIL 1159**
  Timetables, **RAIL 981**
See also Wear & Derwent Jct R
Wellingborough and District Tramroads
  Parliamentary papers, **RAIL 1068**
Wellington and Drayton Railway, **RAIL 719**

Reports and accounts, **RAIL 1110**
Wellington and Severn Junction Railway, **RAIL 720**
  Miscellanea, **RAIL 1057**
  Railway and Canal Traffic Acts proceedings,
    RAIL 1038
  Reports and accounts, **RAIL 1110;**
    RAIL 1116
See also GWR estates and rating
Wellington, Drayton and Newcastle Junction
  Railway (proposed)
  Parliamentary papers, **RAIL 1066**
Wells and Fakenham Railway, **RAIL 721** (Eastern
  Counties R *records*)
  Reports and accounts, **RAIL 1116**
Welsh Highland Railway
  Miscellanea, **RAIL 1021; RAIL 1057**
  Timetables, **RAIL 981**
Welshpool and Llanfair Light Railway, **RAIL 722**
  Miscellanea, **RAIL 1057**
  Prospectuses etc, **RAIL 1075**
  Reports and accounts, **RAIL 1110;**
    RAIL 1116
See also GWR miscellanea
Welsh Railway Union
  Parliamentary papers, **RAIL 1066**
  Prospectuses etc, **RAIL 1075**
Wembury (Plymouth) Commercial Dock and
  Railway (proposed)
  Parliamentary papers, **RAIL 1066**
Wenlock Railway, **RAIL 723**
  Land, **RAIL 1147** (*including predecessor*
    proposed Much Wenlock, Craven Arms &
    Coalbrookdale R)
  Railway and Canal Traffic Acts proceedings,
    RAIL 1038
  Reports and accounts, **RAIL 1110**
See also GWR estates and rating
West and South London Junction Railway
  (proposed)
  Parliamentary papers, **RAIL 1066**
West Birmingham Railway and Canal Company
  (proposed)
  Prospectuses etc, **RAIL 1075**
West Bromwich and Walsall Railway, **RAIL 1201**
  Miscellanea, **RAIL 1057**
  Parliamentary papers, **RAIL 1066**
West Carbery Tramways and Light Railways
  Railway and Canal Traffic Acts proceedings,
    RAIL 1038
West Clare Railway
  Railway and Canal Traffic Acts proceedings,
    RAIL 1038
  Reports and accounts, **RAIL 1116**
See also Irish & English Traffic Conference
West Cheshire Railway, **RAIL 724**
  Parliamentary papers, **RAIL 1147**
West Cornwall Railway, **RAIL 725** (*including*

records of joint committee Bristol & Exeter
R/GWR/S Devon R); **RAIL 630**
   Byelaws and regulations, **RAIL 1001**
   Miscellanea, **RAIL 1008; RAIL 1014;**
     RAIL 1057
   Parliamentary papers, **RAIL 1163**
   Prospectuses etc, **RAIL 1076**
   Reports and accounts, **RAIL 1110; RAIL 1116;**
     RAIL 1117
   Rule books, **RAIL 1134**
   Timetables, **RAIL 981**
See also GWR Secretary's papers
   S Devon R
West Cornwall Railway Joint Committee (Bristol &
   Exeter R/GWR/S Devon R), **RAIL 726** (*includes*
   records of GWR)
   Reports and accounts, **RAIL 1110**
West Coast Conference (Cal R/LNWR), **RAIL 727;**
   RAIL 410
West Cumberland, Furness and Morecambe Bay
   Railway (proposed)
     Maps, **RAIL 1030**
     Parliamentary plans, **RAIL 1071**
West Durham and Tyne Railway (proposed)
     Parliamentary papers, **RAIL 1067**
West Durham Railway, **RAIL 728**
     Reports and accounts, **RAIL 1111**
     Share certificates, **RAIL 1159**
West End of London and Crystal Palace Railway,
   RAIL 729
     Byelaws and regulations, **RAIL 1001**
     Parliamentary papers, **RAIL 1163**
     Reports and accounts, **RAIL 1116; RAIL 1117**
Westerham and Oxted Railway (proposed)
     Parliamentary papers, **RAIL 1066**
Westerham Valley Railway, **RAIL 740**
     Parliamentary papers, **RAIL 1066**
Westgate and South Eastern Junction Railway
   (proposed)
     Parliamentary papers, **RAIL 1066**
West Ham County Borough Tramways
     Reports and accounts, **RAIL 1114**
West Hartlepool Harbour and Railway, **RAIL 730**
   (*includes records of predecessor* W Hartlepool
   Harbour & Dock Co *and* NER)
     Law cases and arbitration, **RAIL 1027**
     Miscellanea, **RAIL 1021; RAIL 1157**
     Parliamentary papers, **RAIL 1067**
     Reports and accounts, **RAIL 1111; RAIL 1116;**
       RAIL 1117
     Rule books, **RAIL 1134**
     Share certificates, **RAIL 1159**
West Highland Railway
     Parliamentary papers, **RAIL 1066**
     Share certificates, **RAIL 1158**
West Lancashire Railway, **RAIL 731**
     Maps, **RAIL 1030**

     Parliamentary papers, **RAIL 1066; RAIL 1163**
     Railway and Canal Traffic Acts proceedings,
       RAIL 1038
     Reports and accounts, **RAIL 1116; RAIL 1117**
     Share certificates, **RAIL 1158**
     Traders' ledger credit agreements, **RAIL 1165**
See also Irish & English Traffic Conference
West London Extension Railway, **RAIL 732**
     Byelaws and regulations, **RAIL 1001**
     Miscellanea, **RAIL 1005; RAIL 1014;**
       RAIL 1057
     Parliamentary plans, **RAIL 1071**
     Railway and Canal Traffic Acts proceedings,
       RAIL 1038
     Rule books, **RAIL 1134**
     Sidings agreements, **RAIL 1167**
     Subscription contracts, **RAIL 1160**
     Timetables
       Public, **RAIL 985**
       Working, **RAIL 986**
See also GWR estates and rating; Secretary's
     papers; miscellanea
     GWR/LNWR/LSWR/LBSCR jt cttees
     Shropshire Union Rys & Canal Co
West London Junction Railway (proposed)
     Prospectuses etc, **RAIL 1075**
West London Railway, **RAIL 733** (*includes records of*
   predecessor Birmingham, Bristol & Thames Jct R)
     Byelaws and regulations, **RAIL 1001**
     Joint committee with:
       GWR/Met R, **RAIL 1134** (rule books)
     Miscellanea, **RAIL 1005; RAIL 1014; RAIL 1057**
     Parliamentary plans, **RAIL 1071**
     Reports and accounts, **RAIL 1110; RAIL 1116**
     Share certificates, **RAIL 1158**
     Timetables
       Public, **RAIL 985**
       Working, **RAIL 986**
See also GWR Secretary's papers
West London Railways Junction Company
   (proposed)
     Prospectuses etc, **RAIL 1075**
West Manchester Light Railways
     Parliamentary papers, **RAIL 1068**
West Metropolitan Railway
     Miscellanea, **RAIL 1057**
West Metropolitan Tramways
     Parliamentary papers, **RAIL 1066; RAIL 1068**
West Midland, Shrewsbury and Coast of Wales
   Railway (proposed)
     Prospectuses etc, **RAIL 1075**
West Midland Railway, **RAIL 734**
     Joint committees with:
       GWR, **RAIL 248; RAIL 284**
         RAIL 617 (Shrewsbury & Hereford R)
         RAIL 759 (Wolverhampton Low Level
          station)

LNWR, **RAIL 617** (Shrewsbury & Hereford R)
    S Wales R, **RAIL 284**
    Miscellanea, **RAIL 1008; RAIL 1014; RAIL 1057**
    Parliamentary papers, **RAIL 1066**
    Reports and accounts, **RAIL 1110; RAIL 1116; RAIL 1117**
    Rule books, **RAIL 1134**
    Timetables, **RAIL 981**
See also Oxford, Worcester & Wolverhampton R
Westminster Terminus Extension Railway
    Subscription contract, **RAIL 1163**
Westmoreland Railway
    Miscellanea, **RAIL 1015**
    Prospectuses etc, **RAIL 1076**
See also Eden Valley R
West Norfolk Junction Railway, **RAIL 735**
West of Fife Railway and Harbour Company
    Share certificates, **RAIL 1158**
Weston, Clevedon and Portishead Light Railways, **RAIL 781**
    Miscellanea, **RAIL 1008**
    Timetables, **RAIL 981**
West Riding and Grimsby Railway (*promoted as* W Riding, Hull & Grimsby R), **RAIL 736** *includes records of*:
    GNR/MSLR (*later* GCR) jt cttee
    Wakefield station jt cttee, WR&GR/MSLR/S Yorkshire R & R Dun Co/MR *later* WR&GR/MS&LR/GNR/MR
    Parliamentary papers, **RAIL 1066; RAIL 1067**
West Riding Union Railway
    Subscription contracts, **RAIL 1160**
West Riding Railway Joint Committee (MSLR (*later* GCR)/GNR), **RAIL 736; RAIL 783** (GNR correspondence)
    Reports and accounts, **RAIL 1110**
See also W Riding & Grimsby R
West Shropshire Mineral Railway
    Parliamentary papers, **RAIL 1147**
West Somerset Mineral Railway
    Maps, **RAIL 1030**
    Miscellanea, **RAIL 1008**
    Parliamentary papers, **RAIL 1163**
    Railway and Canal Traffic Acts proceedings, **RAIL 1038**
West Somerset Railway, **RAIL 737**
    Miscellanea, **RAIL 1057**
    Railway and Canal Traffic Acts proceedings, **RAIL 1038**
    Reports and accounts, **RAIL 1110; RAIL 1116**
West Staffordshire Railway (proposed)
    Parliamentary papers, **RAIL 1066**
West Surrey Railway (proposed)

Parliamentary papers, **RAIL 1066**
West Sussex Junction Railway *see* LBSCR
West Wickham and Hayes Railway, **RAIL 738**
    Parliamentary papers, **RAIL 1066**
West Yorkshire, North and South Union Railway
    Prospectuses etc, **RAIL 1075**
West Yorkshire Railway, **RAIL 739** (*includes records of predecessor* Bradford Wakefield & Leeds R)
    Parliamentary papers, **RAIL 1066**
    Reports and accounts, **RAIL 1116**
Wexford Junction Railway
    Parliamentary papers, **RAIL 1163**
Weymouth and Portland Railway, **RAIL 741**
    Maps, **RAIL 1030**
    Reports and accounts, **RAIL 1110; RAIL 1116**
See also GWR estates and rating; Secretary's papers
Wharfdale Railway
    Share certificate, **RAIL 1159**
Whitby and Pickering Railway, **RAIL 742**
    Miscellanea, **RAIL 1157**
    Prospectuses etc, **RAIL 1076**
Whitby, Redcar and Middlesborough Union Railway, **RAIL 743**
    Miscellanea, **RAIL 1153**
    Prospectuses etc, **RAIL 1076**
    Reports and accounts, **RAIL 1110; RAIL 1116**
    Share certificates, **RAIL 1159**
See also NER
Whitechapel and Bow Railway
    Reports and accounts, **RAIL 1110; RAIL 1116**
Whitechapel and Bow Railway Joint Committee (Met District R/LTSR; *from 1912* Met District/MR)
    Instructions to staff, **RAIL 1135**
    Reports and accounts, **RAIL 1110; RAIL 1116**
Whitehaven and Furness Junction Railway, **RAIL 744** (*includes records of jt cttee with* Whitehaven Jct R)
    Miscellanea, **RAIL 1008**
    Parliamentary papers, **RAIL 1066; RAIL 1163**
    Reports and accounts, **RAIL 1116; RAIL 1117**
    Rule books, **RAIL 1134**
    Timetables, **RAIL 981**
Whitehaven, Cleator and Egremont Railway, **RAIL 745**
    Joint committee with:
        Furness R, **RAIL 118** (Cleator & Furness R)
    Miscellanea, **RAIL 1057**
    Reports and accounts, **RAIL 1116; RAIL 1117**
    Rule books, **RAIL 1134**
See also LNWR
Whitehaven Junction Railway, **RAIL 746**
    Joint committee with;
        Whitehaven & Furness Jct R, **RAIL 744** (jt working)
    Parliamentary papers, **RAIL 1066**
    Reports and accounts, **RAIL 1116; RAIL 1117**

Whitland and Cardigan Railway, **RAIL 747**
(*includes records of predecessor* Whitland & Taf
Vale R)
    Miscellanea, **RAIL 1014**
    Prospectuses etc, **RAIL 1075**
    Reports and accounts, **RAIL 1110;**
      RAIL 1116
    Timetables, **RAIL 981**
See also GWR estates and rating; miscellanea
special reports
Whitland and Taf Vale Railway
    Miscellanea, **RAIL 1057**
    Prospectuses etc, **RAIL 1075**
    Reports and accounts, **RAIL 1116**
    Timetables, **RAIL 981**
See also Whitland & Cardigan R
Whitworth Railway
    Miscellanea, **RAIL 1057**
Wick and Lybster Railway *see* LMSR
amalgamation
Wicklow Mineral Railway
    Subscription contract, **RAIL 1163**
Widnes Railway, **RAIL 748**
    Parliamentary papers, **RAIL 1066**
Wigan and Newton Railway *see* Wigan Branch R
Wigan Branch Railway
    Map, **RAIL 1030** (Wigan & Newton R)
    Subscription contracts, **RAIL 1160**
See also North Union R
Wigan Junction Railways, **RAIL 749**
    Parliamentary papers, **RAIL 1066;**
      RAIL 1147
    Reports and accounts, **RAIL 1110; RAIL 1116;**
      RAIL 1117
    Share certificates, **RAIL 1158**
Wigtownshire Railway
    Reports and accounts, **RAIL 1116**
Wilts and Gloucestershire Railway
    Miscellanea, **RAIL 1057**
    Parliamentary papers, **RAIL 1066**
    Reports and accounts, **RAIL 1116**
Wiltshire, Somerset and Southampton Junction
Railway (proposed)
    Maps, **RAIL 1030**
Wiltshire Railway (proposed)
    Parliamentary papers, **RAIL 1066**
Wilts, Somerset and Weymouth Railway,
  RAIL 750 (*includes records of* GWR)
    Miscellanea, **RAIL 1014; RAIL 1057**
    Prospectuses etc, **RAIL 1075**
    Reports and accounts, **RAIL 1110**
Wimbledon and Croydon Railway, **RAIL 751**
    Parliamentary papers, **RAIL 1163**
    Reports and accounts, **RAIL 1116**
Wimbledon and Dorking Railway, **RAIL 752**
    Parliamentary papers, **RAIL 1066**
    Reports and accounts, **RAIL 1116**

Wimbledon and Sutton Railway, **RAIL 753**
    Parliamentary papers, **RAIL 1066**
Wimbledon and West Metropolitan Junction
Railway
    Parliamentary papers, **RAIL 1066**
Wimbledon, Merton and West Metropolitan
Junction Railway (proposed)
    Parliamentary papers, **RAIL 1066**
Windsor and Ascot Railway, **RAIL 754** (*includes
records of* GWR)
    Parliamentary papers, **RAIL 1066**
Windsor, Ascot and Aldershot Railway (proposed)
    Parliamentary papers, **RAIL 1066**
Windsor Junction Railway (proposed)
    Prospectuses etc, **RAIL 1075**
Windsor, Slough and Staines Atmospheric
Railway, **RAIL 964**
Windsor, Staines and South Western Railway,
  RAIL 755
    Miscellanea, **RAIL 1014**
    Prospectuses etc, **RAIL 1075**
Wirral Railway, **RAIL 756**
    Joint committee with Mersey R, **RAIL 475;**
      RAIL 756 (Birkenhead Pk station)
    Law cases and arbitration, **RAIL 1027**
    Miscellanea, **RAIL 1057; RAIL 1151**
    Parliamentary papers, **RAIL 1066; RAIL 1163**
    Railway and Canal Traffic Acts proceedings,
      RAIL 1038
    Reports and accounts, **RAIL 1110; RAIL 1116;**
      RAIL 1117
    Share certificates, **RAIL 1158**
    Timetables, **RAIL 981; RAIL 987**
    Traders' ledger credit agreements, **RAIL 1165**
See also LMSR amalgamation
Wirral Railways Committee *see* N Wales &
Liverpool R Cttee
Wisbech and Upwell Tramway
    Miscellanea, **RAIL 1005**
    Timetables, **RAIL 981**
See also GER
Wisbech Dock and Railway (proposed)
    Parliamentary papers, **RAIL 1066**
Wishaw and Coltness Railway
    Miscellanea, **RAIL 1057**
See also Garturk & Garion R
Witney Railway, **RAIL 757**
    Reports and accounts, **RAIL 1110; RAIL 1116;**
      RAIL 1117
Wivenhoe and Brightlingsea Railway, **RAIL 758**
    Railway and Canal Traffic Acts proceedings,
      RAIL 1038
    Reports and accounts, **RAIL 1110; RAIL 1116**
Wolverhampton and Cannock Chase Light
Railway, **RAIL 424**
    Maps, **RAIL 1030**
See also LMSR correspondence and papers

Wolverhampton and Cannock Chase Railway
    Parliamentary papers, **RAIL 1066**
See also LMSR Solicitor's records
Wolverhampton and Essington Mineral Railway
    (proposed)
    Parliamentary papers, **RAIL 1066**
Wolverhampton and North Staffordshire Railway
    (proposed)
    Parliamentary papers, **RAIL 1066**
Wolverhampton and Walsall Railway,
    RAIL 1200
    Miscellanea, **RAIL 1057**
    Parliamentary papers, **RAIL 1147**
    Prospectuses etc, **RAIL 1075**
    Reports and accounts, **RAIL 1116**
Wolverhampton, Chester and Birkenhead Junction
    Railway (proposed)
    Prospectuses etc, **RAIL 1075**
Wolverhampton County Borough Tramways
    Reports and accounts, **RAIL 1114**
Wolverhampton, Essington and Cannock Chase
    Junction Railway (proposed)
    Parliamentary papers, **RAIL 1066**
Wolverhampton Joint Committees, **RAIL 759**
    including:
        High Level jt station (Birmingham,
        Wolverhampton & Stour Valley
        R/Shrewsbury & Birmingham R; *after* 1852
        S&BR/LNWR; *after 1854* GWR/LNWR)
        Low Level jt station (GWR/Oxford,
        Wolverhampton & Worcester
        R/Shrewsbury & Birmingham R; *after 1854*
        GWR/OWWR; *after 1860* GWR/W Midland
        R)
        Shrewsbury & Birmingham R/Shrewsbury &
        Chester R through traffic cttee
Wolverhampton, Walsall and Midland Junction
    Railway
    Parliamentary papers, **RAIL 1147**
Wolverton and Stony Stratford Tramway
    Miscellanea, **RAIL 1007**
Woodford Railway (proposed)
    Parliamentary contract, **RAIL 1163**
Woodside and South Croydon Railway and Joint
    Committee (LBSCR/SER), **RAIL 760**
    Parliamentary papers, **RAIL 1066**
    Reports and accounts, **RAIL 1117**
Woodstock Railway, **RAIL 761**
    Railway and Canal Traffic Acts proceedings,
    RAIL 1038
Worcester and Broom Railway
    Parliamentary papers, **RAIL 1066**
Worcester and Hereford Railway, **RAIL 762**
    Miscellanea, **RAIL 1057**
    Parliamentary papers, **RAIL 1066; RAIL 1163**
    Reports and accounts, **RAIL 1110; RAIL 1116;**
    RAIL 1117

Worcester and Leominster Railway (proposed)
    Prospectuses etc, **RAIL 1075**
Worcester and South Wales Junction Railway
    (proposed)
    Prospectuses etc, **RAIL 1075**
Worcester, Bromyard and Leominster Railway,
    RAIL 763
    Law cases and arbitration, **RAIL 1027**
    Reports and accounts, **RAIL 1110; RAIL 1116**
See also GWR estates and rating
Worcester, Dean Forest and Monmouthshire
    Railway
    Miscellanea, **RAIL 1057**
    Parliamentary papers, **RAIL 1066**
Worcester, Hereford, Ross and Gloucester Railway
    (proposed), **RAIL 764**
Worcester Railways
    Parliamentary papers, **RAIL 1066**
Worcester, Shrewsbury and Crewe Union Railway
    (proposed)
    Prospectuses etc, **RAIL 1075; RAIL 1110**
    Subscription contracts, **RAIL 1160**
Workington Railways and Docks
    Parliamentary papers, **RAIL 1066**
Worksop and Bawtry Railway (proposed)
    Parliamentary papers, **RAIL 1066**
Worksop, South Muskham and Newark Railway
    (proposed)
    Miscellanea, **RAIL 1057**
Wotton Tramway
    Timetables, **RAIL 981**
Wrexham and Ellesmere Railway, **RAIL 765**
    Miscellanea, **RAIL 1057**
    Parliamentary papers, **RAIL 1066**
    Parliamentary plans, **RAIL 1071**
    Prospectuses etc, **RAIL 1075; RAIL 1110**
    Reports and accounts, **RAIL 1110; RAIL 1116**
See also GWR miscellanea
Wrexham and Minera Railway Joint Committee
    (GWR/LNWR), **RAIL 766; RAIL 410**
    Miscellanea, **RAIL 1057**
    Parliamentary papers, **RAIL 1066**
Wrexham, Mold and Connah's Quay Railway,
    RAIL 767
    Joint committee with:
        MSLR (*later* GCR), **RAIL 535** (Wirral Rys;
        Dee & Birkenhead *later* N Wales &
        Liverpool R Cttee)
    Parliamentary papers, **RAIL 1066**
    Railway and Canal Traffic Acts proceedings,
    RAIL 1038
    Reports and accounts, **RAIL 1110; RAIL 1116;**
    RAIL 1117
    Rule books, **RAIL 1134**
    Timetables, **RAIL 981**
Wycombe and Oxford Railway (proposed)
    Prospectuses etc, **RAIL 1075**

Wycombe Railway, **RAIL 768** (*includes records of* GWR)
See also Great Western & Wycombe R
Wye Valley Railway, **RAIL 769**
    GWR miscellanea, **RAIL 1014**
    Parliamentary papers, **RAIL 1066**
    Prospectuses etc, **RAIL 1075**
    Railway and Canal Traffic Acts proceedings, **RAIL 1038**
    Reports and accounts, **RAIL 1110; RAIL 1116**
See also GWR estates and rating
Yarmouth and North Norfolk Light Railway
    Reports and accounts, **RAIL 1116**
Yarmouth and Norwich Railway
    Reports and accounts, **RAIL 1110**
Yeovil, Bridport and Exeter Railway (proposed)
    Parliamentary plans, **RAIL 1071**
York and Carlisle and Durham, Westmoreland and Lancashire Junction Railway (proposed)
    Prospectuses etc, **RAIL 1076**
York and Carlisle Railway (proposed) *see* Northern Counties Union R
York and Newcastle Railway
    Reports and accounts, **RAIL 1110**
    Timetables, **RAIL 981**
See also GNoER
    York, Newcastle & Berwick R
York and North Midland Railway, **RAIL 770**
    Joint committees with:
        GNoER, **RAIL 772** (Lease and sale of GNoER)
            RAIL 232 (York station)
        York, Newcastle & Berwick R, **RAIL 773**
            RAIL 232; RAIL 771 (York station)
    Law cases and arbitration, **RAIL 1027**
    Maps, **RAIL 1030**
    Miscellanea, **RAIL 1006; RAIL 1008; RAIL 1016; RAIL 1021; RAIL 1057; RAIL 1157**

Parliamentary papers, **RAIL 1066**
Prospectuses etc, **RAIL 1075**
Reports and accounts, **RAIL 1110; RAIL 1111; RAIL 1116**
Rule books, **RAIL 1134**
Share certificate, **RAIL 1159**
Timetables, **RAIL 981**
See also Leeds & Selby R
    NER
York City Tramways
    Reports and accounts, **RAIL 1114**
York Joint Station Committee (York & N Midland R/GNoER; Y&NMR/York, Newcastle & Berwick R), **RAIL 771; RAIL 232**
York, Newcastle and Berwick Railway, **RAIL 772** (*includes records of predecessors* Newcastle & Berwick R; Newcastle & Darlington Jct R; York & Newcastle R)
    Joint committees with:
        GNoER, **RAIL 772** (lease and sale of GNoER)
        Leeds Northern R, **RAIL 773**
        York & N Midland R, **RAIL 773**
            RAIL 232; RAIL 771 (York station)
    Miscellanea, **RAIL 1008; RAIL 1020; RAIL 1021; RAIL 1057; RAIL 1152; RAIL 1157**
    Parliamentary papers, **RAIL 1066; RAIL 1067**
    Reports and accounts, **RAIL 1110; RAIL 1111; RAIL 1116**
    Rule books, **RAIL 1134**
    Timetables, **RAIL 981**
See also GNoER
    NER
Yorkshire and Glasgow Railway *see* Northern Counties Union R
Yorkshire Dales Railway, **RAIL 774**
    Share certificates, **RAIL 1158**
See also LMSR amalgamation

Appendix 3: List of Designated Repositories

British Transport Commission and British Railways Board Headquarters and Regions 1948–1968

BTC/BRB HQ and subsidiary businesses located in London — London Metropolitan Archive

Regional HQs

Eastern, located London (Liverpool Street) until 1966, then transferred to York — Doncaster (South Yorkshire)

North Eastern, located York, abolished 1966, and merged into Eastern Region — North Yorkshire

London Midland, located London (Euston) until 1985, then transferred to Birmingham — Cheshire

Western, located London (Paddington) until 1984, then transferred to Swindon — Wiltshire

Southern, located London (Waterloo) since 1948 — Hampshire

Railway undertakings nationalized under the transport Act (1947)

Axholme Joint R Cttee	Humberside
Birkenhead R	Wirral (Merseyside)
Cheshire Lines Cttee	Cheshire
East Kent Lt R	East Kent
East London R Jt Cttee	London Metropolitan Archive
Easton & Church Hope R	Dorset
Great Central and Midland Jt Cttees	Doncaster (South Yorkshire)
Great Central and North Staffordshire R Cttees	Greater Manchester
Great Central and North Western Rys Jt Cttee	Cheshire
Great Central, Hull and Barnsley and Midland Cttee	Doncaster (South Yorkshire)
Great Northern and London and North Western Jt Cttee	Leicestershire
Great Western R	Wiltshire
Great Western and Great Central Rys Jt Cttee	Wiltshire
Halifax & Ovenden Jt Cttee	West Yorkshire

Halifax High Level Jt Cttee	West Yorkshire
Hammersmith & City R	London Metropolitan Archive
Hammersmith & City R Jt Cttee	London Metropolitan Archive
Kent & East Sussex Lt R	East Kent
King's Lynn Docks & R	Norfolk
London & North Eastern R	
Central administration	Doncaster (South Yorkshire)
North Eastern Area	North Yorkshire
Southern Area	Doncaster (South Yorkshire)
London Midland & Scottish R	
Central administration (Euston House)	Cheshire
Central Division	Greater Manchester
Midland Division	Derbyshire
Western Division (North)	Cheshire
Western Division (South)	Cheshire
London Midland & Scottish and Great Western Rys Jt Cttee	Cheshire
London Midland & Scottish and Great Western Rys Jt Cttee (Severn & Wye and Severn Bridge R)	Gwent
Manchester, South Jct & Altrincham R	Greater Manchester
Mersey R	Liverpool (Merseyside)
Metropolitan and Great Central Jt Cttee	London Metropolitan Archive
Metropolitan and London & North Eastern R Cos – Watford Jt R Cttee	London Metropolitan Archive
Methley R Jt Cttee	West Yorkshire
Mid-Nottinghamshire Jt Rys Cttee	Nottinghamshire
Midland and G Northern Rys Jt Cttee	Norfolk
Midland and North Eastern R Cos Cttee	Derbyshire
Norfolk and Suffolk Jt Rys Cttee	Norfolk
North Devon & Cornwall Jcts Lt R	Devon
Oldham, Ashton-under-Lyne & Guide Bridge Jct R	Greater Manchester
Otley & Ilkley Jt Line Cttee	West Yorkshire
Shrewsbury & Hereford R	Shropshire
Shropshire & Montgomeryshire Lt R	Shropshire
Shropshire Rys	Shropshire
Somerset & Dorset R Jt Cttee	Somerset
South Yorkshire Jt Line Cttee	Doncaster (South Yorkshire)
Southern R	
Central administration	Hampshire
Central Division	Sussex
Eastern Division	East Kent
Western Division	Hampshire
Southport & Cheshire Lines Extension R	Lancashire
Tenbury R	Hereford
Tottenham & Hampstead Jt Cttee	London Metropolitan Archive
West Cornwall R	Cornwall
West London Extension R	London Metropolitan Archive
West London R	London Metropolitan Archive
Weymouth & Portland R	Dorset
Whitechapel & Bow R	London Metropolitan Archive
Whitechapel & Bow R Jt Cttee	London Metropolitan Archive

Companies amalgamated under the Railways Act 1921

Alexandra (Newport and South Wales) Docks and R	Gwent
Barry R	Glamorgan
Brackenhill Lt R	West Yorkshire
Brecon & Merthyr Tydfil Jct R	Powys
Bridgewater R	Somerset
Brighton & Dyke R	Sussex
Burry Port & Gwendreath Valley R	Dyfed
Cambrian R	Shropshire
Cardiff R	Glamorgan
Carlisle Citadel Station Cttee	Cumbria
Charnwood Forest R Cttee	Leicestershire
Cleator & Workington Jct R	Cumbria
Cleobury Mortimer & Ditton Priors Lt R	Shropshire
Cockermouth, Keswick & Penrith R	Cumbria
Colne Valley & Halstead R	Essex
Dearne Valley R	West Yorkshire
Didcot, Newbury & Southampton R	Hampshire
East & West Yorkshire Union Rys	West Yorkshire
East Lincolnshire R	Lincolnshire
Exeter R	Devon
Forcett R	North Yorkshire
Forest of Dean Central R	Gloucestershire
Freshwater, Yarmouth & Newport (Isle of Wight) R	Isle of Wight
Furness R	Cumbria
Great Central R	Leicestershire
Great Eastern R	Essex
Great North of England, Clarence & Hartlepool Jct R	Durham
Great Northern R	Doncaster (South Yorkshire)
Great Northern and Great Eastern Jt Cttee	Doncaster (South Yorkshire)
Great Western R	Wiltshire
Gwendreath Valleys R	Dyfed
Hayling Rys	Hampshire
Horncastle R	Lincolnshire
Hull & Barnsley R	Humberside
Hull & Barnsley and Great Central Jt Cttee	Doncaster (South Yorkshire)
Humber Commercial R and Dock Co	Humberside
Isle of Wight Central R	Isle of Wight
Isle of Wight R	Isle of Wight
Knott End R	Lancashire
Lampeter, Aberayron & New Quay Lt R	Dyfed
Lancashire & Yorkshire and Great Northern Stations Cttee	West Yorkshire
Lancashire & Yorkshire and London and North Western R Jt Cttee	West Yorkshire
Lancashire & Yorkshire and North Eastern R Jt Ctee	West Yorkshire
Lancashire & Yorkshire R	Greater Manchester
Lee-on-Solent R	Hampshire
Leek & Manifold Valley Lt R	Staffordshire
Liskeard & Looe R	Cornwall
Llanelly & Mynydd Mawr R	Dyfed

London & Blackwall R	London Metropolitan Archive
London & Greenwich R	London Metropolitan Archive
London & North Western R	Cheshire
London & South Western R	Hampshire
London, Brighton & South Coast R	Sussex
London, Chatham & Dover R	East Kent
London, Tilbury & Southend R (absorbed by Midland R 1912)	Derbyshire
Lynton & Barnstaple R (absorbed by Southern R)	Devon
Mansfield R	Nottinghamshire
Maryport & Carlisle R	Cumbria
Mawddy R	Powys
Mid-Kent (Bromley to St Mary Cray) R	London Metropolitan Archive
Mid-Suffolk Lt R	Suffolk
Midland & South Western Jct R	Wiltshire
Midland R	Derbyshire
Mold & Denbigh Jct R	Flintshire
Neath & Brecon R	Glamorgan
North & South Western Jct R	London Metropolitan Archive
North Cornwall R	Cornwall
North Eastern R	North Yorkshire
North Lindsay Lt Rys	Lincolnshire
North London R	London Metropolitan Archive
North Staffordshire R	Staffordshire
Nottingham & Grantham R and Canal Co	Nottinghamshire
Nottingham Jt Station Cttee	Nottinghamshire
Nottingham Suburban R	Nottinghamshire
Penarth Extension R	Glamorgan
Penarth Harbour Dock & R	Glamorgan
Plymouth & Dartmoor R	Devon
Plymouth, Devonport & South Western Jct R	Devon
Port Talbot R and Docks Co	Glamorgan
Preston & Wyre R (jointly owned by Lancashire & Yorkshire and London and North Eastern Rys)	Lancashire
Princeton R	Devon
Rhondda & Swansea Bay R	Glamorgan
Rhymney R	Glamorgan
Ross & Monmouth R	Hereford
Seaforth & Sefton Jct R	Sefton (Merseyside)
Sheffield District R	Sheffield (South Yorkshire)
Shropshire Union Rys and Canal Co	Shropshire
Sidmouth R	Devon
South Eastern & Chatham R Cos Managing Cttee	East Kent
South Eastern R	East Kent
South Wales Mineral R	Glamorgan
South Yorkshire Jct R	Doncaster (South Yorkshire)
Stamford & Essendine R	Lincolnshire
Stratford-upon-Avon & Midland Jct R	Warwickshire
Taff Vale R	Glamorgan
Teign Valley R	Devon
Tottenham & Forest Gate R	London Metropolitan Archive
Vale of Glamorgan R	Glamorgan
Van R	Glamorgan
Victoria Station & Pimlico R	London Metropolitan Archive
Welshpool & Llanfair Lt R	Powys

West Riding R Cttee	West Yorkshire
West Somerset R	Somerset
Wirral R	Wirral (Merseyside)
Wrexham & Ellesmere R	Flintshire
Yorkshire Dales (Skipton to Grassington) R	North Yorkshire

Joint lines

Great Northern and Great Eastern Jt Cttee (Huntingdon–Doncaster)	Doncaster (South Yorkshire)
Hull & Barnsley and Great Central Jt Cttee (lines NE of Doncaster)	Doncaster (South Yorkshire)
Lancashire & Yorkshire and North Eastern Rys Jt Cttee (Leeds New Station)	West Yorkshire
Lancashire & Yorkshire and North Western Rys Jt Cttee (Leeds Goods Station)	West Yorkshire
Lancashire & Yorkshire and Great Northern Stations Cttee (Bradford Exchange Station)	West Yorkshire
Preston & Wyre R (jointly owned by Lancashire & Yorkshire and London and North Western R Cos) (Preston, Blackpool and Fleetwood)	Lancashire
Carlisle Citadel Station Cttee (Carlisle Station)	Cumbria

Bibliography

History of railways

There are thousands of railway history books. 'Ottley' (at the beginning of the following list) is a comprehensive bibliography of the literature.

Ottley, George, *A Bibliography of British Railway History* (Allen & Unwin, London, 1965) (2nd edn, HMSO, London, 1983; *Supplement*, HMSO, 1987; *Second supplement*, by members of the Railway & Canal Historical Society, NRM, York, 1998)

James, Leslie, *A Chronology of the Construction of Britain's Railways 1778–1855* (Ian Allan, London, 1983)

Various authors, *A Regional History of the Railways of Great Britain* (15 vols, David & Charles, Newton Abbot, 1960 onwards; Vol. 16, *Ireland*, Atlantic Transport Publishers, Penryn, 1995). *Each volume is a history of the railways in a particular region from the beginnings to the time of publication.*

Parris, Henry A., *Government and the Railways in Nineteenth Century Britain* (Routledge & Kegan Paul, London, 1965

Gourvish, T. R., *British Railways 1948–73: A Business History* (Cambridge University Press, 1986)

Family history

Hawkings, David T., *Railway Ancestors* (Alan Sutton, Stroud, 1995)

Richards, Tom, *Was Your Grandfather a Railwayman?* (Federation of Family History Societies, 3rd edition, 1995)

Railway historical atlases

British Railways Pre-grouping Atlas and Gazetteer (Ian Allan, London, 1976 and later reprinting)

Jowett, Alan, *Jowett's Railway Atlas of Great Britain & Ireland* (Patrick Stephens, Yeovil)

Index

to chapters 1–7

accidents, 34–35, 47–48, 75, 84
accounts
    annual, 21, 45
    half-yearly capital, 41
    liquidators', 41
Acts *see* legislation
Admiralty, 24, 52, 58–62
    dockyards, 60–62, 103
    station records, 61
    solicitor, 68
Agriculture and Fisheries,
    Ministry of, 67
Agriculture Fisheries and
    Food, Ministry of, 67, 104
Airey, John, 93
airline operation, 22, 25,
    29–30, 39, 65
air raids, 64–65, 67, 100
air raid shelters (tube
    stations), 25, 31–32, 67
Air Ministry, 24, 63–65
amalgamations of railways,
    27
    See also grouping
ambulance trains, 63, 100
armoured trains, 63
Ashton, Stalybridge &
    Liverpool Junction
    Railway, 94
Atomic Energy Authority, 65
Aviation, Ministry of, 65
Beeching, Richard, 9–10, 26,
    34, 47–48, 50
Belfast & County Down
    Railway, 31
Bere Alston & Calstock Light
    Railway, 61
Bessbrook & Newry
    Tramway, 31
Beyer Peacock & Co, 14
Bills *see* legislation
Blythe & Tyne Railway, 96
Bolton & Leigh Railway, 2
Bristol & Exeter Railway,
    99 *illus*
'British Rail', 10, 18

'British Railways', 9, 18, 66,
    69
British Railways Board (BRB),
    9, 15, 26, 34, 54
    custody of records, 11
British Railways Engineering
    Ltd (BREL), 10
British Transport
    Commission (BTC), 9, 12n,
    45, 47–49, 53–54
    custody of records, 11
British Transport Historical
    Records (BTHR), 11–12, 17,
    90
Brunel, Isambard Kingdom,
    4, 36, 56
buses, 22
bye-laws, 3, 20, 35
Cabinet Office, 24, 26–35, 50
Caledonian Railway (Cal R),
    3, 7–8, 19, 36, 62
Cambrian Railways, 8,
    74 *illus*, 75
canals, 22, 41
Canterbury & Whitstable
    Railway, 2
Cardiff Railway, 100
Carnarvonshire Railway, 96
carriages *see* rolling stock
Carter Paterson Ltd, 22
Channel Tunnel and Channel
    link, 25–29, 31, 34, 36, 40,
    44–46, 55, 57, 59,63–64, 66
    Advisory Group, 66
    Study Group, 54
    Working Party, 54
charges, 35, 46–47, 66
Cheshire Lines Committee, 6
Chester & Crewe Railway, 2
Chester & Holyhead Railway,
    38
civil engineering, 12, 21–22,
    43, 48–49
Clifton Extension Railway, 19
closure of railways, 10, 26, 40,
    48–50, 65–67

Cobb, Rev. F.W., 103
commercial railway industry
    see manufacture,
    commercial
Commissioners of Railways,
    5, 35–36
    returns of iron bridges, 36
committees, railway
    company, 18–20
Companies' Registration
    Office, 38, 41
Constabulary, Inspectorate of,
    67, 104
control of railways
    government, 7–8, 43, 46
    wartime, 7–8, 62
contracts, 20, 22, 52
    contract drawings, 92
Copyright Office, 102–103
Countryside Commission, 66
Crown Agents for Oversea
    Governments, 66
Crown estate, 53, 98
Crown Estate Commission,
    66, 98, 103
Customs and Excise, 24,
    55–57
Dean Forest Railway, 52
Defence, Minister of, 25
Development Commission,
    66
directors, railway company,
    18, 21
    lists of directors, 41
drawings *see* maps and plans
Dublin & Kingstown
    Railway, 59–60
Dundalk, Newry & Greenore
    Railway, 3
Eastern & Midlands Railway,
    95 *illus*
Eastern Counties Railway, 85,
    86 *illus*,
Economic Affairs,
    Department of, 66
electrification, 25, 48–49, 54

estates and land, 21, 52–53, 64
Excise, Board of, 55, 57
Explosives Directorate, 66
exports of railway
    equipment, 25, 28–29,
    31–32, 35, 40, 45, 54
    See also Crown Agents for
    Oversea Governments
fares *see* charges
Farnborough light railway
    (RAF), 64
ferries *see* marine
Festiniog & Blaenau Railway,
    75, 77 *illus*
Festiniog Railway, 49
finance, 12, 21, 26, 34, 49,
    51–55, 66, 68
    See also accounts
Forestry Commission, 67
Foxes Bridge and Purton Pill,
    railway between, 61
freight and goods traffic, 6,
    8–9, 26, 28–29, 31, 33, 42,
    50, 57
Friendly Societies, Registry
    of, 67
Furness Railway, 100
Gauge Commission, 4
gauge of railways, 4
Geelong & Melbourne
    Railway, 96
Geddes, Sir Eric, 46
Gladstone, William Ewart, 4
Glasgow & South Western
    Railway (G&SWR), 19
Gooch, Daniel, 96
goods *see* freight
government control of
    railways *see* control of
    railways
Grand Junction Railway, 2, 37
Great Central Railway (GCR),
    6–9, 19, 70–72, 100
Great Eastern Railway (GER),
    7–9, 19, 85, 86 *illus*, 87 *illus*,
    88, 102 *illus*
Great Northern Railway
    (GNR), 3, 6–9, 19, 92
Great Northern Railway
    (Ireland) (GNR(I)), 54
Great North of England
    Clarence & Hartlepool
    Railway, 40

Great North of England
    Railway, 4
Great North of Scotland
    Railway (GNSR), 8
Great Southern & Western
    Railway, 40
'Great Train Robbery', 67, 104
Great Western Railway
    (GWR), 4, 7–9, 11, 17, 19,
    21, 40, 43, 55, 64, 69,
    79 *illus*, 80–81, 96, 100,
    101 *illus*
    New Swindon
    Improvement Co, 21
    Swindon mechanics
    institution, 21
Greenwich & Gravesend
    Railway, 51
Greenwich Hospital estates,
    60
grouping of railways, 7–8, 30,
    46
Halesowen Railway, 19
Hawkshaw, John, 59, 94
Hays Wharf Ltd, 22
Hayward, W.E., 17
Hedley, William, 1
Hexham & Allandale
    Railway, 60
Home Guard units, railway,
    63
Home Office, 67, 104
Home Security, Ministry of,
    67
House of Lords Record
    Office, 13, 15, 20, 91
Housing and Local
    Government, Ministry of,
    67, 104
Hudswell, Clarke & Co,
    95 *illus*
Hull & Selby Railway, 75,
    76 *illus*
Industrial Court, 67
industrial relations, 21, 25–27,
    30–31, 34 , 47–48, 56, 67
    See also Friendly Societies;
    Industrial Court; Railway
    Benevolent Institution;
    strikes; trades unions;
    women workers
Inland Revenue, 24, 55–57
    Valuation Office, 97

inspectors of railways, 3–4,
    35, 42, 52
InterCity, 10
Irish and English Traffic
    Conference, 20
Irish railways, 4–5, 13, 20, 27,
    30–31, 52–55, 57, 62–63
Irish Railway Record Society,
    16
joint railways, 6, 19–20, 78, 80
Jowitt, Sir William, 33
Kenyon & Leigh Junction
    Railway, 2
Killingworth colliery railway,
    1
Lancashire & Yorkshire
    Railway (L&YR), 6–8, 19
Labour, Ministry of, 44, 67
land *see* estates
Land Revenue Record Office,
    98
Leek & Manifold Valley Light
    Railway, 51
legislation
    affecting railways, 3–9, 14,
    35, 38, 44, 46–49, 53, 62
    railway Bills and Acts, 2,
    5–6, 13–14, 20, 27, 30, 35,
    42, 53, 68, 91
Lever, Sir Hardman, 55
light railways, 6–7, 44–45, 52,
    64, 68
Light Railway Commission,
    7, 47
Limerick & Ennis Railway, 36
liner trains, 48
Liskeard & Looe Railway, 2
Liverpool & Manchester
    Railway, 2
Llanelly Railway, 39
local record offices, 13–14, 23,
    91
Locomotive Manufacturers'
    Association, 56
locomotives, 2, 7, 9, 11–12,
    21–22, 26, 29–31, 33–35, 40,
    42, 54, 65, 89, 100, 103
    See also manufacture,
    commercial
London & Birmingham
    Railway, 2, 60
London & Blackwall Railway,
    60

London & North Eastern Railway (LNER), 8, 12n, 19–20, 55, 71–72, 93, 100

London & North Western Railway (LNWR), 2–3, 6–8, 19, 21, 43, 59, 69, 73, 80, 94

London & Southampton Railway, 2

London & South Western Railway (LSWR), 6–8, 59, 69

London, Brighton & South Coast Railway (LBSCR), 7–8, 59, 84, 101 *illus*

London, Chatham & Dover Railway (LCDR), 42–43, 59

London Metropolitan Archives, 12, 15

London Midland & Scottish Railway (LMSR), 8–9, 12n, 19–22, 55, 65

London Passenger Transport Board (LPTB), 8, 33

London, Tilbury & Southend Extension Railway, 59

London, Tilbury & Southend Railway, 100

London Transport (underground railways), 9, 12, 15, 30, 47–49, 53, 55–56, 103–104
See also air raid shelters

London Transport Board, 49

London Transport Executive (LTE), 9, 12

Lord Derby's scheme, 70–72

Manchester & Birmingham Railway, 2

Manchester & Leeds Railway, 36

Manchester, Sheffield & Lincolnshire Railway, 19, 71, 84–85

Metropolitan Carriage & Wagon Co, 96

manufacture, commercial, 14, 35, 40–41, 43–45, 54, 56, 63, 68, 96

maps and plans, 21–22, 36, 38–39, 89–98
Parliamentary deposited plans, 91–92, 98

Railway Clearing House, 5–6, 93–94
wayleave plans, 93

marine, 22, 28, 38, 45, 59

Mersey Railway, 6

Metropolitan Railway, 50, 55

Midland & Great Northern Joint Railway, 6

Midland Railway (MR), 6–8, 19, 51, 92

mobilization in war, 63

modernization plan, 9, 34

Munitions, Ministry of, 7, 67–68, 104

Museum of Science and Industry, Manchester, 14

National Archives of Scotland (NAS), 12, 15

National Coal Board, 66, 97, 103

National Dock Labour Board, 98, 103

nationalization and 'socialization', 7–9, 26–27, 29, 32–34, 47, 54

National Railway Museum (NRM), 11–12, 15, 22, 89, 96, 99

National Register of Archives, 14, 16

Network South East, 10

Newcastle & Carlisle Railway, 2, 60

North British Locomotive Co, 43

North British Railway, 3, 8

North Devon Railway, 60

North Eastern Railway (NER), 3, 6–9, 93

North London Railway (NLR), 72 *illus*, 73, 75

Office of the Rail Regulator, 14

Ordnance Survey, 96–98

Outram, Benjamin, 1

Overseas Trade, Department of, 44

Parliament, records of, 13–14

'parliamentary' trains, 5, 55

passenger duty *see* tax

Passenger Transport Authorities, 49

Pen-y-darren plateway, 1

permanent way, 9, 96

photographs, 12, 22, 62, 99–104

Pickfords Ltd, 22

plateways, 1

Pontop & South Shields Railway, 93

ports, 28, 46, 59, 61

postal traffic, 50, 59,64

Post Office, 50, 52
railway (London), 30

Prime Minister's Office, 24–26

Princes Risborough Laboratory, 103

privatization of railways, 10, 14–15

production, censuses of, 45

Public Record Office of Northern Ireland, 16

Purton Pill *see* Foxes Bridge

radioactive materials, transport of, 33, 65

Railtrack plc, 10, 14–16, 91

Railway Advisory Committee, 55

Railway Assessment Authority, 56

Railway Benevolent Institution, 81, 83 *illus*, 84

Railway Board, 5, 35

Railway Clearing House, 5–6, 47, 90, 93–94

Railway Commissioners *see* Commissioners of Railways

Railway Companies Association, 54

Railway Department (Board of Trade), 5, 35–38, 98

Railway Executive, 9

Railway Executive Committee (First World War), 7

Railway Executive Committee (Second World War) 8

Railway Heritage Committee (RHC), 14–16

Railway Industry National Archive, 15

railway mania, 5

Railway Preservation Society of Ireland, 16
Railway Rates Tribunal, 42
Railway Savings Bank, 54
Railway Training Centre (Army), 65
refreshment rooms, 30
    state management, 67
Resource Centre (PRO library), 13, 20
Regional Railways, 10
Rhymney Railway, 8
roads
    competition with railways, 7, 9, 25, 54
    co-ordination with railways, 26, 34
Robert Stephenson & Co, 96
'Rocket', 2
rolling stock, 12, 21–22, 26, 28–31, 34–35, 55–56, 89, 95 *illus*, 96, 100, 103
    pooling, 7, 20, 55
    See also manufacture, commercial
Romney, Hythe & Dymchurch Light Railway, 62
Rother Valley Light Railway, 53
Rothwell & Co, 99 *illus*
Royal Archives, 27
Royal Commission on Historical Manuscripts (RCHM), 14, 16
safety, 26
Scottish railways, 12
    See also National Archives of Scotland
Scremerston colliery railway, 60
Severn & Wye Railway, 19
shareholders
    lists of shareholders, 41, 45
    meetings, 18
shipping *see* marine
Shrewsbury & Hereford Joint Committee, 78 *illus*, 80
signalling, 9, 94
'socialization' *see* nationalization
Somerset & Dorset Joint Railway, 6

South Eastern & Chatham Railway, 7–8
South Eastern Railway (SER), 42–43
Southern Railway, 8–9, 20
South Wales Railway, 4
Southwold Railway, 100
Spittal & Tweedmouth Railway, 60
staff, 12, 21, 31, 54, 56, 69–88
    loan of officers to government departments, 42
    See also industrial relations
Staffordshire & Shropshire Junction Railway (proposed), 38
Staffordshire County Council, 51
stage carriage duty *see* tax
stamp duty *see* tax
Stamp, Sir Josiah, 65
Stamps, Board of, 51, 55
statistics, 32–35, 45–47, 67
Stephenson Clarke Ltd, 20
Stephenson, George, 1–2, 4, 56
Stephenson, Robert, 2, 4, 36, 60
    See also Robert Stephenson & Co
Stockton & Darlington Railway, 1–2, 81, 82 *illus*
Stothert and Slaughter & Co, 96
Strategic Rail Authority, 14
street tramways, 7, 23, 34, 46–47, 53, 67
strikes, 30, 61, 64, 100
Supply, Ministry of, 65
Swindon *see* Great Western Railway
Taff Vale Railway, 8, 81, 96
Tay Bridge Inquiry, 42, 45
tax, 50, 54–57
    passenger duty, 51, 56–57
    stage carriage duty, 55, 57
    stamp duty, 55–56
Thomas Cook & Son, 31
track *see* permanent way
Trade, Board of, 3, 5, 7, 13n, 14, 24, 35–45, 47, 50–52, 98
    President of, 5, 7, 35
    See also Railway Department

trades unions, 21, 67
    See also Friendly Societies
traffic returns *see* statistics
tramways, 1, 2, 41, 61
    See also street tramways
Tramways Institute of Great Britain, 36
Transport Advisory Council, 45
Transport and Road Research Laboratory, 65
Transport Arbitration Tribunal, 45
Transport Co-ordinating Council for London, 49
Transport Corps, 62
Transport, Ministry of, 7–8, 11, 14, 24, 24, 35–36, 44–50
transport policy, 3–5, 9, 24–34, 46–50, 66
    See also Transport Advisory Council
Transport Users Consultative Committees, 48
Treasury, the, 6, 24, 37, 50–55
Treasury Solicitor, 68
Trevithick, Richard, 1
Tube Shelter Committee, 67
underground railways *see* London Transport
wagons *see* rolling stock
Walker, Herbert Ashcombe, 7
Warrington & Newton Railway, 2
Warrington & Stockport Railway, 96
War Office, 24, 58, 62–63, 100
wartime control of railways *see* control of railways
wayleaves, 2, 93
Welsh Highland Railway, 49
Welsh Office, 65, 98
Wilson, Sir Horace, 44
Wirral Railway, 6
Wissington Light Railway, 67
women workers, 71 *illus*, 72, 100
Wright, Joseph, 96
Wylam colliery railway, 1
York & North Midland Railway, 19